MANCHESTER
MEDIEVAL
LITERATURE
AND CULTURE

READING ROBIN HOOD

Manchester University Press

Series editors: Anke Bernau and David Matthews

Series founded by: J. J. Anderson and Gail Ashton

Advisory board: Ruth Evans, Nicola McDonald, Andrew James Johnston, Sarah Salih, Larry Scanlon and Stephanie Trigg

The Manchester Medieval Literature and Culture series publishes new research, informed by current critical methodologies, on the literary cultures of medieval Britain (including Anglo-Norman, Anglo-Latin and Celtic writings), including post-medieval engagements with and representations of the Middle Ages (medievalism). 'Literature' is viewed in a broad and inclusive sense, embracing imaginative, historical, political, scientific, dramatic and religious writings. The series offers monographs and essay collections, as well as editions and translations of texts.

Titles Available in the Series

Language and imagination in the Gawain-poems
J. J. Anderson

Water and fire: The myth of the Flood in Anglo-Saxon England
Daniel Anlezark

Rethinking the South English legendaries
Heather Blurton and Jocelyn Wogan-Browne (eds)

The Parlement of Foulys (by Geoffrey Chaucer)
D. S. Brewer (ed.)

Between earth and heaven:
Liminality and the Ascension of Christ in Anglo-Saxon literature
Johanna Kramer

In strange countries: Middle English literature and its afterlife:
Essays in Memory of J. J. Anderson
David Matthews (ed.)

A Knight's Legacy: Mandeville and Mandevillian Lore in early modern England
Ladan Niayesh (ed.)

Greenery: Ecocritical readings of late medieval English literature
Gillian Rudd

Reading Robin Hood

Content, form and reception in the outlaw myth

STEPHEN KNIGHT

Manchester University Press

Copyright © Stephen Knight 2015

The right of Stephen Knight to be identified as the author of this work has been asserted by him in accordance with the Copyright, Designs and Patents Act 1988.

Published by Manchester University Press
Altrincham Street, Manchester M1 7JA, UK
www.manchesteruniversitypress.co.uk

British Library Cataloguing-in-Publication Data is available

ISBN 978 0 7190 9526 9 *hardback*
ISBN 978 1 5261 2377 0 *paperback*

First published by Manchester University Press in hardback 2015

This edition first published 2017

The publisher has no responsibility for the persistence or accuracy of URLs for any external or third-party internet websites referred to in this book, and does not guarantee that any content on such websites is, or will remain, accurate or appropriate.

Printed by Lightning Source

Contents

List of figures	*page* vii
Acknowledgements	ix
Note on sources	x
Introduction: drawing an academic bow	1
1 Interfacing orality and literacy: the case of Robin Hood	14
2 Rabbie Hood: the development of the English outlaw myth in Scotland	36
3 Robin Fitz Warren: the formation of *The Gest of Robin Hood*	55
4 Revisiting the broadside ballads	83
5 Romantic Robin Hood	103
6 Robin Hood and nineteenth-century fiction	143
7 The making and re-making of Maid Marian	187
8 Rhizomatic Robin Hood	224
Appendix A	258
Appendix B	263
Bibliography	268
Index	279

Figures

1. A 'Robin meets his match' fight: Thomas Berwick's 'Robin Hood and the Tanner' from Ritson's edition *Robin Hood* (1795), title page. — page 85
2. The almost unknown first Robin Hood novel: *Robin Hood: A Tale of the Olden Time* (1819). — 147
3. Egan the artist provides Gothic elaboration for Egan the novelist: Gilbert Hood sees the spirit of his sister. From Pierce Egan the Younger, *Robin Hood and Little John* (1840), p. 87. — 166
4. Egan the artist and the wedding day of Robin and Marian. From Pierce Egan the Younger, *Robin Hood and Little John* (1840), p. 323. — 168
5. Stocqueler and violence: Marian, her dog and Prince John in disguise. From J. H. Stocqueler, *Maid Marian* (1849), p. 9. — 171
6. Stocqueler and orientalism: Leila dances for the outlaws. From J. H. Stocqueler, *Maid Marian* (1849), p. 89. — 172
7. Emmett and melodrama: Robin rescues Marian. From George Emmett, *Robin Hood and the Outlaws of Sherwood Forest* (1869), p. 54. — 175
8. Emmett and the young audience: Robin meets the Wood Demon. From George Emmett, *Robin Hood and the Outlaws of Sherwood Forest* (1869), p. 37. — 176
9. Pyle's male action: Little John fights the cook. From Howard Pyle, *The Merry Adventures of Robin Hood* (1883), p. 91. — 180
10. Pyle's peacefulness: Robin escapes. From Howard Pyle, *The Merry Adventures of Robin Hood* (1883), p. 306. — 181

11 Rhead's action: Robin and Little John. From Louis Rhead, *Bold Robin Hood and his Outlaw Band* (New York: Harper, 1912), frontispiece. 184
12 Wyeth's action: outlaws shooting to rescue Will. From J. Walker McSpadden and Charles Wilson, *Robin Hood and his Merry Outlaws* (London: Associated Newspapers, 1921), frontispiece. 185
13 1980s outlaws: Michael Praed and Judy Trott in the television series *Robin of Sherwood* (1984). 211
14 Miss Piggy as Marian. From *Robin Hood: A High Spirited Tale of Adventure* (New York: Muppets Press and Random House, 1980), front cover. 217
15 1980s feminism: From *Maid Marian and her Merry Men: Robert the Incredible Chicken* (London: BBC Books, 1989), p. 6. 218
16 The Murdoch *Sun* and the Real Robin Hood: *Sun*, 17 November 1992, p. 1. 233

Every reasonable attempt has been made to obtain permission to reproduce the copyright images. Images have been included, but if any proper acknowledgement has not been made, copyright holders are invited to contact the publisher.

Acknowledgements

Acknowledgements are due to the University of Wales Press, Cardiff, for permission to reprint, in a revised version, Chapter 2, and to Helen Phillips, editor of the collection in which it appeared.

In a book like this which gathers together thoughts and explorations made over a substantial range of periods and places, much is due to many people who have generously contributed their expertise, information or tolerance: grateful thanks to Justin Clemens, Gavin Edwards, Tom Hahn, Kevin Harty, David Knight, Elizabeth Knight, Margaret Knight, Valerie Johnson, Rebecca Munford, Nikko Nonni, Helen Phillips, Peter Roberts, Sean Thompson. I am grateful to staff at the libraries of the University of Melbourne, and to its Vice-Chancellor, Glyn Davies, for a fellowship to sustain my research. I would also like to acknowledge and thank Polly Bentham, Matthew Frost and Fiona Little for their expert professional support.

Note on sources

Early Robin Hood texts pose problems of reference as the ballads often have varying titles, sometimes the same story will differ in detail across versions, and characters' names are often spelled differently. Some of the early texts are hard to date and may well have been lost, while early collections, both ballad garlands and prose lives, can overlap in contents, may be effectively reprints rather than new editions, and themselves can have quite uncertain dates. This study has for the most part used the titles given to ballads by F. J. Child in his *English and Scottish Popular Ballads*, though some revisions have been made in the light of the edition *Robin Hood and Other Outlaw Tales* by Stephen Knight and Thomas H. Ohlgren (see Bibliography for details). Ballads are quoted from Knight and Ohlgren and in some cases, when they are not present in that edition, from Child. The dating of the ballads has been based on the best available information, and caution has been used in arguments about dates and precedence. The names of characters have been normalised on the basis of their earliest appearance – for example Allen a Dale, Marian, Will Scarlett – though when names appear in quotations the original is preserved. To limit referencing, a recurrent source is given in an endnote when it first occurs in a chapter, and further references from it in that chapter are given in the text after quotations.

Introduction: drawing an academic bow

The literary and cultural tradition of Robin Hood differs substantially from other collections of material that might appear comparable. A myth which may have some basis in legend, like that of King Arthur or Tristan and Isolde, it is clearly much more popular than them in both its genres and its politics. The materials do not have the grand status or splendid illustrations of those medieval classics, they do not run on into modern high-status genres like epic poem or opera, and through the myth there is no clear structure of descent or authoritative transmission of the narrative. Modern Robin Hood stories, whether in print or in film, do not, like King Arthur versions, have evident sources which are carefully updated for a new context – rather, as is argued in Chapter 8 of this book, they tend to draw without apparent cultural hierarchy on a scattered range of unranked sources and so are remarkably open to new materials and ideas.

That rhizomatic tendency is itself recurrently regenerated through the way in which the myth itself is of uncertain, even anarchic, nature. Every Robin Hood scholar is familiar with the journalist who only wants to know whether Robin really existed, and some may have spoken on the myth in parts of England where members of the public will confidently identify where Robin Hood was born and brought up – usually close to their own personal locations. Historians and archivists, both professional and overtly amateur, have enthusiastically joined in this reduction of a heroic figure to a mere issue of personal identity – though very oddly (and again anarchistically) the earliest R. Hood of all to appear in the records, who was intriguingly accused of murdering a servant of the Abbot of Cirencester just before 1216, has proved of no interest at all to the 'real Robin Hood' people.

If the myth can be personally empiricised in this randomised mode, it has also avoided serious status through the varied, small-scale, incoherent ways in which it has been recorded for posterity. It was at first apparently oral, in reports, songs and place-names, then was recorded in a couple of unostentatious manuscript anthologies, then became a reasonably popular early print, then withdrew into ephemeral printed broadsides, to emerge in the nineteenth century in a few little-valued poems and a range of unpretentious novels, often with garish illustrations, and in the twentieth century located itself primarily in children's fiction and the new popular disposability of film. This was not the treasured material of great libraries, nor was it enshrined in the genres which would attract moral or nationalistic excitement when, around 1900, literary criticism began to study fiction in languages other than Latin and Greek.

The two main scholarly functions which have proved central to both literary prestige and cultural capital, textual editing and critical commentary, were for long notably absent from the Robin Hood tradition – and when they partly appeared they were redirected in other, primarily historical directions. The sheer popularity of the Robin Hood ballads, including those in small anthologies called garlands, merged in the late eighteenth century with nascent medievalism, first in 1777 by the forgotten Welsh bookman Thomas Evans and then very influentially in 1795 by Joseph Ritson,[1] who basically copied Evans's edition but preceded it with a long introduction which did look like classic-forming respectful scholarship. It referred in its notes to many of the earlier texts, literary as well as popular, but the emphasis lay on the eleven-page 'Life of Robin Hood' (with sixty pages of quasi-empirical 'Notes and Illustrations'), including a genealogical chart tracing his lineage back to the Norman Conquest (when the name was allegedly Fitz Ooth).

In the new mood of biography (the major accounts of Johnson by Hawkins and Boswell came out in 1787 and 1791), this was a life and a legend, but such history itself involved hierarchy. Ritson fully accepted the sixteenth-century gentrification of Robin, turning him from an order-threatening yeoman into an earl true to all hierarchy but opposed to bad King John. Ritson was also for his time a startlingly radical figure – he addressed people as 'Citizen' and, probably even more alarmingly, was a vegetarian – but like many in England at the time, especially looking at events in France, could accept political and social reform only if it were led by a lord. By the 1840s that view had changed, and J. M. Gutch's new anthology,[2] which positioned itself independently by being personally hostile to Ritson, probably because of his radicalism, also, and contradictorily, was more radical than him by conducting a long argument about Robin's having been not a lord but a yeoman, a figure of the people – almost a modern member of parliament, so maintaining Ritson's discursive position on identity and politics but updating it after fifty years.

In much of the nineteenth-century narrative that developed in the novel, historicity still ruled. Robin Hood remains a figure whose exciting deeds are retold only for a political, and so would-be historical purpose – for Scott he is Englishness embodied, and as is outlined in Chapter 6 for others he can be the spirit of Magna Carta rather weirdly combined with the modern English parliament; or among other desirabilities from high liberal politics to low pleasures, he could represent the spirit of English resistance to the French, the natural medieval forest against the alienating modern city, standing up to bullying lords and nasty legal officials, and while fond enough of his wife always keen to kiss a pretty girl. This under-focused para-historical figure oscillating between a trickster spirit and banal nationalism is also behind the finest piece of early outlaw scholarship, the collection and collation by Francis James Child in the early modern period of the early ballads, especially the printed riches, at one penny each. Volume 3 of the five-volume *The English and Scottish Popular Ballads*, which, as part V, originally appeared in 1888, gathers together thirty-eight Robin Hood texts, thirty-one of them broadside or garland ballads (see pp. 83–4),[3] but they are not identified as a theme-focused section. In fact Child links them to the Scottish outlaw of the border ballads by printing 'Johnie Cock' at the start of the volume, then obfuscates the date and coherence of the outlaw texts by offering next the unrelated 'Robin and Gandelyn' and then 'Adam Bell', at best a Robin Hood parallel and recorded later than the early Robin Hood texts which follow.

Child saw the early Robin Hood materials as part of early English national folk culture, and missed their special characteristics, as discussed in Chapter 4. This blurring of boundaries and contents between outlaw texts and folk ballads meshed with his mission – one that was accomplished with remarkable energy and learning, and relied on what would still be impressive world-wide consultation – which was to make widely available in full scholarly mode the early, primarily oral, folk materials of English culture, which were in many instances also part of American culture, and he was implicitly arguing for the richness of these materials that the usual high-culture emphasis on literature and its European antiquities was overlooking. But as well as showing a laudable popularism and an understandable interest in the American cultural past, Child also blurred a crucial generic boundary. The almost comparable scholarship of Bertrand Bronson when he gathered *The Traditional Tunes of the Child Ballads*[4] showed that musically the Robin Hood materials are, as in so many other areas, very different from the norm: their tunes are not ancient and folkloric, they are not medieval, and they are primarily urban and commercial and mostly borrowed – they are new early modern phenomena, and are not of antique folkloric value, neither in the content that Child privileged nor in the form on which Bronson focused.

But no-one at the time in the scholarly or critical professions would notice these malformations of the context of the Robin Hood materials, as almost nobody took any notice of them. The burgeoning number of folklore and folk-ballad people soon realised that the outlaw texts were different, and passed them by for the border ballads and the many early songs of love and loss (the largest category of the Child ballads). The literary people focused on authors who could be felt to rank with the Latin and Greek classics of their earlier education, and in the first half of the twentieth century literary criticism (much to the surprise of people when it is pointed out) was just about Shakespeare and the major poets. The important part of Leavis's intervention was not the shaky moralistic basis and the thematic redirection of authors, but his decision to concentrate on the novel as the major literary art form – *The Great Tradition* is a deliberately challenging title: poetry is superseded. But the outlaw novels were never contenders, being quite without the alienated wit of Austen, the moralising intensity of Eliot or the sensual narcissism of Lawrence.

There were rare instances of scholarly engagement with the outlaw tradition – in 1909 a young American scholar, W. H. Clawson, produced a careful formal study of the major early Robin Hood text, *The Gest of Robin Hood*, and the diligent Oxfordian E. K. Chambers described the early ballads in several studies as part of his literary-historical approach[5] – but no-one followed them up. The first quivers of coherent Robin Hood scholarship appeared after the Second World War in Britain as a debate developed in the journal *Past and Present* about the social and political meaning of the figure and some at least of the texts. Rodney Hilton linked Robin to the so-called 'Peasants' Revolt' of 1381 and others agreed, but then James Holt argued that Robin represented the dissent of small landowners, who were both free yeomen and also minor gentry. Though his interest was clearly political, the conservative Holt could read texts well, and was in fact the first to see ambiguity, even a multiple audience, at the core of the myth,[6] but there were also other nuances. Tom Hahn has shown how this debate was also about how to re-read the English tradition in the light of the post-war leftward move of British politics.[7]

Similar variations in the structures and attitudes of university education led to the actual development of something like Robin Hood studies in the late twentieth century. The move away from core courses, themselves re-creators of a stable hierarchical canon replete with cultural capital, permitted restless-minded people to set up optional courses to study never-discussed issues – like the concerns of women, workers, the colonised and, in this instance, the popular audience. I and others, notably in North America, came across the figure of Robin Hood in courses on ballads, as well as on popular culture and film, and it was immediately obvious that there was no informative secondary material on the tradition, beyond the 'real Robin Hood' obsessionals and the recent extension of that concern into social and political history. One move towards the texts from the historians was the anthology by Dobson and Taylor,[8] but its major value was a lengthy introduction which was the first survey of the textual tradition beyond a few pages in the earlier histories. An indication that a more literary approach would be productive appeared in an essay by Douglas Gray, a classic literary medievalist with wide-ranging and often radical interests, who here thought about the themes and structures of the earliest texts.[9]

It was clear to us Robin Hood ballad teachers that there was more to do to make this tradition, so varied in time and genre, available for coherent analysis. I set out to provide a basically descriptive account, which appeared in 1994 – the subtitle 'A Complete Study' was meant to suggest the old-fashioned descriptivist nature of the project: I was tempted to spell it 'Compleat'.[10] Others were thinking along similar lines: Jeffrey Singman published in 1998 a survey with emphasis on the drama, building on David Wiles's earlier useful though slender book.[11] Kevin Carpenter at Oldenburg University in Germany arranged in 1995 a conference and an essay collection to complement his own fine collection of Robin Hood materials, including visual realisations.[12] Tom Hahn at the University of Rochester joined in with several perceptive analyses as well as organisationally as mastermind of the International Association for Robin Hood Studies, which first met in 1997 and has kept doing so in alternate years, miming the forest spirit by having no subscriptions and no bureaucracy, just a flexible and ad hoc organising group.

Texts for classroom use were another issue, and having separately approached the TEAMS (Teaching of the Middle Ages) series on this matter, Tom Ohlgren of Purdue University and I teamed up and in 1998 produced our *Robin Hood and Other Outlaw Tales*, which has been widely used.[13] A different textual move transpired when, having heard about the discovery in 1993 of the seventeenth-century 'Forresters' manuscript of Robin Hood ballads, I learnt at the British Library, to my surprise, that there were no plans to publish it. I turned to this task – there were no new ballads as such in the manuscript, but a few better versions of broadsides and some new editorially corrected texts. The volume was produced by that fine scholar-turned-publisher Derek Brewer, who proved friendly to Robin Hood – his very wide interests already reached into folklore.[14] Through all this process I realised how hard it was to track down such scholarly and critical materials as had been randomly appearing: Gray's essay, in a Tokyo journal, was one of the easiest to find. Again with the help of Brewer, I produced a plump book of reprinted pieces that have helped many a student write interesting essays on the disparate, challenging but highly rewarding primary material.[15]

Once we had as it were introduced Robin Hood to the groves of academic teaching, it was natural, from genuine interest, as well as meeting (and even ironising) the requirements of the modern university's managerial sheriffs, to develop research output on the English outlaw. The International Association for Robin Hood Studies has produced four essay collections from its meetings; there are other independent ones in process, and a number of scholars have produced essays and books. Much of this work has been a sophisticated form of extending our knowledge of Robin Hood across the genres: Scott Nollen has charted the Robin Hood films, while Kevin Harty has recurrently written on little-known outlaw films, including ones outside the Anglophone world;[16] Linda Troost has analysed eighteenth-century musical theatre, and Lorraine Stock has explored the later work of de Koven;[17] Lois Potter has matched that with a study of the English Georgian Alfred Noyes, as well as reporting on the Sherwood-area poets of the early nineteenth century;[18] Tom Hahn's work on the 'Lives of Robin Hood' will be an important addition to this Robin Hood fieldwork;[19] a major contribution has been Tom Ohlgren's research into the early texts and his re-editing of them, with the sadly late Lister Matheson, in a classic comparative edition.[20]

Another form of critical scholarship has produced striking results as the contexts of Robin Hood materials have been looked at both more closely and more widely. Rob Gossedge has shown that Peacock's *Maid Marian* is not a mere witty frolic, as most have thought, but responds to the royal family's attempt to enclose major parts of Windsor Forest in 1814;[21] Helen Phillips has not only seen a Robin Hood theme deep in the most political Brontë novel *Shirley*, but has also set out in compelling detail the varied and determined ways in which early modern religious controversialists, from St Thomas More on, used the Robin Hood tradition as an instrument in their arguments;[22] John Marshall has examined the events and implications in several of the better recorded early play-games;[23] and I have argued for a fuller understanding of the way in which the play-games link to the French *pastourelle* tradition of 'Robin et Marion'.[24] Laura Blunk, Allen W. Wright and John Chandler have all looked further into the outlaw tradition continuing in modern popular culture.[25]

If moves of those kinds took Robin Hood deeper into the academic libraries, there has also been some sign of transition towards a concept-based treatment of the materials of the myth. This was the Raymond Williams-linked idea behind my book *Robin Hood: A Mythic Biography*, tracing how a changing myth operates politically in terms of its multiple receptive – and in terms of this tradition at least, productive – contexts.[26] Other theory-oriented approaches have appeared: the essay collection that I edited for Brepols in 2011, devoted to serious academic treatments of the outlaw myth, included Valerie Johnson's account of it in terms of Giorgio Agamben's theories, and Alex Kaufman's development of Nietzsche's theories of the horde in terms of greenwood society.[27] There will surely be more of what have been in a tricksterish spirit called 'Robin Hood with brains' ventures, exploring through scholarship and theory how the outlaw materials are not merely a domain of irritating complications, as they were long seen by tidy-minded and effectively conservative scholars, but are in fact a rich field of social, political and intellectual complexity.

The present book is seen as work towards this goal – its premise is to treat the Robin Hood material with the scholarship and the measured, even plodding, tread of analysis that has long been natural to more prestigious literature. These chapters each develop from an area where I have long felt exist elements of unclarity and uncertainty, but have not been able to spend enough time or space to report on them adequately. Most of the chapters have derived from delivered papers which have been too unwieldy or preliminary to publish, though 'Rabbie Hood' did appear in a conference-based essay collection:[28] one of the reasons to continue to miss the late Julian Wasserman is that we never received his promised, or threatened, matching paper entitled 'Rabbi Hood'. This paper, and all the rest, have been worked on and worked up in response to the generous invitation of Anke Bernau and David Matthews to appear in this series which they edit.

The first three chapters focus on enigmas of uncertainty arising in the early materials that have never been properly explored. The first concerns itself with the medium of the early ballads – are they originarily oral, as was long felt, primarily by Child, or are they, as Fowler argued, fully literary?[29] Or do we need to rethink that separation, as the chapter maintains? The second chapter focuses on the curiously frequent and never explained Scottish connections of the early Robin Hood material, which are explored and analysed, in terms, among others, of their capacity to impact on the English materials – the return to the centre of the colonial resistance to repression, as post-colonial theorists would describe it. The third chapter reconsiders the so far unsatisfactorily explained nature and the likely sources and avatars of *The Gest of Robin Hood*, which I have long felt to be both a partial gentrification of the tradition and also needing to be read in the context of other late medieval multi-social-level texts like *Gamelyn* and the 'King and Subject' ballads.

The fourth chapter and its successors deal with existing unclarities in terms of the structure and interrelationship of a sizeable range of texts. The broadside ballads have long been sourced from and largely left for comment to Child – but editing and collating them, both for a text reader and for the Forresters edition, led me to feel that Child's order and sometimes his texts were not always defensible, and that what was needed, but never yet attempted, was a sound analysis of them into dates, types and socio-political meanings. The chapter sorts the broadsides in these ways, and takes this treatment on to the later and much amplified garlands, which lead almost directly to the late eighteenth-century editions of Evans and Ritson. These are then seen as the first stages of what the next chapter surveys and analyses as the Romantic reception and re-formation of Robin Hood, in poetry and prose. This material too has never been sorted properly as a whole, and after some uncertainty I augmented the material by including Peacock's *Maid Marian* in this chapter, rather than in the next one, which offers a similarly unprecedented analytic survey of the nineteenth-century Robin Hood novels. This decision seemed justified when I found surprisingly little, and that largely trivial, influence from Peacock on the novels in the tradition. Whereas I have before commented on some of the more notable novelists, such as Egan and Stocqueler, I sought here as with the broadsides to give a full account of a Robin Hood sub-genre that is in fact remarkably varied and with multiple sources, textual and socio-political.

The last two chapters work across all the materials, from their different thematic viewpoints, one of content and one of form, and both involving reception. This greater range does involve revisiting topics dealt with in the more narrowly focused previous chapters, and as a result there is some reference back to fuller earlier discussions, though in a few instances issues in Chapters 1–6 which are of some importance in the last two chapters have been deferred for fuller discussion until then.

Chapter 7 explores multiplicity across the tradition in both tone and socio-political meaning, considering and analysing the varied ways in which Marian plays a part – and sometimes, in its own way significantly, does not. Placing her realisations last of the chapters that survey material is a temporal climax, because millennial modernity has made her role much more important. But it is still substantially varied, from Jennifer Roberson's Jane-Austenish managerial Marian to the star of televisual feminist farce (as interpreted by Miss Piggy) and on into various forms of female agency, including what can look like post-feminism. Marian's variety over time and within periods is itself archetypal of the multiplicity and anti-hierarchical character of the whole tradition, and this is the topic, from a theorised viewpoint, of the last chapter. It sees, with Deleuze and Guattari, the concept of rhizomatic structure as the way of understanding this tradition whose ever-changing popularity, facility of access, multiplicity of traditions and malleability by contextual forces has long been opposed to, even ostracised by, the canonical tradition which is linear, uniform or, in their terms, arboreal. With Robin Hood you have the forest, not the mere trees.

There might seem to be a misfit in the increasingly common tendency for scholars to impose professional academic methods on this most determinedly rhizomatic of traditions. Is this a fated and innately destructive attempt to fabricate an arboreal structure?

Will we lose sight of the rhizomatic wood? That is not in fact the situation, because criticism itself, especially when it is in the cultural studies and cultural criticism tradition, is not itself linear and arboreal as is so well suited to the hierarchical myths like Arthur or Tristan and Isolde. Brains can operate in rhizomatic mode. The reason why Robin Hood studies have moved quickly and effectively in recent years is that they are themselves of their time, and function through their own unhierarchical non-linear form. Like seventeenth-century balladeers showing in a time of many constraints how Robin speaks for values beyond the city and its sheriff, even beyond the king, like nineteenth-century novel-writers sensing among all the moralising that Robin can be a liberationist symbol of anti-aristocratic reform (as well as some fine fighting and inspirational trickery), the modern Robin Hood scholars are asserting that this various, porous, richly labile tradition is highly appropriate to the modern multi-mobility, generic and personal as well as national and international, that necessarily responds to the alarms, threats, potential oppressions – and indeed the farcical pomposities – of the modern world.

Robin Hood combines clarity of situation – many ballads begin with the isolative absolutism of 'Robin Hood in greenwood stood' – with both great popularity and mysterious power: the much-quoted proverb is 'Many men speak of Robin Hood that never drew his bow.' The cultural scholarship and criticism that is the natural discourse of the humanities in the modern universities, where in the painful present the sheriffs eagerly gather to profit and prevent, is the appropriate way to understand what comprehensions have been implied in the past and present and what aspirations may in the future be invoked by the formations and re-formations of this potent myth of popular freedom.

Notes

1 Thomas Evans (ed.), *Old Ballads, Historical and Narrative, with Some of Modern Date, Now First Collected and Reprinted from Rare Copies*, 2 vols (London: Evans, 1777); Joseph Ritson (ed.), *Robin Hood: A Collection of All the Ancient Poems, Songs and Ballads Now Extant Relative to the Celebrated English Outlaw (to which are Prefixed Anecdotes of his Life)*, 2 vols (London: Egerton and Johnson, 1795).
2 John Mathew Gutch (ed.), *A Lytell Geste of Robin Hode, with Other Ancient & Modern Ballads and Songs Relating to this Celebrated Yeoman*, 2 vols (London: Longman, 1847).

Introduction

3 As is discussed in Chapter 4, 'The Bold Pedlar and Robin Hood' is, while seeming like a broadside or garland, collected too late to be described as such, though it could well be a nineteenth-century creation, as certainly is 'Robin Hood and the Pedlars', which Child printed in spite of his suspicions. Child's decision to call the two radically different versions of 'Robin Hood and the Beggar' separate ballads numbered I and II seems not unreasonable; see F. J. Child (ed.), *The English and Scottish Popular Ballads*, 5 vols, reprint edn (New York: Dover, 1965), vol. 3: for the comment on 'Robin Hood and the Pedlars' see p. 170.
4 Bertrand Bronson, *The Traditional Tunes of the Child Ballads*, 4 vols (Princeton: Princeton University Press, 1959–72).
5 William H. Clawson, *The Gest of Robin Hood* (Toronto: University of Toronto Library, 1909); E. K. Chambers, *English Literature at the Close of the Middle Ages*, Oxford History of English Literature, 2/2 (Oxford: Clarendon, 1945).
6 Rodney Hilton, 'The Origins of Robin Hood', *Past and Present*, 14 (1958): 30–44; J. C. Holt, 'The Origins and Audience of the Ballads of Robin Hood', *Past and Present*, 18 (1960): 89–110.
7 Thomas Hahn, 'Robin Hood and the Rise of Cultural Studies', in Ruth Evans, Helen Fulton and David Matthews (eds), *Medieval Cultural Studies* (Cardiff: University of Wales Press, 2006), pp. 39–54.
8 R. B. Dobson and John Taylor (eds), *Rymes of Robin Hood: An Introduction to the English Outla*w (London: Heinemann, 1976); rev. edn (Stroud: Sutton, 1999).
9 Douglas Gray, 'The Robin Hood Poems', *Poetica* (Tokyo), 18 (1984): 1–19.
10 Stephen Knight, *Robin Hood: A Complete Study of the English Outlaw* (Oxford: Blackwell, 1994).
11 Jeffrey L. Singman, *Robin Hood: The Shaping of a Legend* (Westport: Greenwood, 1998); David Wiles, *The Early Plays of Robin Hood* (Cambridge: Brewer, 1981).
12 Kevin Carpenter (ed.), *Robin Hood: The Many Faces of that Celebrated Outlaw* (Oldenburg: Bibliotheks- und Informationssystem der Universität Oldenburgs, 1995).
13 Stephen Knight and Thomas Ohlgren (eds), *Robin Hood and Other Outlaw Tales*, 2nd edn, TEAMS Middle English Texts (Kalamazoo: Western Michigan University Press, 2000).
14 Stephen Knight (ed.), *Robin Hood: The Forresters Manuscript* (Cambridge: Brewer, 1998).
15 Stephen Knight (ed.), *Robin Hood: An Anthology of Scholarship and Criticism* (Cambridge: Brewer, 1999).
16 Scott Allen Nollen, *Robin Hood: A Cinematic History of the English Outlaw and his Scottish Counterpart*s (Jefferson: McFarland, 1999); Kevin Harty, *The Reel Middle Ages: American Western and Eastern*

Europe, Middle Eastern and Asian Films about Medieval Europe (Jefferson: McFarland, 1999) and 'Robin Hood on Film: Moving beyond a Swashbuckling Stereotype', in Thomas G. Hahn (ed.), *Robin Hood in Popular Culture: Violence, Transgression and Justice* (Cambridge: Brewer, 2000), pp. 87–100.

17 Linda V. Troost, 'Robin Hood Musicals in Eighteenth-Century London', in Hahn (ed.), *Robin Hood in Popular Culture*, pp. 251–64, and 'The Noble Peasant', in Helen Phillips (ed.), *Robin Hood Medieval and Post-Medieval* (Dublin: Four Courts Press, 2005), pp. 145–53; Lorraine Kochanske Stock, 'Recovering Reginald de Koven and Henry Bache Smith's "lost" Operetta *Maid Marian*', in Lois J. Potter and Joshua Calhoun (eds), *Images of Robin Hood: Medieval to Modern* (Newark: Delaware University Press, 2008), pp. 256–65.

18 Lois J. Potter, 'Robin Hood and the Fairies: Alfred Noyes's Sherwood', in Phillips (ed.), *Robin Hood Medieval and Post-Medieval*, pp. 167–80, and 'Sherwood Forest and the Byronic Robin Hood', in Hahn (ed.), *Robin Hood in Popular Culture*, pp. 215–24.

19 Thomas Hahn (ed.), *Lives of Robin Hood*, Teaching of Middle English Series (Kalamazoo: Western Michigan University Press, forthcoming).

20 Thomas H. Ohlgren, *Robin Hood: The Early Poems, 1465–1560: Texts, Contexts, and Ideology* (Newark: University of Delaware Press, 2007); and Thomas H. Ohlgren and Lister E. Matheson (eds), *Early Rymes of Robyn Hood: An Edition of the Texts ca. 1425 to ca. 1600* (Tempe: Arizona Center for Medieval and Renaissance Studies, 2013).

21 Rob Gossedge, 'Thomas Love Peacock, Robin Hood and the Enclosure of Windsor Forest', in Stephen Knight (ed.), *Robin Hood in Greenwood Stood: Alterity and Context in the English Outlaw Tradition* (Turnhout: Brepols, 2011), pp. 135–64.

22 Helen Phillips, 'Reformist Polemics, Reading Publics and Unpopular Robin Hood', in Knight (ed.), *Robin Hood in Greenwood Stood*, pp. 87–117, and 'Robin Hood, the Prioress of Kirklees and Charlotte Brontë', in Phillips (ed.), *Robin Hood Medieval and Post-Medieval*, pp. 154–66.

23 John Marshall, 'Playing the Game: Reconstructing Robin Hood and the Sheriff of Nottingham', in Hahn (ed.), *Robin Hood in Popular Culture*, pp. 161–74, and 'Picturing Robin Hood in Early Print and Performance: 1500–1509', in Potter and Calhoun (eds), *Images of Robin Hood*, pp. 60–81.

24 Stephen Knight, 'Robin Hood: The Earliest Contexts', in Potter and Calhoun (eds), *Images of Robin Hood*, pp. 21–40.

25 Laura Blunk, 'Red Robin: The Radical Politics of Richard Carpenter's Robin of Sherwood', in Hahn (ed.), *Robin Hood in Popular Culture*, pp. 29–39, and 'And for Best Supporting Hero ... Little John', in Helen Phillips (ed.), *Bandit Territories: British Outlaws and their*

Traditions (Cardiff: University of Wales Press, 2008), pp. 196–216; Allan W. Wright, '"Begone, knave! Robbery is out of fashion hereabouts": Robin Hood and the Comics Code', in Phillips (ed.), *Bandit Territories*, pp. 217–23; John Chandler, 'Batman and Robin Hood: Hobsbawm's Outlaw Heroes Past and Present', in Knight (ed.), *Robin Hood in Greenwood Stood*, pp. 187–206.

26 Stephen Knight, *Robin Hood: A Mythic Biography* (Ithaca: Cornell University Press, 2003).

27 Valerie B. Johnson, 'Agamben's homo sacer, "the State of Exception" and the Modern Robin Hood', in Knight (ed.), *Robin Hood in Greenwood Stood*, pp. 207–27; Alexander L. Kaufman, 'Nietzsche's Herd and the Individual Construction of Alterity in *A Lytell Gest of Robyn Hode*', in Knight (ed.), *Robin Hood in Greenwood Stood*, pp. 31–46.

28 Stephen Knight, 'Rabbie Hood: The Development of the English Outlaw Myth in Scotland', in Phillips (ed.), *Bandit Territories*, pp. 99–118.

29 For Child's concept of the originally oral status of the ballads, see the discussion in Chapter 1 below, and Child (ed.), *The English and Scottish Popular Ballads*, vol. 3, pp. 121 and 129; David C. Fowler, *A Literary History of the Popular Ballad* (Durham, NC: Duke University Press, 1968).

1
Interfacing orality and literacy: the case of Robin Hood

Orality versus literacy

In 1844 *The Mysteries of London* by G. W. M. Reynolds began to appear, in weekly eight-page issues costing a penny. There is ample evidence that this very popular work was often read aloud to enthusiastic groups of illiterate people by someone with the skills of reading. At the same time Dickens had great success reading his work aloud, and it has long been known that he even punctuated his work for oral performance. That has usually been written off as part of his theatrical personality but in fact, as with Reynolds, in Dickens's work orality, including a performed orality, was very close to literature; the two modes were interwoven, and for many people the oral was the mode in which the literary took life. The power of orality in electronic modernity may well not be a revival, but a continuation.

While orality had survived as a form of narrative consumption well into the nineteenth century, it was anthropologists and social historians who first asserted the importance of oral culture, with early literary scholars following up by working on the oral character of epics from ancient Greece to the early Germanic world.[1] They were trying to ascertain the orally based structures of an ancient and distant cultural mode, with some success. Historians followed, tracing the transition from orality into their own literary mode, and in the process tending in some way to validate their own position. The titles of Chaytor's *From Script to Print* and Clanchy's *From Memory to Written Record* have a certain self-confidence about them, implying the observable process of the ancient world's passage into the techniques of modernity.[2] Clanchy does have a short sequence on 'Listening to the Word', mostly about the performance of written literature, but this is seen as a transitional stage, ending with printing.[3] Brian Stock is aware of the 'imprecision of the idea of literacy' and the need 'to speak of the occasioned uses of texts' which can leave room for orality, but nevertheless, presumably because he is dealing with theological scholarship, he feels that 'oral discourse exists largely within a framework of conventions determined by texts'.[4] A more sophisticated assessment of the relationship of the two modes comes from Jesse Gellrich, who perceives orality in 'the performative quality of the medieval book' and sees writing as having the status of 'a version of speaking' in the period.[5] A view more fully aware of the complexity of the postmodern period of electronic culture can see the ways in which the power of literacy has been back-projected as a false authority for medieval texts, as when Marianne Boerch writes:

> As for the medieval text, its textuality and authority would have been generated in a complex cultural field featuring a variety of textualities (oral and written, Latin and vernacular, Hellenic and Jewish), power struggles with implications for linguistic usage (clerical/courtly; male/female, aristocratic/bourgeois) and different technologies (orality versus literacy).[6]

This 'complex cultural field' has been over-simplified at times. Despite the perceptions offered by Gellrich, Stock and Boerch that orality and literacy are not simply opposed, the two positions can still be hierarchised, with literacy dominant, and the two modes are separated in a paradigm of historical development. For all Walter J. Ong's sophistications and modulations, a sense that literary supersedes oral is involved in both the broad impact and the underlying thrust of his very influential *Orality and Literacy*. Ong not only speaks of 'the relentless dominance of textuality in the scholarly mind';[7] he also exhibits the tendency himself. He draws a time-line of development from orality to literacy and then back again in the mode of electronic recording into what he calls 'secondary orality',[8] and he also insists on the cognitive, indeed ontologically distinct, character of oral and literary epistemologies. 'Writing Restructures Consciousness' is the bold title of his chapter 4, which takes us with a colonising flourish into 'The new world of autonomous discourse'.[9] Single phenomena that changed the world, whether the wheel, the stirrup, printing, the chronometer, steam, electricity or internal combustion, are intensely exciting to monofocal scholarship, but they are also fetishes: the fetishisation of literacy appears innate to criticism that is itself literary. Joyce Coleman has pointed to the self-validating tendency of these scholars when she comments that 'The story of the eclipse of orality by the strong sun of literacy is a modern-day scholar's creation myth', and she argues for a settled and highly valued condition of 'aurality' in the oral consumption of late medieval texts.[10]

But for all her acute critique of the orality scholars, Coleman is herself only talking about a social and performed mode of experiencing texts, not a system in which orality and literacy actually interrelate. Like the scholars writing in the collection *Performing Medieval Narrative*,[11] she restricts herself conveniently to the late medieval period, where both modes are in fact well known to co-exist and to have social venues of co-existence. What of the post-medieval period, up to Reynolds and Dickens and into what may not be secondary orality, but the original mode continuing? What if literacy were taken merely as an alternative instrument of production, not a self-validating fetish? I suggest that orality and literacy would then appear as dialectical, with phases varying not only through a temporal axis but also through axes which within periods depend on genre, audience and context. That double-axis, or even multiple-axis, view of the situation would of itself explain why in the modern electronic period orality has so readily re-established itself as a major cultural form: it never actually went away, though the self-validating literary scholars wanted to think it had.

The Robin Hood materials are most unusual in that they appear, from the very beginning, to be both oral and literary, and maintain that complexity to the present, with varying intensities of an instrumental and context-driven kind. This is not widely acknowledged as a possibility. In terms of the early materials, the dominant scholarly approach is a simpler version of Ong's time-line and a blunter assertion of the triumph of literacy. That might well seem to be invited by the fact of the length and evident unmusicality of the two long Robin Hood ballads from just after the mid fifteenth century and the even more literary *Gest* from the very end of that century. The earliest Robin Hood songs that certainly survive are from the early seventeenth century – but that is not the only evidence of outlaw orality, as will be discussed below. The major discussion of this piece of literary (or indeed oral) history has an almost obsessive literarity. In his *Literary History of the Popular Ballad* (1968), David C. Fowler does mention 'the supposed autonomy of the oral tradition' but this is not to relate orality dialectically with literacy, but to subordinate the oral to the written.[12] He sees orality as a frayed and decayed version of literacy – what the Germans used to call *herabgesunkenes Kulturgut* ('down-sunken cultural goods'). He assumes that a written record is very close to the date of composition and will dominate the domain of orality – if necessary assuming lost copies to assert this dominance. So in his view the long and literary 'Robin Hood and the Monk' and 'Robin Hood and the Potter', now dated by Ohlgren respectively to c.1465 and c.1468,[13] are themselves the 'rymes of Robyn Hode' referred to in the late 1370s in *Piers Plowman*. This enables him to argue not only that the shorter sung Robin Hood ballads were later, but that in fact all of the sung ballad genre had a parallel literary origin, asserting that 'without the impetus of the Robin Hood repertoire the popular ballad would never have come into being'.[14] He feels the written and printed late medieval Robin Hood ballads gave rise to the much later oral riches that Child printed of over 100 songs about love and war, collected mostly from illiterate or semi-literate lower-class people around Britain and indeed in America. Fowler reverses the earlier folkism of scholars who felt that the sung ballad was a communal product – and of course also reverses their implicit social, even socialist, politics.[15] In this context the striking thing is the almost obsessively writing-oriented nature of his arguments: this is a 'literary history' indeed. Richard Green has argued against this argument, showing the survival powers of orality and its capacity to interrelate with literate modes.[16]

Nancy Mason Bradbury has, in the wake of the 'oral-formula' scholarship, seen oral performative forces at work in medieval narratives in her *Writing Aloud* (1998).[17] She takes her advocacy of the oral so far as to print the later fourteenth-century *Gamelyn* in ballad stanza form rather than the loose pausing four-stress line which, as is shown by the weakness of her alleged stanzas, is the actual form. But attentive as Bradbury is to the separate status of orality, and in pressing it even further than the form of *Gamelyn* in claiming the performative quality of *Troilus and Criseyde* as basically oral (Boccaccio too?), she is inherently and recurrently still faithful to an Ongian historical time-line, and the work of her book is to explore, as in *Gamelyn*, 'the fragmentary written remains of a genuine compositional tradition'.[18] There may be more in the ballads, though, than Fowler's literacy or Bradbury's fragments of orality, and the situation may be continuingly dialectic rather than temporally developmental.

Early references

To look first at the surprising wealth of reference in the early Robin Hood materials, it becomes clear that from the start they can be hard to class as either oral or literate.[19] The term Langland uses in

Piers Plowman, 'rymes', is ambiguous, but has perhaps a tendency towards orality in its stress on rhyming sounds: other very early references are openly dual. In *Dives and Pauper*, of c.1405–10, the poor man, a preacher, speaks about those who 'gon levir to heryn a tale or a song of Robin Hood or of sum rubaudry than to heryn masse or matynes' – this is an elaboration of the *Piers Plowman* 'rymes' as both tale and song, though a 'tale' might of course itself be orally performed. The chronicler Walter Bower, writing in c.1440, speaks of the 'jesters and minstrels who sing' of Robin Hood, and says that people enjoy them above 'all other ballads' – though the Latin word translated as 'ballads' is *romanciis*, not implicitly a song medium, though one capable of being performed aloud.[20]

More unequivocally oral, in 1441 a group of aggressive Norfolk labourers sang 'We arn Robynhodesmen, war, war, war' as they planned to assault the local squire. In the late fifteenth century in *How the Plowman Lerned his Paternoster* some labourers 'songe goiynge home ward a gest of Robyn Hode'; from the same period a burlesque Scottish poem tells how 'the sow sat on hym bank and harpyd Robin Hood'.[21] In John Rastell's *Interlude of the Four Elements* of 1520 Ignorance sings a garbled story, beginning 'Robin Hood in Barnsdale stood'. John Major's chronicle account of Robin Hood, published in 1521, says that his feats 'are told in song all over Britain': the word translated as 'song' is *cantus*, which definitely implies a tune, and as the verb is *utitur*, meaning 'used' or 'enjoyed' rather than the usual translation 'told', this seems to make 'song' much more likely than 'tale'.[22] Thomas More mentions 'a song of Robin Hood' in his *Heresies* (1528); there is a reference to a Robin Hood song in Nicholas Udall's 1542 *Apothegmes*; Lewis Wager's interlude *The Longer Thou Livest the More Fool Thou Art* (1569) has a character called Moros sing a nonsense medley including the lines 'Robin lende to me thy Bowe'; Nicholas Breton's poem 'The Nightingale and Phillis' (after 1596) speaks of how she 'playde Robin Hood' on her lute. A song with the line 'Robin and Scarlet and John' is sung by Justice Shallow in Shakespeare's *Henry IV Part 2*, while Falstaff sings the same song in *The Merry Wives of Windsor* and it is mentioned in Beaumont and Fletcher's *Philaster*.[23]

This evidence indicates that songs about Robin Hood were popular, even usual, in the fifteenth and sixteenth centuries, but none has survived in writing – the narrative song 'Robyn and Gandelyn' from a mid-fifteenth-century Sloane manuscript 2593 is conceivably related, but cannot be claimed as Robin Hood material: its Robin does not have that second name, and as he is killed in the action he hardly plays a Robin Hood-like role in the story. In these references only the two chroniclers, Bower and Major, seem to imply that the songs had a narrative content but both also stress singing – it seems likely that the 'gest' that the labourers sang going home was also a sung narrative. There seems enough evidence to be sure that simple celebratory outlaw songs were common, and were a separate genre in the late medieval period.

It is equally clear that other references suggest that 'tales', lengthy narratives usually performed in some way, are also common about outlaws. This may be what Langland means by 'ryme', and it is a tale that is heard in *Dives and Pauper* (1405–10); tales may also be the genre implied in the common proverb that 'Many men speak of Robin Hood that never bear his bow', first recorded also in 1405–10 in a sermon by Hugh Legat. Bower's account (c.1440) mentions people hearing 'romances' rather than songs: though the word *romanciis* is translated usually as 'ballads' its meaning is clearly closer to 'tale'; a short tale is presumably the genre of the 'gest' that was sung in *How the Plowman Lerned his Paternoster*; in c.1500–10 a Scottish poem has 'Thair is no story that I of heir Of Johne nor Robyn Hude'. There are several sixteenth-century references to tales of Robin Hood that are heard – in Barclay's *Ship of Fools* (1509), and in his Fourth Eclogue (1513–14); in 'The Overthrowe of the Abbeyes', a Reformation allegory using Robin Hood as a basis (1553–58); in Richard Wilson's play *The Three Ladies of London* (1584).

But in addition to song and performed tales, there are also a number of references which suggest people were also reading stories of Robin Hood: these references are all negative projections and, in the spirit of Langland's literary critique, their authors argue that people should be reading more improving matter.[24] William Tyndale, in *The Obedience of a Christian Man* (1528), mentions 'to read Robin Hood' as corrupting; in the same year Jerome Barlowe and William Roye in *Reed me and Be not Wrothe* imply the same judgement; in 1533 Ydelnesse in a polemical poem in British Library, MS Lansdowne 794 takes the same theme; while Bishop Latimer seems to be attacking the play-games in his famous criticism of people celebrating Robin Hood rather than attending church on a Sunday (probably referring to an experience in the 1530s), in a sermon in 1549 he speaks of 'reding profane histories' including Chaucer and Robin Hood. Walter Lynne in *The True*

Beliefe in Christ and his Sacramentes (1550) criticises people who 'reade the fained stories of Robin-hode'; in the same year Robert Crowley, apparently without irony, mentions teaching through 'an A.B.C., a primer, or else Robynhode'; Thomas Churchyard, in 1560, in *A Replicacioun onto Camels Objection*, implies satire of someone whose 'study hath ben of Robin Hood', and in 1593 in *Pierces Supererogation* Gabriel Harvey speaks slightingly of 'idle phantasies' and 'ruffianly jests' that are suitable for 'Robin Hoodes library'.[25]

Through all these references, learned literary people evidently think of Robin Hood in bookish terms, while others seem to experience the outlaw tradition equally in fully oral performance or song. The songs at least may well relate to the Whitsun carnivals involving plays and games, or play-games as they are usually and generally called, when Robin Hood was central to the celebration of summer, a phenomenon that attracts the largest number of references before 1600. No doubt many of the songs were merely celebratory lyrics, but there also seems clearly to be some element of narrative song, apparently referred to with the term 'gest' or 'rhyme'. Somewhere between denigrated reading and popular song, lyric or narrative, stands the relatively uncomprehended process of performing tales which have texts. Here, as apparently in the long early manuscript ballads, the text merely performs a recording function and is without any direct cultural role: that lies in the oral performance, probably to some rhythmic accompaniment. Genre and function are directly linked to context and expectation; orality and literacy can be separate or linked; while the learned, like modern scholars, attempt to impose an evaluative hierarchy, the actual situation is more fluid, dynamic, dialectical.

Early texts

If these conclusions can be drawn from references alone, what can be drawn from the surviving early texts? Non-narrative song appears the most elusive form. There are tunes surviving from song-books from 1592 on for 'Bonny Sweet Robin is All My Joy' and 'Robin is to the Greenwood Gone',[26] but Bronson states that the latter seems to be the same as 'Robin is to the Greenwood Gone' from the French Robin and Marian pastoral love cycle, which has no firm narrative link to the English outlaw, though it may be a source for the south-western play-game tradition.[27] 'Bonny Sweet Robin is All My Joy' seems to be another of these non-outlaw love songs: and in fact Bronson records some thirty references in contemporary songs to Robin, only one of whom is Robin Hood, and that surname may well be an editorial amplification.[28]

There is little help to be found with conjecturing the tunes for the early Robin Hood songs when in the seventeenth century Robin Hood broadside ballads are widely available, often with named tunes: Bronson comments, 'The record of tunes for the Robin Hood ballads is disappointingly meager and uncertain.'[29] The ballad tunes cited for the outlaw ballads are musically uninteresting; many share the same tune (twelve for one of them, even), and most of the tunes are borrowed from elsewhere and in any case show little antiquity. This evidence suggests that the broadside ballads, short narratives with tunes, were not of substantial antiquity, because if they were some at least would have retained earlier modal tunes. It therefore seems that the Robin Hood songs that are referred to in some of the references discussed above, and might well have been old enough to have modal tunes, have been lost. While there is some evidence for sung Robin Hood narratives this is not before the late fourteenth century, and if as I have argued elsewhere the idea of an anti-authority Robin Hood is a later development than the communal and natural hero of the play-games,[30] then these narratives may well be too late to have developed modal tunes, and the absence of old tunes in the seventeenth-century broadside development, when these short outlaw narratives were decidedly popular, is no surprise.

On the basis of this discussion, it seems fairly clear that there are three elements of Robin Hood performativity surviving into the early modern period – lyric songs, completely lost along with their conceivably modal tunes; longish narratives, which have in a few cases been recorded and were also in some way performed; shorter narratives capable of being sung, which survive only through their printed versions as broadsides from the seventeenth century on. However, complexity emerges on closer study of the surviving texts. Nothing more can be known about the lyric songs (though there might be a suspicion that to realise the anti-authority spirit, there had to be some narrative element, and perhaps the purely lyric songs only attended the play-games). Where there is evidence, there is also complication. The relations between the second and third categories, and, more surprisingly, between different versions of the broadsides with different levels of orality and literacy, are quite complex, and orality can even seem to be the more modern feature in the development of the tradition and the hybridisation of texts within it.

Where the broadside texts often have refrains and are in most cases singably short, the earliest of the ballads are far away from such a state. 'Robin Hood and the Monk' and 'Robin Hood and the Potter' are 358 and 423 lines long respectively, and the only other ballad that may be as early, 'Robin Hood and Guy of Gisborne', is 234 lines long.[31] The first two appear in substantial manuscript collections of stories, and the usual explanation is that a professional entertainer compiled them as a resource for performance. A form of orality is clearly present: the first concludes 'Thus endys the talkyng of the munke' and the second begins its second stanza, after the 'summertime' opening it shares with all three ballads, 'Herkens, god yemen'.[32] The most literary of the early material, *The Gest of Robin Hood*, of 1,824 lines, begins in the same way 'Lythe and listin, gentilmen',[33] and the line recurs at line 573, the start of Fitt 3, and at line 1265, the start of Fitt 6 (where it is reinforced by adding 'And herkyn to your songe', line 1266).

But this neat repetition of orality could itself be a sign of enhanced bookishness: it is suggestive of generic change that Gummere found in the *Gest* 'hardly a trace of the leaping and lingering, familiar in the normal ballad', where that technique associated with song and performance is found in 'Robin Hood and the Monk' and 'Robin Hood and the Potter'.[34] Merely to invoke orality does not prove its existence – novelists have often done the same to enliven their literarity. But it does seem to have operated in this case: the usual argument about these stories (often merged with the 'minstrel romances') is that they were performed to some form of musical rhythmicality – a drone or a chord – and this seems what Sir Philip Sidney had in mind when, referring to *Chevy Chase*, one of the lengthy sixteenth-century action texts, he spoke of it being moving when sung by 'some blinde crowder',[35] a minstrel using a stringed instrument. That this form of performance – like a talking blues – is successful has been shown by Bob Frank with his performance of the *Gest*.[36] To accept this puts us immediately in a hybrid situation, as these are written and, very soon, printed texts, yet they are experienced in an inherently oral way though not, because of their length and lack of refrain, in song form.[37]

Not only the mention of orality links the long early Robin Hood ballads to performance. Their episodic structure, a serial 'Gothic' two-dimensional pattern rather than perspectivised aestheticism, and their combination of elision and repetition effects, what

Interfacing orality and literacy

Hodgart and Gummere have identified as 'leaping and lingering',[38] though not found in the *Gest*, are essentially the same as those features when they are found so richly in the ancient epics that were close to full orality. William Nelson has commented on the necessary structural characteristics of the performed text, quoting Tasso's experience, and comments that an Aristotelian unified structure did not work in that context.[39]

A striking number of these lengthy action-based performed narratives thrived in the sixteenth century, many of them printed. They often had historical origins, like the Percy–Douglas stories as in *Chevy Chase*, but even when apparently fictional they were not new. *Adam Bell* is not recorded until 1523, but Dunbar speaks in his early sixteenth-century poem 'Of Sir Thomas Norray' of an 'Allan Bell' in the Robin Hood context, and as early as 1432 there is a memorable marginal entry in a Wiltshire parliamentary roll where outlaw names are written down the margin: Robin and his friends are included but the list starts with Adam Bell, Clyme Ocluw and Willyam Cloudesle, the three heroes of *Adam Bell*, presumably themselves figures from what Langland called 'rymes'. Was there also an Adam Bell song tradition as well as a literary one?

Somewhere between full literacy and full orality, these performed texts, including Robin Hood ones, evidently thrived in print in the sixteenth century – yet it seems that the song tradition of Robin Hood is also alive, as the references indicate, and it can also be in part traced within the surviving texts. With all his experience and his willingness to deploy his personal taste, Child would occasionally claim a ballad as having the true popular tone: he said that 'Robin Hood and the Curtal Friar' 'is in a genuinely popular strain, and was made to sing, not to print' (vol. 3, p. 121), by which he meant those ballads with status going back before the broadside explosion, and so he placed it very early, though it did not survive until the Percy Folio manuscript, when the broadside ballads were well established. He saw this quality elsewhere only in 'Robin Hood and the Pinder of Wakefield', which he said had been 'pretty well sung to pieces before it was printed' (vol. 3, p. 129), referring to the refrain, the direct language and the swift, dramatic action. But he did also stretch a point to make his case about the friar when he edited Percy's second line. In the manuscript the rhyme is identical, 'In May' (line 2) and 'In May' (line 4), but Child makes the first into 'I say' – so inserting an unwarranted orality. In fact the broadside version lacks a refrain and is quite long for singing at

164 lines, and if it does have oral antiquity it may be of the 'talking' kind rather than the song Child had in mind.

A fact he also knew, and may in part have been influenced by, is that the ballads about the pinder and the curtal friar can both also be linked to the sixteenth century because they describe action referred to in the manuscript 'Life of Robin Hood', found in the British Library's Sloane 'Life of Robin Hood', written around 1600 or perhaps somewhat earlier.[40] Both may also relate to another genre that complicates Robin Hood activity, but has no bearing on the orality–literacy interface, or at least not on this discussion of it. The friar story is close – with some interesting differences – to a play printed by Copland at the end of his *Gest* in c.1560, and there was a fighting friar in the play (or in one of the two scenes) from c.1475 preserved in the Paston papers.

Child recognised that this story stood separate from others, noting that the friar is 'never heard of' in 'the truly popular ballads' (vol. 3, p. 122), and it may well be that just as the fighting friar appears to have been added relatively late to Robin Hood's band from the personnel of popular plays, so his story is itself a generic intruder with more oral than literary status, having been developed from the short plays, only one of which was recorded. This may also have happened with 'Robin Hood and Guy of Gisborne', a process that may explain both its air of antiquity and the lack of an early version. The 'pinder' story is also in drama fairly early, in the full-length play *George a Greene* (by 1594, and if indeed by Robert Greene, by 1592), but here the ballad's title, at least, is recorded in the Stationers' Register as early as 1557–59. Interestingly there is a unique expanded, 'talking ballad' version of 'Robin Hood and the Pinder of Wakefield' in the Forresters manuscript, alongside the short, song-like version, so here the more literate form appears to have been developed after the short and more oral form, the reverse of what seems the normal pattern of the few seventeenth-century broadsides where there are earlier versions.

Child also seems to have felt that 'Robin Hood's Death' had antiquity: he prints it between 'Robin Hood and the Monk' and 'Robin Hood and the Potter', and describes it as being 'in the fine old strain', though he knows it is 'found only in late garlands' (vol. 3, p. 103). The story certainly is old: it is found briefly at the end of the *Gest*, and is well known through the sixteenth century.[41] When Bower speaks in c.1440 of 'tragedies' about Robin Hood this is presumably the story he has in mind. The version in Percy's manuscript was, before the pages were ripped, quite long and without a refrain, clearly a performed 'talking' ballad. It is only the eighteenth-century version which, in broadside style, has a song refrain and is short enough to be a song – interestingly, even confusingly, one of the few Robin Hood ballads that may have been sung to the probably old tune of 'The Three Ravens'.[42] But there is no trace of this notional early song being preserved, conceivably because of the evident lack of interest among the public in a tragic version of the outlaw story. The death ballad does not appear in the garlands, and this attitude continues: the fine and finally tragic film *Robin and Marian* (1976) apparently lost money at the box office.

Oralised literacy

So printing and literacy by no means silenced the oral and performative tendency of the medieval outlaw ballad. Rather, they provided resources for that process in the performative mode, and when the song mode developed strongly, with tunes and refrains, in the seventeenth-century broadside ballads, it did so with the support of literacy, not in opposition to it. Sometimes literacy was crude: when Child called 'Robin Hood and the Tinker' 'a contemptible imitation of imitations' (vol. 3, p. 140) he probably referred to the drinking bout and Robin's avoiding paying the bill, but he might have said the same on literary grounds of a stanza like this from 'Robin Hood and Will Stutely':

> 'My noble master thee doth scorn,
> And all thy cowardly crew;
> Such silly imps unable are
> Bold Robin to subdue.'
>
> (Child no. 141, vol.3, p. 186, st. 25)

Here the dialectics of orality and literacy are crass, as they are in the long and literary make-up ballad 'Robin Hood's Birth, Breeding, Valour and Marriage'. This mentions the pinder, Adam Bell, the Gamwell family and Loxley, all from varied sources, and invents for Robin a fairy mistress called Clorinda. That sounds literary indeed, but the final statement that this is a sung ballad matches the burlesque tone as in

> For I saw them fighting, and fidled the while
> And Clorinda sung 'Hey derry down!
> The bumpkins are beaten, put up thy sword, Bob,
> And now let's dance into the town.'
>
> (Child no.149, vol. 3, p. 217, st. 45)

The interface of orality and literacy can be more complex and more dynamic. 'Robin Hood and the Butcher' apparently derives from the early long literary ballad 'Robin Hood and the Potter', with a change of trade (perhaps towards a condensation of nature, violence and vitality more mythically potent in the outlaw context than mere pottery skills? Or perhaps because butchers were more overtly urban than potters?) The earliest survival of the 'butcher' version also seems very much an oral sung version: it begins 'Come, all you brave gallants, and listen a while', ends the first stanza with 'A song I intend for to sing' and uses the 'Hey down a down down' refrain that usually goes with the 'Robin Hood and the Stranger' or 'Arthur a Bland' tune. But just as the phrase 'brave gallant' has a seventeenth-century literary ring to it, so this ballad is not only literary in being printed, but also has an author, being signed T.R. (as are the two versions of 'Robin Hood and the Beggar', sung to the same tune). This is a product of the London literary world, printed by F. Grove of Snow Hill, who worked from 1620 to 1655 – it seems an example of what Child dismissively calls 'char-work done for the petty press' (vol. 3, p. 42). But the world of literacy has in fact generated the oral version, and a clear sign of this is the jingling internal rhyme in the third line, a feature not found in what seem like song-linked earlier ballads discussed above in the same ballad metre, but characteristic of many of the 'make-ups' of the broadside industry from the later seventeenth century.

The other version of 'Robin Hood and the Butcher' is in the contemporary Percy Folio manuscript, but it has older signs: it begins briskly with a version of the 'summertime' stanza found in the fifteenth-century 'talking' ballads: 'But Robin he walkes in the greene fforest, As merry as bird on boughe'; and even though it is damaged, with two half-pages ripped out, it is still 120 lines long, so would have been of the lengthy performed-narrative type. There is no sign of either a refrain, third-line internal rhyme or even anything like the 'lythe and listen' tag which asserts self-conscious orality in these lengthy ballads. The Percy version, it seems, is the transition performed text between 'Robin Hood and the Potter' and the 'Robin Hood and the Butcher' broadside which, being both printed and sung, condenses orality and literacy in functional dialectic. Child prints this early, straight after 'Robin Hood and the Potter', presumably because of their connection: he does not claim antiquity for it, though – curiously like 'Robin Hood and the Curtal Friar' – it first appears in the Percy Folio and the 1663 garland, presumably because both already existed, but have been lost, in the broadside ballad tradition that provided the materials for the garlands.

There are other signs of such multiple status and the interrelation of the literary form with singing in the seventeenth century. Pepys, a devoted singer, had his own collection of broadsides, and they included a version of 'Robin Hood and Allen a Dale', which has a familiar 'literary orality' opening line 'Come listen to me, you gallants so free', and deploys as a refrain a repeated last line of each stanza line. This, however, uses the tune 'Robin Hood in the Greenwood Stood' which Bronson thinks is possibly the 'Bonny Sweet Robin' tune recorded in the late sixteenth century and not itself an outlaw song.[43] No author's initials appear here, and the printer was working later than T.R.'s printer Grove (Cole was active from 1655 on). Other shapes could be visible in this ballad: the highly literary – and also insistently oral – opening stanza seems to be an added frame, as the second stanza has a familiar 'Robin in the summer forest' ring to it: 'As Robin Hood in the forrest stood, All under the green-wood tree'. Pepys's version appears to be a literary transmission of an earlier song, itself primarily literary but derived directly from the talking ballad tradition.

There may be a trace of another sung version of this story in the 1993-discovered Forresters manuscript: this is 'Robin Hood and the Bride', a version which does not mention Allen's name, nor involve Little John in its comic resolution. Those features in fact make the ballad closer to the version of this story that appears in the Sloane 'Life' (though that was about Will Scarlett), and this, as well as the vigorous rhymes and the traces of northern dialect, suggests that the Forresters version of this story may – like other ballads traceable through the Sloane 'Life' or for other reasons to the sixteenth century (see the discussion of dating in Chapter 4, pp. 85–94) – have a sung version as its basis, which has then in its broadside version been titivated with a more literary form of orality – the development process apparently also found in the Pepys version of this story.

A striking instance of the reverse process, sung orality coming from earlier literacy, is the ballad that is best called 'Robin Hood and Will Scarlett', though, presumably for sales purposes, the broadside was named by its printer 'Robin Hood Newly Revived' (also 'Reviv'd') – which may itself imply that there was an earlier version. This gentrifies the outlaw somewhat, as he is discovered to be the cousin of Will, who is himself of a gentry family named Gamwell – a link to the late fourteenth-century literary, if also performable, poem *Gamelyn* seems possible. Having a refrain, this ballad was sung to the very popular tune 'Robin Hood and the Stranger' (itself a variant title of this ballad),[44] but was made substantially literary in broadside form by having attached to it (via a few stanzas of the fugitive 'Robin Hood and the Scotchman') what Child calls the 'pseudo-chivalrous romance' (vol. 3, p. 147) 'Robin Hood and the Prince of Aragon', a ballad of 232 lines printed without refrain and presumably never intended to be sung. But these mercantile (and gentrifying) printing manoeuvres do not seem to have cut the 'Will Scarlett' ballad off from orality: in the nineteenth century J. H. Dixon collected what seems to be a cut-down and strongly simplified 'traditional variation' (Child, vol. 3, p. 154) seeming to link the Gamwell family with a fighting pedlar story, where 'Gamwell' has become 'Gamble Gold', who is still revealed as Robin's cousin. The dialecticality of literary and oral versions of a ballad can extend over centuries.

In these two cases different versions point to different mixtures of orality and literacy. In another case, where there is a more puzzling history, there may be internal signs of multiplicity. 'Robin Hood and Little John' tells the story of their first encounter and the fight at the bridge, which Robin loses, a sequence to be very popular in film. But there is no surviving early version of this story: Child's main text is from a 1723 collection, but he later found and printed, in volume 5, a broadside printed in the late seventeenth century. This was sung to the 'Robin Hood and the Stranger' tune, has the 'Hey down down and a down' refrain and exhibits the internal rhyme in the third line which is characteristic of the seventeenth-century 'written for singing' ballads. So much seems a late piece of literary orality. But there must be some possibility that this highly dramatic action formed part of the lost 'Robin Hood and Little John' play recorded in the Stationers' Register in 1594, and I have argued elsewhere that it may be possible on the grounds of language to see traces of an earlier version in the first part of the 1680s broadside.[45] While some of the text exhibits the language of literary hackwork, at once florid and clumsy (e.g. 'passionate fury and eyre', line 71, or 'the whole train the grove did refrain', line 152), these features seem to dominate the later part of the text, and there could be embedded in the earlier part a version with simpler and more direct language. There may be signs of an earlier sung version which would have fitted the tune of this name found in a 1609 song-book,[46] and which might be expected of such a long-standing and popular figure as Little John – see Chapter 4 (pp. 84–5) for argument about the existence of a sixteenth-century version.

There appears to be another and clearer example of song into literacy in the case of the pinder of Wakefield. The ballad usually called 'The Jolly Pinder of Wakefield' survives from the early seventeenth century: it is short and briskly active, and lacks the wordy later style. Child prints it early, but also with three breaks, as if lines are missing. There is, however, no break in the sense, and it is more likely this is a complete version without evenness of stanza or accurate rhyme – and the fact that it reappears in a number of versions in the same form suggests it was read as being quite adequate in the period. As discussed below (see p. 89) it very likely has sixteenth-century origins, and appears a surviving example of an outlaw song which includes narrative. One of the sources for this view is the recently discovered Forresters manuscript, where it is laid out in four-line stanzas, rough rhyme and all. However, there its fifty-line brevity follows a version with 140 lines, with an elaborated narrative, moderately fancy vocabulary (e.g. 'Clean voyd of Any doubt' and 'doughty Swayne'),[47] and with internal rhyme in the third line. This is a fine example of the fully formed literary version of the earlier oral narrative – the reverse of the literacy into song process evident in the broadsides.

Dialectical survivals

If some later and floridly literary ballads did indeed contain an earlier bolder sung version (which would appear to refute Fowler's sense that literacy gave rise to popularity), that would both symbolise and epitomise the deeply interwoven strands of orality and literacy in this material, both at this time and also in other times and places in the tradition. The highly literary and early printed *Gest*, with its traces of Arthurian dignity in the early Robin and its equally weighty shape of a heroic biography extending to the final death sequence, is also a text to which we are expected to listen. The Renaissance Robin Hood material at its most literary, whether the ponderous gentrification of Anthony Munday or the muscular elegance of Ben Jonson, is directed towards performance, not silent reading. The Robin Hood myth is not only multiple in the possible meanings of his core value of resistance to wrongful authority: it is also multiple in genre and dialectical in mode of delivery.

This is evident even at the heart of literacy: the Robin Hood novels are generically unstable in their dealing with the hero. In

Ivanhoe the doughty Locksley is finally dismissed by Scott specifically back to his world of the ballads – but, saving his own literary position, only to printed ballads; in the wittily learned *Maid Marian* Peacock includes many performable songs, and the musical play of the novel was the major disseminator of this crucial condensation of the respectability of the earl and the vigour of the yeoman. The Robin Hood tradition in the nineteenth century resists in a lively fashion both the moral seriousness and the literary exclusiveness of the English novel tradition.

In the eighteenth century, musical theatre is a major form of transmission of the tradition, along with 'garlands' of printed ballads meant to be singable. In the nineteenth century, while Robin Hood is entombed in a number of three-decker novels full of invented fights and English democracy (including Saxon lords with French names), the oral still lurks: the child-oriented 1841 *Robin Hood and his Merry Foresters* by 'Stephen Percy' (i.e. John Cundall) is five conversations related to the narrator's schoolfriends, themselves based largely on retellings of the broadside ballads. The far more famous American juvenile text of 1883 by Howard Pyle, *The Merry Adventures of Robin Hood*, with much singing and talking as well as very fine illustrations, was, it seems, clearly based on this: Pyle reminisced that his family had a copy of 'Percy', and commentators have assumed he meant Thomas Percy's *Reliques* (though it contains only one Robin Hood ballad), but the link to the 1841 collection is evident from the text (see below, pp. 180–1).

More overtly, and often outrageously, Victorian pantomime picks up the dialecticality of text and voice, and we find, for example, Joachim Stocqueler as co-author both of one of the wittiest pantomimes, rich in music as well as terrible puns and broad comedy (he would surely have included the sow playing a Robin Hood song in church had he known of it), and also of a lively multi-tonal Robin Hood novel of 1849. Tennyson's *The Foresters* (1891) was played and sung to the music of Arthur Sullivan; it was the success of that and the Reginald de Koven musical in the 1890s that helped generate such a wealth of Robin Hood material in early film. Without orality, the silents were energised by performative theatricality, notably gymnastics in the Fairbanks 1922 version, and of course by the insistent music from the pit; when sound came to Robin Hood cinema the original plan to produce a Robin Hood musical with Nelson Eddy and Jeanette MacDonald was shelved (though *Robin Hood: Men in Tights* seems to parody the idea of it in the comically windswept duet scene), but the 1938 version is rich not only with bravura acting and melodramatic action but also the Oscar-winning music of the significant Austrian composer Wolfgang Korngold.

This multi-genre, multi-mode, oral-literary tradition continues: the archetypal Robin Hood film opens not only with Robin rescuing a serf from Norman brutality, but also with music. People still chant happily the theme song from the very widely watched 1950s black and white *Adventures* (though almost all think it was the opening title music, not as in fact sung in older manner over the end credits), and there is often a lute-carrying character as in *The Adventures of Robin Hood* of 1938 (there named Will a Gamwell, wearing scarlet); Disney featured the British folksinger Elton Hayes (as Allen a Dale) to open its 1952 *The Story of Robin Hood and his Merry Men*, and followed up with a singing cockerel (played by Roger Miller) in the 1973 cartoon. Other musical variants occur, such as a rap-format title song in *Robin Hood: Men in Tights* and a dominating electro-folk soundtrack in *Robin of Sherwood*. Story and music united famously in the case of *Robin Hood: Prince of Thieves*, where the theme song 'Everything I Do, I Do it for You' – hardly heard in the film itself – dominated the hit lists for three months in both Britain and America: it might well have been the Robin Hood connections of the video clip that carried this banal song to fame. Even more assertively oral was the title of the novel of this film: it actually reads, or rather says, *Kevin Costner is Robin Hood Prince of Thieves*. A literary title has become PR-speak.

So, in the case of Robin Hood, what might be patronisingly taken as a curious medieval muddle over mode, oral or literary, is in fact a dynamic mix of orality and literacy that has been functional in conveying the rich range of the English outlaw tradition. This case study may well establish a complex dialectic of the two modes, oral and literary, that also holds for other cultural formations, notably those which challenge social as well as cultural stasis, like the myths of the Australian bushranger Ned Kelly and the Welsh trickster Twm Siôn Cati, both outlaw traditions based on resistance to authority, in different colonial contexts.

The dialectical interrelationship of orality and literacy at the core of the Robin Hood materials is appropriate for this hero: he creates in form a resistance to the authoritarian structure of writing as the only mode that the literary sheriffs and evaluative abbots of modernity will allow to be admired, and deployed, in their quest to restrict the liberty of orality, a form of natural lore, and law. Robin Hood may, as in so many things, stand for discoverable freedoms and complex liberties, from a radical yeoman to a moralising lord, not forgetting the harping sow. Like the penny-a-time weekly eight-page serials of Reynolds's huge novel, in cost and function just like a broadside ballad, like so much in narrative both for children and for imaginative adults, like so much in theatre and the electronically captured orality of the modern period, the outlaw myth shows us that orality and literacy are not opposites but can be dynamic partners in an artistically productive dialectic of signs which are meaningful both by being read and by being heard.

Notes

1 A. B. Lord in *The Singer of Tales* (Cambridge, MA: Harvard University Press, 1960) followed up the ground-breaking work of Milman Parry on the patterns of ancient oral epic, and also showed the validity of this approach to Germanic epic.
2 H. J. Chaytor, *From Script to Print* (Cambridge: Cambridge University Press, 1945); M. T. Clanchy, *From Oral Memory to Written Record: England 1066–1377* (Cambridge, MA: Harvard University Press, 1979).
3 Clanchy, *Oral Memory*, pp. 266–72, 293.
4 Brian Stock, *The Implications of Literacy: Written Language and Modes of Interpretation in the Eleventh and Twelfth Centuries* (Princeton: Princeton University Press, 1980), pp. 7 and 12.
5 Jesse M. Gellrich, *Discourse and Dominion in the Fourteenth Century: Oral Contexts of Writing in Philosophy, Politics, and Poetry* (Princeton: Princeton University Press, 1995), pp. 4 and 34.
6 Marianne Boerch, 'Preface', in *Text and Voice: The Rhetoric of Authority in the Middle Ages* (Odense: University Press of Southern Denmark, 1999), p. 12.
7 Walter J. Ong, *Orality and Literacy: The Technologizing of the Word* (London: Methuen, 1982), p. 10.
8 Ong, *Orality and Literacy*, p. 136.
9 Ong, *Orality and Literacy*, p. 78.
10 Joyce Coleman, *Public Reading and the Reading Public in Late Medieval England and France* (Cambridge: Cambridge University Press, 1996), p. 33.
11 Evelyn Burge Vitz, Nancy Freeman Regalado and Marilyn Lawrence (eds), *Performing Medieval Narrative* (Cambridge: Brewer, 2005).
12 David C. Fowler, *A Literary History of the Popular Ballad* (Durham, NC: Duke University Press, 1968), p. 5.

13 Thomas H. Ohlgren, *Robin Hood: The Early Poems, 1465–1560: Texts, Contexts, and Ideology* (Newark: University of Delaware Press, 2007), pp. 40 and 75.
14 Fowler, *Popular Ballad*, p. 65.
15 The notion of ballad as 'the old communal song of medieval Europe', rather than the work of a single author or succession of authors, is outlined classically by Francis B. Gummere, *The Popular Ballad* (New York: Houghton Mifflin, 1997), pp. 43 and 331–4; the concept is discussed in M. J. C. Hodgart, *The Ballad*, 2nd edn (London: Hutchinson, 1962), pp. 151–7.
16 Richard Firth Green, 'The Ballad in the Middle Ages', in Helen Cooper and Sally Mapstone (eds), *The Long Fifteenth Century: Essays for Douglas Gray* (Oxford: Clarendon, 1997), pp. 163–84.
17 Nancy Mason Bradbury, *Writing Aloud: Storytelling in Late Medieval England* (Urbana and Chicago: University of Illinois Press, 1998).
18 Bradbury, *Writing Aloud*, p. 30.
19 The following discussion relies on the list of early Robin Hood references collected by Lucy Sussex and printed as an Appendix to Stephen Knight, *Robin Hood: A Complete Study of the English Outlaw* (Oxford: Blackwell, 1994), pp. 262–88.
20 For Bower's Latin see F. J. Child (ed.), *The English and Scottish Popular Ballads*, 5 vols, reprint edn (New York: Dover, 1965), vol. 3, p. 41. Further references to Child's comments on and editing of the ballads will be inserted in the text.
21 This is usually edited to 'hye bank', but the reading is quite clear and no doubt refers to the hymn bench in the chancel.
22 See John Major, *Historia Majoris Britanniae* (Edinburgh: Fribarn, 1740), p. 128.
23 Child thinks this is the final line from 'Robin Hood and the Jolly Pinder' (vol. 3, p. 129), but it could derive from 'Robin Hood Newly Reviv'd', which introduces Will, especially if as its title may suggest there were an earlier 'Robin Hood and Will Scarlett' form; the line also opens 'Robin Hood and the Prince of Aragon', which was attached to 'Robin Hood Newly Revised'.
24 For a discussion of the religious polemics involved in these and parallel references, see Helen Phillips, 'Reformist Polemics, Reading Publics and Unpopular Robin Hood', in Stephen Knight (ed.), *Robin Hood in Greenwood Stood: Alterity and the English Outlaw Tradition* (Turnhout: Brepols, 2011), pp. 87–117.
25 I am grateful for this new reference to Peter Roberts, who discovered it as part of his work on a PhD at Cardiff University.
26 Bertrand H. Bronson, *The Traditional Tunes of the Child Ballads*, 4 vols (Princeton: Princeton University Press, 1959–72), vol. 3, p. 13.
27 For argument on this point see Stephen Knight, 'Robin Hood: The Earliest Contexts', in Lois J. Potter and Joshua Calhoun (eds), *Images*

of Robin Hood: Medieval to Modern (Newark: Delaware University Press, 2008), pp. 21–40.
28 See Bronson, *Tunes of the Child Ballads*, vol. 3, p. 13.
29 See Bronson, *Tunes of the Child Ballads*, vol. 3, p. 13.
30 Stephen Knight, 'Alterity, Parody, Habitus: The Formation of the Early Literary Tradition of Robin Hood', in Knight (ed.), *Robin Hood in Greenwood Stood*, pp. 1–29, at p. 7.
31 While this ballad is not preserved until the Percy Folio of c.1645, part of its action resembles a play, or scene, preserved in the Paston papers from c.1475, and William Dunbar mentions Guy in c.1500. It is usually accepted as having late medieval roots – or it is possibly a very skilful pastiche: see the discussion in Chapter 4 below, pp. 88–9.
32 For 'Robin Hood and the Monk' see Stephen Knight and Thomas Ohlgren (eds), *Robin Hood and Other Outlaw Tales*, 2nd edn, TEAMS Middle English Texts (Kalamazoo: Western Michigan University Press, 2000), pp. 37–48, at line 355; for 'Robin Hood and the Potter' see Knight and Ohlgren (eds), *Robin Hood and Other Outlaw Tales*, pp. 62–72, at line 5.
33 For *A Gest of Robyn Hode* see Knight and Ohlgren (eds), *Robin Hood and Other Outlaw Tales*, pp. 90–148, at line 1.
34 Gummere, *Popular Ballad*, p. 283.
35 Sir Philip Sidney, A *Defence of Poetry*, ed. J. A. van Dorsten (Oxford: Oxford University Press, 1966), p. 46.
36 Bob Frank performed the *Gest* in slightly modified format at the Kalamazoo medieval conference in 2005, and his version is available on CD-ROM as *A Little Gest of Robin Hood* (El Sobrante, California: Bowstring Records, 2001).
37 Curiously, the short song-like narrative 'Robyn and Gandelyn' speaks in its first line of 'a carpyng of a clerk' as its basis, implying a further dialectical interrelation between the two modes of orality being discussed; see Child, vol. 3, p. 13, st. 1.
38 See Hodgart, *Ballad*, p. 18, and Gummere, *Popular Ballad*, pp. 91–6.
39 See William Nelson, 'From "Listen, Lordings" to "Dear Reader"', *University of Toronto Quarterly*, 46 (1976–77): 110–24, at pp. 110–11.
40 Tom Hahn, who is editing the *Lives of Robin Hood* for a Teaching of the Middle Ages edition, commented at a conference that he feels 1600, the usual date, may be up to a generation too late, which means that the stories used in Munday's 1598–99 plays (the friar, the execution rescue, anti-clericalism, gentrification itself and the death) could not have influenced the references in the Sloane 'Life'.
41 The hero's death was known to Leland in the 1540s, is referred to by Grafton in 1568–69 and is central to Munday's second play, *The Death of Robert, Earle of Huntington* in 1599; see Chapter 3 below, pp. 74–7.
42 Bronson, *Tunes of the Child Ballads*, vol. 3, p. 18.
43 Bronson, *Tunes of the Child Ballads*, vol. 3, p. 51.

44 This is a rare occasion where Child is not correct: he felt Ritson was misled by a much-used tune in giving the ballad this name, but Ritson had no doubt seen, probably in the 1662 prose garland (where it bears different titles on different pages), the text given this name in print.
45 See Knight and Ohlgren (eds), *Robin Hood and Other Outlaw Tales*, p. 476.
46 See Bronson, *Tunes of the Child Ballads*, vol. 3, p. 13.
47 'Robin Hood and the Pinder of Wakefield I', in Stephen Knight (ed.), *Robin Hood: The Forresters Manuscript* (Cambridge: Brewer, 1998), p. 63, line 4, and p. 65, line 49.

2
Rabbie Hood: the development of the English outlaw myth in Scotland

Robin and Rabbie

National heroes can have strange origins. If King Arthur, doyen of English monarchs, had any historical reality it was as a Celtic Briton, speaking Welsh and fighting against the English. Yet cultural heroics can do more than reverse apparent conflicts as the Arthur story does: they can be quite exotic in origin. People with now mature children may well recall the bizarre phenomenon of the Ninja Turtles, where Western child culture crossed both species and the globe to find comfort and delight in heroes doubly displaced in both their Eastern and chelonian kinds.

The cultural mix under discussion in this chapter stands somewhere between Arthur and the turtles, and a mix of methodologies, in part socio-political and in part post-colonial, will be deployed to explore the development of the English hero Robin Hood in a Scottish context, as a figure who was in Scotland hybridised in various ways, and then re-exported to the colonising centre in a different and remarkably successful form.

Any survey of the influences and developments of the Robin Hood tradition over time must soon enough notice the recurrent element of Scottish involvement with the tradition – and yet there has been almost no analysis of this involvement, presumably because of the force of the identification of the hero as English. The Scottish interest has had two major periods, the fifteenth and sixteenth centuries and the time of Scott. The two have some connections: in both periods Scotland developed an interest in and a version of the English outlaw, and it is arguable that in both periods it was in fact the Scottish versions which lay behind major changes in the tradition of the allegedly English hero, changes which of themselves have made it still popular today.

There is no birthright for continued fame for mythic heroes: some of them undergo crucial changes that stimulate re-invention of their myths, while others just fade away. Whatever happened to Guy of Warwick and Bevis of Hampton? Those once sturdy but now forgotten heroes remained unchanged in their fully medieval English forms, and so had only an archaic interest in the early modern period and afterwards. Robin Hood altered a great deal, and so was able to present new ideas about the meaning of resistance to authority. There is a Caledonian flavour to some of the most important of these changes, in both the late medieval to Renaissance period and the time led by Walter Scott. The second period of Scottish interest will be discussed in some detail in Chapter 6 in relation to Robin Hood novels of the nineteenth century: the focus here will be the impact of Scottish interest in the outlaw in the late medieval period.

It has long been known that late medieval Scottish references to the English outlaw exist and that activities linked to the Robin Hood play-games took place in Scottish towns in the late Middle Ages; the role of Scots chroniclers and writers in referring to the English outlaw myth has also been recurrently mentioned by scholars. But these phenomena have not been looked at as a body, and not considered in terms of their wider implications, as I hope to do here. Lewis Spence's brief and quite early essay, 'Robin Hood in Scotland',[1] deals with only some of the material, though it did open up the idea interestingly – but without being pursued by other scholars. Apart from the intrinsic interest and relative neglect of the topic of Rabbie Hood, another good reason to return to it is that the whole phenomenon of a Scottish version of Robin Hood can now be looked at in the light of recently developed knowledge and theorisation about how colonised cultures operate and, most interestingly for this chapter, how the colonial implants may interact with native traditions and how they may in turn, and in return, influence the culture of the colonising power itself. If Robin Hood in Scotland is one of the themes of this chapter, then Rabbie Hood in England is another: as in so many cases of colonialism and post-colonialism, the traffic was by no means one-way. Scottish studies tend to resist post-colonialism on the grounds that Scotland was never a colony of England, just a negotiated ally and federate, but the more complex and contributory role of Scotland to the Robin Hood myth may even in such a delicate context make post-colonial critical discourse conceivably acceptable.

Robin into Rabbie

The evidence of the interrelationship in this outlaw myth between England and Scotland is clear. In the Appendix to my 1994 book on the outlaw, Lucy Sussex gathered together all the pre-1600 references that could be traced.[2] Of some 270 citations, fifty-three are clearly related to Scotland or to Scottish authors. The quantity of the early Scottish references may of course be caused in part by the relatively sophisticated nature of lowland Scottish urban and mercantile life (which extends at least in this context up the east coast to Aberdeen), and also by both the quality and the relatively high survival ratio of their records.

Even in a benign environment for records, about a fifth is still a large proportion, and it is also noticeable that this contains much more than a fifth of the specific and amplified references – many of the English ones just refer to a Robin Hood play-game taking place, or to buying cloth for costumes. The Scots references tend to name characters appearing in the streets and describe their actions, or they are literary references with some detail; and some – and here the Scots have an exclusive claim – are references to apparently real outlaws by chroniclers from Andrew of Wyntoun onwards.

There are no doubt going to be more Robin Hood materials found in the present process of publishing the full records of early drama, but the relative weight and quality of the Scottish references are unlikely to be diminished. The extent, specificity and inherent importance of the early Scottish Robin Hood occurrences clearly indicate that something was going on in this context in the north at that time. How are we to interpret this phenomenon?

Robin Hood is not the only British mythic figure to turn out to have strong early Scottish elements. King Arthur is the obvious candidate, with scholars like Nora Chadwick and Rachel Bromwich thinking his origin as an anti-Saxon leader was very likely among the warriors from north of Hadrian's Wall who had never considered, or been debilitated by, peaceful relations with Rome.[3] But the process was wider. The hero of medieval French romance Yvain was certainly in origin Owain, historical prince of Rheged, centred on Carlisle; Gawain became famous in Europe as Galvaginus, 'the man from Galloway', this name giving rise to his French name Gauvain. Myrddin/Merlin had his origin just south of the border in Cumbria.[4] The scholars who have pursued the northern King Arthur have seen it as a matter of origins, suggesting with some credibility that the real hero operated in the heroic

British north and his tradition was preserved where the language of that area survived, namely Wales. But that does not seem to be a viable model for the dissemination of the Robin Hood myth, and in spite of neo-empiricist, and often regional, passions on the point, the concept of a historic Robin Hood is less persuasive even than that of a real King Arthur (counter-intuitively, the wise man/wizard Myrddin/Merlin has a better case for historicity than either). An originary Scottish Robin Hood, disseminating south, is not in any way suggested by the evidence. Rather, as I have argued in my 1994 book, Robin Hood is a hero of anti-authoritarian myth with multiple locations, who may well be a figure supportive of community when his role is local and organic, but will become involved in opposition to authority when that community comes into conflict with external and intrusive authorities such as those of abbot, sheriff or indeed king – or perhaps when, in the fourteenth century, medical, social and economic crisis becomes widespread.[5] Robin Hood's reality is like that of Santa Claus or Cinderella, representing a functional idea, and one that invites people not to identify him, but to identify with him.

While, as has been mentioned in Chapter 1 (see p. 20), the figure of Robin is traceable to medieval France and to the early play-games of south-western England, the use of the name Robin Hood for public events in south-eastern Scotland clearly shows some cultural transmission through England, quite probably also linking with some French-originated knowledge. Such hybridity is suggested in the name of the ship *Le Robin Hude* which docked in Aberdeen in 1438, itself involved in some aura of criminality: we have the record because the master was accused, as if eponymously, of stealing goods in transit. But the process of Scottish re-localisation of the south-western English play-games is clear in the Scottish records. Aberdeen in May 1508 has a requirement very like those from south-western England that there should be a public and fund-raising celebration where 'all pepil that ar abill within this burghe ... to pass with Robyne Hude and Litile Johnne'. They are to be in costume (many of the English play-game records are notes of the cost of costumes): 'thair arrayment maid in grene and yellow, bowis, arrowis, brass and all uther convenient thingis according thairto'.[6] That is a Scottish relocation or imitation of Robin Hood, but things move towards appropriation and the origins of Rabbie Hood when both the date and the concept of the figure change. In the Aberdeen municipal statutes for that same year, 1508, under 17 November, it says that:

all personiis, burges, nichtbouris, and inhabitaris, burges sonnys, habill to ryd, to decor and honor the towne in thar array conveinant therto, sall rid with Robert Huyid an Litile Johne, quilk was callit in yers bipast, Abbat and Prior of Bonacord, one every Sanct Nicholas day, throw the towne. as use and wont has bene ...[7]

This is a communal fund-raising activity, as is indicated by the substantial fines to be paid by those required to ride but unwilling to do so – twenty shillings to St Nicholas's 'werk' and eight shillings to the 'bailyeis'. The event is an elaborate, prosperous and basically urban version of the English play-games, but the time of year is unusual. The play-games took place in May, at Whitsun. The presence of Robin Hood in May 1508 was a new phenomenon in Aberdeen: in the previous year this May festival was led by the 'Abbat and Prior of Bonacord'. But the greatest innovation is the date of this second Robin Hood event: 6 December. He joins another tradition: St Nicholas's Kirk is the main medieval church in Aberdeen; St Nicholas guilds were associated with clerical performance in medieval England, and December was the time of the 'Boy Bishop' ceremonies, the monastic Feast of Fools with temporary reversal of ranks.

Such elements of carnival were clearly part of the English playgame tradition, but there are no English instances of a winter Robin Hood until his inclusion in a nineteenth-century mummers' play, which is a complete cultural mish-mash – he shares the stage with Lord Nelson.[8] It looks as if the resettlement in Scotland of Robin Hood had also changed the figure significantly, detaching him in part from the strong natural symbolism of the English Whitsun practices – perhaps the bleaker northern weather had an influence there – and making him more a figure of year-round urban harmony as implied in the title Bonacord, itself a local cultural transmission from France. The Abbot of Bonacord had walked in both the summer and winter festivals, so, having replaced him in May, Robin served in the same role again in winter.

Not only is Scottish culture creative with its received material: it can also disseminate its own parallels. There is a clear knowledge in Wiltshire in 1432 of the border outlaws Adam Bell, William of Cloudesley and Clim of the Clough, seen in the Robin Hood context;[9] their story apparently remained popular in ballad form in England throughout the fifteenth and sixteenth centuries and were first recorded in a fragmentary printed text of c.1536. But there seems to have been a more multiple and complex form of cross-border traffic concerning Robin Hood. Rabbie Hood is not simply a quaint kilt-wearing Robin Hood. He is a specialised and syncretic figure. The Scottish Robin Hood, like the nineteenth-century French Robin des Bois, the Hindu Ravi and, most relevantly, the English William of Cloudesley, is not a locally originated social bandit, like the French Thierry de la Fronde or the Indian Bandit Queen, or indeed the Scots William Wallace. Rabbie Hood, by virtue of being borrowed, fits into another world-wide model: the hero from another place who brings external and therefore specially credible values which are used to define a sense of local lack and need. As with Aeneas, the Trojan in Italy, or Beowulf, in Anglo-Saxon England far from his Geatish home, a sense of local weakness (or in Robin's case disaccord) may be calmed by the special powers of the supra-local hero by virtue of his externality. Robin Hood in Scotland means more through his ability to be re-formed for special purposes, starting with Bonacord in November.

The return of Rabbie

The Rabbie Hood formations move well beyond the Aberdeen winter charity street-collector. A particularly striking phenomenon is the remarkable fact that the only chronicle references to Robin Hood before the dawn of English antiquarianism in the mid sixteenth century come from a range of Scottish historians. The references deserve special and separate attention; they have some connections, but each introduces new features, indicating that this is not just a sequence of chroniclers being faithful to each other: each generated a new type of Rabbie Hood.

Andrew of Wyntoun wrote his metrical history of Scotland in the 1420s, which under the year 1283 reads:

> Litil Iohun and Robert Hude
> Waythemen war commendit gud;
> In Ingilwode and Bernnysdaile
> Thai oyssit al this tyme thar trawale.[10]

That is, 'Little John and Robin Hood were praised highly as highwaymen; they conducted their operations during the whole of this period in Inglewood and Barnsdale.' The lines read a little oddly to a textual editor, not simply because John unusually precedes Robin – that is probably just for rhyme. There is a sense of padding about 'commendit gud' and an awkward, expanded feel to the last line: Wyntoun is usually very brisk. A hypothesis worth putting forward is that there was previously a popular jingle:

> Litil Iohun and Robert Hude
> Waythemen were in Ingilwode.

The further hypothesis is that Andrew knew this couplet but, being a good scholar and chronicler as befits an Augustinian canon from a daughter house of St Andrews, he also knew of the Robin Hood of Barnesdale tradition (his source will be a subject of later speculation), so compiled this slightly clumsy elaborated reference.

The date is intriguing: nothing in the surviving Robin Hood narratives can take us back to 1283, though 'real Robin Hood' historians would like to think of a thirteenth-century origin for the tradition. There appears to be an implicit comparison between these admirable outlaws and William Wallace, the Scottish nationalist social bandit who was operating around 1283 and for whom Wyntoun has much sympathy: Joseph Ritson noted this in his influential 1795 account of the outlaw.[11] The clear implication is that Little John and Robin Hood are opponents of the English authorities under Edward I, and so have interests in common with similar figures to the north: the concept of an outlaw from a Scottish viewpoint entails a political and nationalist identity for the figure. Rabbie Hood is emerging.

Wyntoun has no doubt of their existence as real outlaws; he has nothing specific to say about their cultural popularity, though it can be assumed from the sense of 'commendit gud'. The next Scottish chronicler to take up the theme had more to say about culture than about politics. Walter Bower, writing only twenty years later, continued John of Fordun's *Scotichronicon* and re-dated his Robin Hood to 1266. He sums up more severely than Wyntoun:

> Then arose the famous murderer, Robert Hood, as well as Little John, together with their accomplices from among the dispossessed, whom the foolish populace are so inordinately fond of celebrating both in tragedy and comedy.[12]

But Bower also tells a story of Robin's fidelity to the church: he insists on finishing mass deep in the forest before fighting off the sheriff. This might sound simply like a Christianised Robin Hood adventure, but the Latin suggests more. The sheriff is called 'viscount' and Robin is hiding from the 'the wrath of the king and the roaring of the prince',[13] which seems in spite of Bower's dating in the time of Henry III to have a resonance of the slightly later attacks on Scotland by Edward I and his son, and certainly sees Robin as an anti-royal noble on the Wallace pattern, a sense not found in the early English outlaw texts. Rabbie Hood emerges more clearly. As a Scot and a canon himself, Bower sophisticates Wyntoun's story and sets it in another time of resistance to an English king – in the period of Simon de Montfort's resistance to Henry III, an idea much revisited in the nineteenth century, because it could associate this Robin with de Montfort, the alleged founder of the English parliament.

If Bower sophisticates the Scots chronicle tradition somewhat, and directs its idea of an anti-royal Robin back towards England, a third Scottish chronicler completes that process. Written probably in Paris and certainly published there in 1521, John Major's *Historia Majoris Britanniae* not only gentrified Robin somewhat, but took him back into the time of bad King John, so his rebellion against royal rule can itself become fully legitimate.[14] Major probably used the story of Fulk Fitz Warren as a model for this distressed gentleman narrative (as discussed in Chapter 3, p. 70). But in making Robin seem noble, as well as by making him resist a bad king, as is implied by the 1190s date, Major is closer to the Scots anti-royal war-leader model than the popular English hero, who was a plain man among men with no thoughts of nobility or politics beyond robbing a monk, shooting the sheriff and visiting Nottingham for entertainment and danger.

Major makes Robin a 'most famous robber' and a war leader with a hundred ferocious bowmen – a warband fit for a resistant noble like Wallace, not a mere highwayman. He is famous all over Britain (not England); he is noble in manner and also in self – being the 'humanest and the chief' – and the Latin word *dux* here may well have inspired further chroniclers like Grafton, who followed Major closely, to assert that Robin was a nobleman, having 'the noble dignité of an Erle'.[15]

Commentators have stressed the gentrification process in the history of the Robin Hood tradition: class remains an object of fascination, or obsession, for all in Britain. But gentrification is also a different political model, shaping a man who moves on a national political stage, rather than lurking locally in a forest. Major's Robin of 1521 becomes very easily the aristocrat whom Anthony Munday turned him into in the twin plays of 1598–99, *The Downfall of Robert, Earle of Huntington* and *The Death of Robert, Earle of Huntington*: the resistance to a bad prince is already established in Major's dating of the hero to the 1190s. As Renaissance chroniclers like Grafton and Stow absorb this Robin back into the cultural bloodstream, it is as a laudable, aristocratic and national hero. This is a massive reconstruction of the myth which still reverberates throughout the tradition, and appears to derive from a distinctly Scottish reading of the figure – though not yet one that reads the figure as himself having national identity: that lies in the future and the hands of Walter Scott. If Major himself, for all his further Scotticising of the outlaw hero, was also an example of that persisting phenomenon, the Anglophile Celt, the balance was, as usual in such colonial battles, redressed with interest, and Hector Boece and David Buchanan in their later sixteenth-century chronicles firmly restored a fully Scottish viewpoint, Boece even offering the view that Little John was a true giant and was buried in Moray.[16]

To theorise what happened in the case under examination, the destabilised character of the English Robin Hood in Scotland permitted developments which in England would have been blocked because Robin as social bandit was not sufficiently free-floating a figure. In the early English ballads he is empowered by stable and local organic values and is not as fluid a signifier as he became in transmitted and potentially hybrid form. It was in fact the non-local nature of the figure in Scotland, borrowed both in some way from England (as a resister) and in another way from France via the play-games (as a communal leader), which enabled him to be so labile there, and he began to be re-formed in the structure that was to become the distressed gentleman in England. Studying the relationship with Wallace will both confirm and develop the sense of a striking Scottish influence on the Robin Hood tradition, but before that it is relevant to look back at a previously unexplored channel of contact between England and Scotland in Robin Hood matters.

Royal Rabbie

The surprising presence of 'Bernnysdaile' in Wyntoun's chronicle rewards consideration. Robin Hood scholars have long speculated that the Yorkshire Barnsdale, mentioned in *The Gest of Robin Hood*, is an early location of the myth, which became easily conflated with the Sherwood variant, only a good day's travel south of it on the road from York. The existence of other apparent locations for Robin Hood around the country, including Inglewood, has made this seem only more probable. R. B. Dobson and John Taylor, the steadiest of the historians, however, were a little uneasy about Yorkshire Barnsdale, knowing it had never been a royal forest, was too sparse for serious outlaws and so did not really fit the myth, however much the compiler of the *Gest* (by definition operating in a secondary process) might think that was the hero's address.[17]

But there was another forest called Barnsdale, and that originally a royal one, deep in the heart of Rutland. It had never been noticed by the empiricist historians, though if they had driven from Cambridge to Nottingham they would have passed right by it on the A303 from Stamford to Oakham. There are a number of local Robin Hood caves, stones and similar topographic affiliations.[18] But the major surprise is to find that this Rutland Barnsdale, right through the Middle Ages, had belonged to the Earl of Huntingdon, no less. And who was he? He was, no less again, usually a close male relative of the King of Scotland. This was known to Spence, and he speculated in 1928 that an estate near Huntingdon might have been a place for learning the Robin Hood ballads and taking them back to Scotland.[19] He did not seem to know that the Rutland Barnsdale was part of the estate, but the presence of that name in Wyntoun is an intriguing link between the idea of Scottish aristocratic independence and the tradition of Robin Hood. Inglewood too was a royal Scottish forest, and Wyntoun's connection of the two seems, seen from north of the border, fully rational.

Less certain, but interesting enough, is to speculate that perhaps Anthony Munday knew of the Barnsdale–Huntingdon connection. There has never been any explanation of why, when writing *The Downfall of Robert, Earle of Huntington* in 1598–99, he chose that particular title for his newly gentrified hero. To speculate that the concept of hunting is the link seems an example of scholarly despair, especially as Lord Robert never does any hunting. Bevington's argument that the name comes from a pretender to the throne of the 1560s, while more specific, seems even more improbable, though Lisa Hopkins has recently made a case for his views as extended to the third earl, who died in 1595, as 'a credible candidate for the throne' – yet this successor was young, the connection was distant, and it seems unlikely that the time-serving Munday would invite trouble from the queen in such a way, and in any case the play never envisages such a claim for the outlawed earl.[20] Munday does firmly locate his forest exile in Barnsdale, and I strongly suspect that John Stow, the all-knowing Elizabethan antiquarian, an acquaintance of Munday, knew about the Rutland Barnsdale and the Huntingdon connection and gave him the hint – but I cannot find any evidence of that in Stow's writing. A less likely possible link is the 1596 visit by Shakespeare's Chamberlain's Men (rivals to Munday's Admiral's Men) to the heart of Barnsdale at Christmas to play *Titus Andronicus* for Sir John Harington's nine hundred Christmas guests – an early example of Christmas Gothic.

If Munday did know somehow about the title and the forest, then that is another instance of the Scottish connection at the heart of gentrification, but that remains speculation. The Wyntoun connection is stronger. It seems more than guesswork to suggest that he was influenced in discussing Robin Hood partly by the long-standing Scottish royal connection with the Rutland Barnsdale, and partly by the early existence there of local Robin Hood connections – in 1354 a man who was arrested for deer-poaching named himself as Robin Hood in Rockingham forest only twenty miles away.[21]

But should this sound like a mere one-way colonial borrowing, albeit one where the Scots royal house was colonising darkest Rutland, the actual situation appears more complicated, more multiple. If there was a Scottish presence and transmission deep in the east midlands Robin Hood area, there was apparently also an equally mysterious reflex, a soldierly nationalist Robin Hood far in the north. In David Laing's 1872 edition of Andrew of Wyntoun's *Chronicle*, the famous Inglewood and Barnsdale reference is not the only citation to the outlaw in the index. There is also a reference to a certain 'Hwde of Edname' who helped Sir Alexander Ramsay take Roxburgh by storm from the English in 1342. The reference is presumably to Ednam near Roxburgh (though tantalisingly there is also an Ednam in southern Lincolnshire, not far from Rutland).

If the Rockingham Forest Robin of 1354 is likely to be an auto-creation, a man taking the name because he did the appropriate deeds, then why should that in Ednam not be another example, as Laing thought? – though here it was a Rabbie Hood, a noble Robin Hood attached to the Scottish national cause.

Rabbie rampant

The previous argument does not only bear on the issue of how many Robin Hoods, how many Rabbie Hoods. It also stresses inherent multiplicity: if there is a Hood of Inglewood, who can be linked with tales of faraway royal Scottish Barnsdale, there may as easily have been a more martial borderer from Ednam, who also used that name while fighting the soldiers of Edward III. More generally, though, what this implies is the fact that the Scottish reading of the outlaw figure is clearly not the same as the English, especially in terms of national significance. Rabbie and Robin were two different men. In England, Robin represents regularly the local against the national, the village against the sheriff, the people of the forest against the regulating mechanisms imposed by foresters and the whole imagined rural organic community against the cash-oriented nexus of abbot and town business. That is what the Rockingham man represents, while the Rabbie Hwde of Ednam is a nationally conscious freedom-fighter, at home among gentry, a leader of his people.

This notion of different heroes whose stories interrelate is best exemplified in the relationship between Robin Hood and the best-known Scottish national outlaw. It is clear from the epic Scots poem on William Wallace, apparently written by 'Blind Hary', or Henry the Minstrel, that there are close resemblances to events in a number of Robin Hood ballads. But these outlaw motifs in a fully Scotticised form have a powerful political thrust, now embodying resistance to English imperialism. In 'Robin Hood's Progress to Nottingham',[22] the hero is provoked when young into violence and outlawry by hostile opponents: in Wallace's case the cause of trouble is specified as an Englishman, young Selby, whereas for Robin Hood the hostile forces are simply foresters. Both heroes later on save themselves from capture by dressing as a woman with the help of a sympathetic old woman ('Robin Hood and the Bishop', Child no. 143), but where Wallace hides from Selby senior and his English soldiers, Robin escapes the bishop, in a secular-versus-clerical, not national, conflict. Both outlaws rob and (very rarely in Robin's case) kill travellers (*The Gest of Robin Hood*, Child no. 117; 'Robin Hood and the Monk', Child no. 119; 'Robin Hood's Golden Prize', Child no. 147), and both beat off a fierce ambush (the *Gest*), but again only Wallace's opponents have a national denomination. Both outlaws end by having a difficult encounter with the king, tragic and nationalist in Wallace's case, unsatisfactory but negotiated in the instance of Robin. Both die a noble death at the hands of their enemies, and leave an enduring and highly valued memory, but only Wallace's enemies and meaning belong in the domain of national and aristocratic politics. The closest and most interesting of all the parallels is when both heroes play the part of a potter to enter a town, a strong suggestion of motif transference between the traditions ('Robin Hood and the Potter', Child no. 121). Wallace of course penetrates an essentially English borough in this way, but for Robin it is a journey to the hostile heart of urban mercantilism.

The relation between the two traditions is also intriguing in terms of date. In almost all cases the Robin Hood survivals are a good deal later than that of Blind Hary's *Wallace*, and the two earliest Robin Hood ballads seem themselves almost a generation later. According to Ohlgren's new research the manuscript of 'Robin Hood and the Potter' dates from c.1468 at the earliest,[23] and while it contains scribal errors, it does not look as if it has had a long life in literary transmission. The manuscript containing 'Robin Hood and the Monk', which has usually been dated c.1450, has now been pushed a little forward in time by Ohlgren to c.1465: it was formerly dated as the only Robin Hood narrative which could be thought to predate clearly *The Wallace* in written form.

Most commentators (almost all of them English) have assumed that the Robin Hood materials represent motifs that have long been in existence in the outlaw tradition, were used in the apparently oral Robin Hood rhymes that Langland mentioned in the 1370s and Bower in the 1440s and so, by implication, were borrowed in colonial style into the Wallace narrative. However, *The Wallace* lays down very specific versions of a number of major Robin Hood events which are remarkably like those found in English, mostly long afterwards. It is conceivable that Rabbie Hood may in fact in some important sense instigate Robin Hood: 'Robin Hood and the Monk', 'Robin Hood and the Potter' and the *Gest* represent a new literary realisation of the English popular and orally known Robin Hood, and it is entirely credible that these texts were influenced by and textually structured on the model of an existing text, or texts, about a heroic outlaw, especially as both heroes were well known at the same time in Scotland.

The resemblance between Robin Hood and Wallace was long ago noted, though not quite as long ago as Spence thought, relying as he did on a mistaken dating of the document written by a prior of Alnwick who calls Wallace 'Scotico illi Robin Whood', 'that Scottish Robin Hood'. Spence thought it had the sensational contemporaneity of 1304, but the correct interpretation is 1504.[24] That later date, though, has its own relevance to this topic. It is quite clear that the two traditions were circulating more or less together – but only in Scotland. *The Wallace* was printed in Scotland in 1508 and appears to have been in this form in manuscript by 1488, with an originating date of c.1478. These are precisely the years when *The Gest of Robin Hood* attained its present form: it was printed first in the mid 1490s,[25] and constructed not very long before – apparently after 1450. The *Gest* was being printed in the very period when Robin Hood newly walked in Aberdeen.

There are also literary references. As Dunbar's poetry was being printed in Edinburgh at just the same time as the *Gest* appeared (though not, as was once thought, by the same printer, Chepman and Myllar), it is hardly surprising that the poet refers to the English outlaw in 'Of Sir Thomas Norrey' as 'vyld Robeine under bewch' ('wild Robin under bough' – in the wood), but his knowledge is a good deal wider than the *Gest* itself. He speaks of Robin's opponent 'Guy of Gisburne' and also of 'Allan Belle' – presumably Adam – both in the context of archery.[26] At this time the ballad 'Robin Hood and Guy of Gisborne' was nearly 150 years away from its only recording in the Percy Folio manuscript, though a play with some of the same action has survived from c.1475, but it does not name Guy and, being so fugitive, could hardly have been known in Scotland. Other texts clearly were known in Scotland. Another contemporary reference is a simple mention of Robin Hood processions in a poem formerly attributed to Dunbar and dated very early in the sixteenth century, 'Ane Litill Interlude of the Droichis Part of the Play'. Gavin Douglas's *Pallice of Honur*, dated before 1518, mentions Robin and Gilbert with the White Hand – this makes it clear that he knew the *Gest*, the only text where Robin appears with this minor outlaw, at the archery tournament. A Scottish poem recorded in the Hyndford manuscript in 1588 is usually dated between 1500 and 1510, and it says:

> Thair is no story that I of hier
> Of John nor Robene Hude
> Nor yit of Wallace wicht but weir
> That me thinkes half so gude.[27]

It is evident that the English outlaw story is common knowledge in early sixteenth-century Scotland, and that Robin Hood and Wallace are in some ways coterminous, though, for the latter, national identity is dominant. It seems that, in so far as Rabbie Hood exists, he may well, as the chroniclers' presentation suggests, be a hybrid of Wallace and Robin Hood, a nationally conscious gentleman outlaw, royally mistreated by the King of England, noble, resistant, heroic in life and death – all of those features are not in the early Robin Hood story, but are in the Wallace story. And it is far from impossible that as the Robin Hood story is amplified in written and non-sung form in the long literary ballads like 'Robin Hood and the Monk', 'Robin Hood and the Potter' and the *Gest*, elements of plot and structure from the Wallace story, themselves often shared with earlier outlaw stories like those of Hereward, Eustace and Fulk, are employed: Rabbie Hood may even have provided some of the actions and narrative linking for the ungentrified English Robin Hood.

Rabbie continued

The argument, then, is that in Scottish hands the figure of Robin Hood was reformulated. In the English south-west there was probably a first stage where Robin des Bois was adapted as a figure of local festival, but even then he had gained his English surname by a form of cultural colonising. But in Scotland there were more urgent things for a popular hero to resist than a corrupt sheriff or abbot: the targets of natural justice there included a sense of national identity and resistance to a usurping, invading king, neither of which had been central or even of importance to the original Robin Hood. So Rabbie emerged, remodelled along the lines of Wallace, and it may well be that some of the Wallace detail, such as the potter's disguise, was used back in England in Robin Hood ballads. Certainly the greater nobility and greater political weight of the Scotticised figure was the mainspring of gentrification. This figure was returned to England, where he became highly valuable in Renaissance ideology, both to remove what to some powerful people might seem the unappealingly radical element of Robin Hood's resistance to kings and lords, and also to figure a nobleman under pressure from churchmen and bureaucrats, a central element of Munday's late sixteenth-century plays, through which gentrification of the outlaw was strongly disseminated.

This argument makes sense in itself, but may well seem unusual in its return function. Did the Geats get back an Anglicised Beowulf? Was Aeneas repatriated to Troy? Some heroes never return: Welsh-language culture has little interest in the Anglicised Arthur, remaining loyal to its real native leader Owain Glyndŵr. But there are models of this hybrid-transition process in existence: one is the way in which Raymond Chandler hybridised the tough American private eye with his own English-educated aestheticism, and how through the rehybridisation of Hollywood, the complex mix became authoritative in both America and Britain. In the contexts of Robin Hood and of Scotland there are other examples of this process. A striking parallel is in the account given by Robert Crawford of how, to use his fine chapter title, there was in the eighteenth century and especially the nineteenth a 'Scottish invention of English Literature', which then became very influential in England outside the establishment circle of Oxbridge.[28]

A parallel process has occurred actually within the Robin Hood tradition, this time starting in America. Most people of a certain advancing age, on hearing the name Robin Hood, smile and hum the tune of the 1950s television series. The essence of Englishness, surely, was Richard Greene playing the dapper officer-type Robin Hood who, as the song goes, was feared by the bad and loved by the good. The tradition of the popular ballads seemed to have been handed down directly to the modern welfare state. Not so. The dynamic of these stories was American. The company for marketing reasons wanted a drama series, and no-one in Britain knew how to do them. Through Hannah Weinstein, an American producer with left-wing sympathies who had herself moved to London, the company hired some good writers who would work cheaply. The series was shaped by black-listed American writers, principally Ring Lardner, Jr, and Ian McLellan Hunter.[29] In distant New York, without passports, those two created the first left-liberal greenwood idylls that were shot in England, 'with emphasis not just on social justice, humor, and wit, but on the constant threat of informing and betrayal'.[30] Some English writers also followed the lead set from the States as the hero was re-localised with an external re-politicised concept, just as, I am arguing, happened in the late medieval period from Scotland. The film *Fellow Traveller* (1988), written by Michael Eaton, tells this story. Just as Edward I's mailed fist can be seen as the hand behind the Scottish-grounded gentrifying politicisations of the late medieval Rabbie Hood, so Joe McCarthy was the energising daemon behind the ghostwriters of Richard Greene as a newly re-socialised and socialist Robin Hood.

Though the late medieval process of Scottish-located hybridisation did bring Robin Hood into the 1190s, it did not, as most people think, make him a Saxon. That was a later process, and one consistent with other changes to the hero which made him fit for a modern world. It too was guided from Scotland. Walter Scott in *Ivanhoe* (1819) made Locksley a Saxon – albeit a non-commissioned-officer kind of Saxon, illiterate to boot. That is because Scott knew all about and disliked the radical potential of Robin Hood, being familiar with the 1561 Edinburgh riot when, refused the right to a Robin Hood procession, the citizens rebelled, opened the Toll Booth, took the prisoners out and put in the magistrates. Scott refers to the events in his notes to *The Abbot*, and there is some resonance of them in his account of the Porteous Riots in *The Heart of Midlothian*. But he also made Locksley a modern hero, aggressive, competitive and even, through his process of arrow-splitting, sexually potent – and above all nationalistic. In doing all this Scott made a major contribution to the modern Robin Hood, essentially a strong and handsome hero who lives in the woods and represents national honour and ecological value, as well as a marginally acculturated masculinity.

As will be discussed in Chapter 6, Scott had a little-known predecessor in Edinburgh, the anonymous author of *Robin Hood: A Tale of the Olden Time*, published just before Scott started writing *Ivanhoe*. This was more a Gothic novel than an outlaw story or a nationalist text but it does indicate the outlaw myth was still dynamically at work in Scotland. It is often suggested that Scott turned to the period and the topic of *Ivanhoe* to clinch his interest in the much larger market of English book-buyers, but while that makes sense, and the strategy was certainly successful, there is an argument to be made that the confidence of Scott's Edinburgh, its social complexity, its foreign connections and its well-elaborated culture was better expressed through a model which is international, anti-aristocratic and also multi-classed (and indeed multi-racial). The world of the new novel was able to operate as an expression of complex modern Scottish interests in a way that *Rob Roy* was unable to achieve. The generalised sense of national and personal authenticity that *Ivanhoe* expressed, and the influence it transmitted to historical fiction of all kinds, were the most recent of the many contributions by Scottish society and culture to the myth of both Robin and Rabbie Hood.

Notes

1 Lewis Spence, 'Robin Hood in Scotland', *Chambers Journal*, 18 (1928): 94–6.
2 Stephen Knight, *Robin Hood: A Complete Study of the English Outlaw* (Oxford: Blackwell, 1994), pp. 262–88.
3 For a discussion of 'the northern Arthur', see Rachel Bromwich, 'Concepts of Arthur', *Studia Celtica*, 10–11 (1975–76): 163–81.
4 See the discussion of his origins in Stephen Knight, *Merlin: Knowledge and Power through the Ages* (Ithaca, NY: Cornell University Press, 2009), pp. 1–13.
5 Knight, *Robin Hood: A Complete Study*, pp. 113–15.
6 P. Hume Brown (ed.), *Scotland before 1700 from Documents* (Edinburgh: Douglas, 1893), p. 189.

7 Brown, *Scotland before 1700*, p. 190.
8 See R. E. Tiddy, *The Mummers' Play* (Oxford: Clarendon, 1923).
9 See J. C. Holt, *Robin Hood*, 2nd edn (London: Thames and Hudson, 1990), pp. 69–70.
10 See D. Laing (ed.), *The Orygynale Chronicle* (Edinburgh: Edmonston and Douglas, 1903–14), vol. 5, p. 135, lines 25–8. The text is reprinted and discussed in Stephen Knight and Thomas H. Ohlgren (eds), *Robin Hood and Other Outlaw Tales*, 2nd edn, TEAMS Middle English Texts (Kalamazoo: Western Michigan University Press, 2000), pp. 24–6.
11 See Joseph Ritson (ed.), *Robin Hood: A Collection of All the Ancient Poems, Songs and Ballads Now Extant Relative to the Celebrated English Outlaw (to which are Prefixed Anecdotes of his Life)*, 2 vols (London: Egerton and Johnson, 1795), p. ix.
12 See Walter Bower, Continuation of John of Fordun, *Scotichronicon*, extract in Knight and Ohlgren (eds), *Robin Hood and Other Outlaw Tales*, pp. 25–6.
13 Bower, *Continuation*, p. 26.
14 See Knight and Ohlgren (eds), *Robin Hood and Other Outlaw Tales*, pp. 26–7.
15 Richard Grafton, *Chronicle at Large and Meere History of the Affayres of England: And Kings of the Same* (London: Tottle and Toye, 1569), p. 84.
16 For a discussion of these issues see 'The Physical Setting', in Holt, *Robin Hood*, chapter 5.
17 R. B. Dobson and John Taylor (eds), *Rymes of Robin Hood: An Introduction to the English Outlaw* (London: Heinemann, 1976), rev. edn (Stroud: Sutton, 1999), p. 20.
18 See Knight, *Robin Hood: A Complete Study*, pp. 29–32.
19 Spence, 'Robin Hood', p. 95.
20 David Bevington, *Tudor Drama and Politics: A Critical Approach to Topical Meaning* (Cambridge, MA: Harvard University Press, 1968), p. 295; Lisa Hopkins, *Drama and the Succession to the Throne* (Aldershot: Ashgate, 2011), p. 61.
21 See Dobson and Taylor (eds), *Rymes of Robin Hood*, pp. 12–13.
22 F. J. Child (ed.), *The English and Scottish Popular Ballads*, 5 vols, reprint edn (New York: Dover, 1965), vol. 3, no. 119. References to other Child ballads will be given in the text by their numbers in his edition.
23 Thomas H. Ohlgren, *Robin Hood: The Early Poems, 1465–1560: Texts, Contexts, and Ideology* (Newark: University of Delaware Press, 2007): on dating the texts, see pp. 40 and 75.
24 Spence, 'Robin Hood', p. 96.
25 See Ohlgren, *Robin Hood: The Early Poems*, pp. 97–9.
26 William Dunbar, *Selected Poems*, ed. Priscilla Bawcutt, 2 vols (Glasgow: Association for Scottish Literary Studies, 1988), vol. 1, pp. 131–2.

27 Quoted by Spence, 'Robin Hood', p. 95.
28 Robert Crawford, *Devolving English Literature* (Oxford: Clarendon, 1992), chapter 2.
29 On this topic see Steve Neale, 'Swashbuckling, Sapphire, and Salt: Un-American Contributions to TV Costume Adventure Series in the 1950s', in Frank Krutnik, Steve Neale, Brian Neve and Peter Stanfield (eds), *'Un-American' Hollywood: Politics and Film in the Blacklist Era* (New Brunswick: Rutgers University Press, 2007), pp. 198–209.
30 Neale, 'Swashbuckling', p. 200.

3
Robin Fitz Warren: the formation of *The Gest of Robin Hood*

Adjusting the *Gest*

The Gest of Robin Hood has seemed the central text in the long literary tradition of the English outlaw, having been printed and reprinted through the sixteenth century, used as a quarry for some later ballads, and reworked in novel, play and film – though usually without the sad ending. It has seemed the compendium of the medieval tradition, the *Morte Darthur* of the outlaw story, while the sudden lurch towards higher nobility in Munday's 1598–99 play *The Downfall of Robert, Earle of Huntington* has made the earlier *Gest* seem like the sanctuary of yeoman outlaw authenticity.

But the outcome of re-reading the early material in a deliberately literary way (Chapter 4 on the broadside ballads is a parallel to this one) is the view that the *Gest* has been able to go quietly and conceal its own specialist formation by lurking in the shadow of Munday. Contrasting it with the late medieval narrative ballads, and also with the early references, the play-games and the early play-texts, has generated the conclusion that the *Gest* is a careful and consciously upmarket confection, suited to the target audience of early print, and in a number of ways a more radical departure from the established outlaw mainstream than Munday would be. The *Gest*, it will be argued here, draws substantially on the late medieval tradition of sub-chivalric romance, especially as this is found in *Sir Launfal, Gamelyn* and the 'King and Subject' ballads, but it also adds to that essentially medial social cultural material a clear reliance on the narrative of Fulk Fitz Warren.

Both of these source areas are hardly recognised by scholarship on the *Gest*, but the latter may well be the more surprising. It has at times been assumed that the model for Munday's gentrification of Robin as a nobleman displaced from his true status because of justified crimes in the time of bad Prince John, who is forced into the forest until restored to his honour, must be, via John Major, the story of Fulk Fitz Warren. Comparing the texts, however, makes it seem clear that it is actually the *Gest* which owes most to the story of Fulk, that Munday does not derive his distressed earl from Fulk, and that he in fact draws much more fully on the *Gest* itself than on any other source – but does not use not much, if at all, the elements that the *Gest* draws from Fulk Fitz Warren. It is time for the *Gest* to step into the gentrifying light and be contrasted to the preceding (and often succeeding) fully yeomanesque version of the English outlaw.

Fifteenth-century Robin Hood(s)

There are two major sources for the pre-*Gest* image, or images, of Robin Hood. One is the late fifteenth-century texts themselves. But earlier, less focused, and in some ways therefore more interesting and potentially important – as they may represent a wider image than that narrowed to the generic mode and particular context of the lengthy, written ballad – is the set of comments about and references to Robin Hood that can be found from the late fourteenth century onwards.

From the sketchy early references – literary, chronicle, marginal, proverbial, para-legal – a schema of somewhat varied characteristics can be assembled.[1] We hear of a Robin Hood who is a mighty archer, resides in the forest with a small group of male supporters, is seen as hostile to the church (though not to its true values) and to secular authorities (without apparent redeemability), is mobile, may deliver an impact especially in towns near his forest, is evidently of high popular standing, has some elusive and mysterious elements, yet is a congener of comedy and parody and is linked to locations largely in the midlands and north of England.

The play-games appear to offer a less mysterious, less threatening and differently located version of the figure: variant elements are that he is strongly linked to nature and early summer, enters the town in celebratory mode, is involved with money-collection (apparently benignly, and for the local community), is a focal figure for socially competitive games, seems supportive of the local authorities and even the church (though only its buildings), is localised in the English south-west and Scotland. It also appears in the play-games that he is mobile, may originate from the forest, is connected with archery, and is attended by a small group of supporters (including women at times).

From the early ballads and plays there appears a figure with links to both these groups of features, but tending consistently towards the inherent anti-authority position of the references rather than the communal celebratory character of the play-games, or perhaps just mobilising that community temporarily in an anti-authority direction. However, before looking at this evidence in detail, a short excursus is required on the texts to be discussed.

'Robin Hood and the Monk' and 'Robin Hood and the Potter' are certainly before the *Gest*. Ohlgren's recent work dates them a little earlier than has previously been assumed, respectively at c.1465 and c.1468, the latter being the major change (previously c.1490 was usual for 'Robin Hood and the Potter').[2] The very short, cryptic play-text (or two-scene text) linked to the Paston family and dated about 1475 goes along with that period. However, in what follows I will also consider the two plays which Copland attaches to his edition of the *Gest*, c.1560. These are shorter and simpler than the ballads, and so might be taken as performance cut-downs of them. There is, however, no proof, or apparent way of proving, that they are not simple original performance pieces that some literary hand amplified into the more complex ballads – but that issue and possibility seem a side-track at present. The 'Robin Hood and the Potter' play is basically a 'Robin meets his match' conflict; the other play, 'Robin Hood and the Friar', is closer in spirit to the matching ballad, but the latter does not survive until 1625. However, the friar is known in Munday's 1598–99 plays and the probably earlier Sloane 'Life' (see p. 34 n.40 for a discussion of its date): he was apparently a separate figure in outlaw myth (referred to as early as 1417, and appearing in later 'Morris' performances), and he has no link to the *Gest*. I feel that both these plays can be taken as in some way pre-*Gest*: no contentious issues arise from doing that, and they provide some support for patterns found in the early ballads.

More contentiously, I will also consider as pre-*Gest* 'Robin Hood and Guy of Gisborne' – in the text he is usually called 'Sir Guy'. This does not survive until the Percy Folio of the mid seventeenth century, but its action seems an elaborated version of the first scene of the c.1475 play – and its action and language seem very like those of the two early ballads. So much like them, especially in the opening stanza, which could even be a pastiche of the opening of 'Robin Hood and the Monk', that there must be a question of whether this, like 'Adam Bell' and *Chevy Chase*, might be the product of a sixteenth-century archaising literary-historical production, an early piece of medievalism. But its language seems older than that, and different from that of others in that genre, and while I would not want to put heavy emphasis on any evidence it provides, I feel that 'Robin Hood and Guy of Gisborne' is at least citable as an avatar, and probably a fairly early one, of the monk and potter ballads. I will on occasions also refer to other broadside ballads which can be traced credibly to the sixteenth century (see Chapter 4, pp. 88–9, for a discussion of this dating) and which also show no line of descent from the *Gest*, such as the 'execution rescue' ballads, and also the 'Jolly Pinder of Wakefield' as an archetype of the 'meets his match' structure – both of these, like other early examples, have a fully anti-authoritarian positioning.

Taking all these texts together, and viewing some of them with some caution as to the quality of their evidence, there is a substantial amount of material which can be taken to fill out the inevitably sketchy early references and the play-games to establish the fifteenth-century pre-*Gest* image of Robin Hood. From the start it seems important to note some significant absences in the early text materials. Robin in no way derives from noble or property-owning family: the only social identity given for him is 'yeoman'. This has many detailed significations, but excludes both serfdom and nobility. Related to this is that, apparently unlike all other outlaws in story, and many of his later appearances, there is no reason given for his outlaw status. Another unique feature is that where the other medieval outlaws are often described on horseback, even turning round their horseshoes for trickster effects, Robin is not a horseman, and his iconic weapon the longbow cannot be fired effectively from a mounted position.

In terms of positive attributes we find that the natural and summer context is stressed at the start of the ballads (as it is in some lyrics, *chansons d'aventure* and, perhaps pertinently, the 'Robin et Marion' *pastourelle* and *bergerie* tradition).[3] The small group of male supporters is a constant, though it is notable that the process of narrative introduces a new element here not found in the early references or the play-games: there can be discussion and even dissent among them. Much advises Robin to take twelve men with him in 'Robin Hood and the Potter'; they all advise Robin to be very careful of the sheriff in 'Robin Hood and the Potter'; Little John and Robin have a serious disagreement in 'Robin Hood and the Monk', and this is referred to at the end when Robin offers John the leadership of the band to recognise his achievement in rescuing Robin. He declines, but as in the 'meets his match' structure seen in the two c.1560 plays, when Robin is by no means victorious, there is a sense that Robin is an agreed rather than automatic leader. This extends to the band being summoned by Robin's horn ('Robin Hood and the Potter', line 254; 'Robin Hood and the Friar' play, line 93),[4] but on both occasions they are a small number, as were real outlaw bands of the period.

Narrative presents other innovations on or expansions of the hero found in the references. The small outlaw band amuses itself with games, notably with archery contests, including mobile ones ('Robin Hood and the Monk', line 47); it is also clear that fighting with sword and buckler or staff is a recurrent practice, and while this may well have been familiar from the play-games, the activity is substantial in the early ballads. When they meet a stranger, like the potter (whom Little John has fought before, as he has with the friar, another game-like challenger for Robin) or Guy of Gisborne, the contest will have some social meaning – in these instances, one positive, one negative. Robin makes friends with the urban citizen, and defeats the sheriff's enforcers. The ballads about the pinder and Little John himself seem like fairly early versions of this somewhat hostile friendship, but cannot be dated before the *Gest*.

In the case of 'Robin Hood and the Potter' the encounter also involves money-raising – they demand 'pawage' (line 20, also found as 'pavage'), an informal toll for passing through their territory: the 'Robin Hood and the Potter' play calls it 'passage' (lines 147, etc). The Yeovil play-records suggest that something like this, at least in the form of aggressive charity-collection, could happen in the play-game context,[5] and this also seems the rationale of robbing strangers, as Robin has previously robbed the monk who denounces him in 'Robin Hood and the Monk'. This anti-clerical feature, so popular later on as seeming anti-Catholic, is not shown elsewhere in the early ballads or play-texts, perhaps because they have a more strongly focused interest in challenging secular rather than religious authority. The transfer of hostility to the church from the state will be a feature of the seventeenth-century ballads – the Reformation enables withdrawal from a criticism of civic politics, which may in the seventeenth century have become distinctly dangerous. However, because the monk has been robbed, his role in the story is to act as an agent of secular authority impeaching Robin to the sheriff; the other two ballads, like the story that Bower tells and some at least of the early references, identify Robin's primary enemy as the sheriff, enacting as he does royal authority – indeed Bower sees Robin as both anti-sheriff and pro-church.

In each of the long early ballads, the problems raised by engagement with the sheriff are resolved through another crucial feature of outlaw activities, the capacity to go in disguise and infiltrate the apparatus of authority, especially to effect the rescue of an ally. In 'Robin Hood and the Monk' Little John masquerades as the sheriff's agent, then acts as the jailer, to free Robin from jail; in 'Robin Hood and Guy of Gisborne' Robin returns the favour, in Guy's costume and blowing Guy's horn, claiming the right to execute John and in fact cutting him free from his bonds. 'Robin Hood and the Potter' is a milder reversal of this: Robin as the potter offers to lead the sheriff to Robin, but, turning from fake bounty-hunter into outlaw, traps and robs him instead. The c.1475 play seems likely to be a version of the rescue-via-infiltration story, but either this is conveyed by action or the text has not been fully preserved.

A notable recurrent and evidently gratifying conclusion to the infiltration in disguise and rescue story (to be a little later found in the popular 'Robin Hood and Three Young Men') is the fierce violence involved: Little John kills and beheads the monk and his page and kills the jailer in 'Robin Hood and the Monk'; in 'Robin Hood and Guy of Gisborne' Robin kills then beheads Guy, and John sends an arrow through the sheriff's heart – which Percy in his *Reliques* euphemised to 'in to the backe-syde'.[6] The summer-linked tricksterish spirit that the texts in part have is startlingly set aside in these conclusions, which do not relate back to *pastourelle* or *bergerie*, and are rarely found in the later material: they seem to mirror the way villains can be brutally despatched by knights in romance.

This hard-handed approach is presumably seen as a reflex of the hostile violence offered to the outlaws – the sheriff breaches sanctuary in 'Robin Hood and the Monk' and clearly means to execute Robin, though when Much is, early on, worried about Robin's safety if he goes alone to Nottingham, he does not specify the sheriff as a threat. In 'Robin Hood and the Potter' the sheriff's intentions seem very hostile, if he can lay hands on the outlaw; in 'Robin Hood and Guy of Gisborne' the sheriff has let a contract on Robin, and drives his own attack deep into the forest with intent to round up the outlaws.

Both sheriff and monk (though never the friar) are clearly seen as part of an oppressive apparatus, but there is no corresponding enmity for the figurehead of order, the king, though it is true that he plays little direct part in asserting authority. He is seen at the end of 'Robin Hood and the Monk' as capable of admiring the mutual fidelity of Robin and his band, but the outlaws are silent about him throughout. In the religious sphere, Mary is revered by Robin especially, may be implied as helping him in 'Robin Hood and Guy of Gisborne', and is name-checked reverentially in all three ballads, though it is notable that Little John tends to swear only by Christ – perhaps a sign of his more active masculinity.

More could be made of some unusual points, such as Robin's quasi-romance passage with the sheriff's wife (courteous language and the gift of a gold ring and a fine horse seem inherently erotic), and the possibility of mythic ritualism in Guy's horse-hide outfit and his being defaced and beheaded as well. Intriguing as they are, these features seem unsymptomatic, even syncretic. Of more interest is the recurrence of sums of money, in fantastically large amounts: the £10 that Robin pays for the potter's pots (his generous behaviour in selling them also reverses mercantile values); the £20 offered (presumably jointly) to John and Much as 'yemen of the crown' ('Robin Hood and the Monk', line 229); the £100 the monk claims he lost to Robin; the £100 the sheriff fantasises about in 'Robin Hood and the Potter' as being worth paying, first to find Robin, and then to have avoided him ('Robin Hood and the Potter', lines 223, 270).

Needing and exchanging coin was itself part of the developing proto-capitalist socio-economic structure of late medieval England, a newer force than romance or folklore, and the huge cash sums, like the social position of Robin, as both near to and excluded from the developing urban structures, may all point to contextual features of the relation of the fifteenth-century Robin Hood to an emerging monetary economy. However, the size of these sums is hardly realistic, though substantial amounts in cash and valuables were at times transported as 'treasure' in the days before most of the sophistications of banking. But the sums seem to be fantasy figures – a phenomenon which has long continued: in Poe's 'The Purloined Letter' of 1845 Dupin earns 50,000 francs, about four times a professional's annual salary, for understanding where the letter is hidden. The fact that cash can be the medium of dissent between Robin and Little John (as in the disagreement over gambling in 'Robin Hood and the Monk' and the potential squabble at the start of 'Robin Hood and the Potter') can be taken as a prolepsis of what Marx would identify as the fetishisation effect of cash on human personality, which nineteenth-century fiction would realise urgently. It is striking, seeing the recurrent monastic context of cash in the outlaw stories, that Marx consciously uses the term 'fetish' because of its prior religious aura.[7]

Romance, myth and monetarism are exotics in the early outlaw materials, however. Central is the construction of an image that is a focused expression of natural law and freedom: an inherent resistance, courageous, skilled and cunning, righteously opposed to oppressive authority. A utopian position, no doubt, in the nowhere of a nearby forest of urban imagination. And a position that will very soon be given a different location, starting with the *Gest*.

Things done in the *Gest*

Continuity between the early Robin Hood materials and the *Gest* is clear. To guide the above discussion a tabulation was prepared of features found in the early materials. Almost all of these also appear in the *Gest*:

No grounds for outlawry.
Small groups of supporters, even including instances of dissent: Little John shows some 'tene' at Robin's instructions (line 842), and Much wants to debate them (line 273).
Archery and other games.
Feasting/drinking.
Summoning with a horn (but the numbers are higher in the *Gest*: 140 men appear at lines 913, 1555, 1786).
Hostility to authority.
Authority attacks the outlaws' sanctuary in the forest.
Violence used in response to authority.
Disguise for success against authorities (in the *Gest*, Little John only).
Rescue of ally.
Outlaws rob travellers on forest roads.
Mary revered.
No equestrian activity (though in the *Gest* the knight, like the sheriff's wife, is provided with a horse: Robin is said to ride with the king in line 1693, but they also shoot arrows, which is not possible with a longbow from horseback. The issue of the *Gest* wood-cut of a 'mounted Robin' is considered below.)

Less prominent than in the early ballads, but still present, if varied, are:

Natural and summer setting: this is verbal rather than mimetic. In the *Gest*, the famous phrase 'Under the greenwood tree' is used eleven times (including twice as 'this' greenwood tree), and also once as greenwood 'shaw' and once as greenwood 'hore'. Just 'greenwood' appears eighteen times (plus one 'green shawe'). But there is no scene equivalent to the affective May opening of the early ballads.

'Meets his match' activities: found only in displaced form in the *Gest* between Little John and the cook, not in the forest.

Emphasised more in the *Gest* than in the early ballads is:

King respected (found only in 'Robin Hood and the Monk' previously).

And there are some minor modulations:

Tricksterism seems reduced in the *Gest*, and found only of Little John.
In the first part of the *Gest* the church is more emphasised as a hostile force than the sheriff.

There are two major areas of re-formation in the *Gest*. The first is its structure; the other is innovatory materials from another source. Structural discussion of the *Gest* seems to have progressed little since Clawson in 1909 argued that it was composed from no fewer than twelve pre-existing ballads and two *exempla*. His account is learned, though weakened by its interest being ultimately in sources rather than the text (the model is the *Iliad* as based on a series of heroic lays), but Clawson also, if somewhat contradictorily, includes much interesting close analysis of the way the *Gest* works as a narrative.[8] Many of the notional source ballads are hypothetical; some that he feels preceded the *Gest* are known later in what are more likely post-*Gest* cut-down literary broadsides like 'Robin Hood and the Golden Arrow', or substantially later ones like 'Robin Hood's Golden Prize', which Clawson offers as a descendant of the source for the monk-robbery in the forest.

A less Homer-influenced consideration of what exists in the *Gest*, against an awareness of the pre-existing materials, shows a new and substantial double frame in operation. The new outer frame connects the outlaw story to the model of the International Hero. Robin is in the opening stanzas constructed as more authoritative, more whimsical, more quasi-royal than in the ballads and plays, and the obvious model is King Arthur, well known for waiting for a new event to occur or a visitor to arrive before dinner – and a story – can commence. The final frame is from the same International Hero context, as we are told of the betrayal, death and lasting honour of the hero – without here any suggestion of the possible return that is offered with most International Heroes. That was not an essential feature, as is shown by the treatment of Robin Hood alongside King Arthur and other International Heroes by Raglan, where 'Possible Return' is only one of the twenty-two optional heroic 'functions'.[9]

Indicative as it is of some movement up the socio-cultural levels, this International Hero outer frame is not nearly as dominant an element of re-formation in the *Gest* as the inner and much larger narrative frame, which is effectively two major narrative sequences, each in several episodes, in which the outlaw adventures are augmented by an encounter with a higher-class force, first one with a knight and then at the end an equally weighty encounter with the king himself – there is a link as the knight recognises the king and the king restores the knight's fortunes. Between the two sequences are developed the 'outlaws versus the sheriff/church' sequences that survive from the early ballads.

The knight is an underfocused figure. His name is given five times as Sir Richard at the Lee (though not until line 1238), and when still unnamed he is linked to 'Verysdale', identified by both Child and Holt as Wyresdale in Lancashire.[10] It is not clear where he has come from – he is riding south, it seems, through the forest, as he plans to dine south of Barnsdale, in Blyth or Doncaster (line 108), yet is not on his way from crusade: that is a further humiliation waiting for him, he implies (line 224), but elsewhere he says that he and his men have come from the 'see' (line 388).[11] Such blurs are endemic to the knight. He is in difficulties because his son killed a knight of Lancaster and as a result the knight owes the Abbot of York £400 – presumably he borrowed the money by mortgaging his lands to pay a fine. We never see or hear of the son, though we do meet the knight's lady. His castle may well be in Wyresdale, Lancashire, but it also turns up just inside the forest, which cannot be Barnsdale because, though never in the *Gest* named as Sherwood, it is evidently close to Nottingham (whereas in 'Robin Hood and Guy of Gisborne', set in Barnsdale, when he is killed the sheriff is running towards his home in Nottingham).

The knight, it would appear to standard textual analysis, is a ghostly fiction of the text, a figure constructed to elicit responses from characters and readers. Equally striking, and equally unobserved, is the minimal impact he has had on the tradition. Even though several broadside ballads are clearly cut out of the *Gest*,[12] his own story is never retold in that form. He does not interest following authors: as Robin himself becomes landless gentry there is no role for the knight until the scholarly Tennyson in *The Foresters* of 1891 has him as Sir Richard Lea, father of Marian (his trouble-causing son, Walter, is off on crusade). From then on he has a recurrent presence in fiction, and tends to be a fixture in twentieth-century juvenile Robin Hood novels.

It seems easy to hypothesise that like the sub-Latin title, *Gest*, ultimately from *Res Gestae* (things done, 'Deeds'), like the move towards an International Hero in the outer frame and like the more dignified and less trickster-like Robin found in the *Gest*, the knight is there to engage the social aspirations of those who were likely to buy printed texts. As is well known, the great majority of early printed texts peddle the cultural capital of feudal chivalry – Ferguson was generous (or idealistic) enough to call it an 'Indian summer of English chivalry',[13] but a more material analysis would see it as false consciousness at work at the heart of urban mercantilism.

A contemporary commentator might well have had a different take on the knight. Riding alone in wretched misery, met in the forest by a beneficiary, re-established in terms of his moral deserving: this is surely the 'poor knight of romance' trope. When Sir Launfal has been thoroughly humiliated, without any squire, he:

> ... dyghte his courser
> Wythoute knaue other squyer:
> He rood with lyttyll pryde.[14]

As John, Much and Scarloke look into the forest:

> Than came a knighte ridinghe,
> Full soone they gan hym mete.
>
> All dreri was his semblaunce,
> And lytell was his pryde.[15]

The language is too formulaic to suggest direct borrowing, even in 'lyttyll pryde', but the image is certainly familiar, the *Gest* offering the poor knight of romance in a much more mundane, English, version than Yvain or Launcelot driven mad by love. And while Launfal's fate is different, demotic romance can come even closer to the actual *Gest* situation. In another popular poem, driven from home in shame and poverty, Gamelyn wanders in the forest only to meet 'the king of the outlaws', who is unnamed but usually taken to be Robin Hood anonymised to avoid overshadowing the rough-hewn hero. The outlaws' help and inspiration lead Gamelyn, just like the knight, to restoration of his property by standing up to the judicial system, especially his evil brother who has become a sheriff. Where the *Gest* has clear overlap with these texts through the 'poor knight' theme, its link to *Gamelyn* can be even closer: in both texts a character swears by the little-known St Rychere.[16] The *Gest* actually reads 'Richard' but the rhyme requires 'Rychere': it is also a rhyme word in *Gamelyn*. Skeat, when editing *Gamelyn*, favoured St Richard of Gloucester as the reference, but though patriotic this seems lexically unlikely. France offers both Richer de Reims, a medieval scholar, and Richer le Lorrain, a travel-writing monk: perhaps the latter is marginally more likely, though only the former was alleged to be canonised. Curiously, but presumably accidentally, in both cases a villain swears by the saint: the abbot in the *Gest* and the wicked brother in *Gamelyn*.

Nearly as close as the 'Rychere' duplication is when the statement in *Gamelyn*:

> When Gamelyn was crowned   kinge of outlawes
> And walked had a while   under the wode shawes
>
> (lines 691–2)

seems very close to Robin's instructions to the outlaws in the *Gest* to be friendly to any:

> ... gode yeoman
> That walketh by grene wode shawe,
>
> (lines 51–3)

Both of these texts were popular in the late medieval period, and both fit awkwardly with traditional romance – *Gamelyn* is well short of even superficial traces of chivalry, and Bliss remarks on *Launfal* that 'the upper classes are treated with a marked lack of reverence' and there is much 'evidence of a lack of refinement' and 'no hint in the poem of any feeling for morality or religion'.[17] Sands comments in a more nuanced way that '*Launfal*'s appeal would be to the shameless wish-fulfillment of the petty tradesman ... wealth, power and physical satisfaction are unalloyed by any selfless and chivalric ideal'.[18] The knight is a little classier than that (though curiously his meeting with Robin Hood parallels in some detail, and in general effect, Launfal's encounter with his fairy mistress), but the *Gest* insists, as does *Gamelyn*, that it is through throwing in his hand with the forest folk that he regains his position: not only does he return the money, but just as Robin has re-equipped him for chivalry with a horse, so he re-equips the outlaws for yeomanry with bows and arrows.

And then there is the woodcut. The Chepman and Myllar print, sometimes called 'Lettersnijder', bears on the first page a bold cut of a lightly dressed man, not armed, but wearing spurs and carrying a bow, on a big, cavalry-like horse. Scholars are satisfied that this was originally used in Pynson's version of the *Gest*, now reduced to a few stray leaves, and that it came from his *Canterbury Tales* as an illustration of the Knight's Yeoman. It has always been assumed that this is Robin Hood, and Tom Ohlgren has recently put the case, responding to my view that it may not be Robin.[19] Respectfully, I hold to my lonely dissent. Apart from late in the *Gest* when he joins the king to travel to court (and so is non-Robin), Robin does not ride a horse until twentieth-century film, as I have argued elsewhere:[20] only one character rides carrying a bow in the *Gest* and that is the knight – who naturally has spurs (so did Chaucer's Yeoman, to match and keep up with his master, but why would Robin be so equipped?) The longbow is a foot-soldier's weapon, and the horseman must therefore be delivering a bow, a symbolic representation of the knight re-equipping the outlaws. Actually the two cuts are not quite the same: the *Gest* version has trimmed the block slightly, but more interestingly has recut the features so they are, as Marshall says, 'slightly more refined':[21] they also make the horseman seem older. Perhaps this might be evidence of a conscious change of identity?

So I would still argue that the image itself is a sign of the hybridisation of the opening sequence of the *Gest* towards romance: the poor knight is, for his own regeneration, condensed with the pedestrian yeoman. Even gentry Gamelyn walked into the forest. Printers and publishers do not always get their illustrations wrong, and the work of inveigling the knight into the story may well have made the printer aware of the illustration's importance as a badge of the rebadging of the outlaw tradition.

Interwoven with more familiar Robin Hood materials – infiltration of the sheriff's household and trapping him in the forest; a robbery of monks in the forest; an assault by the sheriff on the forest – the knight story eventually resolves itself by coming into contact with the other major innovation in the story, the involvement of the king, mostly off stage in 'Robin Hood and the Monk', as an active figure of authority, at once apparently benign and ultimately threatening. He re-establishes the knight (which seems a largely unnoticed hint for the later 'distressed earl' story), and then engages with Robin.

Much as the 'poor knight' image in humble romance triggers the knight story, so another popular late medieval formation is energised in the sequence focusing on the king. The 'King and Subject' stories are elusive in both editions and criticism, largely as they have no linguistic or amatory-chivalric connections with the adventures of medieval French chevaliers. The archetypal 'King and Subject' story has a late medieval English king journeying incognito; he meets a rough-hewn member of the public – a man of some skill and income, but no sophistication. They develop an amiable rapport and also some social and behavioural dissent. The subject will then, usually when he visits court, recognise the king with some alarm: the king's response varies between liberal tolerance and repressive vengeance, with usually some mixture of the two. The classic text is 'King Edward and the Shepherd', which displays most of the 'King and Subject' features.

Of late fourteenth-century origin, and written in a popular stanzaic style without elaborate or French-oriented diction, this tells how the king, masquerading as a wealthy merchant, meets a shepherd in the countryside outside Windsor (by a river, but the sheep-keeping practice and the attendant wildlife make it clear that this is in fact in the open part of the forest), hears his complaints against the king's officials (not against the king himself, who the shepherd believes does not know about their malign actions) and promises to arrange the return of the four pounds and two shillings that the shepherd is owed. The king then visits the house of the shepherd, who on the way disavows any rabbit or deer poaching because the forester and his bowmen are so fierce. The king and the shepherd then have an elaborate feast, starting with wild birds, which are not protected for the crown, but moving on to rabbit and venison, which are. They also drink a great deal in a ritual game, with special toast-words. Before the king leaves, the shepherd shows him his secret underground chamber, stocked with meat that has been taken illegally.

Next day the shepherd attends court at Windsor and asks for the merchant – whose alias is 'Ioly Robyn', a name found in songs that do not necessarily link to Robin Hood. The king has primed his courtiers, and the shepherd is led in, given his money and feasted – the whole court joins in the drinking game. Finally the king has the shepherd told who he really is: the shepherd is staggered, horrified, and begs mercy – and the story ends with a puzzling aporia: the scribe has written '*non finis sed punctus*' – 'not an end but a stop'. Most other 'King and Subject' stories have the king showing generosity, with some covert menace, to the subject, and that is presumably – but not certainly – the imputable outcome here.

There are clearly strong links to the king and Robin sequences in the *Gest*: the king's disguised visit to a forest outside a major town of royal importance (in the less elaborate 'King Edward and the Hermit' it is actually Sherwood); the concern with poaching and policing the forests; the forest-dwellers' faith in the king and hostility to his agents; the rich feast in the forest at the forest-dweller's residence; the game-based relations that develop between king and subject; the king's keeping of his promise to improve the forester's situation; the welcome to court followed by discomfort; and the unresolved final relationship between king and subject, basically a stand-off.

The *Gest* deploys in its process of elaboration from the early ballads both these late medieval popular forms. It uses the 'poor knight' romance to trace how socio-economic change can threaten the best of the past, and also, via the 'King and Subject' structure, offers a forward-looking eye on emergent areas of difficulty and dissent as trade specialists like millers, tanners and barkers, even shepherds, begin to stake a social claim and are themselves enmeshed in the difficulties of the developing cash-nexus and also the demands of governmental authority.

It is hardly possible to avoid connecting this thematic mix of nostalgia and modernity statement with the world of print, where, as is well known, the suppliers offer both a wealth of now falsely conscious chivalric material and also at least some lower-level popular romance like *Adam Bell*, *Guy of Warwick* or *Beves of Hamtoun*, dealing with upward aspiration and resultant conflicts. Ohlgren's recent study suggests that Pynson's *Gest* is the first of its texts, and he has intimated that he feels that the poem might well have been put together just for this printing.[22] This is highly credible. If there had been a mid-fifteenth-century manuscript ballad-epic about this enormously popular hero it is very hard to believe that there would have been no trace of it in the fairly rich documentation of the late fifteenth century. The greater likelihood is that, like Malory's assemblage of a single-volume Arthuriad, it was a conscious production, very probably for the purpose of printing, and that the 'poor knight' romance and the 'King and Subject' elements were ready prompters to extend the social appeal, both direct and fantasised, of the outlaw story into the areas of wish-fulfilment and cultural capital that were prime mechanisms of attraction for buyers in the new socio-economic regime of mercantile printing.

But there was another source as well for the *Gest*: that long-forgotten, but thanks to French prose and John Leland not quite lost, story of Fulk Fitz Warren.

Fulk Fitz Warren and the *Gest*

The story of Fulk Fitz Warren survives in Anglo-Norman prose, but this has been an ill-fated narrative. All agree that there was an Anglo-Norman verse original for the surviving text, but, as with many other imperial self-validations, there was also a version for the colonised, in this case in English. That too is lost, but the ever-curious traveller, archivist and note-maker John Leland has left a full synopsis, very close to the surviving prose version but with some tweaks: for example, he speaks of Fulco son of Guarine, more ancient versions of the two names, the first Norse and the second Parisian French, rather the Norman Fouke Fitz Waryn.[23]

One of many arriviste warriors who squabbled among themselves and with their own authorities for power and land, especially up and down the borders with Wales and the then still martial Welsh, Fulk has evident relevance to gentrified Robin Hood. He was a nobleman displaced from authority by Prince John who, in story at least, took to the forest with a small band of followers, deployed against the authorities the resistance of both a trickster and a warrior and was eventually restored to authority. It would seem likely that John Major used him as a model in his *Historia Majoris Britanniae* (which elegantly translates as both 'History of Great Britain' and 'Major's British History'). This was published in 1521 though written some years before, not long after the *Gest* appeared. Major for the first time located Robin Hood, a displaced and so in some sense dissident gentleman, in the time of Prince John, and this was followed broadly by Richard Grafton in his 1569 English-language *Chronicle at Large* and, at least in temporal terms, by Munday in his 1598–99 plays *The Downfall of Robert Earle of Huntington* and *The Death of Robert, Earle of Huntington*.

But that is a broad-brush connection, just based on Robin being a Fulk-like lord, around 1200. A detailed look at the story of Fulk will offer a surprising set of connections with the *Gest* rather than with Munday, and it appears that poems like *Sir Launfal* and *Gamelyn* were not the only late medieval English forces that were involved with the extending, elaborating and social elevating of the Robin Hood story in its first printed version. It is a long time since scholars explored the connections. Clawson, publishing in 1909, may have been excessive in source-questing, but he knew the materials very well and, as will be noted, picked up three of the following instances, as did Thomas E. Kelly independently.[24] Before that Prideaux, the far-sighted observer of a Scottish connection for Robin Hood, argued that Fulk was actually a source for Robin Hood, possibly through his 'Amys del Bois' cognomen: Prideaux connects 'Hood' and 'Wood'.[25] A link to *Gamelyn* is as old and as undernoticed: in his edition of that poem Skeat quotes Lindren as seeing it as related to Fulk.[26]

The Fulk story is discussed and translated by Glyn Burgess, in company with the contemporary account of the earlier north French noble outlaw Eustace le Moine.[27] Some features of the Fulk narrative overlap with the pre-*Gest* realisation of Robin Hood found in the early ballads. Fulk is less obsessive about disguise than Eustace, but it would seem that his acting as a Eustace-style monk to divert King John's pursuit is somewhat like Little John's posing as substitute for the monk as a royal agent in 'Robin Hood and the Monk'. There is some similarity between the scene when Fulk delivers for execution a gagged man dressed as himself and the climax of 'Robin Hood and Guy of Gisborne', and a closer resemblance between Robin trapping the sheriff in 'Robin Hood and the Potter' and the scene where Fulk (disguised as a charcoal-burner) catches the king in the forest by offering to lead him to a fine stag. The apparent obsession with beheading in Fulk's story (and in that of Eustace) does mesh with single brutal moments in 'Robin Hood and the Monk' and 'Robin Hood and Guy of Gisborne', but that seems general medieval cruelty rather than a specific link, and this discourse continues in the *Gest*: Little John seeks beheading when injured (lines 1209–20), the sheriff would prefer it to spending another night in the forest (lines 797–800), and later, after the sheriff breaks his vow of peace with the outlaws, Robin beheads him, though this is apparently not itself fatal, but follows his death (lines 1385–92), as with Guy of Gisborne.

These instances might be seen in both Fulk and the ballads as shared use of the medieval outlaw trope collection, along with Hereward and Eustace, and even Reynart, a serial disguiser. But a substantially larger number of episodes, implying a direct connection, link directly only to the *Gest* and clearly suggest that the Fulk story was mined for the elaboration of the early ballads to generate a fifteenth-century outlaw image that provided enough material for a printed text, and one that could speak to the social aspirations of the potential audience.

As has been noted above, the lengthy sequence in which Little John becomes the sheriff's servant and then inveigles him into being caught in the forest by the outlaws might look like a free-hand adaptation of elements of the early ballads, but it in fact follows events in the Fulk story more closely. John de Rampaigne, Fulk's forceful assistant, infiltrates (as a jongleur) the family of Fulk's major enemy Morys fitz Roger and learns enough to enable Fulk's men to trap and kill him on the way to Shrewsbury. Clawson noted this,[28] but did not add that there is no detail about the death in the French prose version: in the English poem, according to Leland, they behead him as Robin does the sheriff in the *Gest*, rare evidence of the English poem being the actual source for the *Gest*.[29] John later uses similar skills of disguise and cunning to free Fulk's henchman Sir Audulf de Bracy: this seems more like 'Robin Hood and the Monk' than the *Gest*, but as there are no other connections, it is presumably accidental.

Other Fulk-like events in the *Gest* occur when the sheriff, after being freed, arranges an archery context and afterwards ambushes the outlaws. In the fight the outlaws have difficulties and flee into the forest to the knight's castle. In just the same way Fulk and his men are ambushed by the king's forces, fight without great success and flee into the forest for refuge at an abbey. In the process of the sheriff's ambush, Little John is wounded, and asks to be beheaded: Robin refuses, and Much carries him to safety. Exactly the same happens in the second royal forest attack with Fulk's wounded brother William (Clawson noted this too).[30] Just as the sheriff entraps the knight in the *Gest*, King John imprisons Fulk's wounded brother William – but both will be rescued.

If this somewhat military milling around in the middle of the *Gest* seems much more like the Fulk action than the very limited physical engagements of the early ballads, then equally related to the Fulk story is the mode in which the 'King and Subject' relations between Robin and the king are introduced to the *Gest*. Like

King John pursuing Fulk, the *Gest*'s King Edward plans to enter the forest to capture the elusive Robin – this is a much more purposive and aggressive legal measure than the casual encounters of the 'King and Subject' genre, and some of the sheriff's earlier King John-like manoeuvres are now reworked in royal terms. The sheriff being tricked by John in disguise is, as noted above, itself linked to the sequence when Fulk, as a charcoal-burner, entraps the king in the forest: the third connection that Clawson observed.[31] As a result of their forest capture both swear oaths of loyalty and peace, the sheriff to Robin and the king to Fulk: both will break them and assault the forest. King John is entrapped a second time: this is when he actually pardons Robin, and in the *Gest* that is also the result of the forest visit by the king.

There are some other suggestive resemblances between the Fulk story and notable features of the *Gest*. Fulk demands truth from those he meets in the forest – though it is Eustace who mirrors Robin's ethic of not robbing someone who tells the truth about his money (a merchant carrying 'sixty pounds in coin').[32] Neither kind of truth-demand is in the early ballads. In a similar evaluative distinction, Fulk will rob merchants only because they are on the king's business – they are merchants who deal in cloth and furs, so adding a conceivable connection with the merchant draper links that Ohlgren has suggested for the context and construction of the *Gest*.[33] Finally, in both the poem and this discussion, the sudden emergence of Robin as claiming to have built a chapel for Mary Magdalene, which seems curious in the light of his earlier avowed devotion to the Virgin (to whom Fulk builds a chapel late in life), has a striking parallel in the fact that Joce de Dynan, Fulk's grandfather, has constructed a chapel to the Magdalene.

More minor and so more suppositious traces of the Fulk story exist in the Robin Hood tradition. Fulk encounters Randolph, Earl of Chester, a magnate who is instructed by King John to arrest him but who proves basically friendly to him, and after Fulk's restoration he joins Randolph fighting in Ireland. Both the *Piers Plowman* reference and the recently discovered Forresters manuscript version of 'Robin Hood's Progress to Nottingham' (there named 'Robin Hood and the Forresters') link Robin and Randolph, though it is conceivable that Langland just lists them as separate heroes of story and Forresters turns this reference into a misunderstood story-motif. A more distant yet very curious contact comes in the ballad 'Robyn and Gandelyn', which Child felt belonged with the outlaw tradition, though

Robin is killed in it. Here the enemy on whom Robin's friend Gandelyn takes vengeance is 'Wrennock', an unusual Welsh or Breton name also held by (G)werenoc, son of Morys Fitz Roger, Fulk's bitter enemy and rival for the prized castle of Whittington/Blancheville.[34] It may seem an improbable further stretch to see some link between the name Gandelyn and that of Gamelyn/Gamwell, as the roles played are so different, but the similarity is nevertheless striking.

To read the Fulk story and the *Gest* together is to experience highly compatible stories, before Robin has been back-located into the period of bad King John. When Fulk is in exile in France he is known as Amys del Bois (Leland says just Amyce, but presumably he is abbreviating) – which seems like a paraphrase of Robin's identity as known in the thirteenth-century *bergerie*. Importing elements of the outlaw vigour and trickery of Eustace le Moine into Britain – a curious parallel to the transition of the 'Robin et Marion' *pastourelle* story into the south-western play-game – Fulk's narrative in its English version seems to have had an unobserved, even disguised, influence on the re-formation of the English outlaw tradition in the *Gest*.

Fulk's Munday holiday

The notion that Munday's gentrification of Robin to the level of earl, so influential in the tradition generally, though having almost no impact itself on the stage – a Stratford reading performance held in 2006 was billed as the first since 1601 – is linked to the career of Fulk Fitz Warren depends essentially on the dating of Fulk's distressed nobility to the period of Richard I's absence and the assumption of rule by Prince John. However, this idea had been put into circulation long before Munday by John Major in 1521, was disseminated by Grafton, and was made a basic idea of later Elizabethan culture in the hands of authors like Leland, Stow and Warner, all before Munday.[35] In Munday's play *The Downfall of Robert, Earle of Huntington* (1598–99) the king's treatment of Earl Robin is a good deal closer to that found of the knight in the *Gest*: mistreated and impoverished by the greedy church, the knight has remained true to the king and resorted to the forest; Robert does all this and then he too is restored to his previous status by the king late in the story – Fulk's forcing John to restore him has nothing like the graceful success of both the knight and Earl Robert.

The only possible specific connection to the Fulk tradition which appears in Munday is that Lord Robin has a partner whose name is Matilda, at least before her forest period as Marian. Fulk was married to Lady Matilda de Cause, a wealthy and beautiful widow and also sister-in-law to the Archbishop of Canterbury, the intriguingly named Hubert le Botiler, who sponsored the match. The story makes Fulk marry her before becoming an outlaw, but in fact this happened after his three-year outlawry came to an end. Diluting the significance of this connection, many noblewomen in the period were called Matilda; the English Fulk poem, according to Leland, knew her as Maude; and Munday's precise source was Drayton's poem *Matilda, the Faire and Chaste Daughter of Lord R. Fitzwater* (1594). It is conceivable that Munday was led to Drayton's text by the name of Fulk's first wife (it was apparently not in the English version, though Munday could read French). If so, that is the only direct link between the Earl of Huntington plays and the story of Fulk.

Much of Munday's detail, if not much of his action, is taken from the *Gest* or the early ballads, often with variations to fit in with the advanced gentrification of the distressed-earl situation, rather than the *Gest*'s mere acquaintance with knight and king. In Munday, Robin's enemy is not primarily the sheriff, but his uncle the Prior of St Mary's of York – a clear transference to Robin from the knight (though the prior was less aggressive than the abbot in the *Gest*). The Sheriff of Nottingham is a position to which Warman, Earl Robert's faithless steward, is appointed, apparently through the influence of the Prior of St Mary's,[36] and he has very little activity in that role. None of this relates to Fulk. Villainy is focused in the Catholic Church and treacherous intimates, a very credible bunch of enemies from the viewpoint of Tudor nobility, enjoying the newly appropriated lands of the church and reliant on expanded administrative staff. The weight of hostility falling on the church is itself a Reformation-based response, and will be seen through the broadside ballads, where the sheriff is rarely the enemy, unless the ballads are cut out of the *Gest*: 'Robin Hood and the Bishop' in fact shows a bishop acting in the role of punitive sheriff. Munday's comment (in the cleric Doncaster's mouth) that Robin is 'still the Churchmens foe' (*Downfall*, line 1391 – 'still' meaning 'always' here) is not entirely inappropriate to the early ballads and the *Gest*, but it has a new emphasis on anti-clericalism like the knight-sequence of the *Gest* that the broadsides will magnify.

This focused hostility to the church in Munday is enhanced when Friar Tuck is himself from St Mary's – which of course a mere friar would never be.

None of this enemy action relates in any way to the story of Fulk, and nor indeed does the representation of Prince John. He is moderately hostile to Robin, but only because he lusts after Matilda/Marian: he is much more an enemy of the Bishop of Ely, Richard's regent. The real villains for Lord Robert are the Prior of York and his henchman Doncaster, 'the envious Priest of Hothersfield' (*Downfall*, p. 350, line 1617):[37] they do not trust John at all, and before long he ends up himself an outcast and, dressed in green, sets off to join the forest exiles under the curious cognomen of 'Wodnet' and has a 'meets his match' encounter with Scathlock. He could be seen as another version of the knight from the *Gest* in his forest misery, and in spite of his dubious nature is welcomed generously by Robin (p. 379, lines 2641–4), a connection which benefits John in his more serious encounter with the fierce figure of the returning King Richard.

There is some familiarity with the ballad material in Munday, but not the manuscript-bound stories of Robin and the monk, the potter or, if it did as seems likely exist by Munday's time, Guy of Gisborne. A sequence of the play is based on the action of what is best known as 'Robin Hood Rescuing Three Young Men', a popular broadside in which, crossing a social range, Robin rescues either three young squires or the sons of a poor widow known to him. This usually begins with Robin exchanging clothes with a beggar and then agreeing to act as the sheriff's hangman before springing the rescue. The prose Sloane 'Life' refers to the opening but not the rest of the story: as noted elsewhere (see pp. 89–90) this was probably already in existence but cannot have provided the rescue narrative. Munday involves Robin in the rescue, but not quite as actively as in the ballad, where he personally frees the men and has the sheriff executed: in the play he merely masquerades as hangman and then blows a horn to call his men (horn-blowing to gather the outlaws is a common enough feature in the early ballads and the *Gest*, but is not found in the Fulk story).[38] Reduced as the earl's activity may be in comparison with the ballad, this is nevertheless his busiest moment in the play and apparently relates to an early version of this ballad. There is a passing reference in *Downfall* to another broadside that was very probably known in the sixteenth century (see p. 89), with effectively a quotation at lines 2509–10 from 'The Jolly Pinder of Wakefield'.[39]

The two prisoners rescued in the play are the brothers Scarlet and Scathlock, a rationalisation of the multiple nature of this name. They are very firmly located to the Nottingham area: they say they have 'raigned uncontrolde, From Barndsdale shrogs to Nottinghams red cliffs' (lines 1281–2), and they provide a highly localised round-up of place-names through Sherwood, Yorkshire and the north. This regional connection for the English outlaw appears to influence both Drayton in *Poly-Olbion* and Jonson in *The Sad Shepherd*,[40] and is itself far from the Welsh border localisation of Fulk. Here Munday's sources appear to be local knowledge: the sequence is a good deal more specific than the *Gest* – which never mentions Sherwood, but does embrace both Barnsdale and Nottingham. However, other elements of Munday's play anchor it firmly to the action of the *Gest*. Friar Tuck leads Doncaster and the prior's men into an ambush clearly in the spirit of Little John tricking the sheriff. Little John's voice is heard directly when he pronounces the 'Articles of Sherwood', a Tudor legislative elaboration of the rules of engagement which Robin passed down in the *Gest*, echoing the knights' collective oath on Arthur's wedding day in Malory. Even more specific is the sequence involving Ely in the forest: the tone is Elizabethan stage farce as he appears disguised as an old rustic, but the fact that he has the royal seal with him is a realisation of his still intact honour and his genuine link with true monarchy. It references directly the moment when King Richard, masquerading as an abbot, reveals the seal in the *Gest* and Robin and his men respect, even worship, 'faire Englands royal seale' (line 2176).

None of this relates to the robust fighting and resourceful tricksterism by which Fulk and his supporters confront and humiliate Prince, or would-be King, John and his numerous incompetent forces. It seems unlikely that Munday had even heard of the story of Fulk, let alone read it, whereas it seems highly probable that the redactor who shaped the *Gest* was as familiar with that story as he was with others such as English popular romances like *Sir Launfal* – and non-romances like *Gamelyn* and *King Edward and the Shepherd*.

The manuscript that contains 'Robin Hood and the Monk' also contains the archetypal 'King and Subject' text 'King Edward and the Shepherd'; that containing 'Robin Hood and the Potter' also offers the more comic cut-down of that model, 'The King and the Barker'.[41] Both manuscripts, strikingly, also include the comical, socially aggressive mock-romance 'The Tournament of Tottenham', which is too comic to be an influence on the *Gest*. The Robin Hood materials, deeply popular and socially multiple, both riding and realising a late medieval wave of social, economic and political innovation, were in touch with many related cultural forces, are marked by them and, most importantly, transmit them.

Languages, nations, nationalities, narratives

Robin Hood bears a French first name and an English surname; it was not until the Christmas of 1819 that a Scotsman made him English, or more exactly Saxon, and so presumptively, and for 1819 attractively, anti-French.[42] Fulk, or Fouke, or most authentically Fulco, was of Norse origin, transplanted to France and then to England, and then to Wales. While such multi-locational identity is still, even increasingly, a reality, there are today still many who prefer nationalist simplifications of human and political relations, past and present. The medieval material about resisting authority does not support such drastic, and as we now know potentially highly destructive, simplifications. Robin Hood the very English outlaw, it seems, originally moved from French lyric poetry to the south-western play-game hero (with a Scottish variant in urban celebration), was reworked in the furnace of the English fourteenth century, was relocated in the wilds of the English north midlands (with another Scottish variant as nationalist outlaw), was redeveloped in terms of a Norse-French baron living in Wales and was reconstructed on a higher social level in a mode initiated by a Scottish scholar long resident in Paris. Tracing the actual formative history of such a potent and still vital political myth takes us around the world of its origins, as much as it projects into the world of modernity and the international outlaw.

To challenge nationalism, and simplicity, and banal empiricism (no medieval creator cared reductively about the 'real Robin Hood') is appropriate, or rather necessary, for those who want to understand seriously the formations of the tradition of Robin Hood. It is with a sense of needing to surprise people into thinking again, into recognising, even valuing, multiplicity, that I have titled this chapter and this hero with the provocative but, as I trust has been shown here not entirely unjustified, cross-class, cross-nation, cross-time and, above all, cross-simplification name that embraces an appropriate hybridity: Robin Fitz Warren.

Notes

1. These references, some 270 of them, were assembled in an Appendix by Lucy Sussex to Stephen Knight, *Robin Hood: A Complete Study of the English Outlaw* (Oxford: Blackwell, 1994), pp. 262–88.
2. See Thomas H. Ohlgren, *Robin Hood: The Early Poems, 1465–1560: Texts, Contexts, and Ideology* (Newark: University of Delaware Press, 2007): on dating the texts, see pp. 40 and 75.
3. See Stephen Knight, 'Alterity, Parody Habitus: The Formation of the Early Robin Hood Texts', in Stephen Knight (ed.), *Robin Hood in Greenwood Stood: Alterity and Context in the English Outlaw Tradition* (Turnhout: Brepols, 2011), pp. 1–29.
4. Line references and quotations are taken from Stephen Knight and Thomas Ohlgren (eds), *Robin Hood and Other Outlaw Tales*, 2nd edn, TEAMS Middle English Texts (Kalamazoo: Western Michigan University Press, 2000).
5. On events at Yeovil, see James Stokes (ed.), *Records of Early English Drama: Somerset*, 2 vols (Toronto: University of Toronto Press, 1996), vol. 1, pp. 411–12, and vol. 2, pp. 970–2.
6. Thomas Percy (ed.), *Reliques of Early English Poetry*, ed. Henry B. Wheatley, 3 vols (London: Sonnenschein, Swan, Lebus and Lowrey, 1886), vol. 1, p. 116, line 236.
7. For fetishisation and the 'commodity relations' generated by cash exchange see Karl Marx, *Capital*, 3 vols (London: Penguin, 1976–81), vol. 1, chapter 2, and vol. 3, chapter 24.
8. William H. Clawson, *The Gest of Robin Hood* (Toronto: University of Toronto Library, 1909); see the summaries on pp. 48–55 and 76 and the structural analysis on pp. 125–7 for details of the twelve ballads he identifies as sources.
9. Lord Raglan, *The Hero* (London: Watts, 1949).
10. Wyresdale is a reasonably credible explanation of the otherwise unknown place-name Verysdale. It is still a very rural district in northern Lancashire and, perhaps linked to the name given to the knight of the *Gest*, includes a village called Lee.
11. An empiricist might wonder where he has come from. Perhaps like Chaucer's knight he has been fighting on crusade in the Baltic and has sailed into Newcastle or Hull. But his journey hardly fits with a base in Wyresdale in Lancashire – though even poor gentry might have more than one landed location. As his castle will soon turn up in the forest close to Nottingham, the knight's placement seems a function of the text rather than late medieval documentary.
12. The later broadsides 'Robin Hood and the Golden Arrow' (c.1750) and 'The King's Disguise and Friendship with Robin Hood' (c.1750) seem clearly based on the *Gest*, as might be 'Robin Hood's Golden Prize' (1623–61). Clawson, *Gest of Robin Hood*,

p. 127, suggests that all three are late-appearing versions of ballads from which the *Gest* was compiled, but their language is too late for this to seem at all likely. However, though the first two only survive very late they were possibly known to the compiler of the Forresters manuscript in c.1670, as he has different versions of their narratives.

13 A. B. Ferguson, *The Indian Summer of English Chivalry* (Durham, NC: Duke University Press, 1960).
14 Thomas Chestre, *Sir Launfal*, ed. A. J. Bliss (London: Nelson, 1960), lines 211–13.
15 *A Gest of Robyn Hode*, in Knight and Ohlgren (eds), *Robin Hood and Other Outlaw Tales*, pp. 80–168, at p. 92, lines 83–6.
16 *Gamelyn*, in Knight and Ohlgren (eds), *Robin Hood and Other Outlaw Tales*, pp. 184–229, at p. 197, line 137; *Gest*, line 362.
17 Chestre, *Sir Launfal*, pp. 42–3.
18 D. B. Sands, *Middle English Verse Romances*, reprint edn (Exeter: University of Exeter Press, 1986), p. 202.
19 Ohlgren, *Robin Hood: The Early Poems*, p. 236, note 30.
20 See Stephen Knight, 'Robin Hood and the Crusades: When and Why Did the Longbowman of the People Mount Up Like a Lord?', *Florilegium*, 23 (2008, for 2006): 201–22.
21 John Marshall, 'Picturing Robin Hood in Early Print and Performance: 1500–1590', in Lois J. Potter and Joshua Calhoun (eds), *Images of Robin Hood: Medieval to Modern* (Newark: University of Delaware Press, 2008), pp. 60–81 at p. 63.
22 Ohlgren does not quite say this in his *Robin Hood: The Early Poems*, though he comes close (see pp. 108–9): but A. J. Pollard records his privately stated opinion that Pynson may well have commissioned the *Gest* in *Imagining Robin Hood: The Late-Medieval Stories in Historical Context* (Routledge: London, 2004), p. 223, note 6.
23 Leland's synopsis is recorded in *Joannis Lelandi antiquarii de rebus britannicis collectanea*, ed. Thomas Hearne, 3 vols (Oxford: E Theatro Sheldoniano, 1715), vol. 1, pp. 231–7. The differences between the texts have been explored by Louis Brandin, 'Nouvelles récherches sur *Fouke Fitz Waryn*', *Romania*, 55 (1929): 17–44.
24 See Thomas E. Kelly's comments under 'Relation to Later Outlaw Tales' in his Introduction to his translation of *Fouke Fitz Waryn* in *Medieval Outlaws: Twelve Tales in Modern English Translation*, ed. Thomas H. Ohlgren, 2nd edn (West Lafayette: Parlor Press, 2005), p. 171.
25 W. F. Prideaux, 'Who Was Robin Hood?', *Notes and Queries*, 7th series, 2 (1886): 421–4; on 'Amys del Bois', see pp. 422–3.
26 *The Tale of Gamelyn*, in *Chaucerian and Other Pieces*, vol. 3 of *The Works of Geoffrey Chaucer*, ed. W. W. Skeat, 7 vols (Oxford: Clarendon, 1884), p. 301.

27 The French text has been studied and translated by Glyn S. Burgess in *Two Medieval Outlaws: Eustace the Monk and Fouke Fitz Waryn* (Cambridge: Brewer, 1997).
28 Clawson, *Gest of Robin Hood*, p. 61.
29 See Brandin, 'Nouvelles récherches', p. 36 for a discussion of difference between Leland's synopsis and the French prose version.
30 Clawson, *Gest of Robin Hood*, p. 81.
31 Clawson, *Gest of Robin Hood*, p. 74.
32 See Burgess (trans.), *Two Medieval Outlaws*, p. 61.
33 Thomas H. Ohlgren, 'The "Marchaunt" of Sherwood: Mercantile Ideology in *A Gest of Robyn Hode*', in Thomas G. Hahn (ed.), *Robin Hood in Popular Culture: Violence, Transgression and Justice* (Cambridge: Brewer, 2000), pp. 175–90.
34 The disappearing initial G may suggest the variation between Norman and Parisian French (e.g. 'warranty' and 'guarantee'), but in fact here depends on the capacity of initial G in Welsh to disappear in circumstances causing initial 'soft mutation': for example, *gwrach*, meaning 'witch', becomes with the feminine definite article *y wrach*.
35 For references to this continuation of the distressed nobleman tradition after Major see Knight, *Robin Hood: A Complete Study*, pp. 40–1 (Leland) and p. 115 (Warner and Stow).
36 Munday, *Downfall*, in Knight and Ohlgren (eds), *Robin Hood and Other Outlaw Tales*, pp. 303–84, lines 537–8.
37 Sir Doncaster appears to be generated from the knight who is in the *Gest* involved with the prioress in Robin Hood's death.
38 Horn-blowing occurs three times, but in ways only linked to Fulk's enemies. The king's knights assault the forest in the guise of horn-blowing hunters (Burgess (trans.), *Two Medieval Outlaws*, p. 154) and on the strange hostile island off Scotland that Fulk visits late in his outlawry: first six giant peasants assemble at a horn and are killed, then Fulk uses the old woman's horn to call two hundred thieves together before slaughtering them (Burgess (trans.), *Two Medieval Outlaws*, pp. 168–9). Where Robin has a positive lead-hunter status, Fulk seems to have a gentry position on horn-blowing.
39 See 'The Jolly Pinder of Wakefield', in Knight and Ohlgren (eds), *Robin Hood and Other Outlaw Tales*, p. 472, lines 45–6.
40 On Drayton see Stephen Knight, *Robin Hood: A Mythic Biography* (Ithaca: Cornell University Press, 2003), pp. 136–9; on Jonson, see Stephen Knight, '"Meere English flocks": Ben Jonson's *The Sad Shepherd* and the Robin Hood Tradition', in Helen Phillips (ed.), *Robin Hood Medieval and Post-Medieval* (Dublin: Four Courts Press, 2005), pp. 129–44.
41 In *Robin Hood: The Early Poems* Ohlgren provides descriptions of the contents of the two manuscripts: for that containing 'Robin Hood

and the Monk', see pp. 31–2, and for the 'Robin Hood and the Potter' manuscript, see p. 70.

42 Scott's *Ivanhoe* was, like many books since, dated a little late, presumably for marketing purposes. Though it appeared, just, for Christmas 1819, it bore the date 1820.

4
Revisiting the broadside ballads

Approaching the broadside forest

Like Sherlock Holmes's pipe and deerstalker hat or Chaucer's narrative art, some things we take for granted are not quite as simple or indeed grantable as they might seem.[1] Since Robin Hood studies started looking at the actual cultural materials, rather than questing possible real Robin Hoods from places or periods of interest to the enquirer, great strides have been made, probing into minor outlaw authors, the possible play-game events, the implications of popular film, the nationalist and sexist and psychological and homosocial elements of the stories. It might seem that hardly a leaf has been unturned in the forest of outlaw culture.

And yet: I want to suggest that what a hundred years ago were seen as the central Robin Hood texts, the broadside ballads, have not been inspected much. F. J. Child did much original work in this field, gathering, sorting and reporting them;[2] the editorial pairs of twins Dobson–Taylor and Knight–Ohlgren have done some pruning and weeding,[3] but basically the ballad garden has since Child been admired from a distance, and rather rarely even visited. After the Forresters manuscript was discovered in 1993, I edited it in the light, or perhaps shadow, of the given body of broadside ballads in Child's edition: that seemed a correct approach at the time, a modest step forward, or perhaps mostly sideways.[4] But it seems appropriate now to take a more distant perspective on the broadside ballads, and as a result a more searching view of them. That can tell us more about how they vary and how they cohere, and how they operated, both in their own period and across time, and also in terms of the continuing construction and reconstruction of the Robin Hood myth.

Child prints twenty-eight ballads that appeared in broadsides (see Appendix A) and three others that appeared only in garlands but may have had broadside origins, 'Robin Hood and the Ranger',

'Robin Hood and the Golden Arrow' and 'Robin Hood and the Valiant Knight'. Two ballads which he printed and which looked as if they were broadside or garland material should be excluded from his numbers. 'The Bold Pedlar and Robin Hood' was collected only in 1842 and so has no clear claim to broadside status, though it may descend from one. 'Robin Hood and the Pedlars' was, it now seems clear,[5] written by the over-enthusiastic collector and archivist John Payne Collier in c.1830 and presented to Gutch as from the seventeenth-century 'Protectorate Manuscript' that he had forged. Child had his doubts about this (vol. 3, p. 170) but inauthenticity was not then proved. Also ignored (but not included in the twenty-eight) should be 'The Birth of Robin Hood' apparently an opportunistic make-up by the ballad-source Mrs Brown of Falkland, based on Child no. 102, 'Willie and Earl Richard's Daughter'. Though it might seem odd that Child regarded the two versions of 'Robin Hood and the Beggar' as different ballads, under that title but differentiated as I and II, the differences that emerge in the two stories do make this seem not unreasonable.

The broadsides can be sorted into two major categories. One is 'anti-authority': Robin and his men resist in some way the force of order, whether secular or religious – the variation there will be of some interest. The other group is best called 'celebratory' – these broadsides do not show the outlaws opposing authority but rather realise and honour the outlaws' status and skills. The 'Robin meets his match' ballads are major examples of this type: they remained popular into the nineteenth century, and figured on the title page of early versions of Ritson's major 1795 edition (see Figure 1). Most of these celebrate the outlaw world without making any specific social comment beyond homosocial celebration, including fighting, so they do not contradict the anti-authority ballads, but rather coexist with them. But there are also some where Robin is involved in celebratory ways with royalty, and so celebration as a mode can at times contradict the anti-authority ballads.

This analysis will also sort the broadsides chronologically (see Appendix B), though the records of dates are by no means precise, often recording only when certain seventeenth-century printers were working, sometimes over extensive periods. There is another difficulty here, because it must be assumed that there has been considerable loss of ballad texts, especially early ones. For example, it is credible that the story of Robin meeting Little John was an early explanatory prequel story, explaining how the band got together in 'Robin meets his match' mode. A lost play *Robin Hood and Little*

Revisiting the broadside ballads

1 A 'Robin meets his match' fight: Thomas Berwick's 'Robin Hood and the Tanner' from Ritson's 1795 edition *Robin Hood* (1795), title page.

John was recorded in 1594, and a ballad of that name was entered in the Stationers' Register in 1624, but a text does not survive until around 1690 (Child found this late, and it is printed in volume 5: until then his earliest example was from the 1723 *Collection of Old Ballads*, but he nevertheless printed it at no. 125 as if it were quite early). After it appeared it was very popular, so probably earlier versions are simply lost. Other similar examples will be discussed below, and it is clear that substantial loss of material remains likely with material up until the later eighteenth century.

Pre-1600 ballads

As is well known, there were Robin Hood texts from the mid to late fifteenth century and references through the sixteenth century to stories and rhymes about him, so it would seem likely that there were printed broadside ballads in the sixteenth century when this form starts to appear. However, it is important to note that in general they are new formations: the old-fashioned idea that the popular ballads descended from folk antiquity is not supported in the case of the Robin Hood materials. As has been discussed above (see pp. 20–1), Bertrand Bronson found the Robin Hood ballads relatively new and uninteresting in terms of the tunes they were linked to, and the broadsides appear to be a new form of orality – albeit literate in mode – perhaps connecting in general with earlier songs and stories, but showing no sign of a strong ongoing tradition from earlier centuries.

In this, Robin Hood is only an extreme version of the usual pattern. There are very few instances of any familiar seventeenth-century broadside ballad, a short narrative with a tune and usually chorus, appearing in print before 1600. The records of the Bodleian Library Sixteenth Century Ballads Project indicate only two Child ballads with tunes surviving from before 1600, and these are both songs, hardly ballads: 'Heigh Ho Holiday' and 'The Shaking of the Sheets'.[6] Without tunes there are a couple of Christian songs, 'St Stephen and Herod' and 'Judas', as well as the secular 'Crow and Pie' and 'Robyn and Gandelyn'. Some quite long narratives, clearly not sung, that Child prints are pre-1600: 'Robin Hood and the Monk' and 'Robin Hood and the Potter', 'The Battle of Otterburn' and 'The Hunting of the Cheviot'. They are all in manuscript, not printed form, but the outlaw story 'Adam Bell' was printed as early as 1505, and 'The Hunting of the Cheviot' does have seventeenth-century broadside versions. The only other printed texts from before 1600 which are mainstream Child ballads are 'Jock o' the Side' and 'Captain Car', also known as 'Edom o' Gordon'. A further six Child ballads were listed in the Stationers' Register as printed, but do not survive from the sixteenth century. Three of them are Scottish, and one, probably, linked to 'Robin Hood and the Pinder of Wakefield', is entitled 'of a Wakefield and a Greene' (1557/58).

The evidence gathered in Carole Rose Livingston's catalogue of sixteenth-century broadsides indicates that the material tends to be separate from the popular traditions which provided most of the Child ballads.[7] She notes that there were about 2,000 broadsides listed in the Stationers' Register, and suggests that about the same number existed but were never listed.[8] Only 260 have survived, and the dominant categories are memorials for important people, religious and moral statements, military events and monstrosities (mostly storms and weird births, human and animal). There is one 'King and Subject' ballad, 'Henry II and the Miller of Mansfield', which might be thought close to the Robin Hood tradition, and a few joking stories, but nothing which seems to be anti-authority or celebrating outlawry in any way (nor any of the love tragedies that dominate Child's collection).

Yet in spite of this extensive negative evidence, there are a few cases, perhaps six, where a later Robin Hood broadside might well have existed before 1600, and the possibilities will be presented in order of credibility. If even half of them are in fact true cases, then this theme was, along with Scottish border events, a major early instance of the sung narrative ballad, as it was recorded in print.

The Sloane manuscript 'Life of Robin Hood', which is traditionally dated at c.1600, is likely to be a generation earlier, c.1580 (see p. 34 n.40); it clearly knows some of the ballads that have survived from soon afterwards – or perhaps just their stories. It refers to the events of 'Robin Hood's Progress to Nottingham' as the cause of Robin's outlawry, and as there seems no other location for the story beyond the broadside, this can be accepted as having a pre-1600 source. It is a popular ballad in broadside form, and a regular in the garlands, notable for its continuing anti-authoritarian vigour:

> Then Robin Hood hee bent his noble bow,
> And his broad arrows he let flye,
> Till fourteen of these fifteen forresters
> Upon the ground did lye.
> ('Robin Hood's Progress to Nottingham', lines 47–50)

Close in situation is 'Robin Hood and Allen a Dale', even though it does not survive in broadside until 1674–79. The Sloane 'Life' clearly knows the story, but offers Will Scarlock as the eventually lucky bridegroom. This story is also found nowhere else, so can be assumed to derive from an early broadside ballad. It seems possible to suggest that this ballad was originally told of Will Scarlett/Scathlock/Scarlock, but when another version of his arrival in the outlaw band became common in 'Robin Hood Newly Revived' (surviving from the early to mid seventeenth century), the hero was switched to Alan, a notion perhaps supported by the fact that the Forresters manuscript of c.1670, calling this story 'Robin Hood and the Bride', does not give the bridegroom a name.

The Sloane 'Life' also refers to 'a fryar called Muchel' fighting Robin and joining his band,[9] but this could have other sources than the ballad 'Robin Hood and Friar Tuck', though it survives as early as 1625 (and as 'Robin Hood and the Curtal Friar' is in Percy, c.1645).[10] Known from the early fifteenth century as a figure of carnival and disorder, the friar appears to have been accreted to the Robin Hood myth. The ballad has overlap with the play from c.1560, which was printed at the end of a new edition of the *Gest* by William Copland. This is basically a 'meets his match' encounter, but the friar maintains the upper hand, eventually dismissing Robin so he can himself 'daunce in the myre' (line 122), whatever that might suggest, with the 'lady free' whom Robin has given him as a dubious inducement to join his band:

> Thou shalt have both gold and fee
> And also here is a lady free:
> I wyll geve her unto the,
> And her chapplyn I the make
> To serve her for my sake.
> ('Robin Hood and the Friar' play, lines 111–15)

The possibility of a *double entendre* on 'serve' is confirmed by the friar's reply:

> She is a trul of trust
> To serve a friar at his lust
> (lines 117–18)

And he characterises himself as

> A prycker, a prauncer, a terer of sheetes,
> A wager of ballockes when other men slepes.
> (lines 119–20)

Child, printing the play as an appendix to the ballad, omitted this as 'ten lines of ribaldry, which have no pertinency to the traditional Robin Hood and the Friar' (vol. 3, p. 128), but this licentious spirit fits with the image of the comic friar known in popular drama, which he sheds to become one of Robin's men. The ballad has a simpler 'meets his match' ending, with the friar joining the band, which is the point of the brief reference in the Sloane 'Life'. Though the play might well have been the source, it seems quite possible, though not certain, that a 'Friar' broadside existed by the late sixteenth century.

The 'Friar' situation might seem somewhat alike in status to 'Robin Hood and Guy of Gisborne' which is found in Percy, c.1645, and has some similarities of action to a very short play (or perhaps just two scenes) of c.1475 in which an unnamed bountyhunter seeks to capture Robin for the sheriff and is killed (this action is not referred to in the Sloane 'Life'). But 'Robin Hood and Guy of Gisborne' does not appear in any other broadside or garland, so is not eligible for this analysis, and in any case remains in historical terms a sort of addendum to the early manuscript ballads. It is much more sensational than either 'Robin Hood and the Monk' or 'Robin Hood and the Potter' – the horse-costume disguise, the beheading, the vengeful final shooting of the sheriff:

> But he could neither soe fast goe,
> Nor away soe fast runn,
> But Litle John, with an arrow broade,
> Did cleave his heart in twin.
> ('Robin Hood and Guy of Gisborne', lines 231–4)

It might be hypothesised that these unusual, even sensationalist features suggest that, especially with its opening stanza so close to that of 'Robin Hood and the Monk', this is a sixteenth-century pastiche, a reworking of an earlier story shown in the play of around 1475. This could just be an instance of very early medievalism, and it would be an unwise argument which depended on this poem for more than merely supportive evidence, as it is used in the first section of Chapter 3.

Another possible early text is 'Robin Hood and the Pinder of Wakefield': the pinder is in some versions called 'jolly'. The Sloane 'Life' mentions Robin's encounter and post-fight alliance with the pinder and as noted above, there was a lost ballad of 'a wakefylde and a grene' registered as early as 1557/58: Robin is not mentioned in the title, but the 1592 play *George a Greene* gives him a large part (though George basically defeats him), and the surviving ballad versions, where Robin defeats the pinder who joins his band, look quite old in language and mode, so a pre-1600 version seems likely. It is a short ballad: Child prints it with three separate gaps where he felt material was missing, but in fact it appears to be complete, and uses a bouncing metre and unstressed rhyme, which may suggest an early oral and musical form: when Robin asks the pinder if he can feed them, he replies:

> 'I have both bread and beef,' said the pinder,
> 'And good ale of the best.'
> 'And that is meat good enough,' said Robin Hood,
> 'For such unbidden guest.'
> ('Robin Hood and the Pinder of Wakefield', lines 37–40)

Child and other commentators say that the Sloane 'Life' knows 'Robin Hood Rescuing Three Squires', but all it actually uses is the initial exchange of clothes with a beggar, which might itself be a free-standing motif that is re-deployed in the ballad to explain how Robin went about the process of rescuing his friends from the gallows. The Sloane 'Life' does not discuss the 'rescue from execution' which is the climax of the ballad and of most of the related 'Robin Hood and the Beggar' versions of the story. Child suggests that this is a combination of two stories, Robin meeting and fighting a beggar and then rescuing his friends (vol. 3, p. 156): he treats this as 'Robin Hood and the Beggar I'. He also prints as 'Robin Hood and the Beggar II' a long and late eighteenth-century ballad where the beggar fights and humiliates the outlaws by throwing meal in their eyes, presumably a much elaborated version of the short episode found in the Sloane 'Life'. Child is kinder to this than to most late make-ups, saying: 'This is by far the best of the Robin Hood ballads of the secondary, so to speak cyclic, period. It has plenty of humour, but the heroic sentiment has gone' (vol. 3, p. 159).

However, the Sloane 'Life' is not the only early evidence here. Munday's *Downfall* of 1598–99 clearly knows the 'rescue from execution' story, and the play of c.1475, brief though it is, has some similarities with the rescue story in its second scene. There is no link between this story and the *Gest* or the manuscript ballads, but the rescue story might, like that of the friar, have been a part of popular drama (as in the c.1475 version). However, there must be some likelihood that there was a print ballad on the 'rescue from execution' theme before 1600. Curiously, though 'Robin Hood Rescuing Three Young Men' is later very popular, like its seventeenth-century variant 'Robin Hood Rescues Will Stutely' (or 'Stukeley'), it is not in fact recorded until the eighteenth century apart from the Percy Folio, presumably another instance of text loss. The Sloane 'Life' and Munday are more likely to have known the story in its 'Robin Hood and the Beggar I' version, which survives from 1623–61.

So far, as candidates for early broadside status, we have as very likely 'Robin Hood's Progress to Nottingham', 'Robin Hood and Allen a Dale' (perhaps focusing on some other bridegroom than Allen, usually Will) and 'Robin Hood and the Pinder of Wakefield', and possibly ballads about the friar, and also 'Robin Hood Rescuing Three Squires', perhaps only in a preliminary version, effectively about Robin Hood disguising as a beggar. It would not be unreasonable to assume that all these existed as texts, quite probably printed, in the sixteenth century.

Some seventeenth-century ballads have thematic links with texts from before 1600 that suggest they might have existed in the sixteenth century. 'Robin Hood and the Butcher' is in the Percy Folio of c.1645, and the first broadside version is from 1623–61 – the long period of activity of the London printer Cole. The essential story is the same as that of 'Robin Hood and the Potter', apart from the change of title and leading role, and in its having in consequence a strong corporate presence of butchers, perhaps a feature linked to the urban guilds. The sheriff wants to buy stock from Robin – is he also a butcher? The butchers eat at his house, but he may very well be an innkeeper, not an uncommon role for a late medieval sheriff. But if a bridegroom can change from Will to Allen, then we should accept a butcher for a potter as being basically the same ballad, and so accept this as probably having a pre-1600 origin. It remains one of the major puzzles as to why the trade is changed so fully. The process does simplify and focus the story, as here the sheriff merely asks if he can buy some 'horn-beasts' (Child no. 122, st. 20, a) from the visiting butcher, and is then shown by Robin 'A hundred head of red deer' (st. 24, c).

The process of developing 'Robin Hood and the Butcher' seems to have had several stages. In the broadside there is no reference to the curious off-stage apparent relationship between Robin and the sheriff's wife found in 'Robin Hood and the Potter', though he does finally say, 'O have me commended to your wife at home' (st. 30 c) – one of the infrequent third lines without internal rhyme, suggesting it might survive from a previous version. Percy's version, though torn, clearly had more about Robin and the wife, as the sheriff there says at the end, explaining his escape:

> 'But I had a verry good wif at home,
> Which made him gentle cheere,
> And therfor, for my wifes sake
> I shold haue better favor here.'
>
> (Child no. 122, vol. 3, p. 118, st. 28)

The sheriff's wife and Robin have met in this version, but their 'cheere' is not recorded: it might well be missing. It would be interesting to have known if they addressed each other here in as courteous, conceivably amorous, a mode as in 'Robin Hood and the Potter'. It seems clear that the Percy version is a transition from 'Robin Hood and the Potter' to the brisker, and rather effective, broadside version: it would have been a good deal longer, partly because the broadside has cut the opening fight; Percy lacks internal third-line rhyme, another sign of its priority. The Forresters text is a good deal closer to Percy than the broadside, having the early fight with the butcher (as with the potter) and even some verbal resemblances to Percy. Here Robin and wife do meet:

> The sheriffs wife filde a pottle of wine
> And to Robin hood dide say
> 'Good sir, drinke to your brethren all
> Theire is Just foure pound to pay.'
>
> Then Robin he tould out eight ould Angells
> And flung them upon her knee'
> Quoth she 'A brauer gentleman
> Did never cum to mee.'[11]

This commercial transaction is less nuanced than the encounter in 'Robin Hood and the Potter', but when Robin lets the sheriff go he speaks of 'thy curteous wife at home', and the sheriff appears to understand the implication, saying finally of Robin

> '... hee shal be welcome to my house
> Whether hee cum to thee or to mee.'
> ('Robin Hood and the Butcher', Forresters version, lines 203–4)

This rather skilful tricksterish story is less multiple than the longer manuscript version of 'Robin Hood and the Potter', but is certainly richer than the printed broadside, is without internal third-line rhyme and may be a good example of the actual transition between the manuscript 'potter' ballad and the broadside 'butcher' version.

It seems rather less likely that there was a separate early ballad of 'Robin Hood's Death', a story found at the end of the *Gest*. The ballad appears in the Percy Folio, c.1645, but, very strikingly, is long unknown in print. It is as rare as a final death scene in Robin Hood films, though its central event is used as a form of structural completion in the later garlands – but the ballad itself is not used there until a garland of 1786. Before that a few stanzas from the end of the *Gest* were in the c.1740 garland (the first survival of the busy London publisher Dicey's expanded version) added to the last text 'Robin Hood and the Valiant Knight', so completing a roughly biographic trajectory for the hero.

In this ballad, the king and 'his bishops and noble peers' (Child no. 153, vol. 3, pp. 225–6, st. 1, d) send Sir William and a hundred men on midsummer day to take 'bold Robin Hood' 'with all his crew' (re-using for Robin's men the negative term used in the outlaw-hostile royalist play of 1661 *Robin Hood and his Crew of Souldiers*). After 'a bloody fray' (st. 16, d) the outcome seems a draw and the parties separate, but Robin 'was taken ill':

> He sent for a monk, who let his blood,
>   And took his life away;
> Now this being done, his archers they run,
>   It was not a time to stay.
>
> Some got on board and crossd the seas,
>   To Flanders, France, and Spain,
> And others to Rome, for fear of their doom,
>   But soon returned again.
>
> Thus he that never feard bow nor spear
>   Was murdered by letting of blood;
> And so, loving friends, the story doth end
>   Of valiant bold Robin Hood.
>
>   (Child no. 153, vol. 3, p. 226, sts 20–2)

The epitaph follows, as found in Martin Parker's 1632 ballad-epic *A True Tale of Robin Hood*. It is curious that only Robin is in the text called 'valiant', though the title allots that quality to his opponent. In the same pro-outlaw way, the viewpoint seems finally that of Robin's 'loving friends'. Yet it is a weak, late effort, replacing the feeling of the 'Death' ballad with banality: perhaps that was too sad to have sold, and this ballad has not survived in a single form, just as the conclusion to a garland. Child's view was sharp and quite radical, saying it was 'Written, perhaps, because it was thought that authority should in the end be vindicated against outlaws, which may explain why this piece surpasses in platitude everything that goes before' (vol. 3, p. 225).

To summarise this survey of likely and possible early materials, we can count from before 1600 four likely broadsides ('Progress', 'Allen a Dale', 'Pinder', 'Butcher'), two possible ('execution rescue, Robin as beggar/hangman' and 'Friar Tuck') and one unlikely ('Death') – 'Guy of Gisborne' being ineligible as not printed. It is very notable that all of the likely items are basically anti-authority, though 'Friar Tuck' is only by implication against the non-friar church, and 'Allen a Dale' is against forced marriage only in the form found in the Sloane 'Life', though its later versions (and some nineteenth-century novels) link a bishop to the elderly knight's appropriation of the beloved. The existence of 'Robin Hood and Little John' in the sixteenth century seems unnecessary to assume as the characters are so strongly represented in the *Gest* (as well as in the two more fugitive fifteenth-century ballads 'Robin Hood and the Monk' and 'Robin Hood and the Potter'). However, none of these tells the story of their initial fight and subsequent friendship, and so if, as seems likely, that is implied by the title of the lost 1594 play *Robin Hood and Little John*, then a preceding ballad, perhaps derived from popular drama, joins 'Friar Tuck' in the category of possible.

The first half of the seventeenth century

Broadside survivals cluster in the first half of the seventeenth century, no doubt in part because they were increasing in numbers, but particularly because the keen seventeenth-century broadside collectors Anthony Wood and Samuel Pepys, and later the assemblers of what became the Douce and Roxburgh collections, looked out for items still available. Some Robin Hood broadsides from this period challenge authority, but this is largely restricted to the church. A popular seventeenth-century broadside 'Robin Hood and the Bishop' (first found c.1650) combines clerical mockery with the trickster energy of Robin disguised as an old woman – and when the bishop arrests the old woman instead she challenges him in the mode of carnival satire to identify her gender, saying, 'Lift up my leg and see' (line 72).

The clerical authority-challenge in this ballad seems unusually political, not just a matter of stealing money from the churchmen: the bishop plays a sheriff-like role in pursuing Robin to arrest him, even though this is in revenge for a robbery. It would seem possible this was a late medieval anti-sheriff story euphemised to being anti-Catholic: the Forresters manuscript has a 'sheriff' version of this that might be the older form. It could also be that if a medieval anti-sheriff ballad was in the Reformation converted to an anti-bishop ballad, then the later 'Robin Hood and the Bishop of Hereford' might have been produced to re-create the simpler 'rob the priest' structure that had been appropriated – it is suggestive of such a history that the two bishop ballads share an opening stanza. The rather straightforward 'Bishop of Hereford' ballad does not survive as a broadside until c.1740, but is in the Forresters manuscript well before that.

Anti-clerical adventures multiply in this period. There is 'Little John a-Begging', both in the Percy Folio of c.1645 and also in a broadside from 1640–65 (a sign either that this is a late-surviving version or, perhaps less likely, that the Percy Folio was recording fairly new ballads). Another is 'Robin Hood's Golden Prize', a clerical robbery, which seems to be a new broadside of 1623–61, because it is signed by L.P., or Laurence Price; it may well be earlier in that period as it is in the garland of 1663. Its literary character is suggested by the antiquarian and anti-Catholic move of Robin posing as a friar.

If the authority of the church is a focus for aggression, the bulk of the material from this period is primarily celebratory. Typical 'meets his match' broadsides which probably derive from before 1650 are 'Robin Hood and the Tinker' (sometimes 'Jovial Tinker' or 'Jolly Tinker'), a broadside from the 1623–61 period, while 'Robin Hood and the Shepherd' dates from 1654–62 and is also in the 1663 garland. The recurrently popular 'Robin Hood and the Tanner' – perhaps exploiting the notorious marginal urban status of the urine-reeking tradesmen – is first dated at 1657,[12] and is a fixture in the garlands. Robin's resistance to authority is not always forgotten: both the tanner and the tinker are acting for his social enemies before they agree to join him, but 'Robin Hood and the Shepherd', like the late eighteenth-century 'Robin Hood and the Beggar II', merely presents a wandering Robin wanting to fight a stranger.

A more exotic celebration is 'The Noble Fisherman', also known as 'Robin Hood's Preferment' (in the sense, presumably ironic, of 'promotion'), and in Forresters simply as 'Robin Hood's Fishing' – being a manuscript, its titles were not seeking sales. Robin goes to sea to make a better living in hard times. He is a poor sailor, perhaps developing the notion that Robin can be less than successful in manly physical encounters apart from archery – but when the ship is attacked by a French pirate, Robin leads the defence potently with bow and arrow, and the English gain £12,000. This broadside survives from 1663–74, and a version was listed in the Stationers' Register for 1631. The ballad remains popular, including in the garlands, and exotic as it may seem, it is structural in the myth: good fighting men were needed for naval battles before the time of long-range accurate cannonry, and earlier outlaws like Fulk and especially Eustace also had maritime adventures.

In social terms the broadsides are firmly loyal to the yeoman Robin, but there are some exceptions. A curious hybrid in both class and gender is 'Robin Hood and Maid Marian', appearing in the 1623–61 period and making Robin an earl, and so having a lady, but also re-using the 'meets his match' structure in that Marian, disguised as a man, meets and fights her lover – doing rather well in the encounter, and taking a while to recognise him. But the yeoman broadside structure asserts itself finally, as they stay, apparently for good, in the forest, and do not plan a return to the noble life:

> In solid content together they livd,
> With all their yeomen gay;
> They lived by their hands, without any lands,
> And so they did many a day.
>
> ('Robin Hood and Maid Marian', lines 82–5)

This is a unique survival which never appears in the garlands, but another somewhat gentrified hybrid is popular as a broadside and a garland entry. 'Robin Hood and Queen Katherine' is a broadside surviving from 1630, which also appears in the Percy Folio, the garlands and the Forresters manuscript (the last of these seems a fuller version, apparently not pruned for a one-page broadside print: Percy's text is damaged). Here Robin, entirely a yeoman still, comes to London to shoot in a royal competition for the queen, and though the king is annoyed, this is only in sporting terms. This ballad is also called 'Renowned Robin Hood' and 'Robin Hood, Scarlet and John', and the pro-royal activity makes it one example of the apparently increasing conservatism of the new broadsides of the first half of the seventeenth century, presumably relating to the fraught political conflict of the period.

The early garlands began with 'Robin Hood's Progress to Nottingham', though the first to survive, from 1663 has, evidently by error, located 'Robin Hood and Queen Katherine' before that – and then repeats it in its usual place half-way through. The collection of prose versions of ballads published in the previous year is a genre that seems to resist explanation, and perhaps shows its links to a more learned or at least more socially elevated tradition, indicated by its title *The Noble Birth and Gallant Atchievements of the Remarkable Outlaw Robin Hood*, and by starting with Robin's 'Noble Parentage'. The ballad garlands lack any such sign of gentrification, just presenting in 'Robin Hood and Queen Katherine' and 'Robin Hood's Chase' Robin's good relations with royalty, or with the queen at least, in a socially elevated parallel to his link with the sheriff's wife in 'Robin Hood and the Potter'. The garlands simply start with young Robin turning outlaw when harassed by foresters, in the very popular 'Robin Hood's Progress to Nottingham', where he is bullied into resistance by the ill-natured foresters. After they have goaded and deceived him, he kills them all and asserts his status:

> 'You have found me an archer,' saith Robin Hood,
> 'Which will make your wives to wring.
> And wish that you had never spoke the word,
> That I could not draw one string.'
> ('Robin Hood's Progress to Nottingham', lines 59–62)

A more socially elevated opening is not recorded until the c.1740 garland, printing at the start 'Robin Hood's Birth, Breeding, Valour and Marriage', which is found in several seventeenth-century broadsides, first from 1681–84. This ballad with a grand-sounding title does link Robin to the gentry: his father was only a forester but his mother was linked to the Gamwell family, and as a gentleman of a sort he becomes connected, indeed married, to a lady he meets in the forest. Because she is Clorinda, queen of the shepherds, she is structurally a version of the fairy mistress who helps out unfortunate knights in popular romances like *Sir Launfal*, but both the bouncy colloquial language and the comic tone substantially reduce the level of discourse. Though 'Her visage spoke wisdom and modesty too' ('Robin Hood's Birth, Breeding, Valour and Marriage', line 115) the action and dialogue locate her in a much more popular mode. They meet eight yeomen 'that were too bold', so John and Robin kill five of the eight and grant mercy to the remainder:

> This battle was fought near to Tutbury town,
> When the bagpipes baited the bull;
> I am king of the fiddlers and sware 't is a truth
> And call him that doubts it a gull.
>
> For I saw them fighting, and fidld the while,
> And Clorinda sung, 'Hey derry down!
> The bumpkins are beaten, put up thy sword, Bob,
> And now let's dance into the town.'
> (lines 173–80)

Child spoke of the 'jocular author of this ballad' (vol. 3, p. 214) and seems unusually tolerant of its literary pretensions: he makes no comment when quoting the 1723 *Collection* anthologist, who called it 'the most beautiful and one of the oldest extant' of the ballads – and titled it 'Robin Hood's Wedding'. As noted above, it is used to begin the c.1740 garland, which, apparently unknown to scholarship, played a very substantial role in guiding both Evans and Ritson in their authoritative transmission of the Robin Hood ballad cadre, though Evans omitted this as the starting ballad. Ritson, presumably in line with his acceptance of a noble Robin, accepted it – and, as will be discussed in Chapter 6, several nineteenth-century novelists basically followed this account of Robin's origins, in terms of his family at least.

The later seventeenth century and after

Most of the ballads that do not appear until the later seventeenth century pursue the gentrified or at least hybrid character of those last two. 'Robin Hood's Chase', a broadside from 1663–65 and a garland regular, follows on from 'Robin Hood and Queen Katherine': the king is angry after his defeat and pursues the outlaw around the country, but the queen brings peace. The outlaw's skill and fortune are finally blessed by royal hands, and the story in that respect echoes the ending of 'Robin Hood and the Monk', though the notion that Robin negotiates authority through friendship with the female consort has a curious resonance of 'Robin Hood and the Potter' and the Forresters manuscript version of 'Robin Hood and the Butcher'.

This kind of conservative hybridisation is evident in a particular ballad complex from the mid to late seventeenth century. There are traces of a fairly early, semi-exotic 'meets his match' broadside in 'Robin Hood and the Scotchman', with some added English nationalism, but its appearance in c.1650 and the 1663 garland derives only from its being used as some linking stanzas in an ensemble, between part 1, the somewhat gentrified 'Robin Hood Newly Revived', and part 2, the royalist military adventure 'Robin Hood and the Prince of Aragon'. As a fully separate ballad 'Robin Hood and the Scotchman' appears only in J. M. Gutch's 1847 edition, taken from a 1796 Irish version: Child comments dismissively that as a link after 'Robin Hood Newly Reviv'd' it has 'neither connection with that ballad nor coherence in itself' (vol. 3, p. 150).

The first part of the ensemble, the popular 'Robin Hood Newly Reviv'd' (also 'Revived'), which was first singly printed in 1660–73 and appears in the garlands from 1663 on, also starts as a 'meets his match' story. A stylish and effeminate-seeming stranger defeats Robin and turns out to be his cousin Will Gamwell, of Gamwell Hall, a low-level gentry connection that seems to bridge the gap between the ballad yeoman and the fully gentrified earl. This ballad was also known as 'Robin Hood and the Stranger': Child's dissent to Ritson's assertion of this identity appears to be his only error of any consequence (vol. 3, pp. 144–5). He felt that this title more likely belonged to 'Robin Hood and Little John' (vol. 3,

p. 133) but it is in fact given to 'Robin Hood Newly Revived' in the 1662 prose *The Noble Birth and Gallant Atchievements*, where Ritson had no doubt seen it.

After the 'Scotchman' stanzas attached to 'Robin Hood Newly Reviv'd' comes 'Robin Hood and the Prince of Aragon', also found as a separate broadside by 1689 or before (it comes from both Onley, working in 1650–72, and Milbourne, Onley and Thackeray, 1670–89). Child calls it 'a pseudo-chivalrous romance' (vol. 3, p. 147), where the yeomen (whose names are sometimes used as a variant title for this ballad, 'Robin Hood, Will Scadlock and Little John') march into battle and humiliate the Prince of Aragon, who has invaded with 'forraign arms' (Child no. 129, st. 12, d), to claim a royal princess. The king pardons them and invites the princess to choose one as her husband: she selects Will, who is revealed as the son of the Earl of Maxfield in a closure at once gentrifying and clumsily sentimental:

> With that a noble lord stept forth,
>   Of Maxfield earl was he,
> Who lookt Will Scadlock in the face,
>   Then wept most bitterly.
>
> Quoth he, I had a son like thee,
>   Whom I lovd wondrous well;
> But he is gone, or rather dead;
>   His name is Young Gamwell.
>
> Then did Will Scadlock fall on his knees,
>   Cries Father! father, here,
> Here kneels your son, your Young Gamwell
>   You said you lovd so dear.
>
> But, lord! what imbracing and kissing was there,
>   When all these friends were met!
> They are gone to the wedding, and so to bedding,
>   And so I bid you good night.
>   (Child no. 129, vol. 3, p. 150, sts 55–8)

This ballad moves towards literary decadence in the broadside tradition, like 'Robin Hood's Birth, Breeding, Valour and Marriage', discussed above. These are all celebratory ballads, and if authority is recognised, Robin favours it to some degree. Two literary broadsides draw on the *Gest* in a similar way: 'The King's Disguise and Friendship with Robin Hood' (not found until c.1750 but dating from well before that and apparently known to the Forresters compiler of c.1670, who has what seems an edited version of the broadside) isolates events from Fitt 7 of the *Gest*, while 'Robin Hood and the Golden Arrow' (also c.1750 and also known to the Forresters compiler, who seems to have reworked this) relates the archery competition, but gives it a rather feeble ending where Robin merely shoots a message-arrow into town to tell the sheriff who won. Resistance has become reduced to off-stage self-advertising, though the letter has a surprising effect, itself conveyed in the stagy literacy of the late broadside:

> The project it was full performd;
> The sheriff that letter had;
> Which when he read, he scratchd his head,
> And rav'd like one that's mad.
> ('Robin Hood and the Golden Arrow', lines 126–9)

Little sign of the socially resistant outlaw is found in three other later seventeenth-century 'meets his match' broadside ballads. The earliest is 'Robin Hood's Delight', from 1655, and is a garland regular from the earliest surviving version of 1663 on: this merely has Robin and his friends fighting for fun with foresters, and lacks the band-joining social coherence theme of most of the 'meets his match' ballads. 'Robin Hood and the Ranger', not surviving until the garland from c.1740, is a fairly thin 'meets his match' ballad versus another forester, so there is some trace of resistance to authority here, but the long 'Robin Hood and the Beggar II', not surviving until the late eighteenth century, is an expanded 'meets his match' story without the second part about the 'rescue from execution' that is usual in the 'Beggar' ballads. It ends with the beggar offering money to the outlaws who have come to help Robin, but humiliating them by throwing meal in their eyes. Although, as noted above, there may well have been a simple early 'Robin and the beggar exchange clothes' story, as used in the Sloane 'Life', it may also be that this recuperation of the beggar story into the 'meets his match' format is another sign of conservative and pro-authority reformation in the later broadsides.

Conclusions

Overall, there are two major formations to observe in the broadside and garland ballads. One is political: the ballads as they survive, and probably as they were published, seem to become incrementally less hostile to authority. Celebration without some anti-authority element is not found up to the Sloane 'Life' of the later sixteenth century, and though the celebration and even the pro-royalty ballads gather after that, it is notable that, throughout the seventeenth century and after, quite hostile anti-authority ballads survive in the garlands, and also appear often in single copies, notably 'Robin Hood's Progress to Nottingham' and the various versions of the 'rescue from execution' story. Martin Parker's ballad-epic of 1632 *A True Tale of Robin Hood* finally both celebrates the resistant outlaw and also notes nervously that things are different today:

> In those days men more barbarous were,
> And lived lesse in awe;
> Now, God be thanked! people feare
> More to offend the law.
> (*A True Tale of Robin Hood*, lines 437–40)

Though it does not confront the dialectic of authority and resistance so overtly, the broadside tradition as a whole in this period appears to be similarly divided, responding to its contexts with that mixture of resistance and acceptance.

The other notable point to emerge is the textual conservatism of the printed tradition: where there are variants, recorded in Child or elsewhere, they tend to be from the Percy Folio or the Forresters manuscript, open to both manuscript and possibly oral tradition, and also to editorial management. The garlands are also faithful to their own tradition: 1663, 1670, 1684–86 and 1689 are the same, apart from the aberrant appearance of 'Queen Katherine' twice in 1663 and a few title changes. Then the amplified c.1740 garland, raising the total number of ballads to twenty-seven, evidently using collected separate broadsides, takes on its own authority as a model, being the structural pattern followed, with very little variation, by the antiquarian anthologies of Evans (1777) and Ritson (1795).

But internal fidelity does not mean internal simplicity or political uniformity. The printed broadsides and garlands are not a mere record of a volatile oral tradition: they are their own complex and conflicted canon, bearing within their structures the multivalent and socially various strands of the Robin Hood tradition that are not only visible across different genres but also within them. The broadsides fire in more than one direction. It would be unwise to take them for granted.

Notes

1 Discussions have shown that Holmes's pipe was not originally curved, that he hardly ever wore a cape: illustrations and especially the 1890s stage version created the iconic image; in the case of Chaucer narrative was a relatively late form in his art and his major narratives end by reversing the trend of their long sequences.
2 Quotations from ballads are taken from Stephen Knight and Thomas Ohlgren (eds), *Robin Hood and Other Outlaw Tales*, 2nd edn, TEAMS Middle English Texts (Kalamazoo: University of Western Michigan Press, 2000) unless otherwise stated. Quotations from those not re-edited by Knight and Ohlgren are taken from F. J. Child (ed.), *The English and Scottish Popular Ballads*, 5 vols, reprint edn (New York: Dover, 1965; originally 10 vols, New York: Houghton Mifflin, 1882–98); this edition has no line numbers, but ballad stanzas are numbered, and these are cited, with lines a–d.
3 R. B. Dobson and John Taylor (eds), *Rymes of Robin Hood: An Introduction to the English Outlaw* (London: Heinemann, 1976), rev. edn (Stroud: Sutton, 1999); Knight and Ohlgren (eds), *Robin Hood and Other Outlaw Tales*: references are made in the text to ballads in this edition, with line numbers.
4 Stephen Knight (ed.), *Robin Hood: The Forresters Manuscript* (Cambridge: Brewer, 1998).
5 On the Collier forgery, see the discussion in Arthur Freeman and Janet Ing Freeman, *John Payne Collier: Scholarship and Forgery in the Nineteenth Century* (New Haven: Yale University Press, 2004), vol. 1. pp. 269–80: they see Gutch as Collier's 'grateful acquaintance and dupe', vol. 1, p. 280.
6 See *Bodleian Library Broadside Ballads*, www.bodley.ox.ac.uk/ballads/ (accessed 9 October 2014).
7 Carole Rose Livingston, *British Broadside Ballads of the Sixteenth Century: A Catalogue, the Extant Sheets, and an Essay* (New York: Garland, 1991).
8 Livingston, *British Broadside Ballads*, p. 789.
9 For the Sloane 'Life' see John Mathew Gutch (ed.), *A Lytell Geste of Robin Hode, with Other Ancient & Modern Ballads and Songs Relating to this Celebrated Yeoman*, 2 vols (London: Longman, 1847), vol. 1, pp. 379–89.
10 For Percy's manuscript see *The Percy Folio Manuscript*, ed. F. J. Furnivall and J. W. Hales, 3 vols (London: Trübner, 1867).
11 See Knight (ed.), *Robin Hood: The Forresters Manuscript*, p. 50, lines 93–100.
12 The English Short Title Catalogue gives 1657 for the first broadside printed by William Gilbertson: there were several other versions soon after.

5
Romantic Robin Hood

Pre-Romantic Robin

In the eighteenth century the Robin Hood tradition extended its variability. Popular publishing saw the broadside ballads and garland traditions thriving, as Robin shot foresters dead, robbed priests with abandon, rescued his friends and other deserving people from the gallows. At the same time, shadows of conformity and even gentrification fell on that robust tradition, as Robin was at times helpful to royalty and revealed some gentry connections of his own, and there was a tendency to play up the merry rural homosociality that made the outlaw experience seem a robust form of pastoral activity. Yet overall, the broadside tradition retained some sense of resistance, and there is a noticeable rise in the incidence of publishing these materials in the later part of the eighteenth century, when various forms of radical ideas were spreading: J. Harris Gable's bibliography lists six garlands in 1700–50 and another six in 1750–75 but sixteen in 1775–1800.[1] The identification of dates and separate versions is less than certain, but the change of figures seems to relate to much more than mere survival rates.

At the same time another popular genre was registering the outlaw tradition, though not with such density and with little idea of resistance to authority. In both late medieval popular drama and the early modern surge of urban theatre, the Robin Hood stories played some role, early on in keeping with the anti-authoritarian tradition; around 1600 gentrification entered the tradition with a conservative implication through Anthony Munday's *The Downfall of Robert, Earle of Huntington* and its sequel about his death (1598–99). Restraint could become constraint: the very short, action-free play *Robin Hood and his Crew of Souldiers*, played in 1661 in Nottingham on the day of King Charles II's coronation,[2] actually dramatised the outlaws yielding without resistance to royal authority. The only surrender in Robin Hood's entire career is a remarkable event, and this must suggest that the links between Robin Hood and the anti-royal cause were more pervasive and consistent than is indicated by the fairly sparse set of references that have been so far assembled, some half a dozen over half a century.[3] The play may have also been meant to warn against future popular anti-authoritarianism of the kind that had assembled around Robin Hood in not yet forgotten past periods. Whether retrospective or prospective in its censorship of dissent, or conceivably both, the threat appeared to work. Theatre was not in the English eighteenth century a major force in intellectual and political liberation, as it would be in early twentieth-century Ireland or in Germany after the First World War. The recurrent, if not frequent, popular Robin Hood appearances on the eighteenth-century stage were not anti-authoritarian in any serious or substantial way, and partly because of that were hardly at all predictive of a Romantic version of the hero and his context.

The old popular play tradition shows signs of survival: in 1717 there was a *Robin Hood and Little John* play at London's summer Bartholomew Fair, conceivably continuing the tradition of the lost 1594 play of that name. In 1724 at Southwark Fair was played *The Adventures of Robin Hood*, which sounds more like a dramatised garland: though the hero was an earl, a subtitle refers to 'His Mate Little John'. These were high summer events in the city, a displacement of the early summer festivals that had formerly featured Robin Hood play-games.[4] In 1730 music entered the tradition, signalled in the title *Robin Hood: An Opera*: Linda Troost suggests this used old ballads, being 'simply one of the old plays retrofitted as a ballad opera'.[5] The new musical element brought with it the need for a soprano female partner in love and song for Robin, and usually at least one other woman, Marian's friend or servant as the contralto. This was performed at Bartholomew Fair on August evenings in West Smithfield, London, and if that suggests links back to the popular tradition, the hero is an earl and his rival for his beloved Matilda (the sister of an unnumbered King Edward) is the Earl of Pembroke, whom Robin finally kills. *The Beggar's Opera* was a huge recent success, and at the same time *The Quaker's Opera* offered the story of the super-criminal Jack Sheppard, but the opera Robin Hood looks towards high-end musical melodrama, not plebeian excitements. But it also offers material for the Bartholomew Fair people: first gender conflict, as Matilda and her friend Marina are caught by outlaws led by Will

Stutely and, until Robin arrives, threatened with pack rape; next comes broad comedy as Little John, caught with the pinder's wife, hides from her husband first under the bed as Towzer the dog and then as the baby in a cradle. Robbing a Puritan called Prim and giving the money to the poor completes the fair-time low-level entertainment element.

Both less elevated and less ludicrous was the 1751 *Robin Hood: A New Musical Entertainment* with book and lyrics by Moses Mendez: this was separated from the ballad tradition and had a new score by the young and very talented Charles Burney (to be father of the writer Fanny Burney). Created for Garrick's Drury Lane Theatre, this was not popular fair material, yet it still had a festival element, beginning the tradition of Robin Hood for Christmas by opening in mid December. It lacks the earldom and in story at least approaches the broadside world as Robin, in the spirit of the Allen a Dale adventure, helps Clarinda (presumably suggested by Clorinda in 'Robin Hood's Birth, Breeding, Valour and Marriage') to escape the plans of her father Graspall to marry her to the unpleasant fop Glitter, and instead to marry her beloved Leander. The tone of urban satire is reinforced as Robin helps achieve this proper outcome by masquerading as Sir Humphrey Wealthy.

By *Robin Hood, or Sherwood Forest* of 1784, with music by William Shield and book by Leonard McNally, Thomas Evans's 1777 *Old Ballads* seems to have brought the ballads back into notice: there is a comic tinker as well as a drinking song. Some traces of Romanticism emerge: Troost feels that Robin exhibits some 'sensibility',[6] and Edwin, a returned crusader, takes up residence in a hermitage, borrowed from Goldsmith's recent ballad 'The Hermit of the Dale'. A pastoral element more picturesque than merry is implied when the four principals sing:

> By greenwood tree and mossy cell
> We merry maids and archers dwell,
> In quiet here, from worldly strife,
> We pass a cheerful rural life.[7]

But the medieval forest setting is also rumbustiously filled with modern theatrical embellishments, as couples find each other and sing duets, and also with the now necessary patriotism. Late in the play Clorinda, here again the love of Robin and now just the baron's daughter, not queen of the shepherds as in the broadside, sings, 'health and success to our country and king Encrease to her honour and fame' (p. 64). This jingoism is especially notable in the light of the fact that McNally, a Dublin lawyer, was in the next decade – still strongly remembered as such in Ireland – notorious as an active government spy against the United Irishmen: the rebels he represented in court were apparently in part convicted because he leaked their defence details to the Crown.

Though the authors of *Merry Sherwood or Harlequin Forrester* (book by William Pearce and lyrics by John O'Keeffe), which was staged for Christmas in 1795, had available the strong anti-authority reading of Robin Hood offered by Joseph Ritson in the introductory 'Life of Robin Hood' in his influential 1795 *Robin Hood: A Collection of All the Ancient Poems, Songs and Ballads Now Extant Relative to the Celebrated English Outlaw*,[8] Ritson's influence was only to give some of the ballads status in the story – the tinker, Allen a Dale, the beggar and the friar all have songs as well as the witch, previously seen in this context in Ben Jonson's *The Sad Shepherd* (c.1635). They appear within the structure of the displaced earl, whom Ritson also transmitted. There is a pastoral element: the opening proclaims 'Our roof is the greenwood tree',[9] but the prime purpose is sheer splendid entertainment – and was recognised as such in a number of new productions for some thirty years. The witch's song introduces this in comic mode as 'the bowman's jubilee' of 'triumphant archery!' (p. 19), and then in the finale the chorus sings: 'In merry Sherwood with blyth Robin Hood Let magic pranks appear' (p. 20). As a Harlequin performance it was evidently very spectacular: the final pageant 'The Triumph of Archery' offers a representation of both classical and modern international archery, with a sequence about the battle of Hastings celebrating the bow and arrow arriving in England to begin their glorious national future.

Though he was a resistant yeoman through the eighteenth century in ballads and garlands, Robin Hood had not in theatre had any coherent identity. In 1788 the comic opera *Marian* by Frances Brooke (better known as the author of the first novel set in Canada, *The History of Emily Montagu*, 1769) dealt with a handsome youth called Robin the Boatman, but he loves Polly the pretty milkmaid and merely helps Marian gain her beloved Edward, a poor clerk: it is as if the outlaw tradition is not well enough known to be a significant influence or interference.

Robin did have other random appearances in the period. Several of the serial collections of criminal characters, including some versions of *The Newgate Calendar*, list him, typically alongside major pirates like Captain Kidd and Henry Morgan. Basically unconnected to the myth was the Robin Hood Society, one of the first of the London weekly debating clubs, flourishing by the 1730s and a formative element in what Habermas identified as the new, and bourgeois, public sphere. The club was primarily Whiggish, and its name apparently drew on 'Robin' as the diminutive of the first name of Sir Robert Walpole, the long-serving prime minister. By the 1790s the same name was being used for one of the more active radical debating societies.[10] In another part of the neo-outlaw forest, Troost argues that the later eighteenth-century fashion for gentry archery parties, for both men and women, was also an element in developing a Robin Hood element in 'the rise of antiquarianism'.[11]

A different late eighteenth-century feature, of some weight and influence, is itself an unrecognised survival of earlier approaches to the outlaw. While the tendency has been to see Joseph Ritson's *Robin Hood* as the foundation for the later development of the outlaw's fame, and it certainly was widely read and reprinted, it is in several ways a backward-looking piece of work, the product of the archival interest in Robin Hood as an important figure in English tradition and even history. Ritson has usually been represented as the first of the strong-minded, even eccentric, scholars who gathered and transmitted medieval materials to the modern period, and like Furnivall and Gollancz he certainly did that and so shaped the path for modern academic medievalists – Gollancz, who became professor of English at King's College, London, was the link between the two groups.

Through Ritson's vegetarianism, his passionate commitment to radical causes and perhaps most gratifying to modern academics his furious rudeness, starting with his savaging of Warton and Percy in the kinds of reviews many might like to write, he offers a compelling personality little diluted by his sad end in insanity, and also casts a benign light on Scott, who both admired his accuracy and was able to manage him courteously in their epistolary and even personal encounters. But the Robin Hood anthology is not primarily original as a collection of earlier material: though it does add the pre-broadside texts to Evans's otherwise full 1777 collection (and both depend substantially on the large garland published by Dicey in c.1740), this sort of archival anthology was familiar through Percy's *Reliques* (1765) and George Ellis's *Specimens of the Early English Poets* (1790): though Ritson made ferociously much of his accuracy, Evans and Ellis were also good reporters.

The thrust of Ritson's originality in the period is as an archivist and a literary historian of a biographically understood figure. His posthumously published *Life of King Arthur* (1825) was a rigorous and largely reliable study of the biographical references and their context and value, and in the same mode was the 'Life of Robin Hood', in which the outlaw is seen as 'this celebrated character' (*Robin Hood*, p. x), and also called, as the 'Life' opens, 'this extraordinary personage (p. iii). Ritson cites as a model Sir John Hawkins, author of the celebrated *Life of Samuel Johnson* (1787). Many contemporaries and followers, notably the nineteenth-century novelists, gained their knowledge of the Robin Hood tradition from Ritson's Introduction and the very full notes he attaches as illustrations of the statements he makes outlining the life. The difficulties he has faced, he remarks, are because there exist in the source materials 'circumstances sufficiently favourable, indeed, to romance, but altogether inimical to historical fact' (p. iii). Biography, not cultural transmission, seems the underlying motive.

In the context of Robin's reconstruction as a figure of Romanticism, Ritson offers remarkably little and touches on very few of the central Romantic tenets. Neither 'Life' nor notes, for all their length, connect the outlaw with nature in any way; there is no critique mounted of eighteenth-century society and attitudes as such; the past is not seen as simpler or wiser than the urbanised and industrialised present; the possibility of a personal, sensitive viewpoint with sensational or picturesque responses is never envisaged. There is perhaps some element of the idea of a powerful individual affecting history, that notion that is in the early period common in German Romanticism, notably that of Schiller, but becomes generalised fairly late in English through Byron's heroic figures and especially Carlyle's lectures on the subject and his book *Heroes and Hero-Worship and the Heroic in History* (1841).

The key impact of Ritson's Robin Hood is not the aggrandisement of feeling or indeed heroic effort towards a sense of national liberation, the Schiller path, but a political innovation that is very much of the present, and a good deal more assertive of populism than Romanticism can usually bring itself to be: Ritson says that Robin 'displayed a spirit of freedom and independence which has endeared him to the common people, whose cause he maintained' (pp. xii–xiii) and sees him as having held 'bishops, abbots, priests and monks, in a word all the clergy, regular or secular, in decided aversion' (p. x), especially because, in a much-quoted passage, they 'consecrated' history to 'the crimes and follies of titled ruffians and sainted idiots' (p. xiii). It is assumed Robin was no friend to the 'ruffians' and 'idiots' whom the church respected and elevated, and most commentators quote that statement to outline Robin the democrat, but that is not what the text specifically says. Robin's focal hostility to the church (itself no innovation) may in fact make easier Ritson's belief in Robin's original and essential aristocratic status, just as the evident interest in the forces of democracy may be the underlying motive for wanting to transmit the texts that communicate the hero noble in both birth and aspirations.

The force of Ritson's Introduction is to present a great history-related and archive-linked real lord Robin Hood: the historicism validates the gentrification. It might seem odd that radical Ritson espoused an aristocratic outlaw, but in fact it was the gentrification of yeoman Robin, stemming from the chronicler Major in 1521 and the playwright Munday in 1598, that stimulated the first stages of this quest for a real Robin Hood. A line of enthusiastic archivists and would-be scholars contributed fragments:[12] figures like Roger Dodsworth, a south Yorkshire loyalist who had heard that Little John 'was an earl Huntingdon', and Nathaniel Johnston, who in the mid seventeenth century drew the famous grave bearing the names 'Robard Hude', 'Willm Goldburgh' and, simply, 'Thomas'. Thomas Gale claimed to have found an epitaph which is in fact only an 'old spelling' version of that found in Martin Parker's 1632 *A True Tale of Robin Hood*. Most elaborate of all, William Stukeley, mid-eighteenth-century Stamford archivist, doctor and parson, produced the extraordinary genealogy of Robin Hood as a Norman Fitz Ooth, which Ritson reprinted, tracing the heroic lineage back through the female line, both to the Earls of Huntington who were part of the Scottish royal family and also to the historical Earl Waltheof, a Saxon, who married the Conqueror's niece Judith. It is remarkable that the ultra-rigorous Ritson, who pilloried so many for taste-led fantasy historicism, would accept this from a man who also claimed that an ancient Celtic King of Bath, Bladud, had founded a university at Stamford in Lincolnshire (where Stukeley lived) before Homer had started the *Iliad*. Not even the Victorian penny-a-liners in love with antiquity, nobility and Britishness would be taken in by such nonsense, which nevertheless survived as a full-page illustration, even in the one-volume version of Ritson's collection.

Ritson's radical politics may belong to modernity, but he is also a major medievalist, valuing the past as a location of value and verity.

He may have been immensely energetic, a notable radical, a man himself of the yeoman class who achieved highly, but the shaping of the Romantic Robin Hood would be in the hands of writers from a similar limited social background who had wider-ranging, more forward-looking and more imaginatively driven sympathies.

Towards Romantic Robin

Just as the entire Robin Hood tradition reveals varying, conflicting strands rather than a single dominant and authoritative structure like that of King Arthur, so the actuality of a Romantic Robin Hood is both multiple and often tentative, a set of gestures towards such a figure rather than a single confident version of it, with contributions by several of the younger Romantics, though not the supposedly major figures of Wordsworth and Coleridge. It was Keats and his colleagues Reynolds and Hunt who made most of the connections, but the elusive Peacock shaped the clearest Romantic image of the hero, with some elements of influence from Shelley. As will be argued here, Peacock's *Maid Marian* (1822), though prose fiction in form, in fact belongs more closely with the Romantic Robin Hood than it does with the less focused and ultimately less influential pattern of the Robin Hood of the nineteenth-century novelists.

The earliest Romantic link, if indirect, with Robin Hood is through Byron. He inherited the family estate and house of Newstead Abbey, close to the western part of Sherwood Forest. His uncle had, as Lois Potter notes in her essay on 'the Byronic Robin Hood',[13] destroyed the trees, but Byron at once replanted an oak and in his 'Elegy on Newstead Abbey' (written by 1806) showed his awareness that this was 'Where Sherwood's outlaws once were wont to prowl'.[14] Byron sold Newstead in 1813, and never used the outlaw tradition as such – though in *Childe Harold's Pilgrimage* (1812–18) he did shape an outlaw in the form of a heroic exile whose values and energy are shared, notably in the novels, by the developed 'great man in history' image of Robin Hood.

It was through local admirers and how they re-energised Robin Hood traditions that Byron's impact was disseminated. Potter shows how the local Quaker couple Mary and William Howitt visited Nottingham, with many other admirers, to honour Byron and touch his coffin before its burial in a family vault in the village of Hucknall just east of Sherwood: the images of Byron as freedom-fighter for Greece and Robin as the local version of just resistance were apparently condensed. The Howitts produced in 1823 a collection of poems named *The Forest Minstrel*: the lengthy title poem, in rhyming couplets, lays out the beauty and value of the forest, notably its bird life, and in the middle speaks of the 'merry outlaws' who might be 'Feasting fair lady or their marvelling king'.[15] The lady does not relate to the broadside tradition, and though the speaker says, 'bold king of outlaws, I honour thy name For thou hadst a generous spirit' (p. 36), he does not retell any adventures, just a sentimental melodrama about the Gilburne family, living in Sherwood. The poem 'Woodnote' also envisages the forest repopulated by outlaws, much as Keats and Reynolds discussed in the poems of 1818 (see below). The Howitts discuss places and areas of the forest, claiming the emotionalised topographical roots which recur through the tradition from Wyntoun's use of Inglewood, the oscillation between Yorkshire and Nottinghamshire in the early texts and the continuing fascination with the specific location of the allegedly 'real' Robin Hood.

In this the Howitts were matched by two other poets connected with Sherwood. Robert Millhouse was a local stocking-weaver, before and after being from 1810 to 1814 a soldier in the infantry regiment that became the Royal Sherwood Foresters. He had strong literary interests, and among other collections published *Sherwood Forest, and Other Poems* (1827). The main poem starts by asserting the value of the forest as it moves

> from the den
> Of Rapine and Misrule, to point the mind
> To love of country.[16]

And the narrator says:

> And when I contemplate that structure grand
> Of Freedom, I behold a part in thee,
> Old Sherwood!
>
> (canto 1, st. 11)

The poem runs through Sherwood's resistant history, from the British Celts confronting Rome and through King Alfred's defence of Wessex and conflicts under the Normans, and arrives in canto 2 at 'the brave Fitz-ooth' who with Marian faced 'the iron hand of tyranny' and supported 'chastity' and 'the poor' (st. 11). As well as generating brave resistance this caused him considerable distress, and 'pondering silently the woods among, Oft would he lose him in the thickest gloom' (canto 2, st. 19), which Potter interprets as a 'conflation of Robin Hood and Childe Harold'.[17] Again there are no specific adventures retold, and Robin is summarised as 'the brave outlaw chief Who swayed with little crime' (canto 2, st. 20). The third canto returns to the natural beauties of the forest, associated with its idea of freedom, with even more topographical detail than is offered by the Howitts.

Millhouse knew well a younger man, Spencer T. Hall, a Quaker and newspaper compositor, and consciously passed his mission on to him: Hall published in 1841 verse and prose pieces as *The Forester's Offering*, and recurrently used the pseudonym 'The Sherwood Forester'. The physical forest is stressed: when Robin walked beneath the Major Oak it was 'in its youthful glory'.[18] Hall makes Robin simply a yeoman, probably being influenced by Scott in this, and he is hostile both to the historicist readings of the character and also to the balladeers who repeat 'all the trash which besmirches the name of Robin Hood and his faithful friend Little John' (p. 38). But he does mention some traditional narratives like that of Allen a Dale and passes on stories that he claims to have received from modern forest residents, who admired Robin's values.

Though Hall and Millhouse, like the Howitts, were humble people, they do not envisage Robin Hood as a radical figure linked to artisan dissent: they see him as a hero of communal populism, deeply involved with nature, and this tradition continued. Hall's work and views were discussed positively by Gutch in his widely known 1847 edition;[19] their work was reprinted, and others joined in, like 'January Searle' (actually George Searle Phillips) with the prose *Leaves from Sherwood Forest* (1850).

There is no sign that this locally nostalgic Robin Hood has any place in the strongly growing spirit of artisan dissent: Robin Hood does not gain a mention in E. P. Thompson's encyclopaedic *The Making of the English Working Class*, and Potter notes that the Nottinghamshire Luddites firmly rejected Robin Hood as too old-fashioned a role model, stating in a song:

> No more chant your rhymes about bold Robin Hood
> His feats I do little admire.
> I'll sing the achievements of General Ludd,
> Now the hero of Nottinghamshire.[20]

Rather than a modern radical force, Millhouse and Hall are offering a different form of serious meaning, itself linked to Romanticism. As Potter comments: 'their Robin Hood is melancholy rather than militant; indeed their true subject is the beauty of the forest and the belief that, as Hall claimed, no-one could be less than virtuous in such a place'.[21] The case for some Byronic influence is made by Potter, but it is also clear that the published Robin Hood work by Keats and Reynolds, coming between the Howitts and the Millhouse–Hall material, is likely to have been a more direct guidance in both celebration and melancholy, two important elements of the Romantic construction of Robin Hood.

Forest days

As John Keats opened his post one cold February day in north London in 1818, the Robin Hood tradition entered the verdant pastures of true Romanticism. His friend John Hamilton Reynolds had sent two sonnets for his consideration, communicating with the past as both an access to natural beauty and also a positive heritage. The first sonnet imagines how the Romantically attuned onlooker might access the presence of Robin and Marian:

> The trees in Sherwood forest are old and good, –
> The grass beneath them now is dimly green;
> Are they deserted all? Is no young mien,
> With loose-slung bugle met with in the wood?
> No arrow found, – foil'd of its antler'd food, –
> Struck in the oak's rude side? Is there nought seen,
> To mark the revelries which there have been, –
> In the sweet days of merry Robin Hood?
> Go there, with Summer, and with evening, – go
> In the soft shadows, like some wandering man, –
> And thou shalt far amid the Forest know
> The archer men in green, with belt and bow,
> Feasting on pheasant, river-fowl, and swan,
> With Robin at their head, and Marian.[22]

The poem begins by invoking obscurity – the grass is 'dimly green', it is 'evening', and there are 'soft shadows', and though the values 'old' and 'good' complete the first line with unalloyed confidence, the octet is all about what is not seen of the 'revelries' of the 'sweet days of merry Robin Hood'. This absence appears to invoke language of Augustan neat formality and social assurance in 'foil'd of its antler'd food' and 'the oak's rude side'. But then the Romantic spell begins to work, and into the vision of this 'wandering man' the archers appear in colour, at a specific feast, and then emerge the two human images with which we make contact.

The sharpening of focus of this highly visual scene – sense-availability, especially of sight, is central to Romanticism – sets up the second sonnet. The two can be read as a double sonnet, and they had the same title: the first was called 'To a Friend on Robin Hood' and the second 'The Same'. This second sonnet moves from vision to value:

> With coat of Lincoln green and mantle too
> And horn of ivory mouth, and buckle bright,
> And arrows wing'd with peacock-feathers light,
> And trusty bow well gather'd of the yew, –
> Stands Robin Hood! – and near, with eyes of blue
> Shining through dusk hair, like the stars of night,
> And habited in pretty forest plight, –
> His green-wood beauty sits, young as the dew.
> Oh, gentle-tressed girl! Maid Marian!
> Are thine eyes bent upon the gallant game
> That stray in the merry Sherwood: thy sweet fame
> Can never, never die. And thou, high man,
> Would we might pledge thee with thy silver Can
> Of Rhenish, in the woods of Nottingham.
>
> (p. 150)

The light and the visionary detail are strong from the start. The first quartet is on Robin, but then eight lines focus on Marian: Romanticism makes her central for the first time, where she was absent in the yeoman tradition and only a supporting player in gentrification. But it is more as a forest spirit than as a physical woman: she is dressed in 'pretty forest plight' – the Augustan touch is here at least positive but then the need to disguise her womanhood as natural 'green-wood beauty' strains the diction back towards the discourse of the last century – and she is watching the deer who are themselves 'gallant': man envelops nature. The underlying masculinism that is a recurrent feature of Romanticism emerges, as Marian has only 'sweet fame' and it is Robin the 'high man' whose drink we would like to share – and this is not yeomanesque ale-quaffing but sophisticated Rhenish white, sipped from silver.

This literary circle was close and dynamic. On the same day Keats wrote the poem that was entitled in published form 'Robin Hood: To a Friend', but in the letter that carried it back to Reynolds was named 'To JHR in Answer to his Robin Hood Sonnets'.[23] Like a good deal in his letters, but little in his poetry, Keats's answer here was initially direct, even decisive, starting with 'No! those days are gone away.'[24] Perhaps this answers a question in Reynolds's lost letter first accompanying the sonnets, or the question in line 6 of the first, 'Is there nought seen', or more likely it is a general response to Reynolds's idea of recuperating the past in a nostalgic present. Keats justifies this negative by insisting the past is past: those days have 'gone away':

> And their hours are old and gray,
> And their minutes buried all
> Under the down-trodden pall
> Of the leaves of many years:
>
> (lines 2–5)

The bright images of the second sonnet and the warmth of Reynolds's re-creation of 'sweet days' in a summer evening are rejected as unrealistic:

> Many times have winter's shears,
> Frozen north, and chilling east
> Sounded tempests to the feast
> Of the forest's whispering fleeces,
> Since men knew not rent nor leases.
>
> (lines 6–10)

These are rich lines. There was very cold weather all through 1816 (known as 'the year without a summer'), and the severe winter of 1817–18 was still present as Keats wrote, but he uses that experience as a medium to express modern socio-economic forces hostile to both the festal and the socially productive aspects of lost rural life, here symbolised in the elegantly assonating feast and fleeces. Morris Dickstein sees this poem as indicating 'the appearance of a certain social consciousness in Keats's work'.[25] Where Reynolds sees the shallower Romanticism of the picturesque and the fantasised in the forest myth, Keats, whom John Barnard here calls the 'less sentimental and more political' of the two,[26] invokes the stronger reading of the past as a critique of the alienated present.

In his first draft the last line read more directly 'Since men paid no Rent or leases', and later lines will pursue the theme of the destruction and dissipation of a free pastoral existence. Keats imagines Robin revisiting in the present when:

> He would swear, for all his oaks,
> Fall'n beneath the dockyard strokes,
> Have rotted on the briny seas;
>
> (lines 43–5)

The destruction of the forest is not seen as a noble patriotic gesture to humiliate the French but as a defeat for nature: the alternative modern use of English ships – to spread a mercantile empire – may also be in Keats's mind and is certainly in tune with Marian's horror when:

> She would weep that her wild bees
> Sang not to her – strange! that honey
> Can't be got without hard money!
>
> (lines 46–8)

This refers to the recent practice of stopping people who rent land from enjoying cost-free the productivity of bees and other natural visitors, and actually charging them for the privilege.

These are views found elsewhere in Keats: Barnard speaks of his dislike of standing military forces and the growing signs of inorganic social structures,[27] and in *Isabella* Keats writes at some length about what he calls the 'ledger-men' of modern Europe.[28] Nicholas Roe, in a chapter entitled 'Song from the Woods, or Outlaw Lyrics', discusses the Reynolds–Keats poetic exchange in the context of the debate at just this time about past rurality as a location and symbol of liberty. He sees 'the greenwood emblem' as 'a focus for Keats's imaging of the traditional liberties of old England as contrasted with the diminished freedom of the present'.[29] It is well attested that the post-war period saw both resistance to social authority in Britain, especially from the artisan class, and increasingly severe responses from the authorities, which would lead in 1819 to the shooting of protestors in Manchester's 'Peterloo Massacre'. The provisions of Habeas Corpus were suspended in February 1817, and there had been much publicity in late December 1817 for the three trials for seditious libel of William Hone: he defended himself successfully, largely by invoking a long British tradition of anti-authoritarian parody and literary resistance, drawing on a wide range of earlier writers.

Marilyn Butler has described in detail under the title 'The War of the Intellectuals' the context and processes in which the conservative position of the older Romantics was challenged by new voices – even Byron, she comments, 'around 1818 … adopts a position more clearly associated with liberalism'.[30] The younger Romantics' idea of a natural, medieval ideal of organic social order was a relatively uncontentious version of the same discontented spirit of the times. It was a common enough Romantic view – in his 'Elegy on Newstead Abbey' Byron had written about medieval 'happy days, too happy to endure' and how 'Nature triumphs as the tyrant dies'[31] – and the specifically political element of their writing was a major reason for the assaults on Keats and Hunt as vulgar 'cockneys' by the conservative *Blackwood's Magazine*.

The development of the Keats poem appears to be an emotive parallel to this argument about reading the present negatively through the past. The initial negative, insisting these days are gone, forlorn in a lost past, is repeated in different ways – there is silence in the forest now, 'no mid forest laugh' (line 15); even in 'the fairest time of June' (line 19) – Robin Hood's high time, Keats evidently realises: Roe shows he knew about continuing May games[32] – and there will now be no-one as in the old play-game days fitting in with 'fair hostess Merriment, down beside the pasture Trent' (lines 29–30).

The sense of absence also recognises the sterner, even anti-authoritarian edge of outlawry:

> Gone, the merry morris din;
> Gone, the song of Gamelyn;
> Gone, the tough-belted outlaw
> Idling in the 'grenè shawe';
> All are gone away and past!
>
> (lines 33–7)

The crisp rhymes link forest pleasure with politics: 'shawe' and 'outlaw' express the two directly. The 'merry morris din' appears to match the noisy end of *Gamelyn* when, supported by the outlaws, the hero restores his fortune and hangs the hostile judge and sheriff. Robin is recalled as 'tough-belted', the memorable epithet insisting on a figure of vigorous active resistance.

Subversive rhyming makes all the more effective the next line, where 'past' rhymes with 'cast' – as Robin is imagined as cast up, reappearing 'Sudden from his turfed grave'. With just the same underlying sense of disturbing rhyme, Marian will indeed 'have Once again her forest days' (line 41), but the rhyme on what Reynolds thought was a lovely revisiting of the lovely past is the harsh word 'craze': modernity invokes disturbance and distortion of discourse.

With the imaginative and verbal brilliance characteristic of his finest work, Keats has doubly negated Reynolds's pleasant but naïve adventures in outlaw Romanticism. It doesn't work like that, Keats says, but it can work as a challenging standard of where we now are. The historicism and the modernity that interface in the strongest Romanticism are brought into the outlaw tradition, and it is in those terms that Keats is, in a gracefully positive coda, willing to celebrate the outlaw myth where the rhymes fall back into positive mutuality:

> So it is: yet let us sing,
> Honour to the old bow-string!
> Honour to the bugle-horn!
> Honour to the woods unshorn!
>
> (lines 49–52)

The final position is to insist the past is past, yet to assent to modern revisitation:

> Honour to bold Robin Hood,
> Sleeping in the underwood!
> Honour to maid Marian,
> And to all the Sherwood-clan!
> Though their days have hurried by
> Let us two a burden try.
>
> (lines 57–62)

It can be argued that this ending implicitly re-creates the political tension previously created by reversing Reynolds's structure, and instead of imagining ourselves simply imagining the delights of the past, in a much more challenging manoeuvre it brings Robin and Marian to the present to deplore our reduced, mercantilised, denaturalised state. It is true that the ending does memorialise elements of the outlaw myth that were instrumentally aggressive – the bow, the bugle, the 'archer keen' and the clearly physical potential of 'tight little John' – 'tight' here evidently meaning fit, ready for action. But it does also finally honour the sleeping Robin and the absence of them all in days that 'have hurried by'.

But if, in courtesy to Reynolds, Keats ended his at times brusque response with some elements of the pastoral idealism that Reynolds offered without nuance or complexity, it is also clear that Reynolds picked up, to some degree, Keats's central political message. He responded very shortly afterwards with a third sonnet – it was published in *The Yellow Dwarf* on 21 February 1818 along with the other two:

> Robin the outlaw! Is there not a mass
> Of freedom in the name? – It tells the story
> Of clenched oaks, with branches bow'd and hoary,

Leaning in aged beauty o'er the grass; –
Of dazed smile on cheek of border lass,
Listening 'gainst some old gate at his strange glory:
And of the dappled stag, struck down and gory,
Lying with nostril wide in green morass.
It tells a tale of forest days – of times
That would have been most precious unto thee:
Days of undying pastoral liberty: –
Sweeter than music of old abbey chimes –
Sweet as the virtue of Shakesperian rhymes –
Days, shadowy with the magic greenwood tree!
(Reynolds, p. 151)

It is a curiously double-voiced poem. The first two lines appear to pick up directly on Keats's politicisation of the myth. The hero is immediately an outlaw, and the statement 'a mass Of freedom in the name' has rich political implications, collective as well as individualistic. But the story the name tells suddenly switches to Reynolds's previous world of sensation-rich male visions, of a pretty girl 'dazed' by the 'strange glory' of the outlaw; even less political, an apparently pleasing image of a dead stag: the rhymes here do proclaim oppositions, but not Keats's politically challenging ones: 'lass'/'morass' and 'glory'/'gory' suggest scopophilia bordering on perversion.

But the sestet reverts to Keats's issues. His phrase 'forest days' is emphasised – it will be picked up by G. P. R. James as a title in the novel tradition, and the outlaw myth is seen, if idyllically, as 'Days of undying pastoral liberty', of a kind 'most precious unto thee'. Politically, this 'thee' sounds like Keats, but in *The Yellow Dwarf* this sonnet is headed 'To E--- with the foregoing sonnets': Barnard suggests that this is Eliza Drewe, Reynolds's future wife, which would further intensify, and vary, the feeling of the poems.[33] But still, these multi-valued days, of forest and liberty, unchanging and pastoral, are better than abbey chimes – Keats and Reynolds were not admirers of any church, especially not the medieval Catholic one. They are even better than 'Shakesperian' rhymes: Roe shows how the major early poets, Chaucer and Shakespeare especially, were used as archetypes of natural liberty by Keats and the London liberal circle.[34] It remains summer in Reynolds's outlaw world, not the wintry present realised by Keats, and the greenwood tree is finally 'magic', but Reynolds has added to his mix of sentiment and idealism Keats's key idea about the medieval forest myth as a test of modern politics.

Between them Keats and Reynolds import crucial Romantic features into the outlaw myth: it is natural, it can be beautiful, we can admire it for that, but we can also learn from it, especially in terms of the liberties it symbolises, which are under threat from various forms of modernity – militarism, state power, mercantilism and (the last clearly implied if not named by Keats and Reynolds) urbanisation. It is an English myth, not from the classics or the recent French enemies. These apparently slight poems create a new realisation of the English outlaw. An especially forceful element, transmitted with all the personalised sensual tremor of Romanticism, is the fact that Robin's body is strongly present and physically very attractive, and so is that of Marian. These fine physicalised figures, set in both history and politics, are ready for the modern mode of narrative and audience engagement, the novel.

While Keats and Reynolds in that cold but productive February did bring Romantic Robin Hood to a richly visible and highly memorable head, they did it in a context that had other elements and other activists. Leigh Hunt was the most overtly political of the Hampstead writers – in 1813 he was jailed for two years for libelling the prince regent – but his politics were also cultural. He had been for a while preparing the collection that he published in early 1818 called *Foliage*, and as Roe discusses, his neighbour Keats would undoubtedly have been familiar with the book's scheme 'to cultivate a love of nature out of doors and sociality within'.[35]

This is more than a programme for good fellowship: John Strachan notes that 'this concept should be read in political terms', and he quotes Jeffrey N. Cox's comment that 'for Hunt and his circle sociability was a way of reclaiming the social and thus the political from what they saw as religious bigots, narrowly nationalistic patriots, and money-driven misers'.[36] The discussion was augmented by a lecture given by William Hazlitt in the same month, 'On Burns, and the Old English Ballads', which as Roe reports discussed the 'adventurous and romantic life' of 'good living and good fellowship'.[37] Reynolds's three sonnets were printed in *The Yellow Dwarf*, edited by Hunt's brother John, on 21 February. Hunt remained interested in the theme: his essay 'On Old May Day' appeared in May 1818 with reference to Robin Hood games, and also discussed Jonson's *The Sad Shepherd*. It developed his thoughts on popular rituals in 'Christmas and Other Old National Merry-Makings Considered', in *The Examiner* for 21 December 1817. But soon he also contributed creatively, publishing four short narrative poems adapting the Robin Hood ballad to the new context and interpretation of the outlaw.

The first came out in a small anthology published for Christmas 1819, the *Literary Pocket-Book*, and the other three appeared late in 1820 in Hunt's new journal *The Indicator*. They would reappear in 1855 when the outlaw myth had found a place both in the novel and in the young person's story, and there Hunt made a few alterations and additions (giving Marian a brief appearance) and added the subtitle 'For Children'. The first ballad's being titled 'Robin Hood a Child' made this change seem easy, but this connection is further-reaching, being part of the recurrent Romantic privileging of the innocence and essential developability of the youthful viewpoint.

Robin's childhood starts with good weather and the pleasures of nature:

> It was the pleasant season yet,
> > When the stones at cottage doors
> Dry quickly while the roads are wet,
> > After the silver showers.
>
> The green leaves they look'd greener still
> > And the thrush, renewing his tune,
> Shook aloud notes from his gladsome bill
> > Into the bright blue noon.[38]

This is a 'Robin's first exploit' story that replaces the savage directness of 'Robin Hood's Progress to Nottingham' with its apparently justified homicide of the fifteen foresters (and the even less defensible mass wounding of Nottingham citizens who come to watch) with a church corruption story of the kind much enjoyed in the seventeenth-century ballads, and clearly to the taste of the decidedly anti-clerical Hampstead literary circle. But it also links up to a degree with the semi-gentrified tone of 'Robin Hood Newly Revived', where Robin encounters his cousin Will Scarlet of Gamwell Hall, though here Will is a servant, not from the gentry as in the broadside.

Robin's mother takes him to see his ill uncle 'the noble Gamelyn' (line 28) – apparently her father. He is an elderly, sickly man but loves Robin's active boyhood, though when the old man preferred it, he would also sit quietly 'And be the gravest of grave-eyed boys, And not a word spoke he' (lines 45–6). This day at the hall they find 'a fat friar' (line 65) who says the squire is dead '"And has made us his whole heirs"' (line 83). Robin's mother weeps, and attends to the dead lord, Gamelyn de Vere: the 'friar' is called 'Abbot de Vere' of Vere Abbey. It is not clear if the abbot is a relation or if the abbey bears the family name: in the 1855 version this is resolved when the uncle is Gamelyn of Shere Wood Hall and the family name is Shere, or 'of Shere Wood', not Vere, but the abbey is still named Vere.

That evening, they leave sadly, and when his mother asks Robin what he is thinking he says '"That if I was a king, I'd see what these friars do"' (lines 128–9). She kisses him, saying '"My own little Robin boy, Thou wilt be a king of men"' (lines 132–3). Much less active than any early ballad, whether secular or anti-clerical, and quite heavily parental as well as gentrified, this was at least made more proleptically physical in the later version when Robin hedges on the need to be a king, adding after that line 'Or if I was a man, which is the next thing', and then after line 129 a new stanza is provided:

'I wouldn't let 'em be counted friars,
    If they did as these have done,
But make 'em fight, for rogues and liars;
    I'd make 'em fight to see which was right,
Them, or the mother's son.'[39]

There are some six-line stanzas in the early version, and this five-line stanza is also aberrant in being the only physical activity discussed except for Robin's reported vigorous games. Like the treatment by Keats and Reynolds, the poem offers a curiously inactive image of Robin the outlaw, which brings to mind the change from the reprint of Ritson's one-volume edition in 1820, which retains from the 1795 edition on its title-page a woodcut of an encounter with quarterstaffs from some 'Robin meets his match' ballad, to, in the 1823 second edition, an entirely passive, even melancholic outlaw, presumably Robin, who sits and reflects as a deer escapes into the forest.

The second of Hunt's new ballads, 'Robin Hood's Flight', is considerably more detailed and active. Robin's mother has long died: he is aware of the poor, 'How they toil'd without their share' (line 26), and how the friars had 'trappings and things as fine as the king's' (line 31). Here the critique extends to 'the King, how he got all his forests and deer' and executed poachers. In the 1820 version it reads that Robin is just 'thinking thus' (line 37), but in 1855 this is changed to 'in angry mood'. He meets Will who is bereft, out gathering feathers to sell for arrows, and calls him '"my dear master that should have been'" (line 43). Robin kills a deer for them to share: Will weeps in gratitude, but suddenly the abbot appears with three foresters and arrests them. Robin shoots two dead, and the abbot gets 'An arrow stuck in his paunch so fat' (line 108): the revised version gives the abbot's weight as 'twenty stone' as he falls from his horse. The third forester asks pardon of '"Sir Robin stout"' (line 118) and begs to follow him. They bury the three dead men in a leafy dell, where to ballad violence Romanticism adds a sense of pathetic fallacy:

> Ankle deep in leaves so red,
>   Which autumn there had cast
> When going to her winter bed
>   She had undresst her last.
>
> (lines 130–3)

Will and the third forester leave, 'With Robin Hood in the middle': Robin weeps at his last sight of 'merry sweet Locksley town' (line 143), but he also feels invigorated: he grasps Will on the shoulder, and that support provides the rhyme as he says: '"Now show us three men bolder"' (line 153).

This seems to be the first appearance of the 'Robin becomes outlaw through helping a poor man' motif: it will form a striking start to Henry Gilbert's widely read novel of 1912, *Robin Hood and the Men of the Greenwood*, and from the 1938 film starring Errol Flynn has become the default opening to explain Robin's outlawry. The secular authorities will replace Hunt's use of the church as central oppressors, but this is an effective explanation of Robin's outlaw position as part of his social generosity, shaping him as a man of action based on morality, so spelling out what had for centuries merely been assumed as embodied in the outlaw figure.

This position is simply celebrated in the short third ballad, 'Robin Hood an Outlaw'. Where readers of the ballad tradition and its titles might expect an adventure – a rescue or a robbery or even both – this simply reports that 'They' (not clarified as church or state, but the church is later named as Robin's enemy) sent men against him without success, as some of them, and others, supported him. Hunt is clearly interested in the idea of political side-changing among the lower orders, a topic which Thomas Miller, a Chartist novelist with real experience of resistant action, will develop in some detail (see pp. 155–8). For Hunt, Robin is popular in the town and even has a few supporters in the religious establishments:

> There was Roger the monk, that used to make
> > All monkery his glee;
> And Midge, on whom Robin had never turned
> > His face but tenderly.
>
> > > > (lines 21–4)

This stanza is more vivid than the preceding ones, and it may well be Hunt had in mind radical sympathisers in the contemporary state apparatus. He goes on in the rest of this short piece to speak personally about those who out of fear or weakness come to change their ideas and politics:

> We cannot bid our strength remain,
> > Our cheeks continue round;
> We cannot say to an aged back,
> > Stoop not toward the ground;
>
> > > > (lines 29–32)

But he ends by insisting on the power of the speaker, perhaps indeed Leigh Hunt as well as Robin Hood, to remain constant to the cause:

> Bur we can say, I never will,
> > Friendship, fall off from thee;
> And, oh sound truth and old regard,
> > Nothing shall part us three.
>
> > > > (lines 37–40)

With its direct statement, avoiding both the narrative of the ballads and the referentiality of Keats – which he to some extent essayed in the first ballad – Hunt speaks here as the most political of the Romantics, and aware that the cause can be too demanding for many. This ballad has no revision in the later version, perhaps because it is short, but also perhaps because it makes its case so sharply.

The last of the four poems returns to outlaw operations to tell 'How Robin Hood and his Outlaws Lived in the Woods'. Their life was essentially natural:

> Robin and his merry men
> > Lived just like the birds;
>
> > > > (lines 1–2)

They exercised at shooting, with sword and quarterstaff; they feasted like 'Princes of the wood, Under the glimmering trees' (somewhat politicised in the revision to 'Under the state of trees'). They even danced to the harp with village girls, who were themselves given consideration: Robin and his men protected the women from harassment, even 'a single kiss unliked' (line 49). After this the 1855 revision inserts two stanzas about Marian, who with Robin 'reign'd as pleasant to all, As faithful to each other.'[40]

This activity was funded by redistribution:

> Only on the haughty rich
>   And in their unjust store,
> He'd lay his fines of equity
>   For his merry men and the poor
>
>   (lines 53–6)

Robin was especially keen on relieving the church of money, and the image used of a friar, that they will 'carve him of his purse' (line 60), effloresces in Hunt's version of Keatsian metaphorical elaboration:

> A monk to him was a toad in the hole,
>   And an abbot was a pig in grain,
> But a bishop was a baron of beef,
>   To cut and come again.
>
>   (lines 61–4)

Robin helped poor men and women, with a whisper of the Marxian theory of labour value, as he told them:

> 'You do but get your goods again,
>   That were altered by the thief.'
>
>   (lines 71–2)

Here as usual Hunt's imagination is directly material, and this ballad and his distinctly liberal, even radical, version of Romantic Robin Hood ends with the cheerful image of the reconstitution of alienated labour, as Robin says to Wat of Lancashire:

> 'Get upon your land-tax, man,
>   And ride it merrily home.'
>
>   (lines 79–80)

Reaching from the excitement of the period that fashioned the figure of Romantic Robin Hood into the mid century when it had become largely disseminated and redirected through the novel – and to some degree in the recurrent pantomimes – Hunt's work lacks the idealism and immediacy of Keats and Reynolds, but it was an important link to, and recuperation of, the ballad form itself, and it also magnified such limited elements of radical analysis as were transmitted from Ritson and Keats. As Hunt's poems show, the limpid suggestivity of the ballad narrative did not fit well with the intensity of late Romantic imagistic argumentation, and it is in that sense not surprising that the climax of this reconstitution of the figure of the outlaw, in a form that has reverberated across period and genres, was in the prime mode of contemporary innovation, fiction – but a kind of fiction that eluded the multiple reiteration of the novel, past or future, and had much in common with the poetic modes of construction of the Romantic Robin Hood.

Peacock and outlaw Romanticism

Thomas Love Peacock's novella *Maid Marian* appeared in 1822,[41] and carried a note, still found in modern editions, which states that all but the last three chapters were written in the autumn of 1818. Peacock's diary and letters make it clear that he was at work on the novel until late in November that year, when he apparently stopped his other activities to work on an essay which would gain him a post with the East India Company early in 1819. Prince John's attack on Arlingford only half-way through the book does seem a little like the siege of Torquilstone in *Ivanhoe*, published in December 1819, and maybe Peacock did some later editing on his existing draft, or even some exaggeration about how far he had got in 1818, but his novella is essentially a substantial part of the high year of the generation of Romantic Robin Hood.

The most action-oriented of his early works, and notable for the comedy and songs that helped it, in J. R. Planché's version, to be a stage favourite right through the century, this is also the least bookish and intellectually focused of Peacock's works. Though it shows knowledge of Ritson's Introduction and especially his notes, the basically populist tone differs from the conversational and referential approach of Peacock's other fiction: J. B. Priestley said that Peacock here 'alternates between high spirits and rather rough sarcasm'.[42] For all these reasons, it would appear, the novella has never figured very largely in academic admiration of Peacock's satirical and contemporarily referential work.

He himself did not see it as lightweight: a letter to his friend Shelley says, 'I am writing a comic Romance of the Twelfth Century, which I shall make the vehicle of much oblique satire of all the oppressions that are done under the sun.'[43] *Maid Marian* can be seen as the first coherent and extended statement of the Romantic Robin Hood, recognising both the natural and sensual aspects of that interpretation and also political elements that only recent research has fully understood. Marilyn Butler has outlined the anti-conservative critique that Peacock makes, aimed at the way the post-war nation states are returning to Burkean conservative positions and even 'the mystique of feudalism'.[44] Rob Gossedge has argued that *Maid Marian* allegorises Peacock's own experience of the forest laws in practice, in the substantial resistance in the Windsor area to the royal family's contemporary moves to exert enclosure over parts of Windsor Forest – a local landowner campaigned against it as Robin Hood.[45] The story's emphasis on natural delight and the underlying link to the Romantic ideal of forest liberty – Peacock certainly knew Hunt's *Foliage* – communicate a real, if inherently implied rather than overt, sense of dissent to conservative modernity.

The title itself must have seemed startling: there is still a sense of challenge in calling a Robin Hood version *Maid Marian*, as with the distinctly feminist, if also comic, BBC television series of 1988, and quite a stir was made when novelists like Jennifer Roberson and Theresa Tomlinson, with some success in the market, made Marian the central figure – and so seemed to downgrade both the importance and the potency of Robin himself. Peacock's representation of Marian lives up to the bid for titular standing – she is vivid, witty, active, brave, charming and beautiful, and the text seems to read her in something like that order. It is hard to believe that Peacock was not in some way modelling her on the highly dynamic Mary Shelley – nor indeed that the lordly radical Percy Bysshe was not to some extent a model for this Robin: they had both left for Europe early in 1818, but Peacock wrote to Shelley about the project, and in *Melincourt* (1817) he had used him as the model for the central and basically impressive character suggestively named Mr Sylvan Forester, a liberal landowner who wins the lovely Anthelia, in spite of the heroics of perhaps Peacock's finest creation, Sylvan's protégé, the orang-utan-turned-parliamentary-candidate Sir Oran Haut-ton.[46]

Romanticism, for all the democratism of Keats and Hunt, is an elite, supra-popular context, and Peacock readily accepts Ritson's account of Robin's biography, making him a lord who has hunted King Henry's deer and resisted his authority, a more radical and Ritson-like ground for royal displeasure than Munday had imagined. The sense of the forest laws as a mode of aristocratic and royal oppression, strongly offered in the Introduction to Percy's *Reliques* and going back as far as Pope's *Windsor Forest* (1713), makes this Robin a clear ally of the people from the start. He is also hostile to the church, being at the start accused of withholding payments from it, though some real quality is found there in the austere but lively Brother Michael, who admires Marian deeply. In this he is curiously like Friar Athelstane in the anonymous Robin Hood novel of 1819 (see pp. 149–51), but any influence on Peacock appears ruled out by the late 1818 date for most of the writing. Brother Michael also stands for English liberties and democracies in a way Ritson would have approved of, but did not include in his comments: in the stage version this was a major role, which the great actor Kemble was happy to play, with substantial success.

The structure of the novella is swift and elegant. The opening scene has Earl Robert and Lady Matilda marrying, but the king's men disrupt events: perhaps Peacock in his final touches was teasing *Ivanhoe* readers when he begins with a quotation from Scott's *Lochinvar* about a disrupted wedding. But in keeping with the unaggressive tone of the whole book, the intruders cause a fight where no-one is shown to be hurt – even though Robert is said to do 'old execution among the pursuers' (p. 10) as he escapes. The leader of the prince's men accuses the earl of forest treason, and this theme recurs in the opening of the second chapter: 'It is sufficiently well known how severe were the forest-laws in those days, and with what jealousy the Kings of England maintained this branch of their prerogative' (p. 21). The forest, however, is not only a space of valued liberty. Hero and heroine are imagined in terms that elaborate and deepen the Reynolds–Keats sense of natural value: Brother Michael sings of them as 'like twin plants of the forest and are identified with its growth' (p. 34). Matilda dominates hereabouts with her qualities of nurture as well as nature. Brother Michael says she has 'beauty, grace, wit, sense, discretion, dexterity, learning and valour' (p. 14): she resists her father with spirit and wit, and Sir Ralph Montfaucon, who is the king's agent but also young and gentlemanly, falls in love with her: the new tension of male rivals that Sedgwick calls the 'between men' phenomenon (see pp. 201–2 below) is itself readable as a containment of the new physical force of the heroine.

As the novel proceeds, events follow briskly, some from the ballads. Sir Ralph's men take Locksley Castle, but cannot find Robin. In spring Sir Ralph goes to Gamwell, following Robin's career in the broadside ballad, and Peacock outlines in vigorous detail the kind of celebration that Hunt and Hazlitt felt was central to the social cohesion and positive 'merriness' of the medieval period, unlike the alienated present. Robin is central to the enjoyment and wins the archery contest; Ralph has too few men to take him, and when the sheriff arrives with fifty, Robin threateningly but pacifically shoots into the ground in front of his horse. In the ensuing mêlée Sir Ralph is wounded in the arm: Matilda helps him, and Robin escapes. When young Gamwell is arrested and set to be hanged, Robin, disguised as a friar, frees him, and finally Sir Guy of Gamwell goes to his northern house – this travel motif will recur in the later novels.

Away from this busy social world, Matilda remains trapped at home, and is pestered by Prince John. He besieges Arlingford to take her, supported by his poet laureate, Harpiton, 'a creeping thing' (p. 127), evidently a reference to Robert Southey, who was disliked by Peacock as a former radical turned deep conservative, and pilloried for the positive financial results of that move in *Melincourt* (1817) as 'Mr Feathernest'. The baron, a sort of Tory radical, burns his castle so that Prince John cannot use it, and Matilda escapes to the forest, accepts the post of queen and is renamed by Brother Michael as Marian. She and Robin marry, but under the forest code of behaviour she will remain a maid.

In this code Peacock develops substantially the suggestions found early in the *Gest*. Little John reads the 'Principles' out as 'Legitimacy, Equity, Hospitality, Chivalry, Chastity and Courtesy' (p. 160), and the political elements mesh with an earlier authorial debate on the new 'most legitimate and most Christian king' (p. 124), Richard I, whose mythical chivalry and daring are seen to co-exist with obsession with seizing property to fund his crusading, and many of his 'zealous adventurers' (p. 124) are said to have had similarly acquisitive aspirations.

But Peacock largely sets aside the anti-Tory possibilities of this material for simple adventure and romance, and the continued enjoyment of active forest Romanticism. Alan a Dale's marriage is retold, and Robin, Marian and the baron go disguised to the north; Ralph pursues them, but when they take refuge in a cottage with people Robin had helped while still acting as an earl, he is beaten in a fight and leaves the story for good. This is the point at which Peacock said he deferred writing for a few years, and events from here on are much more familiar. The ballad-story with the friar follows: Peacock typically adds that he has a special reverence for St Botolph, whom he calls St Bottle, and more adapted ballads appear. Marian, dressed as a boy, meets a knight in the forest and they fight, then go to dinner; a monk who has been robbed is also there, and Robin says that this pays for his loan to a knight a year ago. Then the old knight arrives, and this *Gest* sequence extends into the return of Richard – the knight whom Marian fought.

A similar speedy and light approach typifies the ending of a story that has mixed elegant pace, romantic touches and semi-searching satire. When King Richard dies, Robin and Marian are driven back by King John to 'their greenwood sovereignty' where 'they long lived together' (pp. 261–2) in neo-pastoral peace. Satire again emerges: the last comment is that now Marian's title of maid was 'as much a misnomer as that of Little John' (p. 262), a trivial, even adolescent, note on which to end the most elegant, referential and wide-ranging of the realisations of Romantic Robin Hood. But against that characteristically Peacockian off-hand ending, there survive the glamour and style of Robin and Marian, the witty and searching humour of Brother Michael, the deeply felt sense of natural sociality. All of these are transmitted in Peacock's sparkling prose but, befitting his novella's structural propinquity to the outlaw work of the late Romantic poets, are most fully felt and envisaged in song.

Peacock loved opera, and Butler has pointed out that some scenes have an underlying structure of a song-encounter, where 'Peacock actually seems to think of himself as a librettist':[47] she notes that the four-part scene in chapter 4 is effectively the finale to Act 1, but she might have added the comic spoken duet by the baron and Matilda, and the lengthy sequences of song and harangue by Brother Michael. His song 'It was a Friar of Orders Free, the Friar of Rubygill' refers in title to the very popular 'A Friar of Orders Grey' that John O'Keeffe wrote for the 1795 *Merry Sherwood*, and was very successful on the stage. The friar opens with a witty musical chant celebrating the forest:

> The bramble, the bramble,
> The bonny forest bramble,
> Doth make a jest
> Of a silken vest
> That will through greenwood scramble.
>
> (p. 11)

Later, in more serious romantic mode he sings of Marian and Robin as greenwood trees:

> But this you must know, that as long as they grow,
> Whatever change may be,

You never can teach either oak or beech
To be aught but a greenwood tree.

(p. 20)

Songs follow through the novella, of comedy and feasting, and of love and the forest, and at the end of chapter 11 the social unity of the forest company is celebrated in a full six-stanza song, rich in internal rhyme like the later broadsides, naming the major figures and emphasising their natural connections, especially in the case of Marian:

And what eye hath e'er seen such a sweet Maiden Queen,
As Marian, the pride of the forester's green?
A sweet garden-flower, she blooms in the bower,
Where alone to this hour the wild rose has been:
We hail here in duty, the queen of all beauty,
We will live, we will die, by our sweet maiden Queen.

(p. 86)

This is closer to Reynolds than Keats in its nostalgic celebration, and that sentimentally positive Romanticism flows through to the end, when the friar finally sings of forest delights, including:

Ye pleasant sights of leaf and flower:
Ye pleasant sounds of bird and bee:
Ye sports of deer in sylvan bower:
Ye feasts beneath the greenwood tree:

(p. 139)

Butler suggests in a striking conclusion to her account of the novel that Marian in fact represented for Peacock a force of natural idealism close to religious experience,[48] and the intensity of these celebratory lyrics overwhelms the final sarcasm about Marian's now unmaidenly status and asserts the strength of Peacock's *Maid Marian* as a full, rich and primarily Romantic celebration of the outlaw life as natural, youthful, sensual, essentially English, and offering ranges of freedom beyond the reach of narrow modernity. Yet the novel also critiques the neo-conservative positions, as Butler has also shown, and Gossedge traces Peacock's personal links to modern exploitative enclosure: in his late-published essay 'The Last Days of Windsor Forest' Peacock describes how he watched the final round-up, by Royal Horse Guards, of the last of the free-running forest deer. Gossedge notes that although he is in name an earl, Peacock's 'Robin has identified himself with the yeoman foresters'[49] and, another important development, 'Neither does the value of the forest lie in outlawry.' Rather 'Robin is here the focal point and facilitator of forest harmony'[50] – that force which is idealised in Marian.

This deployment of the idea of 'the forest' was not a general and bland romantic idea as most commentators have thought, but bears coded reference to a detailed and dramatic social conflict of the period, important enough to Peacock to inspire a modal change in his writing. Gossedge finally suggests that it was simply to realise this past but still highly valued social formation through narrative and symbolism that Peacock here abandoned his usual, and usually admired, form of referential satiric conversation as the structure for a novella.[51] Instead, in *Maid Marian* he realised an early, strong and pervasively influential version of nineteenth-century medievalism – a mode notably pervasive in the theatre – that gathered and focused the interests of the other late Romantics in this theme and this figure. On the basis of the wonderful year of 1818, the Romantic revision of the image and meaning of Robin Hood has remained one of the major themes of the English outlaw tradition.

Romantic outlaw aftermath

It is both fair and unfair that Robert Southey figures in Peacock's *Maid Marian* as the boring time-serving bard Harpiton. Politically and stylistically he may have deserved the sharp edge of Peacock's wit, much as in *Nightmare Abbey* Coleridge earned the name Mr Flosky and the melancholic Byron was figured as Mr Cypress. But in Robin Hood creativity, at least, Southey was in advance of Peacock, as he was thinking of working in the field well before 1818. There is no sign that his early liberal years included an interest in the outlaw, though he would have read Ritson and may perhaps have contemplated Robin as a parallel to his well-remembered – by ironic radicals at least – play *Wat Tyler* (1794), or his unfairly forgotten epic poem *Joan of Arc* (1796), a vigorous realisation of the national leader born from the ordinary people that is more radical than Schiller's *Die Jungfrau von Orleans* (1801). But as early as 1808 Southey was writing notes for a Robin epic which combines the ballad stories with the gentry outlaw, much as Ritson had: this seems surprising, as in 1804 he had written to a friend that he was thinking of an English epic, and was drawn to King Arthur, because 'I am afraid there cannot be found another for an English poem except Robin Hood, and that lowers the key too much.'[52] It appears that by thinking of gentrified Robin, perhaps through

Ritson's 'Life of Robin Hood', but overlooking its radical element, he was reconciled to the theme.

His surviving 1804 note is brief and out of order, but this seems the planned story:

> The wicked Sir Hugh returns from crusade and sends off Marian (probably the miller's daughter and apparently Robin's love already – her brother is his friend) 'to be married to a villain'. Robin's cousin Annabel is forced into a nunnery by Sir Hugh, refusing to let her marry the squire she loves. Robin storms the nunnery, rescues her and is outlawed. King Richard has returned from captivity and Robin rescues him from Prince John's men; in return Robin's lands are restored by the king but he prefers to continue as Robin Hood and gives his lands to Annabel.[53]

There are later notes which add elements, including some from nature: in 1814 Southey says that 'Marian is a skylark, Annabel a nightingale – or a turtle dove', and it will be a 'rich live pastoral book'. The story will go through to Marian's death and the old age of Robin, and a separate note, predicting Hunt, mentions Robin's 'boyhood'.[54] Then there is an 'Original Sketch' of several pages, undated but, as a reference to *Ivanhoe* indicates, no earlier than 1820. By now some names have changed – Annabel is Aveline and Hugh is Reginald – and there is a striking, even far-sighted, innovation in that Robin refuses to go on crusade because an Arab whom his father brought back has 'taught the youth to long for Arabian liberty'.[55] The new material has some enhanced sentiment – Marian will die 'at about five and twenty' – but also more historicism. Probably because Scott has by now pre-empted King Richard, the story links with King John and the barons: Robin will work with the barons against him, a view looking forward to the novel tradition, as is the detail about English politics, and there is a draft sequence about preparing for crusade.

Southey was active on this project in late 1823 when he wrote to the poet Caroline Bowles, later to be his second wife, suggesting that she 'form an intellectual union' with him. They met to discuss the project: she recorded that as she demurred at 'battle scenes and such like, "the women and children, and forest" were assigned to my management'.[56] He soon sent her his first section, nearly 400 lines of opening (including a 'women and children' element of Robin's childhood); she drafted and then re-drafted a forest sequence of nearly 300 lines with a little action. There the project stalled, and though Southey often planned to return to it he did not, and then suffered mental illness: in his last period, somewhat better, he again hoped to produce more. But he died in 1843, and *Robin Hood: A Fragment* was published, with Caroline's sad Preface, in 1847.[57]

This may well be, like Jonson's *The Sad Shepherd*, a generic misfire in outlaw literature. Though Southey thought it was an epic, they settled for Caroline's favourite metre, the difficult, sombrely lyrical technique of Southey's 'Thalaba', a lengthy unrhymed stanza with no set number of metrically varying lines. Robert usually keeps it going with a martial pace, but can drift into something much more prosaic than poetry:

> Full six score spears hath Sherwood sent:
> Thirty have joined from Lindsey and from Kyme;
>   The rest are on the way,
> And with the men of Huntingdon,
>   Will on the march fall in.
>
> (Pt I, st.xx)

Caroline manages well some emotional and metrically mobile effects:

> The holy stillness of the hour,
>   The hush of human life,
> Lets the low voice be heard –
>   The low, sweet, solemn voice
> Of the deep woods –
>   Its mystical murmuring,
> Now swelling into choral harmony –
>   Rich, full exultant.
>
> (Pt II, st.ii)

But she moves very slowly through a series of somewhat automatic responses to nature and childhood. As a whole the poem is rather turgid, each lengthy stanza making a separate point or scene, and it consistently thrusts sentiment upon the reader. It seems hardly surprising that the project did not arrive at any substantial action, let alone outlaw action: Peacock's response on its publication would have been interesting.

A much more restrained, but also more potent, reconstitution of the image of the elusive forest figure, which relates to the radical element of Robin Hood, is found from the also unlikely-seeming hand of Charlotte Brontë. Helen Phillips has argued that though *Shirley* (1849) makes only two specific references to Robin Hood, these are part of the novel's 'multiply-stranded exploration of power, submission and rebellion'.[58] Brontë was personally familiar with two Robin Hood sites, Kirklees, where he allegedly died, and Hathersage, where Little John's very long tomb is still to be inspected, but this is a new reading of the myth. Where the Southeys lost touch with the active resistance to authority in their wandering sentimental stanzas, Brontë refocuses the themes for her own quite specific purposes. Phillips shows that she reverses the myth of the faithless prioress, as she 'gives the name of Mrs Pryor to the mother-figure in Caroline's story',[59] and links her to the contemporary issue of unmarried mothers. In a parallel displacement Brontë, through her phrase 'Robin Hood's haunts' and placing him in 'an antique British forest',[60] relates him to 'supernatural beings, epitomized in the figures who inhabited the woods now threatened by industrialization'.[61] She also links this to her female themes by naming the forest Nunnwood – and in addition debates the forces of modern Luddite resistance to industrialisation (which she also knew from the Kirklees region). So Brontë in general suggests that the 'ancient woods imply, like the figure of the national outlaw-hero, that freedoms – the freedoms demanded by radicalism for workers and women – may be more ancient than oppression'.[62]

Writing in 1848, Brontë, an inveterate reader, would probably have known the Southey *Fragment* of the previous year, but her version of the Romantic Robin Hood is both more fragmentary and better focused, a clear sign that the figure, as he evolved through many hands, is now well known and available for reworking – but her treatment is strikingly linked back to Keats's admiring, yet also quite political, reading of the possible meaning of the forest tradition.

Other late Romantic treatments were less socially pointed, though capable of memorable effects and of disseminating further the generalised impact of late Romanticism. Tennyson is the only writer to have honoured both the Arthur and the Robin Hood traditions with substantial contributions: his play *The Foresters*, written by 1881, is a good deal slighter than *The Idylls of the King*, but is still the work of a major poet, and someone who undertook research thoughtfully. Tennyson wrote it for performance by Henry Irving, but he felt it was not suitable for his self-assertive style: however, as Potter has shown, in an extravagant production by Augustin Daly and with music by Sir Arthur Sullivan it was very successful in America in 1892.[63] It was less popular in England and has hardly been noticed since, but in terms of both politics and poetry it contains elements that deserve respect.

Tennyson basically accepted Peacock's pattern of a lordly hero enjoying life and exercising his generous instincts in the forest, but does this with some sense of history: he follows liberal, if inaccurate, contemporary history in feeling that this was a 'great transition period in the making of England, when the barons sided with the people and eventually won for them the Magna Carta'.[64] But much of the most memorable thrust of the play is Romantic: as in so much in *The Idylls of the King*, morality and its opposite are interpreted through nature. Robin hates Prince John as one

> that can pluck the flower of maidenhood
> From off the stalk and trample it
> And boast that he hath trampled it.[65]

There is traditional outlaw material involving the knight from the *Gest* (who in keeping with the family interests of the Victorian novel, including the outlaw novel, is Marian's father), and Little John and his sweetheart Marian's maid offer relatively unfunny comedy, as does Robin's posing as an old woman. Some fake beggars are dealt with firmly; also in the spirit of Victorian times some honest business folk, called 'Citizens', are supported, rather than the deserving poor, and the foresters sing a thumpingly patriotic song, 'There is no land like England' (p. 756). The play strongly picks up the nature theme: early on Robin praises 'this free forest life' as offering him a new world:

> 'For while I sat
> Among my thralls in my baronial hall
> The groining hid the heavens; but since I breathed,
> A houseless head beneath the sun and stars,
> The soul of the woods hath stricken thro' my blood,
> The love of freedom, the desire of God,
> The hope of larger life hereafter, more
> Tenfold than under roof.'
>
> (p. 757)

And even though at the end of the action he admits, '"we must hence to the King's court"', his heart remains behind as he adds:

> 'I trust
> We shall return to the wood. Meanwhile, farewell
> Old friends, old patriarch oaks. A thousand winters
> Will strip you bare as death, a thousand summers
> Robe you life-green again.'
>
> (p. 782)

Marian, in a final speech, asserts the natural-world Romanticism of the tradition:

> 'We leave but happy memories to the forest.
> We deal in the wild justice of the woods.
> All those poor serfs whom we have served will bless us,
> All those pale mouths which we have fed will praise.'
>
> (p. 782)

The political – or at least liberal – note of Keats's poem is remembered, and the phrase 'wild justice', poised between resistance and savagery, like Reynolds's phrase 'a mass of freedom', catches the attraction to and distance from overt politics characteristic of most of the Romantics. Marian goes on to offer a more Reynolds-like reading:

> 'And here perhaps a hundred years away
> Some hunter in day-dreams or half asleep
> Will hear our arrows whizzing overhead,
> And catch the winding of a phantom horn.'
>
> (p. 782)

The idea of poets half asleep or day-dreaming might have been created for the early twentieth-century Georgian poets, and the neo-pastoral Robin Hood was of interest to most of them. Their Ritson equivalent as transmitter was Sir Arthur Quiller-Couch, who produced from Oxford University Press a collection of *Robin Hood Ballads* in 1908 and then dedicated a substantial section to 'The Greenwood' in his influential *Oxford Book of Ballads* in 1910. The creative element of this Romantic aftermath was most richly realised by Alfred Noyes, though John Drinkwater and J. C. Squire were also involved. Noyes's widely anthologised poem 'Sherwood', first published in 1906 (and sometimes called 'A Song of Sherwood' to differentiate it from his verse play *Sherwood* (1908), which was revised as *Robin Hood* (1926)), follows closely the tone of the speech that Tennyson gives finally to Marian. It begins, 'Sherwood in the twilight, is Robin Hood awake' and celebrates the national and the natural together:

> Merry, merry England is waking as if old,
> With eyes of blither hazel and hair of brighter gold:
> For Robin Hood is here again beneath the bursting spray
> In Sherwood, in Sherwood, about the break of day.[66]

While the medieval is used, as in Keats, implicitly to critique modernity, here there is no political edge or sense of a need to confront any issues: the medieval is gesturingly recalled in phrases like 'grey goose feather', redolent of national (or nationalist) glory at Agincourt and Crécy, and Noyes can equally, and about as realistically, celebrate while 'Round the fairy grass-rings frolic elf and fay' (p. 46). The sensual body of Romanticism is present, in male mode, and if the representation of Robin with his hazel eyes and bright gold hair is homosocial, even on the edge of homosexual, there is also robust masculine excitement as the 'outlaw troupe' passes:

> from aisles of oak and ash
> Rings the Follow! Follow! and the boughs begin to crash,
> The ferns begin to flutter and the flowers begin to fly,
> And through the crimson dawning the robber band goes by.
>
> (p. 46)

Because they are, unlike real forest outlaws, mounted, they seem more like well-bred gentlemen out hunting – reminiscent of another Georgian Robin Hood author, J. C. Squire, who combined editing a literary magazine with running a gentlemen's cricket team, given to country sports and quaffing ale. He wrote for the stage *Robin Hood: A Farcical Romantic Pastoral* (1928), where an ironic tone spices the nostalgia, and Noyes with *Sherwood* and Drinkwater with *Robin Hood and the Pedlar* (1912) also created Robin Hood drama. Playlets and story collections were very widely published in both Britain and the USA for use in schools in English classes, and in them the natural, the patriotic and the Romantic all converge. Sir Henry Newbolt was a major figure in English literature education, notably with *The Newbolt Report on the Teaching of English in England* of 1921, and his 1925 book of essays *The Greenwood* was published in a series called Teaching of English. In an essay entitled 'The Old English Greenwood' he said of this 'national legend' that in his time only Alfred Noyes 'has succeeded ... in dreaming it to life again'.[67]

If the Georgians finally disseminated the Romantic Robin Hood in his least political, most patriotic and even partly numinous form, it appears that some at least of that aspect of the figure was even more influentially re-created in film. Fairbanks with his vigorous, elf-like representation is one aspect of that figure, and Errol Flynn in the tightest of green tights conveyed the directly Romantic masculinity attractive to cinema audiences, though at the same time the great tree that comes to life with ambushing bandits, Korngold's late Romantic score and Michael Curtiz's innate sense of the power of folklore connected with the deeper traditions that ran from Reynolds through Tennyson.

Romantic Robin Hood remains an available and potent part of the outlaw repertoire: Kevin Costner and Russell Crowe may trudge through versions of historicised political modernity, but in the very successful 1980s television series named *Robin of Sherwood* in the UK and just *Robin Hood* in America, when Ray Winstone, playing Will Scarlett like a real East London outlaw, asked what all this effort and risk was really all for, Michael Praed, as student-radical Robin, flicked back his shoulder-length hair, spun around, waved his arms at the tree-rich landscape and cried, 'For this!' The figure of Romantic Robin Hood who first emerged that cold day in February 1818 has thrived, and flourished.

Notes

1 J. Harris Gable, *Bibliography of Robin Hood*, University of Nebraska Studies in Language, Literature and Criticism, 17 (Lincoln: University of Nebraska Press, 1939).
2 For a text and a discussion of this play see Stephen Knight, 'Robin Hood and the Royal Restoration', *Critical Survey*, 5 (1993): 298–312.
3 For a review of these references see Christopher Hill, 'Robin Hood', chapter 5 of *Liberty against the Law: Some Seventeenth-Century Controversies* (London: Lane, 1996), pp. 71–82.
4 For these details see Linda Troost, 'Robin Hood Musicals in Eighteenth-Century London', in Thomas G. Hahn (ed.), *Robin Hood in Popular Culture: Violence, Transgression and Justice* (Cambridge: Brewer, 2000), pp. 251–64.
5 Troost, 'Robin Hood Musicals', pp. 251–2.
6 Troost, 'Robin Hood Musicals', pp. 256–7.
7 William Shield and Leonard McNally, *Robin Hood, or Sherwood Forest* (London: Almon, 1784), p. 28. In the American-published *Songs in the Comic Opera Robin Hood, as Performed at the New Theatre in Philadelphia* (Philadelphia: Carey, 1784) this line reads in a more Gothic way, as 'By dark grove, shade or windy dell'. There are other major variations to the lyrics throughout, and Troost, 'Robin Hood Musicals', gives details of some reworking during varied productions: see pp. 257–8.
8 Joseph Ritson (ed.), *Robin Hood: A Collection of All the Ancient Poems, Songs and Ballads Now Extant Relative to the Celebrated English Outlaw (to which are Prefixed Anecdotes of his Life)*, 2 vols (London: Egerton and Johnson, 1795).
9 John O'Keeffe, *Airs, Duetts and Choruses in the Operatical Pantomime of Merry Sherwood or Harlequin Forrester* (London: Longman, 1795), p. 4.

10 On its vigour in the 1790s see Donna T. Andrew, *London Debating Societies, 1776–99*, www.british-history.ac.uk/report.aspx?pubid=238 (accessed 10 April 2013).
11 Troost, 'Robin Hood Musicals', pp. 254–5.
12 For a discussion and illustration of the Johnston grave and the Stukeley genealogy see Stephen Knight, *Robin Hood: A Complete Study of the English Outlaw* (Oxford: Blackwell, 1994), pp. 16–21.
13 Lois J. Potter, 'Sherwood Forest and the Byronic Robin Hood', in Hahn (ed.), *Robin Hood in Popular Culture*, pp. 215–24.
14 Lord Byron, *Poetical Works* (London: Oxford University Press, 1933), pp. 31–2, at p. 31.
15 William and Mary Howitt, *The Forest Minstrel* (London: Baldwin, Cradock and Day, 1823), p. 33.
16 Robert Millhouse, *Sherwood Forest, and Other Poems* (London: the author, 1827), canto 1, st. 3.
17 Potter, 'Byronic Robin Hood', p. 221.
18 Spencer T. Hall, *The Forester's Offering* (London: Whitaker, 1841), p. 63.
19 See John Mathew Gutch (ed.), *A Lytell Geste of Robin Hode, with Other Ancient & Modern Ballads and Songs Relating to this Celebrated Yeoman*, 2 vols (London: Longman, 1847), vol. 1, pp. ix–xvi.
20 See 'General Ludd's Triumph', in Roy Palmer (ed.), *A Touch on the Times: Songs of Social Change, 1770–1914* (London: Penguin, 1974), pp. 286–8; see also Potter, 'Byronic Robin Hood', p. 224.
21 Potter, 'Byronic Robin Hood', p. 223.
22 J. H. Reynolds, *Poetry and Prose*, ed. George L. Marsh (London: Oxford University Press, 1928), p. 150.
23 See John Barnard, 'Keats's "Robin Hood", John Hamilton Reynolds, and the "Old Poets"', *Proceedings of the British Academy*, 75 (1989): 181–200; reprinted in Stephen Knight (ed.), *Robin Hood: An Anthology of Scholarship and Criticism* (Cambridge: Brewer, 1999), pp. 123–40, at p. 126.
24 John Keats, 'Robin Hood: To a Friend', in *Collected Poems*, ed. Jack Stillinger (Cambridge, MA: Harvard University Press, 1982), pp. 169–70, line 1.
25 Morris Dickstein, *Keats and his Poetry: A Study in Development* (Chicago: University of Chicago Press, 1971), p. 159.
26 Barnard, 'Keats's "Robin Hood"', pp. 126–7.
27 Barnard, 'Keats's "Robin Hood"', p. 128.
28 See Keats, *Poems*, pp. 324–5, especially sts xvi–xviii.
29 Nicholas Roe, *John Keats and the Culture of Dissent* (Oxford: Clarendon, 1997), p. 140.
30 Marilyn Butler, *Romantics, Rebels and Reactionaries* (Oxford: Oxford University Press, 1981); for the Byron comment, see p. 149.
31 Byron, *Poetical Works*, p. 32.

32 Roe, *Keats and the Culture of Dissent*, p. 151.
33 Barnard, 'Keats's "Robin Hood"', p. 134.
34 Roe, 'The Chaucerian Key', in *Keats and the Culture of Dissent*, pp. 134–40.
35 Leigh Hunt, *Foliage, or Poems Original and Translated* (London: Ollier, 1818), p. 8; on this see Roe, *Keats and the Culture of Dissent*, p. 141, and Barnard, 'Keats's "Robin Hood"', pp. 196–7.
36 Leigh Hunt, *Selected Writings*, vol. 5: *Poetical Works, 1801–21*, ed. John Strachan (London: Pickering and Chatto, 2003), p. 211 and note: the Cox reference is to Jeffrey N. Cox, *Poetry and Politics in the Cockney School*, Cambridge Studies in Romanticism (Cambridge: Cambridge University Press, 1998), p. 87.
37 Roe, *Keats and the Culture of Dissent*, p. 142.
38 Hunt, *Selected Writings*, vol. 5, pp. 288–91, lines 1–8.
39 Hunt, *Selected Writings*, vol. 5, p. 340, notes 14 and 15.
40 Hunt, *Selected Writings*, vol. 5, p. 342, note 46.
41 Thomas Love Peacock (originally 'By the author of Headlong Hall'), *Maid Marian* (London: Hookham and Longman, Hurst, Rees, Orme, and Brown, 1822).
42 J. B. Priestley, *Thomas Love Peacock* (London: Macmillan, 1927), p. 57.
43 *The Letters of Thomas Love Peacock*, ed. Nicholas A. Joukovsky, 2 vols (Oxford: Clarendon, 2001), vol. 1, p. 156.
44 Marilyn Butler, 'The Good Old Times', chapter 5 of *Peacock Displayed* (London: Routledge, 1979): pp. 140–55 for the Peacock section, reprinted in Knight (ed.), *Robin Hood: An Anthology*, 141–54; for 'the mystique of feudalism' see Butler, *Romantics, Rebels and Reactionaries*, p. 147.
45 Rob Gossedge, 'Thomas Love Peacock, Robin Hood and the Enclosure of Windsor Forest', in Stephen Knight (ed.), *Robin Hood in Greenwood Stood: Alterity and Context in the English Outlaw Tradition* (Turnhout: Brepols, 2011), pp. 135–64.
46 See Nicholas Joukovsky, 'Peacock's Sir Oran Haut-ton, Byron's Bear or Shelley's Ape', *Keats–Shelley Journal*, 29 (1980): 173–90.
47 Butler, 'The Good Old Times', p. 150.
48 Butler, 'The Good Old Times', pp. 158–9.
49 Gossedge, 'Thomas Love Peacock', p. 162.
50 Gossedge, 'Thomas Love Peacock', pp. 162 and 163.
51 Gossedge, 'Thomas Love Peacock', p. 163.
52 The comment is in a letter to Charles Williams Wynne, 30 December 1804, National Library of Wales, MSS 4811–15D. I am indebted for this reference to Dr Gavin Edwards.
53 See Robert Southey, *Later Poetical Works, 1811–1838*, vol. 4: *Fragments and Romances*, ed. Tim Fulford and Rachel Crawford (London: Pickering and Chatto, 2012), p. 311.

54 Southey, *Later Poetical Works*, vol. 4, pp. 311–12.
55 Southey, *Later Poetical Works*, vol. 4, p. 312.
56 Southey, *Later Poetical Works*, vol. 4, pp. 287 and 288.
57 Robert and Caroline Southey, 'Robin Hood', in *Robin Hood: A Fragment* (Edinburgh: Blackwood, 1847), pp. 1–36, at pp. 15, 22–3.
58 Helen Phillips, 'Robin Hood, the Prioress of Kirklee, and Charlotte Brontë', in Helen Phillips (ed.), *Robin Hood Medieval and Post-Medieval* (Dublin: Four Courts Press, 2005), pp. 154–66.
59 Phillips, 'Robin Hood, the Prioress of Kirklees', p. 158.
60 Charlotte Brontë, *Shirley*, World's Classics Series (Oxford: Oxford University Press, 1979), p. 237.
61 Phillips, 'Robin Hood, the Prioress of Kirklees', p. 159.
62 Phillips, 'Robin Hood, the Prioress of Kirklees', p. 161.
63 Lois Potter, 'The Apotheosis of Maid Marian: Tennyson's *The Foresters* and the Nineteenth-Century Theater', in Lois J. Potter (ed.), *Playing Robin Hood: The Legend in Performance in Five Centuries* (Newark: University of Delaware Press, 1998), pp. 182–204.
64 See Hallam Tennyson, *A Memoir of Lord Tennyson* (London: Macmillan, 1897), vol. 2, p. 173.
65 Alfred Tennyson, *The Foresters*, in *Poems and Plays*, 2 vols, Oxford Standard Authors (Oxford: Oxford University Press, 1965), vol. 2, p. 573.
66 Alfred Noyes, *Sherwood*, in *Collected Poems*, 4 vols (London: Blackwood, 1928), vol. 1, pp. 45–7, at p. 45.
67 Sir Henry Newbolt, *The Greenwood*, Teaching of English Series, 40 (London: Nelson, 1925), p. 213.

6
Robin Hood and nineteenth-century fiction

A novel Robin Hood

The hero is at home in rural surroundings, moves easily among people of different social levels, is of considerable interest and appeal to others, confronts his opponents with some courage but triumphs in part through his force of character, faces the threats of town life with courage and eventual success, and returns to his authoritative nature-girt location having proved his true nobility and evidently going to continue a positive and productive life.

This is Tom Jones, of course, archetypal hero of the English novel, but it might just as easily be Robin Hood as he had developed by the later eighteenth century. Yet essentially Fielding's hero was a redirection or masculinist gentry appropriation of the unruly forces of the novel, variedly adventurous between city and desert island in its Defoeian origins and readily routed into feminine-oriented feeling and sensational anti-rationalism in the Gothic novel. In keeping with that volatility the three earliest Robin Hood novels, all deriving from exactly the same period just after the end of the war with France, are strikingly different in tone, genre and ideological direction, giving quite different accounts of the social origin, the characteristic deeds, the final appearance and the political implications that attach to the outlaw hero in a new century and a new genre.

Like Tom in his progress, Robin takes time to settle down as the patriotic, masculine, leaderly hero of the mid-Victorian popular novel. The three early and varied texts are the anonymous *Robin Hood: A Tale of the Olden Time*, published in Edinburgh by mid 1819; Walter Scott's *Ivanhoe*, usually dated 1820 but in fact appearing just in time for Christmas 1819; and Thomas Love Peacock's *Maid Marian*, published in 1822 but, a preliminary note insists, with all but the last three of its eighteen chapters written in late 1818.

They share two striking features, one clear and one quite puzzling. They are all in evident ways guided by the material in Ritson's 1795 anthology, with substantial variations among their responses. All three accept the period of Richard I and his troublesome brother Prince/King John, but only Peacock makes real use of the ballads themselves: Scott re-uses some of the *Gest* material, mostly that to do with the king, and Anon develops a quite different story with ballad narratives showing up occasionally. The three Robins have different social origins – Scott's is a very sturdy yeoman, even a plain Saxon peasant, and Anon has him the illegitimate son of a knight, while Peacock accepts the biography of a displaced earl. For Anon he loves the fair Ruthinglenne, whatever she claims her name is; Scott's outlaw has no interest in women; only Peacock re-uses the gentrified tradition of love for Marian Fitzwater. Scott alone has any interest in the importance of race and nationality, heavily emphasised, and his tone is strongly historical and exhortative throughout, supported by a steadily developing united narrative; Anon has a lighter tone, more Romantic than Gothic, with much intercutting of scenes and time periods; Peacock is as ever witty, brisk and light all at once, in both tone and structure, with fine songs and jokes as well as some incisive liberal commentary.

Those links and disparities are readily enough understood as being the result of three very differently positioned writers working in the tradition of Ritson's *Robin Hood* in their own potent ways. The puzzle is to explain why they should all have appeared more or less together, and why Ritson's impetus took a generation to operate. As has been outlined in the previous chapter, poets were at work in the same period as these novelists, but there had been very little outlaw recension in the generation before that. Ritson's anthology was certainly about and consulted: it was reprinted in 1820 and there was a second edition in 1823, but that seems more likely to have related to the new interest itself than to have been a trigger to sudden productivity. What was new in the post-war period that made people stimulated by Robin Hood? One element might well be the removal, with the defeat of France, of the threatening character of the idea of resistance to authority – which made Ritson in the time of his original publication seem to be touching on distinctly dangerous themes in his hostility to kings and lords. Another may well be the evident post-war social and economic distress, to which liberals and reformers were reacting strongly.

But that hardly explains why Scott, a decided Tory, or Anon, who seems likely to be an author, probably female, of some seriousness and restraint, and Peacock, a genuine enough liberal but hardly a street-fighting radical, should be drawn to this myth that offered a mix of independence, stubbornness and some style. It is most likely that this is the liberal-nationalist wing of early medievalism, standing mostly against the constraints of eighteenth-century and internationalist manners, and so valuing true feeling – Anon and Peacock; direct manly national courage – Scott mostly; and nature-focused intensity – Peacock even more than the others.

Robin Hood does have a place in the radical end of new medievalism: a Chartist like Thomas Miller would see the importance of the story for his own reformist principles, and in 1846 *The People's Journal* reprinted the *Gest* as a memory of radical continuance. But that was only one of the threads of meaning that would be drawn out of the initial triune establishment of the outlaw myth in the form of the novel, and it would be matched by other themes just as far from the thrust of these first three novels, that, with the éclat and impact characteristic of the period, first brought Robin Hood into imaginative prose.

A multiple tradition: 1819–43

While Ritson and his generally overlooked predecessor and model, Thomas Evans, were the major transmitters of the outlaw tradition into the nineteenth century, neither of them imposed a dominant form of the tradition. The nineteenth-century coverage of the outlaw story seemed in most instances to be re-created every decade or so with new focal interests and new techniques to realise them. While the idea of a nobleman turned outlaw for honourable reasons was outlined by Ritson and reinforced by Gutch in 1847 (in spite of his dislike of Ritson's radicalism), this was not a permanent or well-developed element in the story. The association of Lord Robin with the time of bad King John was itself challenged, especially by the idea that he was involved in the events that, liberal ideologues liked to assert, saw Simon de Montfort as a founder of the cherished institution of parliamentary democracy. There was a not uncommon parallel idea that Robin was somehow a force connected with Magna Carta, a notion still present in the 2010 Robin Hood film. But there were many more elements of vigorous vitality than that, including sympathy for Chartism, interest in magic or at least superstition, confident assertions of xenophobia, hostility to Catholicism and fascination with manliness, including fighting and flirting with girls, but also re-creations of greenwood homo-sociality, crass humour (usually associated with Friar Tuck and Little John), occasional celebrations of hunting, traces of Romantic feeling for the natural environment and concern with models for the young – though young men only, it only appears.

In its previous generic variations the tendency has been for the first surviving example of a Robin Hood genre to dominate in mood and tone, like the early ballads in the yeoman tradition or Munday's work in the gentrified domain. But later the textual tradition's variety only grows: the post-seventeenth-century stage tradition is quite heterogeneous, and, among the novels, those discussed in this section are remarkably different, taking varied political and tonal positions and not accepting any authoritative model of topic for their material from earlier traditions. Robin Hood does not enter the novel in anything like popular mode, though he will by 1840 arrive and flourish there: the first two authors are notably literary in tone, both exhibiting remarkable skill and confidence, though one has a major reputation, and one is intriguingly elusive.

There might seem to be good reason for taking Scott first, as *Ivanhoe* is so important a historical novel, where he first broke into the field of English history and the very lucrative English market; and his massive impact on fiction world-wide might seem to justify some sense of priority. But although unacknowledged by *Ivanhoe* scholars, and indeed almost unknown to scholarship in general, including Robin Hood studies, *Robin Hood: A Tale of the Olden Time* was published in Edinburgh before Scott was at serious work on his novel, and it deserves to be discussed first (see Figure 2).[1] Assigning Scott to a mere place in the list puts into some perspective the innovative element of his topic, though it does not dilute his powerful influence and his assertive insistence on the themes of nationalism, or rather racism, and his imputing of an equally assertive masculinity to the outlaw hero. Indeed not only does it seem very likely that Anon is notable not only for linking the Robin Hood novel to the Romantic Gothic tradition, but, from the lack of interest in fighting and the central role and viewpoint given to women, it seems extremely likely that the writer was a woman.

This novel set in the Middle Ages begins, it seems following Scott's established practice of explaining the origins of his historical narration, with a lengthy 'Introductory Chapter' of around 15,000 words, nearly a fifth of the novel, explaining how the narrator, a lawyer educated in Edinburgh and Oxford, gained access

ROBIN HOOD;

A TALE

OF

THE OLDEN TIME.

> There's some will talk of Lords and Knights,
> And some of Yeomen good;
> But I will tell of Will Scarlet,
> Little John, and Robin Hood.
> *Old Ballad.*

IN TWO VOLUMES.

VOL. I.

EDINBURGH:

OLIVER & BOYD, HIGH STREET;
G. & W. B. WHITTAKER, AVE-MARIA-LANE, LONDON;
AND W. TURNBULL, GLASGOW.

M.DCCC.XIX.

2 The almost unknown first Robin Hood novel: *Robin Hood: A Tale of the Olden Time* (1819).

to this story. He met an elderly village teacher of Welsh origin, Goody Clifford, who played the harp and told many 'amusing tales of the olden times with which her forefathers entertained the knights and squires, and fair ladies of the days of yore' (vol. 1, p. 22). Apparently modelled on women like Mrs Brown of Falkland, who provided old ballads for the recent collectors, but through her Welshness having a national range (though not it seems a Welsh one), she will tell the novel's story, but not before a lengthy debate is held on the value of literature itself. Mr Sharp, surely named for aggressive modernity, is against literature, but Mr Greville is in favour. He likes Scott and speaks of Robin Hood and his men as having status like classical warriors, with him being even 'another Cataline' (vol. 1, p. 54). Along with the classical learning (if at times a little vague, as with the spelling and the relevance of Catiline) there is recurrent reference to the role of women in culture and story, and thoughtful contributions from women present, notably Mrs Greville. Robin Hood is thought of as taking from the rich and giving to the poor, being especially generous to women, and this Ritson-linked element of gentrification has some resonance, with the outlaws being thought of as having become 'freebooters', but also 'still knights' (vol. 1, p. 55).

With the scholarship and Scottish framing cleared away, Goody starts her story in a decisively melodramatic tone: 'The night was dark and stormy', it begins (vol. 1, p. 81), looking forward to Lytton's famous opening of *Paul Clifford* (1830). A young woman seeks entrance to an abbey. Goody, we have heard, has Hugh Walpole and Mrs Radcliffe prominent among her books, and the tone, especially of the opening, is recurrently Gothic. The young woman at the abbey is Ruthinglenne, who says she has walked from Huntingdon: she is very beautiful and is received by a stern abbess called Elgiva; her abbey confessor becomes Father Athelstane, who is very interested in her, though not in any improper way, and feels she is not of peasant stock.

The names must give some pause. Elgiva is Saxon, belonging to a tenth-century queen and saint at whose tomb illnesses were cured; later in the book the nun is a number of times called St Elgiva, presumably a simple error. Ruthinglenne is surely linked to the memorable name given to the hero of Isabella Kelly's eponymous novel of 1801: Kelly was of well-born Scottish family and a minor Romantic poet and Gothic novelist; she had fallen on difficult times and by 1819 was in London and apparently had become a teacher. She must be a credible candidate for authorship: she wrote little by this time, apparently nothing coming out after 1823 – though she lived on until 1857, when she was ninety-eight. Then Athelstane is, with the same spelling, a major figure in *Ivanhoe*, the Saxon of royal blood to whom all but the Norman lords defer. The *Edinburgh Review* records this novel as being published in March–July 1819 by Oliver and Boyd,[2] and it also appeared in London and Glasgow. Scott was at this time suffering severely from gall-stones, but was also finishing *The Bride of Lammermoor* for the third of the series Tales of My Landlord, and by June his agent was beginning to negotiate terms for what would become *Ivanhoe*. He apparently began dictating it by early July, and in spite of more illness made rapid progress, with volume 1 nearly finished by 19 July and volume 2 done by late August.[3] It seems very likely that it was the work of Anon that suggested to Scott important elements of his first English topic.

There are other arrivals at the abbey. An old woman and a blind minstrel appear: he talks nonsense and sings what he says are Chinese songs coming from the Black Sea. In the next chapter a horn blows, and the outlaw band arrives, led by a Robin Hood benefiting from the tendency of the novel genre to give detailed physical descriptions: he was

> a young man apparently about twenty-five years of age, tall and elegantly formed; and of a countenance distinguished by an unusual degree of masculine beauty. His dress was green, like that of his companions; but it was enriched by a purple scarf thrown across his shoulders and by a knot of plumes of a similar colour, which waved in his cap. (vol 1, p. 131)

With parallel distinction he takes over the plot. The strange entertainers were Allen a Dale (the minstrel) and Little John, there to open the gate to the band so that they could steal the silver image of the Virgin from the altar. It is not a sequence from the outlaw tradition, but the mix of disguise, infiltration and theft from the church, as well as comic disguising, is fully within its spirit. But when they discover that the image was the gift of Queen Eleanor, and she is herself staying there, Robin desists and they leave politely. When Ruthinglenne hears about this, she greets Robin's name with 'a deep groan' (vol. 1, p. 136) and says she believed he was dead: the adverb 'faintly' is repeated.

The narrator takes us back in time for explanations. Gilbert Hood, a handsome Nottinghamshire ranger, loved Alice Pevys, daughter of Sir Robert Pevys. Banished, Gilbert became a Northamptonshire farmer, and Alice eloped with him from the castle. When their son Robin is fifteen he and his mother go to try to make up with her brother, now Sir John. Robin falls out with Will Scarlet, Sir John's illegitimate son, but Sir John promises Robin his estate, and Will only money. Seven years later Gilbert Hood dies and Alice is seized with grief: Sir John is ill but Robin will not leave his mother. When she dies he goes to the castle: Sir John is already dead, and Will, with the abbot's support, has seized title, lands and money (though the abbot has some of the last). Robin goes off to be a soldier with Little John, a senior servant from the castle. A beautiful lady falls from a white horse: they take her home to Nottingham Castle; Robin loves her, Claribel, and her father Sir Walter Le Clare approves. But when he hears about Robin's disinheritance that changes, and Robin and Little John leave. Riding through beautiful Sherwood Forest they meet the merry men mourning their leader. They live in an ancient ruin, say they are respectable and ask him to lead them – he will have a silver bow and a purple scarf and plumes. He agrees.

Rapid action follows, some touching on ballads. Allan a Dale appears: his beloved, niece to the Bishop of Hereford, is being forced to marry Sir William Pevys, formerly Will Scarlet. The outlaws go and sort things out. Then Claribel arrives in the forest, dressed as a boy: she has discovered that her father separated them. Robin shows her 'the romantic habitations formed in the ruin' (vol. 2, p. 57): they marry and stay in the forest. Robin has a large reward on his head and is arrested in Nottingham: his men go to rescue him, but no fighting is needed – they meet him outside the town, freed by Sir Walter, who feels he is partly to blame and does not know that Robin has married his daughter. Back at the forest, Claribel has disappeared – Robin had heard in town she was marrying Sir William, but thought it nonsense. The outlaws see the pair together on horseback: she dismisses Robin brusquely; the outlaws plan to steal the silver image from the abbey.

The final sequence is as well paced and skilfully interwoven. At the abbey Ruthinglenne tells Father Athelstane she is Robin Hood's wife. She fled when he was arrested, to help him by hiding the marriage, but thought he was executed (hence the previous faint). She sends Robin a message saying she is his wife under an assumed name, and will meet him and explain all in six days. But it is Little John who turns up, saying Robin is off obtaining money for the outlaws.

Soon there is a crisis at the abbey. Ruthinglenne has failed to do her duty and seems odd: they find her hair is now not shaved off. She is sent to the dungeon, and King Richard arrives to take his mother to Oxford. A lady arrives to see him – it is Ruthinglenne. A while ago, the outlaws took Sir William Pevys as he was carrying a message from Prince John to the King of France (that is where Robin was when Little John replaced him at the abbey). Claribel was with Pevys – she is Ruthinglenne's twin sister. Ruthinglenne loved Robin at the castle and went to the forest to him, as Claribel. Robin has exchanged the two at the abbey so he can be with Ruthinglenne.

Both sisters plead to the king for their husbands. He forgives Sir William, and the queen begs for Robin so that his men can form her guard, apparently a memory of 'Robin Hood and Queen Katherine'. Ruthinglenne is released from the abbey: because she was married she was ineligible to take a nun's vows. Little John ends the novel by saying, 'Fear God – honour the king – relieve the poor – forbear to envy the rich; and do as you would be done to by all mankind' (vol. 2, p. 221) – a distinctly feeble form of outlaw ethic.

This is a love mystery turning on the double-identity themes beloved of Gothic and Romantic fiction, with a double heroine as well as good and bad male quasi-fraternal leads. It is plotted with theatrical skill and uses very little of two major themes of the nineteenth-century outlaw novel, the beauty of the forest and the pleasure of manly fighting. Robin's gentry connections do not have any continuing meaning, and he has no social restoration: he is always a man of feeling, for his mother and then both the sisters in turn. A handsomely produced two-volume novel, the work plays almost no part in the new outlaw novel tradition. Though it does bring Gilbert Hood and the Clare name into the tradition, its rejection of the major issues of class, race and masculinism cut it off from the mainstream concerns – though it must seem a great pity that no Hollywood story-boarder has come across what would be a great vehicle for a twin-playing melodramatic actress, let alone a youthful Robin with scarf and plumes, who could even double, less well dressed, as his enemy.

At the very end of that year Edinburgh book-buyers could enjoy another piece of Scots-based English medievalism, with a distinctly different Robin Hood in very varied action, and set in a remarkably altered emotional and ideological context. Selling at thirty shillings for three volumes, and moving 10,000 copies in two weeks, *Ivanhoe* took Scott to the summit of the international novel.[4] The pattern he had previously developed is readily traced back, as by James Chandler,[5] to Scottish Enlightenment historiography and its thinking about the stages of history through which developing cultures, and nations, proceed. This is not a 'great man' approach to history: his characters like Waverley himself or Jeanie Deans tend to be the viewpoint from which the novel observes the processes at work. This is also the pattern of *Ivanhoe*: the title hero is distinctly underexciting, as several film actors have found in spite of their efforts, and its theme of English vigour largely rests on the dynamic character of Robin Hood.

But what Ivanhoe represents is still potent. Scott's account of history is never naïve or simple: this is not about the way the Norman French took over England. It is about what nineteenth-century writers would increasingly see as the continuing conflict between French-originated lords and the residual English self-defence that Victorians liked to feel led to the defeat of the House of Lords and the rise of the House of Commons and the common law. Scott was no radical, disliked Luddites and knew about the 1561 Edinburgh Robin Hood riots (with a disapproving note on them in *The Abbot*, 1820), and as he was working on *Ivanhoe* wrote firmly in support of the military action at Manchester's 'Peterloo Massacre' where fifteen people died and hundreds were injured. He still stood for a form of democracy, with at least the *haute bourgeoisie*, like urban lawyers and writers, having a large say in public rule and in political debate – a moderated anti-aristocratism which made the novel so popular in France, perhaps especially with the final accent and rising intonation in their title, *Ivanhoé*. This new conception made the figure of Robin Hood a firm symbol of the English liberal political struggle over time. However imaginary that connection was, the succeeding novelists would be convinced, and would rework it in various modes, not being as learned or as speculative in their history as Scott and certainly not finding room for his distinctive imagining of the urban Jewish financier and his clever beautiful daughter as a medieval version of the engaging modern forces of urban internationalist mercantilism.

But Locksley, tough illiterate commander of peasant soldiers and fearfully accurate with bow and arrow, is not the only element in the novel that comes through Ritson's transmission of the outlaw tradition. The titular hero is a brave returning crusader, stripped of his lands by Prince John and his minions, separated from his long-intended bride, loyal to the true king, supported by a band of peasant patriots and finally returned to his rightful position. This sounds every inch gentrified Lord Robert – but is in fact Ivanhoe himself: his Saxon identity is the main reason for his dispossession. It seems very likely that Scott found Robin Hood the resistant yeoman too threatening to use him as the noble Saxon, and neatly substituted an invented hero, with an Anglo-Saxon name taken from an English midland village – for some time Scott liked the idea of calling him Harold, but he decided that Byron's *Childe Harold's Pilgrimage*, finished in 1818, pre-empted the idea. The Robin of the other 1819 novel is of gentry birth, and at one point in the story regrets his involvement in crime, so that representation might even have stimulated Scott's reshaping of the heroic noble figure.

Apart from his existence as the deep-laid identity of Ivanhoe, the outlaw appears in only four major sequences. He is an emergent man of the people in the early tournament scene, a 'stout, well-set yeoman, arrayed in Lincoln green, having twelve arrows stuck in his belt' (p. 80). He is named Locksley, in apparent euphemism. Prince John feels he is insolent, but when the archery contest is called, Locksley stands up to the prince's bullying and then humiliates his chosen French archer. Symbolism is rich here: Hubert's grandfather shot at Hastings – the fatal arrow there is glanced at (however unlikely this is to have occurred), and Locksley gets personal when Hubert hits the bull, saying, 'I will notch his shaft for him, however' (p. 152), and performs the famous feat of splitting the arrow. Scott had already used this of the Douglas in *The Lady of the Lake*. It is of course impossible, and comes from 'splitting the peg' or hitting the wooden centre that attached a target to its base. It is hard to separate Scott's interest in the alleged feat from the idea of phallic competition, especially as for him, like the other Romantics, Robin is a strongly masculine presence.

Locksley's next major appearance is when the Saxons, with the Black Knight, peasants and outlaws, prepare to attack Torquilstone Castle to free their friends, including Rebecca. He says he is 'a nameless man; but I am the friend of my country and of my country's friends' (pp. 212–13), and with Ivanhoe speaking his love for 'England and the life of every Englishman' (p. 212), both talk and action bring to a head the most potent element of Scott's novel. This re-articulation of the meaning of Robin Hood is in line with the potent and fairly new force of nationalism. Usually seen as a later eighteenth-century development when the pan-European power of aristocracy and Catholicism weakened, and having been strongly fostered in German aspirations to nationhood and French revolutionary assertion of a new self-conscious identity, this new nationalism finds its primary English-language ideologue in Scott, and this will reverberate through most of the outlaw novels, even in the naïve and thoughtless forms that history has shown to be characteristic of popularised nationalism and its product, racism.

Scott still seems reluctant to make the figure of Robin Hood central: he is one of the leading figures in managing the siege; his ballad tradition is appropriated as they send Wamba in, disguised as a friar, to save the Saxon lord Cedric (Scott's version of Cerdic), and he does organise and launch the crucial infantry assault on the castle – but there is no narrative outcome of this. Yet he is not absent, and speaks last after the castle is taken, to call his yeomen to share the spoils together 'at the trystng tree in Harthill Walk' (p. 346): Scott as ever mixes fidelity to tradition with modernisation. We later see the outlaws, like peaceful citizens, bring all the spoils and share them quietly, under Locksley's 'laudable impartiality' (p. 356): the scene never suggests the discussions and disruptions of democracy. Locksley has said to the Black Knight/king, 'In these glades I am monarch' (p. 348), and the king has noted 'the justice and judgement of their leader' (p. 356). Locksley remains somewhat recessive as an oppositive figure, concealing from the king his own 'mystery', not offering any explanation of how he came to the forest and offering, as in the other 1819 novel, some regret about being an outlaw (p. 375).

The final Locksley scene occurs when the Black Knight blows his horn for help – the king has himself entered the world of the ballads – and is rescued. Locksley finally gives his name as Robin Hood when the king's favour makes him no longer an outlaw and the king calls him, in politically euphemistic terms, 'King of outlaws and Prince of good fellows' (p. 465), but at least Robin has 'the natural and rough sense' (p. 472) to prompt the dilatory king to go on his way and to his business. Richard gives him 'full pardon and future favour', and Scott touches on the English liberal tradition by saying, 'the charter of the Forest was extorted from the unwilling hands of King John' (p. 475). But there is no Marian, no future action, not even a hero's tragic betrayal and death in this story: as if returning to his innate distaste for this peasant powerhouse, Scott sends him off to a career ending in 'the tale of his treacherous death' in the literary world of the 'black-letter garlands' (p. 475), well away from this drama of human history and nationalist self-identification.

Scott's strong, steady style and rare capacity to create memorable, meaning-laden scenes have brought into the novel a Robin Hood far more potent than the charming young man whose story emerged in the same year in the same city. The fact that in some ways the outlaw was too strong a figure for Scott to make central did not in any way diminish the impact that *Ivanhoe* had on the English novel and national attitudes. And yet it was not Scott's image of the tough illiterate non-commissioned officer, good both in war and at putting the nobility in their place, that was pursued by the mainstream tradition. The idea of an English hero, and one about whom people bought books, was Scott's major gift to the novelists to come. They had their own additions to make, often following, if lamely, Scott's historicism and nationalism. The pattern of a fully new tone and context, not a reworking of the ballad tradition, did not end with Scott and Anon. The brilliance and influence of Peacock's *Maid Marian*, that other product of 1818–19, have tended to make it seem the source of the novel tradition, but its impact operated slowly, first occurring in print with Egan in 1840, and not substantially appearing in the later novelists. This tends to confirm, or at least justify, the decision to treat him in this study along with the other Romantic handlers of the outlaw tradition, not among the novelists. But two other writers were close to Scott in using Robin as a powerful, but not central, figure in a plot guided by a medievalist political agenda, of compatible but also quite different kinds.

Ritson, Hunt and to some extent Keats had seen Robin Hood as a figure capable of being linked to modern liberal reforms, and the use of the name by Luddites, and for the highly active radical Robin Hood Society,[6] also located him on the emergent left. Scott avoided that connection, Anon ignored it, and Peacock had transmuted any idea of resistance into elegantly muted satire. But Thomas Miller was a more serious radical: he would become a dedicated Chartist and by the end of 1837 turned from his successful rustic and naturalist writing to *Royston Gower, or The Days of King John: A Historical Romance* (1838),[7] a historical three-volume novel that had been carefully researched – including in the British Library, he says in his lengthy Introduction.

There were links to his recent work as what he called a 'rural sketcher' (vol. 1, p. vii) in *A Day in the Woods* (1836) and *Beauties of the Country* (1837), both synopsised in the end-papers of the first edition of *Royston Gower*. He says that now 'the principal intention of this work is to show the tyranny of the Norman Forest Laws' (vol. 1, p. xiv) and that concern with the past appropriation of nature as part of 'a tyrannic mandate' on a 'brave yet oppressed people' (vol 1, p. viii) is understood as parallel to the contemporary destruction of nature. He speaks of writing some of the book when visiting Sydenham Woods on the edge of London, but he found Penge Wood already blighted by trains, and it was clear that 'Trade and tumult, and buildings will increase' (vol 1, p. xxiv).

Miller accepts Ritson's dating of events and his view of kings and lords as oppressors, but firmly resists making Robin Hood himself noble. He also does not make Robin as central a figure as he has been in Anon or Peacock: much as in Scott, he is an often off-stage facilitator of events. The gap between Saxon and Norman is of major importance, but Miller adds a strong sense of class: the Saxons, highly aware of their lost power, tend to be fugitive or elusive, essentially in opposition to the Norman lords. Royston Gower is, despite his name, a Saxon, a plain soldier who reconnects with his class and racial origins, and is a channel for the awakening radical conscience which is Miller's prime target.

This is a lengthy novel with an elaborate plot, and its theme operates through a range of characters. Miller creates well a complex social world, the pattern of the contemporary novel – he proved a good choice in 1848 to continue the rich multi-plot pattern of George Reynolds's *Mysteries of London* after Reynolds fell out with the publisher. The focal strand of *Royston Gower* concerns Geoffrey de Marchmont, a lord in the Sherwood area who wants to marry Edith of Lincoln, a high-born Norman beauty with a Saxon mother, and also take the estate of Hereward the Ready – a name epitomising Saxon vigour. But Edith loves the Saxon Henry of Gloomglendell, heir to an earldom. Geoffrey de Marchmont's beautiful daughter Margaret loves a Saxon, at present pretending to be Geoffrey's page but actually Edwin, son of Gurthric of Clifton (although Saxon, also a crusader), and claimant to Geoffrey's lands, including Nottingham. Documents held by the Prior of Newstead will prove the right of Gurthric and Henry and dismiss the Norman Geoffrey from power.

Robin Hood, usually called 'the outlaw', hates Geoffrey de Marchmont because he has hanged some of his men, but is still honourable enough, disguised as a messenger, to save him from a violent death when the fierce outlaw Walter the One-Handed is about to throw Geoffrey out of his own castle window. The outlaws often support and protect the Saxons and the sympathetic part-Norman women, and a larger role than Robin's is played by Elwerwolf, an elderly wise woman (with a brave dwarf son named Druth) whose knowledge and advice can be important, and who makes a major speech of Saxon defiance against the Normans who 'revel in idleness and luxury, are all knights or nobles; while we eat of the bitter bread, nor look for aught beyond the appeasing of hunger' (vol. 2, p. 263).

Royston Gower, who appears late in volume 1, once served Gurthric (including on crusade) and is now among Geoffrey de Marchmont's soldiers. Ordered to jail Margaret's lover Edwin, he is reluctant, and when Elwerwolf explains who Edwin is he takes him and Margaret to the forest, she dressed as a page. Royston then fetches Robin and his men to rescue Edith, who has been abducted for Geoffrey. When Royston is eventually captured by Geoffrey's men, he refuses to save his life by killing Edwin – but his guards follow his model of aroused self-consciousness, refuse to kill him and go over to Edwin and the outlaws.

The complicated story ends with a major 'trial by battle' scene between Geoffrey de Marchmont and Edith's beloved Henry of Gloomglendell. Geoffrey is badly wounded, and after his death Royston relates his brave crusading deeds: Geoffrey has always been in part admired as a man of action and spirit, especially overseas. There seems a whisper of masculinist, even imperialist, admiration here, but Royston's final image is as the emblem of muscular Saxon virtue. The story predicts that when Edwin and the Saxonised Margaret die they will be buried beside Royston, and the text provides the future epitaph for him, in Saxon and English translation, both written by Edwin. Miller would later write *A History of the Anglo-Saxons* (1848), and his commitment to the theme is already strong.

The regained inheritance story is very common from the period, and here it is given both racial and political meaning, notably as a means of re-asserting popular right. Robin Hood acts more as a facilitator than as an active agent in the process, though he does at the end marry Elfrida, daughter of Hereward, the Saxon landowner whose difficulties have interwoven through all the events. Almost as marginal to the major story as Robin is King John, who fumes and rants a fair amount but is also capable of seeing, if not reason, at least good policy. The historical Cardinal Langton also appears; Miller represents in a scholarly way the period of the Interdict, when the pope placed England under sanction for John's misdeeds towards the church. A rich set of minor figures of some weight appear, such as John of Chester, a corrupt instrument of Geoffrey of Marchmont, outlaws like the very handsome Will, and the very tough Walter the One-Handed, but also Hugh de Lacy, a Norman lord sympathetic to good order and Saxons, and the beautiful Queen Isabelle, who is a friend to Edwin, and the sensible Elfrida – her name, we are told, means 'may rain' (vol. 3, p. 249) and links Robin back to nature rather than natural law.

This long novel, with extended scenes of dialogue and description, loops back consistently to the forest laws, yet curiously gives all the villains some trace of honour – even John of Chester, who lusts seriously after Edith, is betrayed by Geoffrey de Marchmont and ends up being beaten for penitence by some hard-handed friars. Central are two ideas: Saxon virtue is prime, and linked to it is the possibility of the agents of Norman oppression realising that their interests are with the other side. It is a powerful message for its time, but one that because of its inherently reformist political character has little interest in the idea of outlawry as natural law or justified resistance. That is for the future: at the end the outlaws are complaining that there is too little action, but Walter the One-Handed says the barons are organising against the king. Little John complains, 'we shall have no share in the feast', and they agree to wait to see, as the outlaw Pinder puts it, if 'the time may yet alter' (vol. 3, p. 256).

Another post-Scott outlaw novel is politically differently positioned. In *Forest Days*,[8] G. P. R. James developed his position as a well-known producer of popular historical novels for the general public – Thackeray cuttingly linked him to bourgeois arrivisme and inauthenticity by calling him 'G. P. R. Jeames', but he was quite learned and was even appointed by King William IV as Historiographer Royal, a largely honorific post. He travelled widely and in the 1850s emigrated to the USA, where in 1852 he was appointed British consul in Norfolk, Virginia. Evidently concerned with historical conflict – his first success was with *Richelieu* (1829), in which he was encouraged by Scott – he became interested enough in Robin Hood to take up the notion that he had been involved with the events connected to Simon de Montfort and the alleged establishing of what would be parliamentary democracy in his tussles with Henry III. This idea was evidently drawn from a lengthy essay by the yet unidentified 'G.F.' in the *London and Westminster Quarterly* in March 1840 that went back to the dating first found in Bower (though it quoted it as by Fordun).

James was quite conservative, being well known to the Duke of Wellington, and he shapes a version of the story opposed to Miller's, in the dating and, more importantly, in both the respect shown to the true aristocrats who dominate the novel and the lack of interest in the idea of Saxon resistance to exploitative French lords. As a result James also makes Robin Hood rather recessive, so not gaining the title of the novel – presumably James was too cautious to privilege the aristocrats in his title as Miller had the peasantry, and so used the romantic phrase *Forest Days*, apparently taken from Keats's poem, or possibly Reynolds's third sonnet, and in any case largely inappropriate, as after a sequence in volume 1 little of the action takes place in the forest, and there is almost no sign of the theme of natural beauty as national value that had emerged in the Romantic writers and already thrived in the outlaw novel.

This is another three-volume novel, with ample plot, if not one quite as intricate as Miller's. The core of the action focuses on two small noble families: the elderly Earl of Ashby, with his daughter Lucy and son Alured (which may be meant to be an Anglo-Saxon name), and their troublesome 'kinsman' Richard de Ashby. The name may recall Scott's use of Ashby-de-la-Zouche as the site for the tournament. Close to them are the Earl of Monthermer, noble and generous, and his nephew Hugh, kind, handsome and learned, who loves Lucy. The earls are both de Montfort supporters, though friendly with Prince Edward, who will become Edward I, the warrior and proto-imperialist king very important in the English national myth at this time.

The dubious Richard de Ashby is a king's man and has some influence on Alured, who is not a strong personality. In the opening action Richard causes dissension in a village near Pontefract where in heavy disguise (with a hunchback and a purple nose) a man called Hardy watches, and warns a Monthermer servant about Richard. Next day, May Day, when Richard harasses a pretty barmaid and starts a fight, 'Hardy' and his men in Lincoln green deal with him and his servants: Richard gets an arrow through his bonnet with 'Scathelock' written on it – James evidently knows this can mean something like 'cut-hair'.

The text develops the outlaw theme, celebrating 'the infinite variety of the forest' (vol. 1, p. 102), and we hear of Robin robbing monks and friars as well as 'the petty tyrants of the neighbouring shire' and – a new touch – 'wealthy and ostentatious merchants' (vol. 1, p. 104). The outlaw leader is homoerotically described, from 'the full and swelling muscle that clothed his limbs' to 'the eyes giving a keen and eagle-like look to a face in every other respect frank and gentle' (vol. 1, pp. 108–9). This paragon meets Monthermer and indicates he supports the earls, and Monthermer says he did his best to have his outlawry revoked but the Earl of Gloucester was his enemy: there is no further discussion of a restoration. His name, equally unemphasised, is Robert of the Lees, suggesting kinship with the knight of the *Gest*.

Lucy has been abducted from the woods near Ashby's castle; Hugh looks for her, and Robin takes him deep in the forest to a house where she is protected by Tangel, who looks like an ape-like child. Alured, rather hostile to Hugh, takes Lucy under protection, and the characters move towards the west, where war is developing between de Montfort and the earls against the king and the Earl of Gloucester, Gilbert de Clare (a historical name, apparently not drawn from Anon). Alured is now with Ashby and the king, to oppose Hugh and his party.

The battle of Evesham is treated in some detail, and after much marching and counter-marching and a brutal account of the action, de Montfort dies bravely, Hugh is taken prisoner by Prince Edward at Eltham Palace, and Robin Hood conveys the wounded Earl of Monthermer, who has been outlawed, to safety. The text says that 'mourning spread through the middle and lower classes of the people ... and through the greater part of the barons who claimed a genuine English descent': de Montfort was the man who 'had protected their rights and liberties' (vol 2, pp. 125–6).

Prince Edward is friendly towards Hugh, but Richard de Ashby plots against him, as does Guy de Mangan, who desires Lucy and has been beaten by Hugh for mistreating her. Richard plans to kill the Earl of Ashby and pin the blame on Hugh, and this apparently happens, though the earl wounds one of de Ashby's men badly. Hugh is already condemned to death for his part in the rising, which is seen through his enemies' urging as treason, but Robin sends Tangel with a ladder and a disguise to rescue him. Though the earl's body has disappeared, Richard persuades people that the now free Hugh committed the murder. Alured has doubts, and with Princess Eleanor's sympathy (she is a friend of Lucy) Hugh will face trial by battle against Alured. Meanwhile Kate, the mistreated barmaid of the early stages, has taken a dying confession from Richard's assassin, whom the earl wounded. Alured sees this, but feels compelled by honour to fight Hugh, though knowing him innocent – he thinks he will probably die, and Hugh be vindicated, so this appears highly honourable.

When de Mangan tells de Ashby that Alured is weakening, they try to poison him, but his servant drinks most of the poison and dies. An ill Alured turns up for the trial by battle. But Hugh and his uncle appear, with the Earl of Ashby being carried. He survived the murder attempt and then had the outlaws' help. Richard de Ashby, who is now arrested, begs pardon from the king, and as Prince Edward declines to speak on either side (an interesting example of royalty being above the action, guilt-free), Richard is pardoned and exiled: he curses Hugh and the others. The novel ends as, from a distance, a man shoots Richard dead, crying, 'This for the heart of the murderous traitor Richard de Ashby! – Whom kings spare, commons send to judgement!' (vol. 3, p. 302). The arrow has written on it 'Robin Hood'.

This is essentially a gentry melodrama, with most lords being noble, one bad, Richard, and one fairly weak but ultimately noble, Alured. So in social terms, nothing needs changing. The mistreated nobleman Hugh is eventually reinstated with help from true lords and the outlaws, and will gain his appropriate love Lucy: it is structurally a replay of *Ivanhoe*, though there are disappearances, violences, treacheries, letters, forgeries, poisonings and confessions that seem to look towards the new genre of mystery writing, with Robin Hood playing a role not unlike the detective of dubious social origins but strange powers, including disguise, cunning and recurrent legal surprises like producing the old earl alive at the trial. James had produced an early version of mystery fiction in *Delaware: or The Ruined Family* (1833), though there, as here, the quasi-detective was subservient to an officer-class gentry figure.

Though in the first volume there is a creation of the outlaw, and in the battle of Evesham there is some definite memory of his military capacity as in *Royston Gower* and *Ivanhoe*, Robin plays only a minor supportive role from then on. The Preface spoke of him as 'One English yeoman of a very superior mind ... outlawed, in all probability, for his adherence to the popular party of the day' (vol. 1, p. vi). But he is not a focus of value in the text, which seems uninterested in whether he was Saxon or not – he is certainly patriotic, singing to the Earl of Monthermer at a forest feast a song about 'Merry England' where 'My dear island home Veils not the crest to Rome' (vol. 1, pp. 184–5), which may just laud Anglicanism, but quite possibly sees England as the new classical-style empire.

One thrust of the text is its detailed historicism, in both the events of the time and the recurrent commentary on matters like the warmer weather in the Middle Ages (vol. 1, p. 146, though the idea of vines in Northumbria is apparently a myth), the history of ladies leaving a dinner party to the men (vol. 2, p. 188), and a discussion of the external nature of public evaluation – 'What may be called representation was a part of that epoch ... a great part of everything in that period was effect' (vol. 1, pp. 168–9). In thematic terms the text offers a generally nostalgic positive medievalism – the pre-industrial world is innately good with 'a spirit of sylvan cheer and rustic hardihood' (vol. 1, p. 1), and then there was real strength in 'the natural affections of the heart, the sound judgement of right and wrong and the high emotions of the immortal spirit within us' (vol. 1, p. 37). But James's basic thrust is to urge noblemen to behave in an appropriate way and so earn the endless loyalty of the people. Robin Hood and Hugh debate this at some length in the forest: Robin says the nobles need to 'remember the oath of their chivalry', and in a two-page speech Hugh insists that it is the nobles who have 'stood forward against tyranny wherever they found it': they have 'shed their blood in defence of the rights of the people', and it is through them 'that such a thing as human bondage is disappearing from the island' (vol. 1, p. 277); he finally insists that it is the nobles who will 'stand between the people and oppression and wrong' (vol. 1, p. 278). At first Robin is silent, with his eyes downcast: then he says that he hopes all the nobles will remember this and not disgrace their standing – and finally seems to exculpate weak lords by saying that only Jesus was perfect.

James's semi-patron, the Duke of Wellington, himself still a leading Tory lord, would not have objected to this kind of bold outlaw, and the ultimate thrust of the novel is strongly in keeping with the 'Young England' idea of a strong alliance between nobles and commons in the face of threatening modern change. That rewrites Miller's re-shaping of the outlaw story in almost every way, but change continues in the tradition. James's retrospective values are not shared by the subsequent series of outlaw novels, which are more fully focused on the actions and meanings of the forest hero himself, and extend their scope a good deal more widely, and sometimes more erratically, than the theme-focused versions of the Robin Hood novels examined so far.

The ballad tradition had, outside Peacock, played very little role in the Robin Hood novel so far. It was not forgotten: garlands were still appearing; Ritson's edition was widely available and would in 1847 be updated and in some ways surpassed by J. M. Gutch's edition, which commented on 'the constant reprinting of Robin Hood Garlands'.[9] The new genre of children's literature showed early interest in retelling the ballads. *Robin Hood and his Merry Foresters* (1841) by 'Stephen Percy',[10] a pseudonym for the prolific John Cundall, appears to be the first outlaw collection specifically aimed at the emergent youth market. Dedicating 'These Stories of my Boyhood' to his sister, the narrator remembers how 'forgetting for a while Caesar, Cicero and Virgil' his school-mates would ask for 'some tale of Robin Hood' (p. 2), and in a suitably rural setting, near a little village, he recounts what followed. First, to a single boy, he tells the 'progress to Nottingham' story, with quotations, ending by relating how Robin Hood, born Fitzooth, takes to the wood and becomes leader of the outlaws through 'his superior skill in archery and his prowess at all manly exercises' (p. 8). There follow the stories of his meeting Little John and Will Scarlet and between them the story, with plenty of quotations, mostly dialogue, of 'Robin Hood and the Butcher' – perhaps chosen because it lacks the adult feature of Robin and the sheriff's wife of the potter version.

The story-telling is so successful that next day there are six schoolboys, who hear 'Robin Hood and Allen a Dale', 'Robin Hood's Golden Prize' with some full quotations, 'Robin Hood and the Ranger' quoted complete and a synopsis of 'Robin Hood and Guy of Gisborne'. This lacks any mention of St Mary and the beheading, but still has plenty of violence. At the end the assembled foresters shoot many arrows at the sheriff and his men, but they escape, with not even the arrow in the backside which for the earlier Percy euphemised the sheriff's death – but the sheriff does take Will Stutely a prisoner, and the text hurries on to describe his rescue, followed by the version of 'Robin Hood and the Beggar' without a rescue, where the beggar fights lustily against Robin and his men.

On the next evening outlaw sports are described, followed by accounts of Robin's encounters with the friar and the Bishop of Hereford, which has added to the text 'smoking haunches of venison' (p. 82). On 'Our Half Holiday', in the wood the narrator tells a version of 'Robin Hood and Queen Katherine' entitled 'Robin Hood in Finsbury Fields'. This uses Henry II and Queen Eleanor (perhaps suggested by her presence in Anon's 1819 novel – James's novel where she figures was not yet available and she appears in none of the ballad versions, though she could simply have come from Munday via Ritson). This version draws on Scott to add Robin splitting the arrow of his opponent Clifton, and there is another linking as the Bishop of Hereford appears, loses a bet against Robin and refers to the action of his own ballad. Linking develops further when 'The Fifth Meeting' tells a ballad of 'Reynolde Grenelefe' which is the archery tournament with only Little John starring and then being employed by the sheriff, with consequences as in the *Gest*. Then, as also in the *Gest*, the monks are robbed and the knight arrives – the man he helped on the way was called George a Green, from another ballad, 'The Pinder of Wakefield'.

On 'Our Last Evening', the 'golden arrow' story is retold, and this links into a fight with the sheriff's men as in the *Gest*, and then the outlaws rescue the knight and kill the sheriff. The king is in the forest, the *Gest* scene is quickly retold, and Robin goes to court, where 'our brave hero assumed his title of earl of Huntingdon, and lived in most noble style' (p. 151). The final sequence is also adapted from the *Gest*: Robin leaves for the forest but the king, much as in Parker's 1632 *A True Tale of Robin Hood* (to be found in Ritson), sends two hundred men after him. Robin is wounded fighting in Sherwood and goes to Kirklees: a final quotation from 'Robin Hood's Death' has him buried where his arrow lands, and the epitaph follows, as found in Parker, and also in Ritson.

The narrator says that he 'was obliged to hurry the latter part of my stories more than I could have wished' (p. 154) and the school bell called them 'to our less pleasing, but more important pursuits' (p. 154). In one more sentence the holidays arrive and the text ends with 'we all returned HOME' (p. 154).

A fairly faithful and lively dissemination of the ballads and, until almost the very end, of yeoman Robin Hood, this was, it appears, to have substantial influence, especially through the work of Howard Pyle. It and its many descendants in schoolboy story-telling kept alive the simple, energetic ballad figure with his innate resistance to oppression and his general sense of vitality, vigour and natural law. It is without the overlay of national values and historicism that had already entered the tradition and would be substantially supported by the novelists to come. Starting with Egan, they wove the ballads back into their narrative largely because they lacked the specialist positions, whether political or in the case of Anon primarily literary Gothic, that had led the earlier novelists to keep Robin mostly out of the centre of the narrative and to see his yeoman adventures as of little interest.

Robin Hood in the popular mainstream

All the Robin Hood novelists examined so far have had aspirations behind their reworkings of the story – Scott is a high-level historicist, James a more modest practitioner in that field, Anon is a Gothic Romantic, Peacock a wit-focused Romantic, Miller offers a political lesson to ordinary people, and Percy entertains schoolboys and educates them in their English popular cultural heritage. Pierce Egan the Younger operates more simply, as a popular writer, son of the well-known author of boxing fiction and the very successful serial *Life in London* (starting in 1821), a pioneer in fictionalising London.

Egan the Younger started as an illustrator, and his *Robin Hood* includes his own illustrations, always naïve and sometimes almost charming. It may well be this lack of a special interest that led him simply to accept the task of retelling the Robin Hood story and using the hero's name in the title – which strangely enough was, with the exception of Stephen Percy's backward-looking juvenile redaction, the first time the outlaw's name had graced a novel title. Early on Egan worked in Scott's medieval tradition – his second novel was *Wat Tyler* (1841), about the Peasants' Revolt, and his *Robin Hood and Little John: or, The Merry Men of Sherwood Forest* started to be serialised in 1838 and appeared as a novel in 1840.[11] It was 'hugely popular and was reprinted many times',[12] was clearly imitated by Stocqueler in 1849 and provided the basis for the popular *Robin Hood, prince des voleurs* (1872) and *Robin Hood le proscrit* (1873) by, or at least claiming to be by, Alexandre Dumas.

The first straight novelising of the Robin Hood tradition in close contact with the ballad events, this is of very full length, some 400,000 words, in the new mode of serial publication and then appearing in a single volume retaining the small type and the double columns of the weekly episodes, with one illustration for each eight-page issue. The market is popular and major, where the other early novels, with a couple of hundred words a page, wide margins and three expensive volumes speak to a wealthier audience, even if they are invited, as by Miller, to espouse radical reformism. In the same popular mode, Egan's novel teems with brisk, direct action without lengthy speeches and authorial interventions. The outlaw tradition has returned to its popular roots, and it flourished there.

From the start we see both familiar Robin Hood material and also contemporary innovations running through this popular medievalism. Robin, the heir to the earldom of Huntingdon, is delivered as a baby to the cottage of Gilbert Head (later known as Hood, a feature apparently drawn from Anon), a Sherwood forester, by de Beaseant, his father's uncle who desires the title, and gains it after Robin's father soon dies. His mother, who died bearing him, was the daughter of Sir Guy of Gamwell Hall. Soon de Beaseant dies and the Abbot of Ramsey seizes the estate. Robin grows up and as a handsome fourteen-year-old saves from an attacking archer Allan Clare (another name from Anon) and his sister, Marian: Allan loves Christabel, daughter of Baron Fitzallan, Earl of Nottingham, who is opposed to the idea and has set the archer onto them.

This mix of traditions, with Peacock and Anon both marginally evident, also goes back to Ritson – and indeed represents him. Ritson is the name of the other man who brings the baby Robin, and it is also he who threatens Allan and Marian, and has already killed his lover Annie, Gilbert's sister. She reappears as a ghost (see Figure 3) and terrifies him, and he will die in pain after Gilbert's dog bites him severely. Both radical and famously cantankerous, Ritson had not left an image positive for many: he was lampooned here and attacked in Gutch's 1847 Introduction. When young Robin's arrow pins his hand to his bow, it seems a comment is being made on his literary achievements with that very hand.

The following action moves with spirited rapidity between romance, violence and farce. Marian (already loved by Robin) is pursued by a thug (from Ritson again), and is saved by Little

3 Egan the artist provides Gothic elaboration for Egan the novelist: Gilbert Hood sees the spirit of his sister. From Pierce Egan the Younger, *Robin Hood and Little John* (1840), p. 87.

John, a forester, who takes her to the home of his uncle, Sir Guy of Gamwell. Robin is imprisoned after standing up to the baron, but Maude Clare, the warder's daughter (no relation to Allan and Marian Clare, whose father has been banished for supporting Thomas Becket), likes him and he escapes (though he is still fourteen). But he already loves Marian and will later persuade Maude to go with Will, who loves her. As Robin leaves, also rescuing Christabel, he shoots Caspar Steinkopft, the baron's enforcer, to death, through the eye, in a sort of revenge for Hastings; for his own vengeance the baron sends his men to the forest, and they hurt Allan and kill Gilbert's wife. The author explains that such bloodshed was very common then (p. 155). Among these sober events the baron is trapped up a tree by a wolf, falls on the wolf and kills it.

Six years pass and the action starts up with book 2. A good deal of fighting is detailed with gusto: Robin and his friends fight, with little rationale, against some returned crusaders, and Gilbert is killed; Little John takes to his quarterstaff against a Norman soldier; a major battle occurs as three hundred Normans attack Gamwell Hall, defended by the Saxon villagers and Robin and his friends. After nearly twenty pages of conflict the Normans prevail, and the Saxons take to the forest. Little John says they need a leader; the men shout for him, but he declares for Robin as a great archer and really an earl. Sir Guy of Gamwell and some of his sons go north, and five more years pass.

In all that action there has been one short sequence of ballad material where Robin meets and fights the friar (who also loves Maude), but in the following sequence there is more familiar outlaw activity. Clerics are robbed, there is much merriment, the Will Scarlet story is told, as is a fight against foresters, and then come a gallows rescue and the Allan a Dale wedding story, both in adapted forms. Egan also offers his own contribution: Christabel is being forced to marry her father's friend and banker Sir Tristram Uggleretsch – weird comic names are themselves part of the popular mode. There are also signs that the pattern of a romantic novel is closing on the forest action of the tradition. When Robin visits Marian in Yorkshire she has an admirer, Sir Hubert de Boissy: Robin fights him and he leaves, but is later killed by the foresters. Also in romantic mode, after Allan and Christabel marry, Robin marries Marian in a major forest social event (see Figure 4), to live with him in the forest, as in the ballad 'Robin Hood and Maid Marian', and Will marries the still fairly reluctant Maude.

As book 3 starts other outlaws marry and some have children: both 'Robin and Will Scarlet became fathers to two fine boys' (p. 328) – but this son and heir of Robin's is forgotten, even when Marian makes her lengthy dying speech. The outlaw band remains of primary interest: Robin's forest rules have a distinct, if wordy, link to the *Gest*, as he proclaims:

> 'All Saxons are free, gentle and simple, and even our courtesy may be extended to such Norman knights, who not being of such a grasping, avaricious nature as their brethren, have little more fortune than their sword, and who do not, by overbearing conduct, merit wholesome and seasonable chastisement.' (p. 329)

After this the action becomes more traditional: the story of the knight from the *Gest* is recounted as another family drama, and there follow the stories of the Bishop of Hereford, Robin disguised as the old woman, Robin versus the friars, and Little John and the

4 Egan the artist and the wedding day of Robin and Marian. From Pierce Egan the Younger, *Robin Hood and Little John* (1840), p. 323.

beggars, and by way of variation Little John tells Will the story of 'Robin Hood and the Butcher' – and Robin will shortly relate his meeting with the tinker.

At the same time, modernity invades: early in book 3 there is a surprising amount about Robin flirting with and kissing the pretty castle servant Grace, and domestic material emerges about Maude and Marian in Barnsdale. Little John and Much, with their chosen partners Winifred and Barbara, are there too, and lengthy debates occur about the value of family life. Those two pairs will soon marry and there are to be more weddings: Will, wanting to get all his six brothers married, lines up likely willing 'damsels' (p. 388), and on one day eight marriages assert Will's highly Victorian statement that 'It is every man's duty to try to make women happy, they are gentle tender things, with nobody to look after their wants and welfare but us' (p. 379).

Finally, the forest action darkens as the story follows first 'Robin Hood and Guy of Gisborne' (ending with the sheriff merely shot in the backside as in Thomas Percy's version) and then the *Gest* from Little John's wound through to the death of the sheriff – and here he is beheaded. The outlaws stay in the forest, and 'So far as lay in his power, Robin Hood relieved the heavy burden of the poorest classes around him' (p. 438). Time passes: Prince John's men attack the forest but fail to find the outlaws; King Richard returns, and as in the *Gest* he visits the forest and goes to Nottingham with Robin, who says they have improved the breed and numbers of deer in the forest. Both the knight and Robin, as earl, are reinstated, but the king leaves, and the Abbot of Ramsey holds onto the Huntingdon estate; Richard dies and King John assaults the forest again. The outlaws beat the king's men off but Marian dies.

In a coda, the band is gloomy and Robin very sad, so he goes to Scarborough and the action of 'Robin Hood's Fishing' occurs. He returns to Barnsdale, where he and Little John live like brothers – John's wife Winifred has died in childbirth. The outlaws, with up to seven hundred men, fight against the excesses of King John across the north and finally, aged fifty-five (Little John is sixty-five), Robin is weary and goes for treatment to Kirklees where his prioress cousin has previously healed him. But now she is involved with Gisborne's brother: the 'death' ballad is followed rather than the *Gest*, and he dies on the spot where the arrow lands, but then they bury him back in Sherwood beside Marian. His long final speech stresses that he was a Saxon, was loved by the poor and held the affection of the outlaw band.

Egan finally quotes 'that sweet poet John Keats' on 'Honour to bold Robin Hood' (p. 474), which seems appropriate, because as Keats transformed the myth in Romantic poetry, Egan, for all his ramblings, is the first novelist to adapt the outlaw tradition to the forms and concerns of the nineteenth-century novel, especially offering guarded sexuality constrained by the ideology of marriage alongside physical conflict routed through liberalism, masculinity and nationalism.

The wordy style, the naïve illustrations, the multiple but also dawdling plot, these all belong to the process of serial publication which both dominated and reshaped fiction in the mid-century period, and out of that dynamic matrix came a new image of Robin Hood, a nobleman with the common touch, a brave and resourceful fighter for popular causes, a committed husband with a wandering eye, handsome, well-spoken, admired and loved, a true Englishman, whatever that might mean. Both novelists and children's writers would exploit Egan's re-creation of the central figure of this enduring and changing national myth.

Joachim H. Stocqueler was of Portuguese family: like Peacock, he joined the East India Company in 1819, but served in India and became a journalist there. After returning to London in 1843, he wrote about travels in the East and Europe, notably

Germany. He had a busy life with four marriages (the first two ended in divorce), bankruptcies and many books, and died in America in 1886. International themes do emerge in his Robin Hood novel, but of more weight is his experience in writing for the popular stage, including a part in creating the very entertaining pantomime *Robin Hood and Coeur de Lion* (1846). It features puns, jokes, comic songs, a witty Macbeth parody to open (with the witches replayed as writers), a substantial role for the Algerian nationalist leader Abd el-Kader, as 'The Old Man of the Mountains', and, best of all, a scene where Little John bursts into tears and is affectionately led off stage by Robin Hood – both being played by no doubt tall women with their fine legs in tights, as indeed are Richard's minstrel, Blondel, and all the outlaws. Against that theatrical gallimaufry, Stocqueler's fictional follow-up to Egan seems almost staid, though as a novel it stretches many boundaries. Answering Egan's title by being named *Maid Marian, the Forest Queen*,[13] it directly claims to be 'A Companion to "Robin Hood"'. It is shorter, has fewer, but broadly similar illustrations and basically avoids as far as possible replaying Egan's material.

Robin is away on crusade, and the second chapter describes at length the siege of Acre. Meanwhile, Marian is acting as the leader of the outlaw band, but is involved in a set of perilous adventures with Prince John and a villain named Hugo Malair (see Figure 5; for details of her difficulties see pp. 206–7).

Stocqueler's theatrical confidence with melodrama is clear, and this sequence is basically Act 1, interspersed with Robin's adventures at Acre and his rescuing King Richard from death. As a reward he is allowed to return to his 'merrie men' (p. 20): the king says he would restore Robin to his title now 'were not the example dangerous' (p. 19) but promises generosity when they meet again in England. Nearly a third of the way through the novel Robin returns, bringing with him Suleiman, an Arab, and his lovely daughter Leila – he rescued them from the sack of Acre.

After he tells his adventures, with some stress on his time in Germany, as in Stocqueler's recently published travel writing, the plot develops. Prince John is raising money, but Nottingham citizens give their Saxon loyalty as grounds for resistance, though their leader's name is the distinctly Norman William Fitzosbert. Staying with *Ivanhoe*, Prince John's men attack Reuben the Jew for money, rough up his eleven-year-old daughter Hagar and hang him upside-down – he soon dies. The outlaws and five hundred

5 Stocqueler and violence: Marian, her dog and Prince John in disguise. From J. H. Stockqueler, *Maid Marian* (1849), p. 9.

townsmen fight the prince's men; Fitzosbert joins the outlaws, and describes the work he and his brother Richard have done for Saxon resistance. He will soon leave the outlaws for London, along with the tough outlaw Brand, who misses women.

Alongside this mix of Scott (the nationalism) and Egan (the local squabbles), another plot line is developed. Suleiman is sulky but Leila is popular, dancing for the outlaws (see Figure 6). Marian begins to be jealous of her with Robin. Minnie Eftskin, the forest witch – the theatre tradition again – wants Leila's jewels and Reuben's hidden money: she feels her plans will be helped if she wipes out the outlaws. Because of the presence of the Arabs and her own interference, 'the sylvan society was in a state of disintegration', with 'a universality of distrust' (p. 118). Minnie has been giving Marian love-philtres for Robin and provides herbs to burn 'to restore happiness to the boys of the greenwood' (p. 131) – but

6 Stocqueler and orientalism: Leila dances for the outlaws. From J. H. Stocqueler, *Maid Marian* (1849), p. 89.

they are poison. A dog dies, but the outlaws all survive, and villainy is removed: Suleiman, suspected of the poisoning, escapes to Nottingham, and Minnie accidentally burns herself to death in her hut. Leila meets the again disguised Prince John in the forest, and he invites her to his castle.

In what follows, appearing much like Act 3, Stocqueler seems to be working hard to find material. The story moves to Southwell Hold, owned by Baron Fitzmowbray: Sir Wilfrid Cotherstone returns from the Holy Land, having been sent by Richard to check on the situation – he too talks about Germany, and likes the baron's daughter Rosa. Stocqueler comments on differences between her boudoir and contemporary versions of female furnishing. There is a tournament at Nottingham, meant to kill Sir Wilfrid. Prince John's man Sir Brian de Mainfer (p. 187, but named Main de Fer at p. 94) attacks him treacherously, but fails. The outlaws and Baron Fitzmowbray's men face Prince John's forces without success, and they all escape to the forest. Hearing that Prince

John is on the way, they go by boat (most unusual in Robin Hood stories) to Southwell, which Prince John then besieges: in the end the baron is killed, Wilfrid goes missing, Marian is taken, and Robin and others escape to the forest.

They rescue Marian through the help of Robin's town friend William of Goldsborough – the name alleged to be on Robin Hood's seventeenth-century grave: Stocqueler has been reading Ritson (or perhaps Gutch, who spells the name Goldesborough).[14] Marian and her father leave: he appears to have overcome his doubts about Robin and says he will try to have him restored to his title.

Soon the outlaws save King Richard from the prince's men: the French king has warned John of his presence. Robin seeks the king's help to bring back Marian and also to christen Hagar, whose inheritance has been restored by William of Goldsborough, about to be Nottingham's mayor. Sir Wilfrid, who has reappeared, marries Rosa, and Hagar marries Rosa's brother Edwy (a curiously Saxon name for a baron's son). Finally Robin gets Marian from her father at Arlingford (her home in Peacock). Stocqueler sums up briskly, avoiding Robin's end (though Kirklees is mentioned in passing) to concentrate on the heroine of his title. He says he differs from Egan in that she died before Robin, being eventually poisoned by Prince John and (also as in Munday) buried at Dunmow.

Rich in detailed action and theatrical episodes, this presents very little traditional Robin Hood activity – no ballad sequence is re-used, the *Gest* is never reworked. Peacock is referenced at times, and Scott is behind the siege, the tournament, the Jewish material and the jester's name Gurtha, condensing Wamba and Gurth from *Ivanhoe*. Invented historicist figures carry a good deal of weight, especially in the second half, and the interest in the Arab characters links to Stocqueler's own internationalism. It is tempting to see the sudden nineteenth-century interest in Robin's role on crusade – something the medieval and early modern periods were either bored with or wary of – as a reflex of empire, and Stocqueler's own positioning would seem to make that persuasive. Certainly Sir Wilfrid, unlike Wilfred of Ivanhoe, seems much like the imperial returnees, from Thackeray's Jos Sedley to Doyle's Dr Watson, who take a central role in representing for English society the values and risks of empire in the mid to late nineteenth century.

In that respect, as in his story's sadism, sexism and vague nationalism, Stocqueler both develops Egan's positions and also continues some of them in entertaining but hardly subtle modes. Something of a tangential development of the outlaw tradition as it is, *Maid Marian, the Forest Queen* kept the outlaw novel before the public gaze, deflecting further the radicalism of Miller in the very period of mid-century reformist intensity, and channelling a distinctly tame account of outlaw politics on to the next, fuller, and more serious, if also distinctly heterogeneous, version of the Robin Hood novel.

Most of George Emmett's often short books were world-wide adventures suitable for stimulating boys and disseminating the imperial spirit, like *Midshipman Tom* (c.1875) and *Frank Fearless* (c.1875 – the dates are rarely given in these popular texts). He was not above imitating earlier writers – his first novel was *Black-Eyed Susan* (1868), drawing on Douglas Jerrold's play, and later there would be a *Young Tom's Schooldays* (c.1885). *Robin Hood and the Outlaws of Sherwood Forest* (1869),[15] serialised from 1868 in *The Young Englishman's Journal*, which started in 1867, is basically in that category because it covers ground similar to Egan and at times James, and takes a parallel if rather vague historicist-nationalist stance.

Nationalism is heavy from the start: the ballads, the Introduction tells us, expressed 'in good Saxon language a love of all that is manly and brave', and Robin Hood 'hated, with a thorough Saxon hate, the Norman oppressors of the English nation' (p. 2). Emmett speaks of his research and name-checks major sources dealt with by Ritson. He has also looked at the earlier novels, as he dates the story in the time of Henry III, with G. P. R. James, and Little John is, as in Egan, of the Gamwell family. Robin is an earl from the start, but Marian is of simpler status, niece to Much the Miller, here a serious tradesman.

The structure of the novel is decidedly piecemeal, being governed by its eight-page weekly issues, each with an illustration, rather than the book-by-book structure of more dignified novelists or the quasi-theatrical partitioning that came naturally to Stocqueler. The opening sequence draws on James to show noble Robin fighting beside Simon de Montfort at Evesham, withdrawing his men from defeat in good order, taking to Barnsdale as outlaws in strength – with over seven hundred men (matching the figure given late in Egan). They are attacked by the Earl of Mortimer. Robin eventually beats him in a swordfight, and they become friends in the forest. But trouble continues: the sheriff is de Lois, a king's man whose uncle is Abbot of St Mary's. They have a spy in the outlaw camp whom Robin's generosity wins over to his side, and the sheriff also harasses Marian, a Saxon of

Robin Hood and nineteenth-century fiction

7 Emmett and melodrama: Robin rescues Marian. From George Emmett, *Robin Hood and the Outlaws of Sherwood Forest* (1869), p. 54.

'wondrous loveliness' (p. 63), but Robin, heavily moustached, arrives through the window to rescue her (see Figure 7). The outlaws capture both abbot and the sheriff on their separate attempts to trap Robin and entertain them in the forest, with traces of the 'Bishop of Hereford' ballad, but the sheriff is ransomed, swearing not to harm Robin.

Mortimer is now arrested as being a friend of Robin, who breaks into the castle to rescue him with the help of the daring Madge Stukeley, whom Little John will admire. All this seems like a vivid re-creation of the medieval spirit, but there are lurches away from it: in the dungeon Robin and Mortimer find a spectre who shows

8 Emmett and the young audience: Robin meets the Wood Demon. From George Emmett, *Robin Hood and the Outlaws of Sherwood Forest* (1869), p. 37.

them a skeleton, so they bury it. Before long Robin in the forest will meet a Wood Demon (see Figure 8), who offers him perfect archery in return for his soul: they fight, and in the end Robin's mother's holy ring saves him.

Outlaw coming and going continues, with the friar fighting well and killing a few of the sheriff's men; Robin is caught, tied to a tree and then rescued; he wins the silver arrow at a *Gest*-style archery contest, and they fight their way out of the sheriff's trap, with Marian killing a man about to take Robin's life. They catch the abbot again, and rob him; they celebrate in the forest; they hunt, Marian included.

A variant strand is gentry visitors to the forest: quite early Sir Richard Wykeham, with a friend Maria Danvers, is looking for Robin to help them against the sheriff who has seized his land – they are apparently Saxons – and they remain to enjoy themselves; then the Duchess of Lancaster appears on her way to the king's court with her entourage, including a fool: she shoots with Marian and dances with Robin. From G. P. R. James comes a visit from Princess Eleanor, who in a highly Gothic sequence is threatened by a couple of villains digging up a body. Robin sees through her disguise, knows she is to marry Prince Edward, who 'is not a favourite with the Normans' (p. 238), and escorts her to safety in Leicester.

After this, the action speeds up even more: ballad stories are enacted of the butcher, the tinker, the three foresters and the rescue of three squires. Prince Edward begins to enter the story: the sheriff is afraid he will favour Robin as he 'espouses the cause of the people' (p. 210), and soon the king himself appears in the forest, fights Robin at quarterstaff and behaves rather as in the *Gest*, but then rejoins the sheriff. This may seem odd for the less than military Henry III, but even more bizarrely, Edward's men torture a Jew to death for his money, and the prince will continue this practice. An odd quasi-Masonic moment occurs, when a farmer joins Robin Hood's resistance – they share a secret handshake. Marian is again imprisoned, but escapes by shooting a man with a crossbow. Characters multiply – a Moorish jester who poses as a knight; a new villain called D'Anville, definitely Norman; a mysterious bearward in the forest who is a royal spy; an old wise woman who foresaw Marian's arrest has a vision that Robin is to be poisoned; and a conspiracy develops to do just that by the sheriff, D'Anville and others.

Dark events gather: Robin is alone in 'gloomy abstraction' (p. 392); Much is made an archer in the castle and hears two knights arguing over their determination to 'have' Marian (p. 407), and shoots one. The other, D'Anville, takes her off to Brittany, so Robin becomes a fisherman (the ballad story is located late in the story, as in Egan) and rescues her. The king is very angry, and sends men to the forest. The outlaws are routed but Much burns their base, rescuing Marian and their treasures. Robin is wounded and bled to death at Kirklees. Little John buries him there, and in a strange, almost casual, ending, despairing of seeing Marian again, he simply leaves, 'the last that was seen of the Outlaws of Sherwood Forest' (p. 414).

The ending has the same lack of perspective as the whole fragmentary narrative, which is full of fights, casual killings, sudden actions and lurches in the plot. Some sequences are inconsequential, like the gentry wandering in the forest, Stukeley the chief warder's madness and side-changing, and the disappearance from the action of his brave and attractive daughter. Very little is made of robbing to give to the poor (but as later in

Tennyson local businessmen receive help at times), and though the villains are firmly Norman there is no clear Saxon-based animus against Normans and lords in general – yet Robin is not taken seriously as a nobleman either. The period is observed in general, but nothing historico-political is made of this as was the case in Miller and James. Presumably the *Young Englishman's Journal* connection lies in the lack of marriages and kissing, the occasional supernatural event and the wealth of physical activity, as well as the emphasis on drinking, joking, singing and swearing: Friar Tuck likes to swear 'By the bones of St Hubert' while Little John is free with an enigmatic expression of surprise, 'Wep with a wenion' – the rare colloquial word 'wenion' appears to mean 'vengeance'.

In a more general sense what Emmett shows is that the Robin Hood novel has now seriously joined the lower levels of the publishing mainstream in this casually episodic novel, with simplistic attitudes and garish illustrations – and some notable errors: one of the illustrations shows two young men in nineteenth-century costume, clearly from another of that week's issues; several others have nothing to do with the action of that issue. The text can read weirdly at times – the miller asks Robin 'Hadst thou not better change thy garbage', rather than using the word 'garb' (p. 295). But the novel was evidently popular, being reprinted in the 1880s, and it is a busy, vigorous, if less than sophisticated, account of outlaw events. In fact so much emphasis is laid on the dangers of the castle and the city – and in the final sequence Robin faces danger in London itself – and so much stress falls on the disturbing impact of the lust for money, that the overall meaning could be read as a medievalisation of the dense urban anxieties of the new genre of the mysteries of the cities that was apotheosised in *Dombey and Son* and *Bleak House* and was most fully represented by the work of George Reynolds – and curiously one of the minor outlaws is called 'Reynolds' (p. 175), relating perhaps not so much to Little John's alias in the *Gest* of Reynolde Grenelefe as to the master of the eight-page weekly serial himself.

Long, dense, devoted to shaping a medieval version of Victorian ideologies of masculinity, nobility and above all Englishness – and the things that could confuse or threaten those valued states – the popular mainstream novels by authors like Egan, Stocqueler and Emmett who established Robin Hood so firmly in the thronging double-column style of the popular novel just as firmly relocated the outlaw hero in modern medievalism. He would be reconnected with his origins and his romantic past before he entered the calmer waters of the classic early twentieth-century juvenile novel.

Modern Robin Hood fiction: Pyle to the present

If you buy a modern English-speaking child a book of Robin Hood stories in the bookshop, newsagent or supermarket, it is very likely that the small brightly coloured book will contain a text cut down, legally or not, or derived in some way from Howard Pyle's 1883 edition of *The Merry Adventures of Robin Hood, of Great Renown in Nottinghamshire*.[16] A coherent set of stories more than a novel, but enfolding the values of a generally apolitical historicism, the value of natural surroundings and male high spirits, this is the Robin Hood garland for modern times.

It was very widely read throughout America and elsewhere and effectively became the default Robin Hood for some fifty years, as the outlaw myth became a mainspring of the English heritage myth, a central feature in school education and an important strand in films – the dialogue for the Robin–Little John scene in the 1938 film comes directly from Pyle.

The impact was to a large degree visual. Unlike Arthur and his knights, medieval Robin Hood had not been amply depicted, not being of prime interest in the past to the wealthy or clerical people who employed illuminators, and while the broadsides often carried woodcuts they were both clumsy and static. Scott's royal romanticism did give Maclise a fine subject for his much-reproduced painting of the king in the forest, but the outlaw was too rough-grained to attract the Pre-Raphaelites. Pyle was a young American professional illustrator looking for material, and wrote his own text in which to foreground his black and white full-page etchings of dramatic action, both happy and sad, with elegant borders that varied according to the theme. He was a great admirer of Dürer, and coupled design and drama in these medievalist drawings so well that William Morris himself warmly approved. The original book was quite large and expensive, as the publisher gave it a properly handsome treatment, and Pyle's tradition lived on, being developed by Louis Rhead and Pyle's pupil N. C. Wyeth, who produced fine colour versions of outlaw action, which also had an impact on the 1938 film, newly in Technicolor (Figures 11 and 12).

Pyle's equally remarkable achievement was in creating a text that could live up to his elegantly vigorous illustrations. He had a certain outlook and attitude to guide him: his family were Quakers,

9 Pyle's male action: Little John fights the cook. From Howard Pyle, *The Merry Adventures of Robin Hood* (1883), p. 91.

and he and his mother were great readers, with a notable interest in medievalism.[17] He has a positive idealism about this always 'merry' England 'wherin no chill mists press upon our spirits' as he says in his Preface (p. vi). There is plenty of manly fun and fighting, as when Little John brawls with the cook (see Figure 9), but his Quaker values exclude the sadistic elements that run through some of the novels, and Robin can be pleased to escape at times (see Figure 10). The story does start, garland-like, with the story of young Robin being abused by the foresters, and he does finally kill the worst of them, but 'his heart was sick within him, and it was borne in upon his soul that he had slain a man' (p. 6). Years and chapters later he recalls, 'never do I wish to slay a man again, for it is bitter for the soul to think theron' (p. 47). Pyle is an American, and there is none of the English love of a lord here: this Robin is proud of being a yeoman, and though he is made Earl of Huntington at the end by the king, it seems that this comes from Stephen Percy.

When he was already planning this book, having just arrived in New York in 1876, Pyle wrote asking his mother to send their

10 Pyle's peacefulness: Robin escapes. From Howard Pyle, *The Merry Adventures of Robin Hood* (1883), p. 306.

family 'Percy'. Scholars have thought he meant Thomas Percy's *Reliques*, but that includes only one Robin Hood ballad. As he uses the 'Queen Eleanor' version of 'Robin Hood and Queen Katherine' and the late and seven other ballads in Stephen Percy (as well as three not there), it seems very likely that this was his garland-type source, though it also appears he read Emmett: Little John here swears 'Marry come up with a wanion' (p. 201), and the oppressor of the *Gest* knight is here called the Prior of Emmett, apparently continuing the tendency to name-check an author's source; there is also evidence, discussed below, that Pyle knew Egan's novel.

Also consistent with Pyle's family and context is the firm early statement of Robin's charity: 'country people round about came to jolly Robin in time of need' (p. 3); as the band gathers it agrees to 'despoil their oppressors' and 'help the poor folk' (p. 7). But most of the text is taken up with cheerful outings, striding through forests, fighting lustily with strangers, rescuing fellow-outlaws, celebrating with manly fun and drink. It is a very male environment: Robin does think early on of 'Maid Marian and her bright eyes' (p. 3) but she does not appear. Little John, when disguised as a friar, is admired by several 'lasses', who even drink his ale, but this is a devotedly homosocial world, true in that way to both the original ballads and the gender-separation of contemporary education.

Some have found Pyle's medievalism a little overdone with its insistence on the 'jolly' side of things, its determined antiquity in language like 'quoth' and 'smote' and its naïve yearning for a simpler, better past:

> The good old times have gone by when such men grow as grew then; when sturdy quarterstaff and longbow toughened a man's thews till they were like leather. Around Robin Hood that day there lay the very flower of English yeomanrie. (p. 101)

But the concept, like the phrase 'good old times', is close to that of Peacock and Scott, and Pyle has some at least of their scholarship: the outlaws swear by Anglo-Saxon saints, and his character Gaffer Swanhold, who rules by proverbs, has an almost Peacockian wit. There is also some acuity in plotting: Robin meets here a corn engrosser, a proto-capitalist with money hidden in his shoes, and this is a much more radical encounter than Tennyson offers with the merchants in his almost contemporary play *The Foresters*. The separate ballads are linked together with some skill – he would have found that in Stephen Percy, and like him uses the Bishop of Hereford as a recurring figure: the bishop, conferring with the sheriff, sets Sir Guy onto Robin late in the story, as it darkens towards its end, as happens in Egan.

Sir Guy is only the second man whom Robin kills, his outlawry is so earnest, and Pyle's Quakerism so firm. Unlike Percy, Pyle inserts in the fight with Guy Robin's original appeal to Mary (p. 329) and, here, with Egan the likely source rather than Percy's *Reliques*, Little John shoots the sheriff merely in the bottom. As also in Egan (as well as Stephen Percy) the *Gest* is used to bring the king to the forest, though now, always a social creature, Pyle's Robin goes to court with numbers of his band as in Stephen Percy. The ending is less bleak than usual. With Richard dead King John attacks the forest, and when some of his men die Robin is so upset that he catches a fever. Even the prioress is not really an enemy: she is upset that Robin has surrendered the earldom and is also afraid of King John, so bleeds him to death in fear for herself. Robin is buried by Little John in the usual way, but the last we hear is that the yeoman outlaws scatter and because of 'a more merciful sheriff' they were able to 'abide in peace and quietness' (p. 375), and that they handed down the stories we have been reading, and admiring in visual form.

Imposing in its visual splendour and literary richness, and immensely popular in cheap forms across the world, Pyle's version is the archetype of Robin for the twentieth century – a popular hero, more in nature than in history, English in an unemphasised and less than racist way. Pyle gave style and weight to the transition into juvenile literature that had been going on for some time – just before Emmett's rather ponderous effort in the *Young Englishman's Journal* there appeared in 1865 a *Life and Adventures of Robin Hood* by 'Peter Porrence' (actually Richard Lewis), a short novel for sixpence, and just after Emmett's novel appeared *The Outlaws of Sherwood Forest* by 'Forest Ranger' of 1870, in forty numbers.

There were two more London-published full-length forest novels in nineteenth-century mode. Edward Gilliat, a master at Harrow School, produced *In Lincoln Green: A Merrie Tale of Robin Hood* in 1897, a somewhat wordy mix of ballads and the *Gest* ending, but without Robin Hood's death and with an intermittent presence in the forest by Marian; J. E. Muddock, also a popular crime writer, published in 1892 *Maid Marian and Robin Hood*, a somewhat mechanical and sentimental reprocessing of the materials. As both give some prominence to Marian they will be dealt with more fully in Chapter 7.

By the late nineteenth century Robin Hood publishing was increasingly set into a model that lasted for nearly a century. Pyle epitomised the quality juveniles, which would continue through writers like James Walker McSpadden, Richard Lancelyn Green and Antonia Fraser, and he also had some of the historico-political tradition that would continue through Henry Gilbert's quite radical *Robin Hood and the Men of the Greenwood* (1912), the more conservative Carola Oman in *Robin Hood* (1939) and the decidedly left-wing Geoffrey Trease's *Bows against the Barons* (1934). Those patterns would continue to the present, with variation by feminist writers like Robin McKinley and Theresa Tomlinson and alternative historicist accounts whether romantic-nationalist like those by Parke Godwin and 'Nicholas Chase' or re-formations like Steven Lawhead's melodramatic Wales-based King Raven trilogy, *Hood* (2006), *Scarlet* (2008) and *Tuck* (2009), or Adam Thorpe's 'real Robin Hood' exercise in scholarly irony, *Hodd* (2010).

But Pyle's restitution of the ballad to the mainstream was in its own first years already being supported by reprints of earlier texts, from single ballads to major anthologies like the fifth part of F. J. Child's *English and Scottish Popular Ballads* (which appeared in 1888, the series running from 1882 to 1898), with some half of its entries Robin Hood-related; or Arthur Quiller-Couch's *Robin Hood Ballads*, published by Oxford University Press in 1908 and much of it absorbed in his *Oxford Book of Ballads* (1910), which had a section on 'The Greenwood'. The strong heritage element of that and similar publishing (including work by the late Romantic Georgian poets) was paralleled by the amount, as notable in the USA as in the UK, of material presented specifically for use in schools, plays as often as stories. Only the grim years of war, 1914–18, interrupted that flow of heritage-oriented Robin Hood materials, which served nostalgic adults and developable children, as it has done to the present. Often with fine illustrators like Rhead emphasising masculine melodrama (see Figure 11) or Wyeth

11 Rhead's action: Robin and Little John. From Louis Rhead, *Bold Robin Hood and his Outlaw Band* (New York: Harper, 1912), frontispiece.

12 Wyeth's action: outlaws shooting to rescue Will. From J. Walker McSpadden and Charles Wilson, *Robin Hood and his Merry Outlaws* (London: Associated Newspapers 1921), frontispiece.

dramatising forest action (see Figure 12), this material has linked powerfully with the impact of film. It is only in the last twenty years that there has been some growth in scholarly and critical material which has explored the contexts and the social and even the political meanings of the Robin Hood myth, just as this chapter has tried to disentangle them from among the many currents of entertainment, narrative, thought or simply feeling that were evident in the richness, and sometimes the poverty, of the Robin Hood novel in the nineteenth century.

Notes

1. Anon., *Robin Hood: A Tale of the Olden Time*, 2 vols (Edinburgh: Oliver and Boyd, 1819).
2. See 'List of Publications March to July 1819', *Edinburgh Review*, 32 (1819–20): 257.
3. Edgar Johnson, *Sir Walter Scott: The Great Unknown*, 2 vols (London: Hamish Hamilton, 1970), vol. 1, p. 680.
4. Walter Scott (originally 'The Author of Waverley'), *Ivanhoe: A Romance*, 3 vols (Edinburgh: Constable, 1820).
5. James Chandler, *England in 1819* (Chicago: University of Chicago Press, 1998), pp. 127–8.
6. On its vigour in the 1790s see Donna T. Andrew, *London Debating Societies, 1776–99*, www.british-history.ac.uk/report.aspx?pubid=238 (accessed 10 April 2013).
7. Thomas Miller, *Royston Gower, or The Days of King John: An Historical Romance*, 3 vols (London: Colburn, 1838).
8. G. P. R. James, *Forest Days: A Romance of Old Times*, 3 vols (London: Saunders and Otley, 1843).
9. John Mathew Gutch (ed.), *A Lytell Geste of Robin Hode, with Other Ancient & Modern Ballads and Songs Relating to this Celebrated Yeoman*, 2 vols (London: Longman, 1847), vol. 1, p. xxii.
10. Stephen Percy, *Robin Hood and his Merry Foresters* (London: Tilt and Bogue, 1841).
11. Pierce Egan the Younger, *Robin Hood and Little John: or, The Merry Men of Sherwood Forest* (London: Forster and Hextall, 1840).
12. J. W. Ebsworth, revised Megan A. Stephan, 'Egan, Pierce Junior (1814–80)', *Oxford Dictionary of National Biography* (Oxford: Oxford University Press, 2004), www.oxforddnb.com/view/article/8578 (accessed 10 April 2013).
13. J. H. Stocqueler, *Maid Marian, the Forest Queen, being a Companion to 'Robin Hood'* (London: Peirce, 1849).
14. See Gutch (ed.), *A Lytell Geste*, vol. 1, p. 47.
15. George Emmett, *Robin Hood and the Outlaws of Sherwood Forest* (London: Temple, 1869).
16. Howard Pyle, *The Merry Adventures of Robin Hood, of Great Renown in Nottinghamshire* (New York: Scribners, 1883).
17. See Stephen Knight, 'Afterword', in Howard Pyle, *The Merry Adventures of Robin Hood* (New York: Signet, 2006), pp. 377–88.

7
The making and re-making of Maid Marian

Robin and sometimes Marian

Pairs of lovers' names have had different fortunes. There is no Romeo without Juliet, and for most people the same is true of Tristan and Isolde, though the medieval prose romances can, as with Malory, ramble for many pages through the solitary endeavours of the powerful knight from Cornwall. For most modern cultural consumers Robin and Marian are a matched pair, though only rarely as tragedy-oriented as other amorous combinations. But a visit to the medieval and early modern world of the outlaw ballads will offer very little sight of the lady, and there are other elements of the early outlaw tradition where Marian does not appear, such as the play-games found mostly in the south-west of England and the brief references and proverbs about the hero, where he is just a name attached to some usually mysterious manliness.

In addition to her recurrent and genre-related absences, Marian is also unlike her partner in that through her intermittent appearances the meaning given, whether social or personal, to her identity and actions does not have the same kind of consistent core that belongs to Robin. He is always in some way anti-authority; her role and meaning have no such constant vanishing-point. A naïve response might be that she changes as an expression of his variety, whether, for example, he represents a noble lord or a Victorian national hero, but that hardly explains how Marian can become for the Romantics, early and late, an image of ennobling desirability or in a modern feminist context the opposite, a model of competence and even dominance. Marian is, it appears, primarily invoked by the gender-related concerns of the social environment in which she appears: she does not resist authority so much as represent a changing alternative to it.

The history of Marian in the Robin Hood tradition is both the history of form, seen through generic change, and also the history of content embodied in a range of ideological meanings, elisions and illusions from early medieval French song to twenty-first-century media. Along the way there are many variations and applications of beauty and braveness, vulnerability and virtuosity – and also the eerily recurrent shadow of the 'False Marian' to realise the negative pressure of the gender-oriented forces to which this volatile heroine vigorously responds.

Pastourelle Marian and *bergerie* Robin

To read widely in early French poetry is soon enough to discover the name of Marian, often spelt Marion and found in diminutive form as Marot, even Mariet, for an attractive young peasant in the lyrical narrative known as *pastourelle*: she is usually a *pastoure*, a shepherdess. When she has a recognised partner, other than the knights, clerks and wandering riff-raff who are keen to engage with her, he is called Robin. These songs, found across France, were gathered and elaborated in a full-length semi-opera by Adam de la Halle, using traditional themes and tunes, named *Robin et Marion* (c.1283).

But the apparent fit of the names and period does not mesh easily with the English tradition. This Robin is not an outlaw, though he may help resist the wandering gentry who make advances to Marian, and there is no surname like Hood, though he may be Robin des Bois, as is still common in France. He is a working peasant, usually a shepherd, perhaps a ploughman: he has a number of friends, and they are given to simple celebrations. French scholars tend to sort the poems into two groups. The *pastourelle* proper is where Marian meets an intruder who shows some form of sexual interest and Robin may – or more usually may not – be involved in responding to this incursion; the *bergerie* focuses on rural social activity and celebration, where Robin plays a significant role and Marian is often not present. Scholars suggest that *pastourelle* and *bergerie* are not separate genres, but focus on different aspects of the fiction of peasant pastoral, the sexualised *pastourelle* and the communal *bergerie*: Adam de la Halle represents both in *Robin et Marion*.

However, neither form is simple or repetitive. In the *pastourelle* a knight or similar insurgent offers Marian/Marot his attentions, but with widely varying outcomes. Sometimes the knight just rapes Marian and she ruefully accepts the situation. In reverse, sometimes she simply accepts the knight as better than Robin, and may give Robin a brisk account of the new situation. Occasionally she firmly rejects the knight in favour of Robin, and sometimes Robin chases him away with varying degrees of violence – though his more common kind of rescue is saving her sheep from a wolf. Once Robin and two shepherd friends defend her against a knight, and once Robin, here called son of Foudrier, beats off the knight with an apple-club and the support of a crowd. The range of outcomes and apparent messages is very varied, much as there are quite extreme variations in the direction and residual meaning of the parallel urban form with a non-gentry focus, *fabliaux*.[1]

In the *bergerie* songs Robin is consistently associated with the forest – so Robin des Bois – and on occasions he is linked to the hazel-tree and the willow.[2] There are some connections with the later English outlaw. He can wear a green hat and usually has a company of friends and relatives for security and celebration. He is on foot – his only horse will pull a plough. Mostly this Robin celebrates in *bergerie* revels with his friends and cousins: they include Gautier the Hothead, who is very strong but less than subtle (his idea of cultural fun is a farting competition) and seems an avatar of Little John. There are other friends, including young women, as well as Marian – and even on a few occasions a rival called Guiot, conceivably the origin of Sir Guy. Robin and his friends act out the patterns of *bergerie* – games, dances and songs relating to early and simple sub-aristocratic and non-moral pastoral, though there can also be quite strong class-based satirical elements. Their activities often end with a dance or a feast, or both.

The *bergerie* events sound much like what can be deduced of the practices of the Robin Hood play-games, a connection made by E. K. Chambers.[3] Mostly in the English south-west, a village or small town would, at Whitsun time, early to late May, hold processions focused on Robin Hood, often from the forest to the social centre, where Robin would preside over games and sports, and then a feast, frequently called a Robin Hood ale. Robin's supporters would collect money for village facilities like roads and bridges, and occasionally church buildings. In general Robin of the play-games is a positive communal focus for the celebration of the coming summer.

While it seems improbable that the party who travelled with Robin Hood into the social centre, who danced with him and feasted with him, did not include women, there are in the records very few signs of female presence. Kingston in 1509–10 has the earliest reference to Marian – but there are not many after that in the play-games.[4] It would seem that as the play-game appears close to the *bergerie*, not the *pastourelle*, there is no sub-generic requirement here for Marian's presence, and there is certainly no sign in the play-game records of any intrusive knight – even the sheriff only appears once, at Yeovil in 1572–73,[5] and as he is being bought a green silk ribbon like Robin and John, he is presumably a benign presence. In the play-games it is the seasonal and natural celebration that is central, being focused on a Robin linked to the woods in the early summer context of May. The threat of external authority, masculine or social, is not relevant, so the *pastourelle* characters and events, including Marian, remain off stage.

But just as the *pastourelle* story could have surprising outcomes, the topic of Marian and the play-games can develop strange connections. When her name appears in popular records it usually relates to a Morris dancer, partnered by a friar, but even this is recorded late, though as Forrest notes, as early as the Kingston records Robin and the friar and Marian seem to be involved in parallel activities: he also points out that by the late sixteenth century Marian in the Morris is expected to be played by a man.[6] Equally far from the traditional Maid Marian is the figure who appears in the short play appended by the printer William Copland to *The Gest of Robin Hood* in c.1560. The friar is, by way of introduction to the band, presented with a woman: he is very pleased, and dismisses the outlaws so that he and the girl can have fun, declaiming:

> 'Here is a huckle duckle an inch above the buckle.
> She is a trull of trust to serve a friar at his lust,
> A prycker, a prancer, a tearer of sheets,
> A wagger of ballockes when other men sleeps.
> Go home ye knaves and lay crabs in the fire
> For my lady and I will dance in the mire.'[7]

This is comic popular, even vulgar, theatre – a 'huckle-duckle' is an artificial phallus, which the friar no doubt dramatically reveals as preliminary to his appreciation of the wench. Some commentators have called her Marian, but only in rare and late Morris dances is there a Marian in a mode anything like this. Such an exotic figure cannot be linked in any functional or authentic way to the play-games, which are an area of significant absence for Marian as a figure of social and personal meaning, and as such they are like the best-evidenced early Robin Hood material, the yeoman ballads.

Absent outlaw, fifteenth to sixteenth centuries

The absence of Marian continues as the English outlaw tradition is formed and Robin is hostile to authority, as shown in early references and ballads. It remains a matter for debate whether this change of Robin's stance relates to more violent practices of social interaction in Britain than in France (though this is not found in the play-games) or, more probably, to the dark impact of the pressures of the fourteenth century, developing through bad weather, plague and war and generating major social changes involving liberated serfs, growing towns and mercantilism, and including the imagining of liberty for ordinary men and yeomen.

There were plenty of actual outlaws in medieval England, normally declared as such by the law, which made them subject to casual litigious brutality: the idea of choosing outlawry as Robin Hood appeared to have done was in itself a boldly imaginative image of freedom. In reality, men tended to be outlaws in summer, and in small groups, often with relatives and friends, and they did not take their womenfolk to the wilds with them. The image of Robin in the summer forest with a few trusty friends is a cultural re-imagination of the reality of outlawry, and there is no place for a female partner. It might seem no accident that Robin's only loyalty across gender is to the Virgin Mary and that there is a revealing touch in his story to the king at the end of the *Gest* in which he has created a chapel in the forest to St Mary Magdalene, who might perhaps be called the good outlaw of the New Testament. It is possible to read either of these religious Marys as a stand-in for Marian, bringing limited aspects of the female into the forest story, but they do not of course survive the Reformation.

The lack of Marian or other woman as a character in the classic ballads is a specific response to a real situation. Even when in the seventeenth-century broadsides the tradition develops rapidly, and there are clearly many new, often pot-boiling, authors involved in their creation, women play very limited roles: the queen favours Robin from some distance in 'Robin Hood and Queen Katherine', and two peasants are briefly involved, a mother pleased by a gallows rescue in 'Robin Hood Rescuing Three Young Men' and a wry crone who is arrested after exchanging clothes with Robin in 'Robin Hood and the Bishop'. Two women have full roles in the broadside ballads: a bizarre deutero-partner for Robin appears in 'Robin Hood's Birth, Breeding, Valour and Marriage', where he becomes the partner (and husband) of Clorinda, Queen of the

Shepherds (a downmarket version of the fairy-mistress romance), and there is just the one appearance by Marian herself in 'Robin Hood and Maid Marian', which has survived in only one text and needs to be discussed in the context of the sub-genre of gentrification from which in this form she derives.

Lady Marian, sixteeenth century onwards

Marian's return to Robin and her arrival at the centre of the English outlaw tradition occur in the context of the development usually called gentrification. In the sixteenth century there were many moves towards controlling what seemed disorderly elements of the past, from burning witches to enclosing common land, and in this spirit Robin Hood was reconceived and the anti-authority yeoman of the early ballads became an earl who rebelled against bad Prince John and was reinstated by good King Richard. Suddenly the outlaw's vigour becomes substantial support for hierarchy and the newly reformed church.

The yeoman social bandit did not disappear: he was still celebrated in ballads through to the eighteenth century and remembered after that, but there were now two social layers of the outlaw myth – and basically there still are, between the liberal Lord of Locksley as seen in the form of Kevin Costner in the 1991 film *Robin Hood: Prince of Thieves*, and the peasant rebel like Michael Praed as the star of the 1980s British television series *Robin of Sherwood* (in the USA simply *Robin Hood*). When he is made a lord, with a land, Robin, or now Robert, from the sixteenth century on has a lady. Her forest name is Marian, as his is Robin, and in her first appearance of any substance her name is that of a true-blue Norman aristocrat: like Henry II's mother, she is Matilda, and she appears in the ground-breaking double play by Anthony Munday, *The Downfall* and *The Death of Robert, Earle of Huntington* of 1598–99. Matilda/Marian is Robin's faithful aristocratic lady, lusted after by Prince John, and before her forest exile is known as Lady Matilda Fitzwater, as derived from Michael Drayton's 1594 poem *Matilda the Fair and Chaste Daughter of Baron Fitzwater*.

Munday's Marian does not influence successive stories much: in this version she survives Robin's death very early in the second play and is pursued by Prince John to her own tragic fate. Marian as martyr did not catch on (though there will be examples in nineteenth-century fiction, deriving from the summary of the plays in Ritson's Introduction to his 1795 ballad collection), but Munday introduced a very striking motif which has seemed almost compulsive for authors who give Marian a substantial role. This is the false Marian, a witch-like betrayer of Robin.

In Munday's *Downfall* Queen Eleanor, mother to King Richard and Prince John, lusts after Robin as much as John does after Marian, and early on, as Robin and Marian flee, she persuades her to change clothes – ostensibly for Marian's safety, but in fact because the queen desires him. This feature will recur: it seems that the more sexually aware and active is the love of Robin and Marian, the more likely there is to be a malign double for her. The false Marian motif appears to relate to the masculinist anxiety that woman can be delusive and dangerous as well as – or instead of – being passive and supportive. This keeps going through the tradition, right on to the 1991 film with Uma Thurman as Marian, where the sheriff's mistress is her malign double.

Munday's Marian is first seen in a thoroughly controlled light: the dumb show that opens the play speaks of Robin and Marian as 'This youth that leads yon virgin by the hand'.[8] She is re-invented to bear the role of titled lady, little more than a cipher in a world of male property: she takes to the woods, but does nothing there. Robin does apostrophise her, but only as a distant pastoral lover, with none of the direct desire or physicality of the *pastourelle*. The emphasis of the text asserts in fully pastoral mode that the forest is a natural and free version of the court, and any mention of Marian's beauty is as an aspect of the beauty of the forest, to be loved in entirely reified form. Robin's finest poetry is addressed around rather than towards her:

> For Arras hangings and rich Tapestrie
> We have sweet natures best imbrothery.
> For thy steele glass, wherin thou wontst to looke,
> Thy Christall eyes, gaze in a Christall brooke.
> At court, a flower or two did decke thy head;
> Now with whole garlands is it circled.
> For what in wealth we had, we have in flowers,
> And what wee loose in halls, we finde in bowers.
>
> (lines 1374–81)

Marian continues to play an entirely secondary role as she mourns Robin, and is then pursued by John through most of the second play: she is here as secondary as she is in comic mode in the Admiral's Men's multi-authored follow-up *Looke About You* of 1600, where her strongest impact is when Robin borrows her nightgown and turban to appear in very bizarre disguise, and as a result is wooed by King Richard as a distinctly comic, if perhaps homoerotic, false Marian.

But woman and forest could have a quite different and much less passive association, more actively classical. The image of a Diana-like huntress was another direction for the notion of a lady of the forest, and Michael Drayton, in his 1622 version of *Poly-Olbion*, in the Sherwood section, represented her as Robin's partner:

> his mistris deare, his loved Marian
> Was ever constant knowne, which whersoere shee came
> Was soveraigne of the Woods, chief Lady of the Game:
> Her Clothes tuck'd to the knee, and daintie braided haire
> With Bow and Quiver arm'd, shee wandr'd here and there
> Amongst the forests wild; Diana never knew
> Such pleasures, nor such Harts as Mariana slew.[9]

The mix of local figure and classical huntress would go further when Ben Jonson developed *The Sad Shepherd*, published in 1641: this was unfinished, most commentators feel because of Jonson's death in 1637, though he seems to have been interested in the topic and the region well before that.[10] His Marian is more than a mere possession as in Munday or a sportswoman as in Drayton. She is for once fully a lover, and Jonson pursues the classical idea of the bow and arrow as an amatorial image. As Marian returns from hunting, the forest lovers meet and exchange enthusiasm, affection and what seems like an off-colour joke about the part of the deer called 'the inch-pin':

> MARIAN: How hath this morning paid me, for my rising!
> First, with my sports; but most with meeting you!
> I did not half so well reward my hounds,
> As she hath me today: although I gave them
> All the sweet morsels, Calle, Tongue, Eares and Dowcets!
> ROBIN: What? And the inch-pin?
> MARIAN: Yes.
> ROBIN: Your sports then pleas'd you?
> MARIAN: You are a wanton.
> ROBIN: One, I do confesse,
> I wanted till you came. But now I have you,
> I'll grow to your embraces, till two soules
> Distilled into kisses, thorough your lips
> Do make one spirit of love.
> MARIAN: O Robin! Robin! [11]

The making and re-making of Maid Marian

In spite of this frank affection – or perhaps because of it? – Jonson strongly develops the false Marian motif with a wicked witch called Maudlin: she is sometimes called Maud, which, interestingly, and probably not accidentally, is the short form of Matilda, so suggesting a black/white splitting in the figure of the outlaw heroine. Maud impersonates Marian with some success, not in this case seeking personal pleasure like the queen in Munday, but suggesting that Marian is a whimsical and cruel cause of trouble: as this negative stereotype of woman, the false Marian is both elusive and aggressive, and as a result manages to confuse and alarm Robin. These problems and other complications were to be reconciled by the end, according to Jonson's surviving act synopses.

The vigorous real Marian does ultimately defer to Robin's authority, both aristocratic and male, but she is also represented as having real agency, including physical and gendered power. This is Jonson's imagination at work, not a new generic formation: in gentrification Lady Marian's potential power will be largely deferred, and the special nature of the semi-classical heroine produced by Drayton and Jonson is indicated when contrasted with the version of Munday's creation which is found among the broadside ballads of the seventeenth century onwards.

This very popular Robin Hood genre basically deploys the woman-free world of the yeoman outlaw, though as has been argued in Chapter 4 some elements of gentrification in the broadside ballads do approach the forest figure, and there are occasional instances of women figures. But only one broadside survives with a gentrified context and a full appearance from Marian – and this is never fitted into the routinised model of the garland collections.

'Robin Hood and Maid Marian' appears to be a version of 'Robin Hood and Will Scarlett' with Marian playing the Will role: in both cases a person enters the forest looking for Robin and fights lustily with him; they call off the fight, and become close. This is here re-gendered and to a degree up-classed – Robin is an earl, though the Will Scarlett story does have some elements of gentrification as Robin's cousin Will is himself of minor gentry origin. But 'Robin Hood and Maid Marian' starts with full gentrification. In love with the outlawed Earl Robin, Marian follows him into the greenwood dressed as a man and well armed:

> With quiver and bow, sword buckler and all,
> Thus armed was Marian most bold,

Still wandering about to find Robin out
Whose person was better than gold.

But Robin Hood hee himself had disguisd,
And Marian was strangely attir'd,
That they provd foes, and so fell to blowes,
Whose vallour bold Robin admir'd.

They drew out their swords, and to cutting they went,
At least an hour or more,
That the blood ran apace from bold Robins face,
And Marian was wounded sore.

'Oh hold thy hand, hold thy hand,' said Robin Hood,
'And thou shalt be one of my string,
To range in the wood with bold Robin Hood,
And hear the sweet nightingall sing.'

When Marian did hear the voice of her love,
Her self shee did quickly discover,
And with kisses sweet she did him greet,
Like to a most loyal lover.[12]

They end up agreeing affectionately, but the all-male forest-based yeoman ballad asserts its structure at the end. Marian finally fits into the normal homosocial world of the forest as Robin includes his lady, in Will Scarlett's usual role, when, after celebrating, the yeomen stroll together in the forest, and here Robin:

> went to walk in the wood,
> Where Little John and Maid Marian
> Attended on Robin Hood.
>
> (lines 79–81)

There is further integration with the yeoman tradition. This is a very rare gentrified text where Lord Robin and Lady Marian do not return to their social world of wealth and position: the ballad ends:

> In solid content together they livd,
> With all their yeomen gay;
> They livd by their hands, without any lands,
> And so did many a day.
>
> (lines 82–5)

Gentrification is enormously influential on the social conception of Robin Hood, if not on the actual content of the stories – it is only rare and usually dissenting later instances that insist on his yeoman or, rarely, peasant origin: the default Robin is some form of gentleman, often with some element of place-name like Locksley or Huntington to suggest his connection to property. Yet gentrification is also a weak force in terms of narrative: it is the idea of nobility that is disseminated, not any specific narrative incidents. Munday and indeed Jonson transmit no story-elements to the tradition. When the genre remains theatre, Marian is a figure of much reduced importance as the impact of gentrification is itself reduced, in part through the popular nature of the stage and its audience, but also because as soon becomes clear, in eighteenth-century outlaw musical theatre a variety of forces interact, with little sign of coherence or consistency, particularly with regard to the figure of Marian.

Stage partner, eighteenth century

The Marian who appears occasionally in eighteenth-century ballad opera is not the belligerent Rosalind avatar that the yeoman ballad briefly admits. When in 1730 *Robin Hood: An Opera*, using old ballad tunes and new text, was performed the plot was elaborated with elements of gentrification but also theatre routines, including male rivalry. Matilda is the sister of a King Edward, who is unnumbered, as he is in the *Gest*, and while she is devoted to the Earl of Huntingdon there is, for theatrical purposes, a rival, the wicked Earl of Pembroke.

Lord Robin will eventually kill him and finally sing with his own beloved, and there is also a characteristic theatrical doubling of this plot – you need a contralto and a bass to match the leading couple of soprano and tenor. Matilda has a friend Marina (perhaps generated by anagram) who loves Huntington's lordly friend Darnel, who will in the forest play Little John. A darker side of gendered theatre also appears: Will Stutely, an outlaw associated with displaced Lord Robin, at one stage seizes both Marina and Matilda and feels he has the right to rape them: 'You are my prisoners by the right of Armes, and I must make bold to try my Manhood upon you.' The foresters themselves think this is a good idea and feel the women could be 'shar'd in Common'.[13] Robin soon puts a stop to this – perhaps the sequence is a comment on the uncontrolled privilege of aristocratic entourages, but it may also be a relatively recent brutish contemporary response to the presence of women on the stage.

Later theatrical versions are unusual in a more acceptable way. In 1751 the Drury Lane Theatre produced *Robin Hood: A New*

Musical Entertainment, which develops the ballad 'Robin Hood and Allen a Dale', with updated characters: the heroine Clarinda may in name come from 'Robin Hood's Birth' but her father 'Graspall' is from modern satire, as is the wealthy man-about-town Glitter, whom he wants her to marry. Robin himself masquerades up-to-date as Sir Humphrey Wealthy, to bring about the desired match and a musical 'come all ye' ending.

In the fuller 1784 comic opera *Robin Hood, or Sherwood Forest* there is a good deal more amatory activity, with Allen and Scarlet partnering Margaret and Stella, and a new melodramatic love-pair, Edwin and Angelina. Robin joins in, but here too Clorinda is his lady, and their relationship is as much national as personal: their final appearance is with the words:

> Strains of liberty we sing
> To our country, queen and king.[14]

Later in the century Marian returns, if only as a minor figure, in the major 1795 success of *Merry Sherwood or Harlequin Forrester*, with some reliance on the yeoman ballads, now again known through the anthologies of both Evans in 1777 and also Ritson's new one of 1795. Overall, as is common in eighteenth-century Robin Hood theatre, Marian plays an almost invisible role. That is also largely true of Ritson's long Introduction, where she is mentioned once in passing in connection to Morris dancing, and then in connection with the two Munday plays as 'an important character',[15] but she is quoted only when she mourns Robin's death. Ritson makes no mention of Drayton's play and poem or Jonson's masque with their vigorous representations of Marian. In general the eighteenth century did not find Marian an inspiring figure, largely because she was the product of gentrification and this had very limited impact. New concepts, especially relating to the role of women, will give Marian renewed power.

Novel heroine, nineteenth century

This reticence about Marian will change as the outlaw tradition enters the genre which played such a large part in realising women's roles, both as characters and as authors – the novel. The key treatment of nineteenth-century Marian, which survives to the present, is as the noble but vulnerable woman, that prime way of both enhancing and validating the status of her male consort. As has been argued in Chapter 6, a range of themes appear in the outlaw novel, notably national history and a validation of forms of liberal resistance to undue authority, usually royal or aristocratic. But there is also the physical realisation of hero and heroine and some representation of their emotional links, which usually falls short of any seriously sensual interchange – Ben Jonson's pair of lovers equal in activity and passion is quite forgotten, or effectively censored.

Before the novel begins its work some aspects of both feeling and physicality for Robin and Marian are evoked through Romanticism in the poetic exchange between Reynolds and Keats on Robin Hood, discussed in Chapter 5. The first sonnet Reynolds sent, while offering Romantic medievalism in reflecting on 'the sweet days of Robin Hood', is almost entirely masculine, focusing on 'archer-men in green' until the final word, where 'Marian' seems an afterthought to produce a slightly forced rhyme:

> Feasting on pheasant, river fowl and swan,
> With Robin at their head, and Marian.[16]

In terms of attention at least, the second sonnet makes up for this, moving in the second quartet on to the lady:

> and near, with eyes of blue
> Shining through dusk hair, like the stars of night,
> And habited in pretty forest plight,
> His green-wood beauty sits, young as the dew.
> Oh, gentle-tressed girl! Maid Marian!
> Are thine eyes bent upon the gallant game
> That stray in the merry Sherwood: thy sweet fame
> Can never, never die.
>
> (p. 15)

The physicality of Romanticism, as well as its sexist use of woman as an object to admire, is evident. Not even Munday's containment of Marian was as passive or the gaze of the poetry as consuming as this: her 'sweet fame' is a merely girlish honour, and it is only Robin, the 'high man', whom 'we' are invited to 'pledge' in the final lines.

However, in his poem in response to Reynolds's two sonnets, Keats does involve Marian in a form of action and even imagines that she might have a voice. Just as Robin will regret what has happened under mercantile imperialism to his beloved oaks, so she will have a sharp political response to a bleak feature of the present world:

> And if Marian should have
> Once again her forest days
> ...
> She would weep that her wild bees
> Sang not to her – strange! that honey
> Can't be got without hard money!¹⁷

Keats also, in his farewell, pays equal respect to both characters:

> Honour to bold Robin Hood,
> Sleeping in the underwood!
> Honour to maid Marian,
> And to all the Sherwood-clan!
>
> (lines 57–60)

However much Reynolds learned from Keats's responses in his final sonnet, it was not related to Marian or gender. She is quite absent from his third sonnet, and the only feminine reference is a socially lower and even more belittling piece of observation than she was accorded in the second sonnet: the fifth line (where Marian was introduced in the second sonnet) merely includes a reference to the impact of Robin Hood as 'A dazed smile on cheek of border lass'.

If Reynolds seems struck to silence by Keats's notion of a heroine with some agency, Leigh Hunt's treatment is more understandably completely without Marian. His four ballads focus on reworking the politically oriented ballad yeoman, and so she is absent, though she does have a presence in the post-1855 revision, which inserts into the final ballad 'How Robin Hood and his Outlaws Lived in the Woods' two stanzas about Marian, who with Robin 'reign'd as pleasant to all, As faithful to each other.'¹⁸ This sounds like the 'Marian as queen of the forest' idea which had by then arisen in several novels, notably Stocqueler's of 1849, but was also, a more likely source for Hunt, in Peacock's 1822 *Maid Marian*. Through this late addition Hunt can be acknowledged as having some limited recognition of the role of Robin's partner in life, but only Keats has imagined this in any detail.

The existence of such a figure is recognised, but not as Marian, in the first but little-known Robin Hood novel, *Robin Hood: A Tale of the Olden Time* of 1819, appearing just as Scott was working on *Ivanhoe*. The heroine is Ruthinglenne: she loves Robin, goes to the forest to meet him, has difficulties, is brave, does her best to help him in his own problems and is finally reunited with him and will share the recognition of his social status. It is like a parallel, or even parody, of the Marian story found in Munday, but the name Marian is never used and the whole story is made much more Gothic by her having to hide in a nunnery and marrying Robin while pretending to be her twin sister – who herself is folded into the traditional story by being married to the relative who has seized Robin's lands.

Two major writers produced Robin Hood novels just after the Gothic one: Peacock was at work in autumn 1818, but did not finish and publish until early 1822. Scott's *Ivanhoe*, out for Christmas 1819, represented one Marian option in the outlaw tradition by not mentioning her at all. His tough yeoman Locksley has, ballad-style, no lady, though in compensation Ivanhoe, clearly a version of the gentrified outlaw, has two, both a respectable Saxon wife-to-be Rowena and an exciting Jewish lady-friend Rebecca. Peacock offers a lively version of the Munday tradition, condensing it through his characteristic elegant pithiness with a range of ballad stories. Peacock's version went immediately onto the stage in the hands of J. R. Planché, and played all through the century – the scholar George Saintsbury vividly remembered seeing it in c.1880.[19] Here Marian did take to the stage fully, and she would appear regularly in the pantomimes and grandiose operettas that flourished through the century.

Peacock's version has in general become either directly or indirectly the default Marian, and yet did not totally influence the novels to come. His heroine is capable of vigorous action and strong values, but is also foreclosed by the masculine world. She does have point of view, but Robin comes to control it; she can shoot, and fight, but she needs rescuing in a crisis; she is lovely and vital, and an object of desire for Prince John's follower Sir Ralph Montfaucon, a good fighter and quite noble kind of man.

Montfaucon's rivalry with Robin initiates a new context for Marian, one briefly raised but then dropped in the 1730 musical play, which invites analysis in terms of Eve Kosofsky Sedgwick's ground-breaking book *Between Men*. Noting that around the start of the nineteenth century literature embraces a new fable, the rivalry of two men for a woman, she argues that this is actually a coded way of realising homoerotic attraction between two men, merely mediated by a woman.[20] She makes her case well from the texts she discusses, but had she looked at the Robin Hood material, from Peacock through to modern films, she would have been delighted by the evidence available, such as the moment in the fight between Errol Flynn and Basil Rathbone in the 1938 film when, at the climax of their combat, they almost kiss.

Marian is in this way made both a subject in her own right and the potential object of a foregrounded, and complex, male desire, and in the same way Peacock's prose both privileges and gazes at its heroine:

> Matilda, not dreaming of visitors, tripped into the apartment in a dress of forest green, with a small quiver by her side and a bow and arrow in her hand. Her hair, black and glossy as is the raven's wing, curled like wandering clusters of dark ripe grapes under the edge of her round bonnet; and a plume of black feathers fell back negligently above it, with an almost horizontal inclination, that seemed the habitual effect of rapid motion against the wind.[21]

This is the first work in the Robin Hood tradition where Marian is given the title.[22] That might in part be a response to the 1819 Robin Hood title, and commercially oriented versions of such variation would appear, but Peacock, an admirer of Mary Wollstonecraft and her daughter Mary Shelley, has the proto-feminist standing and also the strength of attention devoted to Marian through the novel to justify her providing the title. She is witty, active, brave, charming and beautiful, and the text seems to read her in something like that order. As noted above, it is easy to think that Peacock was in some degree modelling her on the highly dynamic Mary Shelley, whom he had seen a good deal in the year before starting the novel.

In the early action Marian, as Matilda, dominates, resisting her father with spirit and wit, and Sir Ralph falls in love with her. Brother Michael says she has 'beauty, grace, wit, sense, discretion, dexterity, learning and valour' (p. 14); he admires her deeply, but not improperly: he admires Robin nearly as much. For a while Matilda remains trapped at home and is pestered by Prince John, who besieges Arlingford to take her. The baron, a sort of Tory radical, burns his castle so that John cannot use it, and Matilda, renamed by Brother Michael as Marian, escapes to the forest and accepts the post of queen. The forest is not only a space of liberty: hero and heroine are imagined in positive natural terms. Brother Michael sings of them being 'like twin plants of the forest and are identified with its growth' (p. 34). She and Robin marry, but under the forest code of behaviour she will remain a maid. She helps and supports people (the probable source for the late Leigh Hunt insertion about her), but she can be active too. When she and Robin, and her father the baron, are attacked in a hut by the sheriff's men, as they prepare for battle man and woman are equal:

'Robin and Marian each held a bow with the arrow drawn to its head and pointed in the same direction' (p. 206). They shoot and then fight with swords, against odds, and the man turns out somewhat stronger:

> Robin now turned to the aid of Marian who was parrying most dexterously the cuts and slashes of her two assailants, of whom Robin delivered her from one, while a well-applied blow of her sword struck off the helmet of the other, who fell on his knees to beg a boon, and she recognised Sir Ralph Montfaucon. (p. 210)

As in Munday, who provides the under-text of this whole story, King Richard returns and reinstates them as earl and lady, but to accommodate the myth of bad Prince John, even more important to English liberalism than to the Robin Hood tradition, Richard dies, Prince John resumes hostilities, and they return 'to their greenwood sovereignty' (p. 261). In its final words the novel comments that 'in merry Sherwood they long lived together, the lady still retaining her former name of Maid Marian, though the appellation was then as much a misnomer as that of Little John' (p. 262).

Peacock presumably wanted to end by privileging his bold new title, though his apparently irresistible habit of second thoughts and undercurrents of irony emerges in the final comment on her name. Though he has established Marian as a figure of real power in the tradition, which will in general persevere, and she as much as Robin is the recipient of the force that derives from Peacock's brilliant condensing of the authority of gentrification and the activity of the yeoman tradition, there remains a whisper of masculinism in the final comment, even perhaps a slight trace of suggesting she might be a duplicitous, if not quite false, Marian.

The potent model that Peacock offered was not automatically adopted by novelists who took up the story. The earliest have no place for Marian as Robin's consort but realise different political interests in primarily historical novels. In 1838 Thomas Miller, a basket-weaver and Chartist, produced *Royston Gower*, speaking up for Anglo-Saxon liberties, which are represented by Robin and his outlaw but also by characters like the half-Saxon half-Norman beauty Edith who loves Henry of Gloomglendell, son of a fully Saxon earl, who is being sidelined by the intrusive Norman baron Geoffrey de Marchmont, with the help of Prince John. Family, gender and race are interwoven, as is reform: the title goes to a Saxon soldier who, like some others in the story, steadily recognises he should stop serving his inauthentic masters and stand up for both native freedoms and the rights of the ordinary people.

A parallel lack of Marian and somewhat off-stage presence of Robin mark G. P. R. James's more conservative, though still essentially liberal, historicism in *Forest Days* (1843) – days which Keats gave to Marian as moral custodian: here she is missing and the forest itself is not emphasised. James tells a story of aristocratic virtue, with one easily swayed and ultimately regretful noble semi-villain, and privileging the love between Hugh, nephew of the Earl of Morthermer (and in spite of his name, a noble-souled Saxon), and Lucy, daughter to the equally noble Earl of Ashby. The story is set in the thirteenth-century period of Simon de Montfort, who, through his hostility to Henry III, was seen by liberals as a hero of very early parliamentary-style reform. This highly improbable proto-democrat dies early in the novel at the battle of Evesham, where Robin and his men fight bravely, and the rest of the story simply works out an aristocratic family drama with nationalist and broadly liberal political implications, both some way downhill from Scott. Robin remains mostly a useful assistant to the plot, notably in the final scene when with an arrow from a distance he personally takes vengeance on the bad lord, who is about to be set free by the vacillating Prince of Wales, not yet become Edward I.

Just as Miller and James displace the Peacock-renovated Robin and Marian outlaw romance into different characters of more immediate political appeal, so 'Stephen Percy' in his 1841 *Robin Hood and his Merry Foresters* relies on the past social world of the broadside ballads, which through their own origins as well as their intended juvenile audience lack the implications of love and intergender companionship inherent to the elaborated Robin–Marian story. But for the world of the mainstream three-volume romance, with an audience clearly including women and a main thrust towards family values of a traditional and sometimes sensational kind, the outlaw's consort is of recurrent value, and this pattern works out through the socially lowered, politically unsophisticated and underfocused narrative by Pierce Egan the Younger, *Robin Hood and Little John: or, The Merry Men of Sherwood Forest* (1840, but serialised from 1838).

The hero is central, and the story opens with his arrival as a fosterling to a forester in Sherwood, where he rapidly grows up and – no doubt in part looking towards the burgeoning youth market – is for the early part of the novel a sturdy teenager. Soon he saves from a bow-bearing criminal the young Allan Clare from Nottingham

Castle and his sister Marian, who earns some 500 lines of intense physical description. A fifth is on the clothing 'displaying the beauty of her form deliciously': the same amount dwells on her 'choice mouth', matched by her 'large dark hazel eyes' while her 'eyelids were full and long', with a 'beauteous profusion of hair and a 'small-white-tapered hand, the softest of the soft'.[23] Her brother Allan loves Christabel, daughter of the Earl of Nottingham, who has set the archer onto them. The names Clare and Christabel point back towards the 1819 anonymous novel, though little here will be as tensely dramatic as that story.

Marian is loved by the young Robin, but she is again pursued by a thug, and this time saved by Little John, a forester, who takes her to the home of his uncle, Sir Guy of Gamwell. Then Robin, still fourteen, is imprisoned after standing up to the earl, and a curious sequence follows. Maude Clare, the warder's daughter (apparently no relation to Allan and Marian Clare), likes Robin: he is happy to kiss her, and he escapes from jail. But he loves Marian and will later persuade Maude to go with Will, who loves her, and she comes to accept this. Presumably this is Egan's version of a popular hero, and the Maude sequence seems to link to excitable events on the popular stage, but it also tends to confirm Marian's role as either a vulnerable visitor or at best a less than exciting wife – though it would be possible to read Maude here as a false Marian whose purpose is to release the spirit of sexuality into the text.

Six years pass: Marian is at Gamwell Hall in Yorkshire (where unwanted characters are sometimes sent in these novels); she has an admirer, Sir Hubert de Boissy, but Robin visits and fights him and he leaves, to be later killed by the foresters – the sidelined male violence perhaps matches Maude's female excessiveness. Now adults, Marian and Robin declare for each other, but she is kept out of the ensuing action, much of which is simple violence, military rather than outlaw operation. Eventually in book 3, when the action is mostly the recounting of ballads, including the knight sequence from the *Gest*, Allan and Christabel marry, and then Robin marries Marian, who comes to live with him in the forest: Will is married to the still fairly reluctant Maude. In one passing comment Robin and Marian are said to have a son, but Marian does not develop at all as a mother, merely remaining the threatened and eventually tragic heroine.

The narrative winds up quickly with Richard's return, but here there is no real restitution of Robin; though Richard re-establishes him as earl, he delays leaving the forest and Richard dies. King

John soon attacks, and Marian is accidentally shot when his men just as accidentally find the outlaw stronghold. She dies with Robin beside her, and the story finally ends with Robin's death at Kirklees – but he is buried back in Sherwood beside Marian, after speaking as he dies of his Saxon heritage.

Egan's novel was quite successful, and gave rise to one from 1849 by Joachim H. Stocqueler which answered Egan's title by being named *Maid Marian, the Forest Queen*. It claims to be 'a Companion to "Robin Hood"', and that is also the status of Marian herself. She is the daughter of Baron Fitzwalter and Robin's partner in the forest – Stocqueler tends to go back to Munday and Ritson to vary Egan's innovations. She acts as the leader of the outlaw band while Robin is on crusade: the first chapter is called 'The Forest Maiden', and as 'The Forest Queen' she reclines theatrically in green tunic, boots and hose in the beautiful forest where 'the oak, in its ancient majesty, spread its fast and protecting branches cross the humbler members of the arborial tribe'.[24] Though Little John is her 'trusty lieutenant' (p. 3) and she 'paraded her men and inspected their appointments' (p. 36), she is still vulnerable: she has already been confronted by a pressing 'man of rank' (p. 4) disguised as a bearded pilgrim, to be saved by her dog and Little John, in that order (see Figure 5); later she is inspected by the evidently villainous Hugo Malair, and, after she is gored by a wild boar in a distinctly sadistic scene, he abducts her in a sack.

Malair's daughter Edith, one of Prince John's mistresses, helps Marian escape, to her own harm: she is taken by the prince's men thinking she is Marian, and when, with a knife, she threatens the prince, he simply throws her out of the castle window to her death in the moat. In similarly melodramatic mode, Robin returns from crusade with two Arabs, Suleiman and his dancing-girl daughter Leila: Marian begins to be jealous of her with Robin. Another sensational character, Minnie Eftskin the forest witch, who is hostile to everyone, has been giving Marian love-philtres for Robin and also provides poisoned herbs to burn, she says 'to restore happiness to the boys of the greenwood' (p. 131). The outlaws all survive, and Robin and Marian vow to each other that they 'will live and die in the greenwood' (p. 150). Marian, for all the novel's melodrama, never attracts a false Marian, though perhaps her virtue stimulates the negative female stereotypes that surround her.

When the outlaws escape from Southwell Hold, besieged by Prince John, Marian is taken prisoner, but eventually they rescue her – she climbs down a silken ladder that Robin has shot into her cell – and for safety she goes home to Arlingford (as in Peacock), where her father is apparently overcoming his doubts about Robin, and says he will try to have him restored to his title. But his hostility returns, and only finally does Robin gets Marian back. Stocqueler sums up briskly, bypassing Robin's death, though Kirklees is mentioned, for the fate of his title's heroine. He says he differs from Egan, and she dies before Robin, being, as in Munday, poisoned by Prince John and buried at Dunmow.

Stocqueler offers both major sensation and a structure oscillating between Munday and the opposite of Egan, with Marian more like the girlish Juliet than the womanly Isolde. A good deal less planned is the next major outlaw lovers' saga, George Emmett's *Robin Hood and the Outlaws of Sherwood Forest* (1869). Marian is of simpler status, niece to Much the Miller, who is here an earnest tradesman. She is a Saxon of 'wondrous loveliness',[25] and the sheriff, named de Lois, harasses her, but Robin arrives, through a window, to fight him off (see Figure 7). Marian plays an intermittent role in forest activities, helping Robin and the outlaws fight their way out of the sheriff's trap, and she kills a man about to take Robin's life. A little later they catch the abbot and rob him, and when they sing and celebrate in the forest, and then hunt, Marian is an active member of the party.

Marian is also used in the mode of popular melodrama as a vulnerable heroine. She is abducted to help the king extort money from Robin by a new villain called d'Anville, but she finds her own way out by shooting a man with a crossbow. In a final sequence she is, after escaping a lustful friar, again in the castle dungeons: Much, currently a castle archer, hears knights arguing over their determination to 'have' Marian (p. 407), and shoots one. The other, d'Anville, takes her off to Brittany – so Robin becomes a fisherman: the story is from the ballad 'Robin Hood's Fishing' but he rescues her rather than taking a French ship by his deadly archery. In the end the outlaws are routed, and Much burns their base and rescues Marian and their treasures. Robin is wounded and bled to death at Kirklees. Little John buries him there and, in an almost casual ending, despairing of seeing Marian again, he simply leaves, 'the last that was seen of the Outlaws of Sherwood Forest' (p. 414): the curiously open ending of the story seems to match the erratic treatment of Marian throughout the novel as part dynamic heroine, part melodramatic victim.

The Marian-free ballad tradition was re-energised, especially in America, by Howard Pyle's briskly told and splendidly illustrated

The Merry Adventures of Robin Hood (1883): it relies firmly on a sequence of broadside ballad stories with some added links, and the only reference to the heroine is that early on Robin thinks of 'Maid Marian and her bright eyes'.[26] But the rambling Robin and Marian novels did not disappear in England. Edward Gilliat, a master at Harrow School, produced *In Lincoln Green: A Merrie Tale of Robin Hood* (1897): boys' school propaganda is rife, and Robin and Marian have a summer holiday at Whitby. Reduced until very late from his earl status, Robin is a miller and cattle-drover, and Lady Marian, a 'buxom young woman' with 'flaxen hair',[27] has a son Walter (his schooling is emphasised) and a daughter called Rosalind. As in Marian's only ballad appearance, she goes into the forest disguised as a squire and has a fight – but her opponent is, as in Peacock, King Richard, not Robin, and there is no tragic end, just happy parenthood for the once more noble outlaws.

A different compromise of traditions is *Maid Marian and Robin Hood* (1892) by Joyce Muddock (the real name of a male author of many popular novels, including thrillers). The daughter of a Saxon yeoman and formerly a major landowner, Marian, or Mariana Walstone, is a blonde beauty 'deeply skilled in woodland lore'.[28] She arranges that Ulf the giant swineherd liberates Robin from execution for killing a man who pestered her, but she is then mostly off stage. When the outlaws take to the forest she is sent home for safety and meets a handsome Norman soldier, St Vallerie, who both loves her and tries through jailing her to make her betray Robin's whereabouts. Eventually he changes sides, and halfway through the novel she rejoins Robin and they marry, she becoming 'a true wood nymph' (p. 187), but before long she and Robin fall out when she tries to stop him risking all to rescue Will Stutly from the gallows. Angry, she leaves the forest, and for three years she has dire misadventures, until finally her Norman lover brings her and Robin together to die.

Recognising Marian's presence as partner, but negotiating her absence so that the ballad action can flow, is also a feature of Henry Gilbert's well-known *Robin Hood and the Men of the Greenwood* (1912).[29] Again based largely on ballad action, this makes Marian often marginal to the action: the niece of Sir Richard of the Lee, the knight of the *Gest*, early on (and apparently from Muddock) 'Fair Marian' is threatened by an evil knight, whom Robin kills. When he takes to the forest he sends her home, as, though they love each other, the forest is not suitable for 'a maid'. She reappears when Allen a Dale's chosen bride is a friend of hers and then, worrying about Robin, she visits her father's friend Friar Tuck, dressed as a squire. Eventually Robin and she marry, and when King Richard returns they live on her inherited lands for sixteen years. Robin is a Saxon, and his family were once earls, but his inheritance is long lost – though in a sort of possessionist compensation he is close to the benign forest trolls. Finally an old family enemy, a villain new to the tradition grandly named Sir Isenbart of Belame, kills her, and the novel follows Robin to the end of the story in the *Gest*.[30]

Gilbert exemplifies the way the novel tradition, after its rather politicised start, has focused on ballad adventures, but also found a place, though often marginal, for Marian alongside Robin, with occasional influence from the early Romantic treatment. That early approach recurs in the late Romanticism of Tennyson's *The Foresters* (written by 1881), where she is treated with considerable respect as a secondary and helpful figure, accepting the queenly role that Guinevere refused to play. This ideal wife is the purest of the pure, as her husband Robin insists:

> The high Heaven guard thee from wantonness
> Who art the fairest flower of maidenhood
> That ever blossom'd on this English isle.[31]

Though Marian does have some energy it is no more than ethical and charitable, and though she finally speaks in the plural of what they have achieved, claiming some joint agency, the only name mentioned is that of her lord and husband:

> And yet I think these oaks at dawn and even
> Or in the balmy breathing of the night
> Will whisper evermore of Robin Hood.
> We leave but happy memories to the forest.
> We dealt in the wild justice of the woods.
> All those pale serfs whom we have served will bless us,
> All those pale mouths which we have fed will praise us
> The widows we have holpen pray for us
> Our Lady's blessed shrines throughout the land
> Be all the richer for us.
>   (vol. 2, p. 782)

Tennyson, scholarly and sensitive as ever to tradition, has stressed the Keatsian love of nature as well as the love of Mary, but this limits the human love of Marian and Robin that the novelists did explore. The Georgian poets follow a similar path, both stimulated by Tennyson's treatment and also appreciating the tradition's capacity for the homosocial patriotism they admired – the cast-list of J. C. Squire's 1928 play *Robin Hood* sees Marian as 'Rosalindish, vivacious, but more daring and male'.[32] Alfred Noyes's well-known anthology poem 'Sherwood' does not mention Marian, nor, but for a passing reference, does John Drinkwater's rather elegant masque-like play *Robin Hood and the Pedlar* (1914), but Noyes's verse play *Sherwood* (1908, revised 1926) activates her through its basic use of the Munday story – though curiously he makes Elinor into Prince John's sister, not mother, and she, as a nun, will bleed Robin to death: not as in Munday a false Marian, Elinor adopts a different female villainy. Lady Marian, here red-haired, marries Robin but within months, having been surrounded by fey forest spirits rather than outlaw action, they are dying together in a secularised Tennysonian ambience: the final song states, 'The Forest has conquered',[33] and Robin and Marian reappear as embodied spirits in a love and death ending of classically antique Romanticism.

In early film the figure common to both the novels and Romanticism of Marian as faithful wife can become transmuted into a flapper-like spirited young woman, a medievalist Pauline in Peril. The 'between men' triangle of Robin, Marian and a vigorous villain relates to the generic patterns of stage play and film, but it also redefines the role of the woman and provides her with both glossy appearance and, for all her charm and often wit, the role of a prized object of exchange. These Marians do not, however, usually appear as the sorceress-like false Marian; the possibilities of violence are to be only passively received, and any capacity for desire is firmly under the control of noble sentiment. This is the children's fiction Marian, the Hollywood lady and the heroine of the 1984 *Robin of Sherwood* television series, which in other respects was politically, racially and musically radical in presentation, but had a teenage Laura-Ashley-style Marian, with pale skin, big eyes, waves of hair and long white dress, mostly decorative and vulnerable, and essentially subservient to the handsome New Age Robin of Michael Praed (see Figure 13).

Robin's lovely vulnerable partner could at times become a little more steely. In the 1922 Douglas Fairbanks film she is at first negatively so, as 'The Queen of Beauty' who frightens the boyish Robin, a sort of super-Marian rather than a false one, but after he rescues her from Prince John they bond in common interest, rather than love. Later she assumes a more positive strength, calling Robin back to save his country, and fakes her own death to save herself – at which point he does move on to loving her. In

13 1980s outlaws: Michael Praed and Judy Trott in the television series *Robin of Sherwood* (1984).

the 1938 film starring Errol Flynn, Olivia de Havilland not only wore dresses of apparently rigid satin but also was capable of some management to help her man, assisted by the comically busy and friar-ogling Una O'Connor as her maid Bess. The very successful and, at least in its theme-song, unforgotten television series starting in 1955 had a Marian who seemed modelled on the woman air-force officer of British war movies – much as Robin himself has been called Squadron-Leader Robin Hood. Marian was played in series 1 and 2 by the handsome, straight-speaking, Bernadette O'Farrell, and was for the final third of the episodes replaced by another Irishwoman, Patricia Driscoll, who, perhaps because she came out of children's television, seemed a little less formidable but still held her ground credibly.

However, beauty verging at times towards capability has not been the only modern Marian. Like gentrification, Romanticism, nationalism and liberalism, feminism has also had a clear impact on the outlaw tradition, and there has been in recent years a striking range of Marians who are more or less – often less – energised in terms of contemporary ideas of women's roles and capacities in action and what they might well call a relationship. They do love Robin and seek to support his ambitions, but they focus more on what the pair might do together, where she has agency and a voice – there are also for the first time formations where Marian is very clearly the major figure and Robin recedes somewhat, if very attractively, into the background.

Marian in charge, late twentieth to twenty-first centuries

The first sign of a newly invigorated Marian was in the non-aggressive form of Audrey Hepburn in Richard Lester's film *Robin and Marian* of 1976. This Marian is wiser, calmer and much more far-seeing than the limited and soldier-like Robin and Little John, and it is she, knowing that his wound will incapacitate him seriously, who decides they should die together from drinking a potion she provides. The witch-like prioress of the *Gest* becomes a wise woman, and through this reversing of the false Marian phenomenon she has for the first time a major part in both plot and meaning.

Elements of agency were, as Lux outlines, visible in the two major Robin Hood films made in 1991.[34] Both give Marian a more significant role in general than did the 1938 film, and involve her in active scenes, though neither offers her as much actual political impact as she had in the 1922 Fairbanks film. 1991 saw both *Robin Hood: Prince of Thieves* starring Kevin Costner and *Robin Hood* with Patrick Bergin. Very successful though it was, the Costner vehicle has gained few favourable critical opinions, and Maid Marian studies would also see little reason to prize it. True, the first view of Marian is in armour fighting Robin, more like Joan of Arc than the sword-wielding Marian of the broadside ballad. The novel of the film puts it like this:

> Robin hurled the deer's head at his assailant and threw himself after it. He managed to grab the hand holding the dagger, spun his assailant round, and smashed the hand against the wall until the dagger fell from numbed fingers. They struggled together, and Robin

quickly realized he was by far the stronger. He waded into his assailant with both fists, and the masked man collapsed. Robin stood over him for a moment, panting for breath, and then reached down and tore off the metal mask. Long hair tumbled free, and Robin stared blankly back at the beautiful woman staring back at him.
 The door flew open and Azeem burst in, scimitar at the ready. Robin looked round, startled, and the woman seized the opportunity to punch him viciously in the groin. Robin sank to his knees beside her and smiled with clenched teeth.
 'Hello, Marian.'[35]

It is not explained why, having previously heard he is Robin, Marian fights him at all; still less why, when seeing him in front of her, she hits him in the groin. Perhaps it is a move towards a double Marian, first fiercely aggressive and then sweetly supportive. Certainly, by the end of the film she is as usual imprisoned, in need of rescue, and ends enfeebled in a stereotypical gender position:

> He took Marian into his arms, and for a long moment they stood together, losing themselves in each other. Marian raised a trembling hand to Robin's face, as though half-afraid he might disappear like a dream.
> 'You came for me! You are alive!'
> Robin held her eyes with his. 'I would die, before I let another man have you.'
> They kissed as if they were never going to stop. (pp. 232-3)

The 1991 Patrick Bergin as Robin film had, along with a lower budget and a simpler story, a more roguish hero and a more dynamic Marian, with Uma Thurman, initially playing as self-willed, refusing the husband chosen by her guardian. From the start she gazes repeatedly and secretly at the handsome Robin, reversing the usual scopic relishing of her beauty. This Marian herself, when disguised as a boy, frustrates the false Marian, and then as she and Robin escape she, still a boy, plants a warm and initially gender-disruptive kiss on his mouth. Nevertheless, it would hardly be true to describe this as a feminist figure: essentially she is a spirited but eventually submissive Marian. Her feeling and vigour are naturalised, elided into a sort of mythic womanhood, as she finally says of Robin, 'he makes the bees buzz in my breast', and they are married in a distinctly fertility-linked May ritual context.

As in other popular genres, such as crime fiction, it is in the novel, not film, that the most extensive feminist movements have been made, though progress has been fairly slow. While there have, as David Blamires records, been plenty of sensitive and suffering young female leads,[36] some children's writers have given Marian substantial roles like the forceful omni-competent heroine created by the historian Carola Oman in 1939 or Antonia Fraser's Marian, both adventurous and vulnerable (including to the false Marian of Black Barbara) in 1955, or Bernard Miles's more recent (1979) robust semi-feminist tomboy. A serious attempt to represent Marian differently was Robin McKinley's *The Outlaws of Sherwood* (1988), where as Robin's well-born lover she visits him in the forest, knows its topography better than any of the newly arrived outlaws and is best with a long-bow. She wins the archery tournament disguised as Robin Hood (like the *Robin and Marian* prioress, a positive false Marian), and at the end King Richard wants her to be the new sheriff when the pardoned outlaws go with him on crusade. The idea of Marian as a competent professional woman is new, and involves for the first time – with the partial exception of Peacock – giving her a good deal of the narrative focalisation of the text. But at the same time she is seen as more a facilitator than an agent; she is never really one of the outlaws, and it is they who provide the title of the book.

A shift towards Marian as central figure is indicated in the title of Jennifer Roberson's novel *Lady of the Forest* (1992), the strongest of the Marian-focused texts. Her father died on crusade and his message to her, brought back by Robert of Locksley, son of the Earl of Huntington, is that for her protection she should marry the sheriff. She comes to admire, then love, Robin, but the sheriff is not an ogre and is difficult to avoid: one of Roberson's purposes is to show in convincing detail how a woman, including one of beauty and breeding, is constrained by a set of protocols, duties and social expectations. Something of Jane Austen is present in the sense of limitations imposed by social expectations on a clever and energetic woman, though the writing is simple and even prone to melodrama, as when Marian, in the sheriff's prison, names herself to him as 'Robin Hood's whore. And grateful for the honor.'[37] In general, Roberson's Marian is a rather responsible figure, as if McKinley's concept has been made central to the plot and the focal intelligence of the book.

Gayle Feyrer's *The Thief's Mistress* (1996) marks a new stage in Marian's renovation partly by making her a serious and successful fighter and also by following the explicit lines of recent fiction in terms of violence and sexuality. In the opening sequence Marian fiercely kills the man who has trapped and murdered her mother. She has deliberately taken a lover as part of maturing herself for this vengeance, and is already acting at the French court as an espionage agent for Queen Eleanor of England. Her new assignment – the James Bond pattern seems influential here – is to infiltrate Nottingham Castle, where the sheriff is a supporter of Prince John, but on the way she is ambushed by Robin Hood: he, struck as all are by her beauty, kisses her instead of robbing. She is both stirred and shaken by the experience – she might even be moving on to a post-feminist position.

In this novel Sir Guy is a modern man – he takes her shopping in Nottingham market – and he is also handsome and decisive: Marian is attracted to him, again perhaps in post-feminist mode, though she hopes to gain information from him, even to win him to the queen's cause. For both reasons she decides to take him as her lover, and some steamy scenes ensue. But she does not forget the frisson of Robin's kiss and goes to meet him, again partially for good espionage reasons: though she feels impelled to pull a knife on him, soon they feel 'a strange bond of desire'.[38] She returns to Nottingham, and the plot unfolds, mostly around the sadistic sheriff, until finally, with King Richard returned and Marian forbidden by him to fight, Robin and Marian join together as if in the 'ancient land of Faerie' (p. 423) – again a less than feminist resolution in spite of the evident reference to Bradley: post-feminist conservatism may be rearing its head.

This novel is not as crass as some of its sequences suggest: both it and Marian deserve a stronger title than *The Thief's Mistress*. Because of the move towards the romance genre, made first by Roberson, the novel can locate Marian at the centre of the plot without the difficulty McKinley faced, and the explicit notion of Marian as Amazon and sexualised woman, however sensationally handled, is a valid counter to the structures of past versions of popular masculinism.

Theresa Tomlinson liberates Marian in a different direction in her serious-toned juvenile novel *The Forestwife* (1993), developed into a trilogy (also called *The Forestwife*) with *Child of the May* (1998) and *The Path of the She Wolf* (2000). Marion Holt is central: she escapes from a forced marriage into the forest, and works for and then succeeds the Forestwife, offering advice, and support, mostly medical, to the poor. In this she gains the help of a handsome but distinctly limited peasant youth, Robin. Strongly set in place and time, the first novel presents a credible account of a young woman finding her identity by working for others and also having a loving and supportive man. In the later novels the story gains wider political range as Robin and his friends, including several strong women, become involved in resistance to King John.

Tomlinson's historical strength and firm focus on women's issues make this the most feminist of all the Marian novels so far, though new ones give her a fair level of activity and independence. Elsa Watson's *Maid Marian* (2004) is basically a medieval mystery as Marian resists being forced to marry her dead husband's brother: Queen Eleanor is behind the idea, and Marian thinks they mean to murder her for the inheritance. Robin becomes involved, first as a quasi-detective, and then emotionally with Marian: with his help the plot is foiled (in that sort of language) and they end up happily married, with a baby on the way. If the feminist Marian can in that way be absorbed into traditionalism, the most vigorous extension of her agency can through other populist modes consume the character entirely, as in *Robin: Lady of Legend* (2012) by R. M. Arcejaeger. Also entitled *The Classic Adventures of the Girl who Became Robin Hood*, this is about a noble young woman named in fact Robin, who becomes the outlaw hero, cross-dressed, helps her sister Marian, and falls in love with Little John and ends happily with him.

The most self-conscious moves towards film feminism have been made through comedy – which implies euphemisation of the theme. In *The Zany Adventures of Robin Hood* (1984), apart from a less than heroic Robin, with George Segal in ill-fitting green tights and a relaxed spirit, there is a Marian out of *Valley of the Dolls*, played to the hilt by Morgan Fairchild: languishing in a negligée she cries out, in wry frustration, 'I'll soon be Old Maid Marian.' Humorous as it is, this is nevertheless about as feminist as the wishful wrigglings of Amy Yasbeck as Marian in Mel Brooks's *Robin Hood: Men in Tights* (1993), which as its title indicates, is more interested in exploring, if only in fun, the possibilities of a homosexual aspect to the outlaw tradition, among many other elements of burlesque.

Another comically contained version of Marian's frustrations (see Figure 14) appears in *Robin Hood: A High Spirited Tale of Adventure* (1980), a Muppet production in comic book, not film, form. Robin is 'a bold and chivalrous frog'[39] who is seized by Sheriff Gonzo. But there is hope:

> Maid Marian was in truth an extremely glamorous pig who had fallen in love with Robin Hood and had come to live in the forest to cook and sew for her frog and his merry men. The problem was that she hated living under the greenwood tree, or any trees for that matter ... However, at this moment of crisis she surpassed everyone

The making and re-making of Maid Marian

by quickly organising a brilliant campaign to rescue their leader. 'We go to the Sheriff's castle and take him back.'

Leading a band of courageous chickens – the sight of them unmans Gonzo – she rescues Robin. Yet her reward is slight:

> 'Nice work, guys,' said Robin to his merry men. 'I knew you could do it.'
>
> 'Ahem, Robbie,' said Maid Marian. 'It wasn't all done by the guys, mon cher. So how about an itsy-bitsy kissy for moi, your lady fair and mastermind of this gallant rescue?'
>
> She closed her eyes and puckered up her lips, expectantly. Robin Hood leaned towards Maid Marian, then picked up her hand and shook it heartily.
>
> 'Thanks a lot, Maid Marian,' said Robin. 'Now I've got to rescue the Judge.'[40]

14 Miss Piggy as Marian. From *Robin Hood: A High Spirited Tale of Adventure* (New York: Muppets Press and Random House, 1980), front cover.

The Muppet version equally satirises forceful females and feeble Robin Hood plots, but another project aimed primarily at children put Marian fully in charge, though also in a farcical and diminishing context. The BBC television series of 1988, challengingly named *Maid Marian and her Merry Men*, placed her, played vigorously by Kate Lonergan, in charge of a rag-bag of dissidents among whom the last and definitely least is a fragilely handsome dress-designer named Robin of Kensington. With her sleeves rolled up, Marian runs the band very effectively in spite of male expectations (see Figure 15), but in a context so improbable and with plotting so ludicrous that any possibilities of a feminist effect are heavily carnivalised – in spite of some playfully liberationist lines as when Marian plans to recruit a band of 'highly attractive respectable young men who are just a *little* bit rough'.

15 1980s feminism: From *Maid Marian and Her Merry Men: Robert the Incredible Chicken* (London: BBC Books, 1989), p. 6.

In more recent visual versions Marian's capacity for agency is assumed, but not of prime interest. In *The New Adventures of Robin Hood* (1997), a US production well downstream from *Xena the Warrior Princess*, a posturing matinee-idol Robin has as partner a busy, stocky Marian, dressed usually in leather shorts and skimpy blouses. Just as lurid, in a less unselfconscious way, was Disney's *Princess of Thieves* (2001), where the young Keira Knightley played Gwyn, daughter of Robin Hood, who leads a geographically very improbable resistance against bad Prince John and ends up as willing mistress to an invented King of England, Phillip I. The film appears to have been excluded from Knightley's CV, though she continued with para-masculinity in *Bend it Like Beckham* (2002).

A more serious updating of the story and of Marian was involved in the BBC television series *Robin Hood*, which ran for thirty-nine episodes from 2006 to 2009. Robin, young and undershaven, returned from crusade in disgruntled and apparently post-Iraq mood, was played with surly intensity by Jonas Armstrong. Lady Marian, cross that he had left her for crusade (a memory of *Robin and Marian*), is the daughter of a former sheriff of Nottingham and initially feels that Robin's outlawry is self-indulgent and he should work within the system. But more than any previous Marian she has an active role, in part by miming Robin in being the 'Night Watchman' delivering food and help to the poor, and also, looking back to the feminist novelists, by becoming somewhat involved with the older and semi-criminal Guy of Gisborne, who supports the sheriff and loves her, if in an uncertain way. These complications remain unresolved, and throughout she supports Robin, if somewhat erratically, but at the end of the second series, when actually in the Holy Land, she finally rejects Guy and he kills her – only for her to reappear in spirit to kiss Robin as he is dying.

Brisk and handsome rather than vulnerable and glamorous, Lucy Griffiths plays both a figure for modern times and one who like Robin and his friends is aimed at the young teenagers who were the advertisers' focus: one of the production team privately expressed delight that they had hit the market audience for 'make-up and trainers'. Other effective communicators were Richard Armitage as the world-weary Guy, attracting loyal support among an older and female audience, while a more complex message was sent by the small, dynamic Anjali Jay, playing Djaq, a Saracen girl in England who joined the band as her dead brother – a variant of Stocqueler's belly-dancing Leila, even a politically acceptable false Marian.

The polyvalent young Marian of this series may have been in the mind of the producers of the 2010 film *Robin Hood* when they originally cast the worldly-wise *gamine* Siena Miller as Marian, but by report Russell Crowe, playing Robin, felt the difference in age would be embarrassing, and Marian was eventually played by Cate Blanchett, nearly unrecognisable as a mature, almost plain and deeply earnest woman: she does help free some mistreated resisters in King John's England and supports Robin in his move towards early popular representation (Thomas Miller is the antique parallel) but lacks the energy and flamboyance of modern feminist Marians.

The film had originally planned to show Robin as in fact a sheriff, and its title was to be *Nottingham*: the formative context was the post-9/11 heroisation of the security services. But this intriguing departure was abandoned, apparently largely by the director Ridley Scott – his English origins may have been influential – and the story was steadily rewritten to bring Robin back to the position of a good democratic outlaw, but brutal modernity seems to make romance no longer appropriate. Marian has been married to Loxley, a knight who dies on crusade and whom Robin impersonates to return safely from the crusades, so their relation is at best one of growing trust and mutual acceptance in the context of a gender politics where Marian is back to her nineteenth-century support role.

After her long journey through trivialisation, anonymity and instrumentality, the liberated Marian has some way to go. Caught between romance, farce and the role of a forest Martha, as a heroine she can be multi-class, forest-loving, resistance-supporting, bow-wielding, cross-dressing and brave, and some of the more potent of these elements are recently exemplified, but have not cohered. At the moment the re-gendering of the Robin Hood legend seems unfinished business – it would not be difficult to imagine a feminist version of the outlaw story going far beyond the recent nervously comic ventures, and exploiting the existing Marian-liberating novels, perhaps like Tomlinson moving into the domain of mysticism a little.

That suggests a title like *The Mists of Sherwood*, and the novel seems the only likely genre for Marian's further advancement. But the failure of any substantial film effort to exploit Marion Zimmer Bradley's huge popularity must make it doubtful that outlaw feminism could manage more than limited television or specialist film. There have been some high points, as in the self-management of the *pastourelle* heroine, the bravura of Jonson's Marian and the dazzling capacity of Peacock's heroine, and Marian has made some moves into modern mature independence. But whatever does come up in the way of new Maid Marian fictions, it is still very unlikely that from now on Marian's role will be as absent or insignificant as it was before the impact of generic change and feminist thinking began the outlaw heroine on her long, slow and still uncertain progress towards a position and an impact as important as that of her consort.

Notes

1 The major sources for *pastourelle* are K. Bartsch (ed.), *Altfranzösische Romanzen und Pastourellen* (Leipzig: Vogel, 1870) and Jean-Claude Rivière (ed.), *Pastourelles*, 3 vols (Geneva: Droz, 1974–76). A translation of many of the texts is found in William Paden (ed. and trans.), *The Medieval Pastourelle* (New York: Garland, 1987).

2 Presumably this is Chaucer's 'joly Robyn' whom Pandarus speaks of as playing in the 'haselwode'; see Geoffrey Chaucer, *Troilus and Criseyde*, in *The Riverside Chaucer*, ed. Larry Benson (New York: Oxford University Press, 1988), vol. 5, p. 1174.

3 E. K. Chambers, *English Literature at the Close of the Middle Ages*, Oxford History of English Literature, 2/2 (Oxford: Clarendon, 1945), pp. 176 and 175.

4 Costs are recorded for Marian's 'huke' or cloak and (with Robin) her gloves: see W. E. St Lawrence Finny, 'Mediaeval Games and Gaderyngs at Kingston-upon-Thames', *Surrey Archaeological Collections*, 44 (1936): 102–36, at p. 123.

5 See James Stokes (ed.), *Somerset: Records of Early English Drama*, 2 vols (Toronto: University of Toronto Press, 1996), vol. 1, p. 411.

6 John Forrest, *The History of Morris Dancing, 1458–1750* (Toronto: University of Toronto Press, 1999), pp. 153, 168–9.

7 'Robin Hood and the Friar', in Stephen Knight and Thomas Ohlgren (eds), *Robin Hood and Other Outlaw Tales*, 2nd edn, TEAMS Middle English Texts (Kalamazoo: Western Michigan University Press, 2000), pp. 286–90, 115–23.

8 Anthony Munday, *The Downfall of Robert, Earle of Huntington*, in Knight and Ohlgren (eds), *Robin Hood and Other Outlaw Tales*, pp. 303–84, line 86.

9 Michael Drayton, *Poly-Olbion*, in *The Works of Michael Drayton*, ed. J. William Hebel, vol. 4 (Oxford: Blackwell, 1961), song 26, lines 352–8.

10 See the discussion of the origins of *The Sad Shepherd* in Stephen Knight, '"Meere English flocks": Ben Jonson's *The Sad Shepherd*

and the Robin Hood Tradition', in Helen Phillips (ed.), *Robin Hood Medieval and Post-Medieval* (Dublin: Four Courts Press, 2005), pp. 129–44.
11 Ben Jonson, *The Sad Shepherd*, in *The Cambridge Edition of the Works of Ben Jonson*, ed. David Bevington, Martin Butler and Ian Donaldson, 7 vols (Cambridge: Cambridge University Press, 2012), vol. 7, pp. 417–80, Act 1, scene 6, lines 1–13.
12 See Knight and Ohlgren (eds), *Robin Hood and Other Outlaw Tales*, pp. 494–6, lines 34–53.
13 *Robin Hood: An Opera* (London: Watts, 1730), p. 26.
14 William Shield and Leonard McNally, *Robin Hood, or Sherwood Forest* (London: Almon, 1784), p. 28.
15 Joseph Ritson (ed.), *Robin Hood: A Collection of All the Ancient Poems, Songs and Ballads Now Extant Relative to the Celebrated English Outlaw (to which are Prefixed Anecdotes of his Life)*, 2 vols (London: Egerton and Johnson, 1795), p. xx.
16 J. H. Reynolds, *Poetry and Prose*, ed. George L. Marsh (London: Oxford University Press, 1928), p. 15.
17 John Keats, 'Robin Hood: To a Friend', in *Collected Poems*, ed. Jack Stillinger (Cambridge, MA: Harvard University Press, 1982), pp. 169–70, lines 48–9, 54–6.
18 Leigh Hunt, *Selected Writings*, vol. 5: *Poetical Works, 1801–21*, ed. John Strachan (London: Pickering and Chatto, 2003), p. 342, note 46.
19 See George Saintsbury, 'Introduction' to Thomas Love Peacock, *Maid Marian* (London: Macmillan, 1895), pp. vii–xxix.
20 Eve Kosofsky Sedgwick, *Between Men: English Literature and Homosocial Desire* (New York: Columbia University Press, 1985).
21 Thomas Love Peacock, *Maid Marian* (London: Hookham and Longman, Hurst, Rees, Orme, and Brown, 1822), p. 26.
22 A comic opera named *Marian* by Frances Brooke was staged in 1788, including 'Robin the Boatman', but it has no relation to the outlaw tradition at all: see Stephen Knight, *Robin Hood: A Complete Study of the English Outlaw* (Oxford: Blackwell, 1994), pp. 151–2.
23 Piers Egan the Younger, *Robin Hood and Little John: or, The Merry Men of Sherwood Forest* (London: Forster and Hextall, 1840), p. 19.
24 J. H. Stocqueler, *Maid Marian, the Forest Queen, being a Companion to 'Robin Hood'* (London: Peirce, 1849), p. 2.
25 George Emmett, *Robin Hood and the Outlaws of Sherwood Forest* (London: Temple, 1869), p. 63.
26 Howard Pyle, *The Merry Adventures of Robin Hood, of Great Renown in Nottinghamshire* (New York: Scribner, 1883), p. 3.
27 Edward Gilliat, *In Lincoln Green: A Merrie Tale of Robin Hood* (London: Seeley, 1897), p. 88.
28 Joyce E. Muddock, *Maid Marian and Robin Hood: A Romance of Old Sherwood Forest* (London: Chatto and Windus, 1892), p. 25.

29 Henry Gilbert, *Robin Hood and the Men of the Greenwood* (Edinburgh: Jack, 1912).
30 Did Richard Carpenter, creator of the 1984 television series *Robin of Sherwood*, read Gilbert? His first villain is Robert de Bellême, another unpleasant Norman.
31 Alfred Tennyson, *The Foresters*, in *Poems and Plays*, 2 vols, Oxford Standard Authors (London: Oxford University Press, 1965), vol. 2, p. 753.
32 J. C. Squire, *Robin Hood: A Farcical Romantic Pastoral* (London: Heinemann, 1928).
33 Alfred Noyes, *Sherwood*, in *Collected Poems*, 4 vols (London: Blackwood, 1928), vol. 1, pp. 45–7.
34 Sherron Lux, 'And the "Reel" Maid Marian', in Thomas G. Hahn (ed.), *Robin Hood in Popular Culture: Violence, Transgression and Justice* (Cambridge: Brewer, 2000), pp. 151–60.
35 Simon Green, *Kevin Costner is Robin Hood Prince of Thieves* (New York: Berkely, 1991), p. 66.
36 David Blamires, 'Maid Marian in Twentieth-Century Children's Books', in Helen Phillips (ed.), *Bandit Territories: British Outlaws and their Traditions* (Cardiff: University of Wales Press, 2008), pp. 44–57.
37 Jennifer Roberson, *Lady of the Forest* (New York: Kensington, 1992), p. 16.
38 Gayle Feyrer, *The Thief's Mistress* (New York: Dell, 1996), p. 250.
39 *Robin Hood: A High Spirited Tale of Adventure* (Los Angeles: Boom Studios, 1980), p. 18.
40 *Robin Hood: A High Spirited Tale of Adventure*, p. 18.

8
Rhizomatic Robin Hood

Firing the canon

The politics of a myth do not arise only from the nature and status of the characters involved, their relations with others and the outcome of the story. There may be among those elements potent content-based issues like failed royalty and fated love to shape the headlines of myths like those of King Arthur or Queen Isolde, but there is also a more elusive and pervasive force embedded in the form of a myth. In the past this is found in the ways in which they are preserved and communicated, but also, even less visibly, in the differing ways in which the myths are found comprehensible to commentators. Content, form and reception are related but frequently separate and mis-related domains of meaning in myths and parallel cultural fields, and in all three areas the myth of Robin Hood is very unusual. Where much of this study has been focused on content and to some extent on form, this chapter will explore the form and the reception across time of the outlaw materials and argue that the entire formation is essentially rhizomatic, or linear, in structure, quite different in both pattern and ideological implications from other myths and from the general shape of canonical literature. While the Robin Hood content is not yet widely understood, and the form has been little considered, its reception processes have been the most obscure area of the whole domain: these are a good place to start, but to do so requires first some preliminary clarifications, or revelations.

Within cultural traditions there is a hidden structure of considerable power, which has usually tended to support views of human relations that are both conservative and hierarchical. For example, there has long been an area of literary study that has seemed both staid and serious – so much so that it was for decades the disciplinary area which future researchers had to undertake to qualify for their postgraduate and notionally professional status. Text-editing was the subject, taught by austere senior staff practising deep in a great library. Here you learnt about the difference between a bad quarto and a good folio of Shakespeare, and how to establish a text of acknowledged authority from the error-filled manuscripts and clumsily printed versions that have come down to us knowledgeable people. The self-privileging of modernity is evident, even while it offers an interest in the past, but contemporary self-indulgence is not the central ideology of the editing process.

The language of the process of textual editing is based on that of inheriting property through a family: wealth through time, the need to protect it, to maintain rights and to seize your proper deserts in it is the recurrent implicit theme. W. W. Greg claimed scientific authority in the title of his classic guide, *The Calculus of Variants*, but the real meanings of his 'genealogical method' were property and lineage, as the language revealed. Manuscripts were sorted into a 'family'; each had its 'predecessors' in a 'genetic group'; 'the filiations of descent' were demonstrated by the scholars who eluded all 'corruption' in this process of 'inheritance' from the 'common ancestor' and its cultural riches.[1] The text has a specific value that scholars, like archivists, or perhaps more like bank clerks, will cherish – and in fact produce. No-one at the medieval time had any cognition of an authentic or first edition of *The Canterbury Tales*, including its author: he kept on working, and never got to finish, though he did produce an ending, of a kind ('The Parson's Tale' basically rejects almost all the tales that have been told), and a copy was spun off whenever someone was interested in having one made. The not very authoritative author might even keep revising and reworking the whole, as with William Langland and his *Piers Plowman*, of which there were long alleged to be three quite different versions: recently the number went up to four, and it threatens to dissipate into many severely varying and overlapping recensions.

Both the idea of a single authentic text, and also the language in which we seek to establish this, are in fact individualistic fetishisations of a previous world's actively engaged and interactive communications with no perceived value beyond communality. While this ideological basis was quite clearly shown in the 1980s,[2] the processes of editing have not been in any way changed, nor have their individualist and property-obsessed implications been opened to criticism to a significant degree.

But if the texts that bear literary content can in this way be treated or re-created as a hierarchised fetish, so can the literary myth itself as a whole. It is a familiar idea that traditional attitudes and teaching practices set up and basically defended, by exclusion of others, a series of literary texts as the 'canon' of literature, the hierarchy of material which should be dealt with, studied and perpetuated, itself transmitted as property, with its rights and inheritances embedded in a hierarchical institution that you might yourself, via education, join, and so share in the cultural capital. One issue of interest is how this theoretically uniform and perennial canon has radically changed. So for example English literature, miming its classical avatar, became canonised only from about the beginning of the twentieth century, when other national and nationalistic English institutions like the Tate Gallery and Everyman's Library were founded. Even then it was not until after the Second World War that the novel found its way into the canon – before that it was only poetry and Shakespeare, and the canonical acceptance of the novel is recent, in large part a forgotten and lasting impact of F. R. Leavis. His title *The Great Tradition* was in itself a challenge to the existing canon as the only tradition, and the challenge was entirely successful – modern students find it very hard to believe that novels were not seriously studied until after the Second World War.

But in the present discussion the matter of most interest – and it needs stressing because it has not been a topic of public discussion – is how each element of the canon was itself canonical in mode and origin: the Shakespeare slot in the canonical sequence went back to that ultimate fetish, the first Folio, that book that editing processes were to protect and perfect. It is, though, quite possible to talk about the changing formations of the Shakespeare myth. From the later seventeenth century women took the stage in what were now much smaller theatres, and the tradition was re-gendered and both physicalised and sentimentalised. Davenant staged *Much Ado about Nothing* and *Measure for Measure* as one play named *The Law against Lovers*; Dryden turned *Antony and Cleopatra* into *All for Love*. In the twentieth century the rise of professional criticism privileged the problem plays – and of course the central social challenge of such genius realised by a provincial glover's son has been rejected by those who find another better-qualified author. And in case that might seem simply based on English class-obsessions, it is worth noting that the bulk of the 'who was Shakespeare?' people are wealthy Anglophone Americans apparently bothered by potentially downmarket elements of their own cultural inheritance. But all through the variations of the Shakespeare myth the original texts have a canonical authority, for the Stratford deniers a sacred one.

This formal canonicity has its parallel in the shape of other major myths which do not have a single textual origin. The myth of King Arthur is effectively a succession of great books, and no doubt its topic – an ideal world of royally directed order is disrupted and destroyed from within – was of consuming interest to the kinds of people who patronised and funded the production of great books in the past. Geoffrey of Monmouth's powerful Latin quasi-chronicle, the first major text about Arthur as a monarch of European grandeur, was written for Norman princes in the time of Henry I, then translated and transmuted into French for the baronial cultural centres of high medieval France. The bookish link with the powerful continued, if variably – Malory's dominating English version is a manuscript produced over some time that was quickly transitioned by Caxton into the new print-based book culture, itself thematically focused on dreams of chivalry as a fantasy aristocratic form of life in the new mercantile cities where book sales thrived in consumer mode. Arthur had a para-authoritative presence as the ideal of grandeur which Spenser's *Faerie Queene*, like Queen Elizabeth, put into practical action, but then the king of chivalry failed as a canonical representation. Jonson, Milton and Dryden all planned to tell his mighty story, but other issues and ideologies prevailed, though Dryden at least did keep the heroic myth alive with his 1691 play that re-interprets Arthur's notional war against the Anglo-Saxons in terms of his own period's political and religious conflict and compromise. In the eighteenth century Arthur did slip out of the canon: he appeared in Fielding's *Tom Thumb* (1730), a comic parody of courtly (and Whig) grandeur, and when his grand vizier Merlin appeared in the period it was often in musical theatre as compère of a group of very lightly dressed ladies, there to sing and dance, not to engage in anything more traditionally chivalrous or romantic.

But medievalism in England resurrected the king – not as early or as confidently as some think. Barczewski's account of both Arthur and Robin Hood as leading English nationalist figures seems unaware both of Scott's potent intervention on behalf of Robin and of the even more surprising use of Arthur as a national figure only by Welsh and Cornish, and a few Scots, around the year 1800.[3] There is an intriguing by-product, also apparently unknown to the public or allegedly professional scholars, in the minor English Arthur of the period who operates in the far north, even the Arctic, as an image of English domination which is neither Mediterranean nor Catholic – a quasi-imperial hero of the Northern Gothic.[4]

But though Malory had not been reprinted since 1634, copies were still about – early books had a remarkable power to survive, through both a general care for the past and their own sturdy qualities – and his work was reprinted in the early nineteenth century along with much other medieval material, often seen as a basis for criticising mercantile modernity and urban ugliness. But there was very little new Arthurian material until Tennyson created *The Idylls of The King*, with elements first appearing in 1859 and all of the work finally published by 1885. Arthur was still grand, but he adapted to modernity in part by having a troubled marriage and also by finding that those he relied on to order the kingdom were not sufficiently trustworthy – Tristram in particular is a morally lax modern cynic, not the ancient ardent lover. But the literature of the grand, troubled and ultimately tragic king was re-established, notably in very popular novels like T. H. White's *The Once and Future King* (1938–58), engaging as it does with mid-century political issues, including war, and the equally dynamic *The Mists of Avalon* (1981) by Marion Zimmer Bradley, which deployed the female wisdom and also conflicted authority of his half-sister Morgaine in a powerful assessment of woman's possible role at the height of secular authority.

As a result of the literary succession, interrupted as it was for more than a century between Dryden and Tennyson (apart from the essentially off-stage efforts of the Arctic Arthur), when you write about or teach in the Arthurian tradition, you can always trace the sources, see who has been reading what, and then identify what that author has done with the tradition, and so speculate why. Tennyson for example makes Arthur a much more energetic figure than the *roi fainéant* he became in the French romancers and in Malory, as he saw modern-style royalty as more potent, and so more focal, than did the courts of medieval great, but not royal, barons. Equally, White tells a story tracing Lancelot's attitudes and beliefs from his childhood, making little of his love for Guinevere, reworking the Arthuriad as a script about psychological pressures in human – and male – life and offering Merlin as an all-knowing, all-purpose guide, a fantasy of an Oxbridge tutor.

This Arthur canon has, like royalty and aristocracy themselves, its own structure of inheritance and authority: what Arthur has tragically lost is culturally recuperated in his myth and in the continuing respect that the reading public has had for its relational and comprehensibly changing nature. This is the normal situation with the canon, even in its public and popular manifestations: there has recently developed a substantial academic specialisation in adaptation, looking at, for example, how Jane Austen is rendered in film. Her authority is still there, reworked, re-interpreted, but visible in the changes that her inheritors have made with her potent and reified works, like descendants rebuilding the stately home, but never changing its location or indeed their own share in its authority.

However, this does not work with Robin Hood. It has long been evident that there is a different essential formation in this long-loved and highly dynamic cultural myth, compared with the high-end stories which are enshrined in the upmarket genres of five-act play, opera, art novel. This became sharply clear to me recently when a friend invited me to speak on Robin Hood at an adaptation conference. In the end I was unable to make the date, which was something of a relief, because I had come to realise that it was simply not possible to make, in this field, a comparative study of text and source with learned and insightful comments on the differences and their own contextual meanings. There was no clear succession of sources and variations in the Robin Hood tradition. It was not just that it was excluded from the canon: it did not have the structural characteristics evidently required for canonical status.

That perception meshed with a previous realisation about the Robin Hood materials. When I was developing and then teaching a course simply called 'Robin Hood' at Cardiff University there were a number of ways in which the activities were different from a standard, one might say routine, English literature course. First, you had to decide whether this was a normal-length module option, or one requiring double effort – and providing double reward. The usual candidates for double status (department wits called it duplicity) were Shakespeare, Chaucer and that ilk. From the start I aligned Robin with them, feeling that I wanted students to read quite a lot of material, not just select a few items for study, and, as double modules had an early essay, would have to work on the medieval material. With that structure in place, there was an issue about sources, but that will be discussed later: in terms of methodology the striking variation was the type of essay question you could set. As experienced academic teachers will know, the essential question on one of the greats is simply 'Explain the genius of writer X in the text Y.' You can dress this up variously, but no matter, the issue is that the work has been done by the writer in providing moments of brilliance which the student will in some way excavate; some would say exhume. But the Robin Hood materials very often do not have authors, and in any case have no tendency to offer, or interest in offering, brilliant, nearly secret patterns of imagery, insight, symbolism, mature judgement or other instruments of alleged immortality.

Rather, being texts in cultural studies rather than literary elitism, the Robin Hood materials offer views of what narratives and forms of representation have been popular at any given time; the patterns to be found in them all feed out into their contexts and do not remain sequestered inside their textual confines, only to communicate with the individual reader. That this contextuality is also found in all allegedly great literature is perfectly true, but it is not an approach that literary criticism has much liked to offer, being deferred both by the tradition of scholarship which isolates, edits and facilitates entry to these fetishised objects, and also by the insistence of evaluation across time (the greatness-based ahistorical principle) and towards the equally, and in parallel fashion fetishised, individual reader.

I found it striking that when for the first time I was constructing a set of Robin Hood essay topics early on (the department had the benign habit of handing these out before students chose courses in the spirit of 'this is what you are up for'), I was not able to name texts, but rather had to indicate varied approaches that might be applied to a thoughtful selection of texts. Instead of 'The Franklin's Tale contradicts the Marriage Group: discuss' or 'In *Bleak House* Dickens uses for structure a vanishing point, not a plot: discuss', it proved necessary to offer conceptually generic topics like 'Discuss male interaction in the outlaw materials' or 'Discuss location and value in the outlaw materials.'

I basically understood the need for this generalised approach from the start, but was not always convinced. In the first years I did occasionally try and name a major text: 'Discuss the role played by the *Gest of Robin Hood* in at least two later versions.' But this proved a prolepsis of the adaptation aporia: students who were tempted to fall back on their familiar techniques would find themselves discussing crucially different texts like the *Gest* and either the Errol Flynn or the Douglas Fairbanks film (both of which lack the *Gest* ending), or Peacock and Tennyson with equally disparate versions: in all cases the texts to be compared with the *Gest* seemed to cover much the same ground but in fact differed consistently in meaning and function. The pairs were parallel, not convergent, and the students were faced with writing essays that could only contrast, not compare.

If the lesson drawn from constructing an essay list was that the Robin Hood material is quite without the textually connected coherence of other and canonically established traditions, then the secondary lesson drawn from that, as from my non-venture in adaptation, was that the texts basically stand alone in terms of each other, and also are connected firmly to their contexts. But those contextual connections can be both compared and contrasted and the texts' varying interrelationships between materials and social setting can be isolated, and then those comprehensions of the meanings of each version of the materials can be informatively compared.

That understood, and with an opening address to students on the difference of approach that these materials require, I received a remarkable number of excellent essays over the years, quite a few of which have contributed quite substantially to my own understanding of the Robin Hood tradition. Comprehension of these materials has itself been non-hierarchical.

Going back further in time (disrupting chronology can be a good way of understanding structures as it disavows the alleged forces of development), my own approach to Robin Hood studies and the provision of materials through which to enable those studies was in itself counter to existing academic structures and orders of thought. At Sydney University I worked in a very large English department – over fifty staff and in those days of under-promotion (and so *hoi polloi* communality) only three professors – with many specialised options and specialists to deliver them (we even had our own, quite good, cricket team led by the useful medium-pacer and Test-standard Shakespeare critic Derrick Marsh). I developed and taught a course on the Child ballads, enlivened by my colleague the Canadian poet Phil Roberts, who gave some lectures and especially played and sang ballads to his own accompaniment on the harmonium (not harmonica). We always did a few weeks on the Robin Hood ballads: the students found them of great interest, and asked questions I could not answer about their contexts, meanings, references and so on. So I went in search of material, and found only the quite useful but also general Introduction by Dobson and Taylor and the very suggestive, but necessarily not very detailed, essay by Douglas Gray, well known both as a friend of friends at Oxford and of course as one of the last, and one of the best, of the extraordinary body of medievalists that New Zealand donated to Britain – reverse colonisation at its most potent.⁵

There was no Robin Hood ballad-study shelf in the library – even the ballad scholars (and there were a few with folkloric names like Child, Gummere, Hodgart) did not see the outlaw texts as of much importance in the whole ballad context. Both the students and I wanted more detailed data than that for our interests, and were especially dissatisfied with the fact that the only sign of activity was among two kinds of historicism. One then and still was the naïve and individual-focused empiricism of the 'real Robin Hood' industry much loved by journalists (and quite fairly lampooned in the tongue-in-cheek pages of Murdoch's American supermarket paper *The Sun*; see Figure 16). More interesting, though still with no interest in the texts as such, were the historians trying to understand the political and social context for the outlaw figure. The last kind had valuable elements: Tom Hahn's essay linking the *Past and Present* debate on this topic to post-war English politics is a classic contextual reading, treating the historians as his texts.⁶ But we wanted to think about the interrelation of the texts, with their contexts and – at that time still thinking in a formally canonical mode – with each other. So I started developing a field of study which turned into the survey of the Robin Hood materials, published in 1994, on the basis of an Australian research grant and with the expert research assistance of Lucy Sussex.⁷ While that positioned me for both further research and teaching, the idea of the latter invoked the question of texts. In those pre-internet days courses were handcuffed to publishers: if it was not in print, forget it. I did not feel that Dobson–Taylor had enough range or literary/cultural studies style of commentary, and in any case it was inappropriate to set for classes, being then only a costly hardback, so I made an approach to the TEAMS series and teamed up very positively with Tom Ohlgren, who had already suggested a similar idea, and we produced by 1997 a bulky anthology with all the early texts, a full selection of broadside ballads and – a contribution from the comparative literature tradition still strong in America – quite a few other early outlaw stories, some in translation. I used the proofs of that to start my Cardiff course in 1996, and it worked very well.

That left noticeable a space in the secondary reading needed for serious study. Since the arrival of the photocopier in the mid 1960s university teaching had significantly raised its game. In the old days before machine copying and when libraries usually had only

16 The Murdoch *Sun* and the Real Robin Hood:
Sun, 17 November 1992, p. 1

one copy of each title, your lectures had to begin with an author's birth and death dates: New Criticism was a fine adaptation to the situation, as a mimeographed page of Shakespeare sonnets could be solid work for an hour for a very large class, and they could follow up with their own sonnet-reading. But suddenly we could provide copies of critical essays, however rare, and expect good students to read, compare and apply them – which they did with some spirit: the senior undergraduates could produce models of postgraduate research, and I have seen perfectly publishable third-year essays. But there were difficulties in letting Robin Hood studies follow this highly positive path. Not only were there few essays that did not debate some irrelevant late medieval citizen named R. Hood, but those that did exist were far-flung – Gray's fine piece was published in Tokyo – or buried in some hard-to-access collection – Lord Raglan's classic essay on Robin as an International Hero was in *The Hero*, last reprinted in 1949.

So with the support of a publishing house set up by Derek Brewer, the learned and genial British medievalist, to do more than Oxford and Cambridge University Presses ever dared, I gathered a rather plump collection of material that would make it possible to write decent outlaw academic essays. Some were literary, like Jess Bessinger's epic-oriented survey of approaches to the *Gest*, or Douglas Gray's major contribution; another section reached into the notional history with the political pair to left and right of Hilton and Holt, and others like Maddicott and Richmond extending the field. The range spread wider with Joseph Nagy's classic essay on outlaw folklore and John Matthews's more excitable account of modern mythicism; and just a few taking the cultural history approach that I felt was focal to the thrust of this work, such as Richard Tardif's essay on the audience of the early ballads, from his MA work at Sydney, and Christopher Hill's investigation into what Robin Hood might have signified in the century of the English revolution. A couple of surveys on film, by those fine scholars Jeffrey Richards and Rudy Behlmer, filled out the collection for modernity, and finally came my own piece on *Robin Hood: Men in Tights*, which I felt fulfilled the conceivably serious, possibly just annoying, role of Chaucer's 'Tale of Sir Topas'.[8]

So a general survey was published, sources primary and secondary made available, and there began to be seen Robin Hood teaching and the emergence of conferences and essay collections, led by Tom Hahn at the University of Rochester, and supported in lively fashion by those whom Lorraine Stock memorably called 'the merry men and women' of the International Association for Robin Hood Studies, a body which has successfully modelled itself on the myth in having no elected officers and never charging a fee – though when a Canadian university required payment, our revered colleague Richard Green (itself a notable name in the field) tapped for finance not a passing abbot or sheriff but Robin Hood Flour of Canada. Such as they are, Robin Hood studies were under way. Or was it, as the dictionaries suggest, under weigh? There is difference everywhere.

Especially in the Robin Hood tradition. The more work that was done, by researchers, by students, by continuing creative engagement through novels, television and film, the clearer it became that while it was easy enough to treat this as what seemed an intriguing and relevant subject of study, the politics of myth, in fact Robin Hood just came out differently from other figures in the field like King Arthur, or Jeanne d'Arc, or Sherlock Holmes. The lack of an authoritative textual centre was one recurrent variation, but that was matched by a lack of coherent hierarchical structure in the tradition itself. The myth could have parallel, even contradicting, forms at any one time, and could also exhibit sudden start-ups of new shapes and structures that seemed to have no real contact with the preceding patterns – the shape and feel of the Robin Hood materials across time was as if the Arthurian eighteenth century of abdication and randomisation had continued all the time.

We had become in twenty years quite good at handling the detailed occurrences of the Robin Hood myth, the text–context contiguities were widely discussed, and that cultural history method was spreading steadily through the material – as in Rob Gossedge's essay on Peacock's *Maid Marian* or Lois Potter's on Alfred Noyes's play *Sherwood*.[9] It seemed time to go in the other direction and look at the overall conceptual understanding of this myth that was not in itself canonical or hierarchical. Where was the back of a match-box description to be found, where was the key to all the outlaw mysteries? *Naturellement*, it was in Paris.

The rhizome rises

Another way of seeing both the idea of a canon and also a textualised hierarchical tradition is to use the term 'a grand narrative', meaning the kind of structure that postmodernism in general, and Lyotard's very influential statement of postmodernism's tenets in *The Post-Modern Condition* in particular, sees as a grandiose fiction, a falsification of events and phenomena into rigid and exclusive patterns of comprehension.[10] For Lyotard, the opposite to that hierarchical fiction was a free inspection of data, and for many this seemed to mime democracy: the appeal of postmodernism in modern America seemed to be consistent with multicultural plurality, even a lack of constraints on personal freedom, and the idea was widely adopted as the basis for a free-for-all reading of social and cultural forces – such as a trend in late twentieth-century crime-fiction criticism.

If this could be taken as the structural principle of a modern cultural supermarket, without any awareness of the neo-liberal economic and political model behind it, a more fully comprehended model of multiplicity and potential freedom was offered by the ever-productive and ingenious authors Deleuze and Guattari. The model they offered for cultural production was a viable alternative both in its actual dissemination through the created world and also in its presentation of a structure of the development of and interrelation between cultural elements that was neither inherently hierarchical nor disciplinary in formation and implication.

This was the idea most fully presented – the terms 'developed' and 'argued' would not be appropriate for their insistent invocations of an idea – in *A Thousand Plateaus* (1980). They assert that the traditional 'rational foundation for order' is 'arborescent',[11] suggesting that the coherence, interconnection, upward and onward movement and capacity to spread are all understood as being a single structure like that of a tree. The contradictory model is a rhizome, a widely spread, invisible root-system which drives plants upwards through the ground from any point. It has both connectivity and heterogeneity – 'any point of a rhizome can be connected to anything other, and must be' (p. 7). If understood in cultural terms the rhizome has polyvalent powers: it 'ceaselessly establishes connections between semiotic chains, organisations of power, and circumstances relative to the arts, sciences and social struggles' (p. 7). It is not as simple as 'a semiotic chain' or a 'language', and there is 'no ideal-speaker-listener' (p. 7). The rhizome is inherently something of 'multiplicity' and can expose the 'pseudo-multiplicity' (p. 8) of basically aborescent forms. The arborescent tendency can be traced as operating in and through and upon social systems and legal systems, in modes of bureaucracy and especially in thought-systems.

Through this argument there hovers the threat that a rhizome is simply a different form of organic structure with a variant but operative force of creation and dissemination. But Deleuze and Guattari make it clear that they are using the image as a metaphor of comprehension, not as an underlying description of real construction: they offer 'linear' as the model of linkage in a rhizome, rather than the upward and socio-intellectually ordered features of an arborescent model. They develop this flat-thinking concept to suggest, as in their title, that the significant space of the rhizomatic production is a plateau, understood as a self-existent domain, of, referring to Gregory Bateson, a 'region of intensities whose development avoids any orientation toward a culmination point or external end' (p. 22). Or, a little more clearly, in their own words, the rhizomatic plateau, or textual field grown large, is 'any multiplicity connected to other multiplicities by superficial underground stems in such a way as to form or extend a rhizome' (p. 22).

This utopia without grandness or narratives is read as a form of, or at least a domain for, intellectual anarchism where one can 'overthrow ontology, do away with foundations, nullify endings and beginnings' (p. 25). That may seem an excitable over-statement, but it is in fact strikingly apposite in outlining the effects of the Robin Hood tradition. It is recurrently necessary to note how this cultural field rejects individualist ontology – no Hamlet-like soliloquies here; dispenses with foundations (except for the empiricalistic historians and their search for a real Robin); recurrently avoids dramatically tragic endings of *Morte Darthur* style (the fine film *Robin and Marian* lost money); and does not routinely begin with an explanation of where we are and how we got here, but in rhizomatic fashion the story just commences and then continues.

To think about the Robin Hood tradition in terms of a rhizomatic structure where the coherent determinants of time, place, class and power, as well as their servants in terms of literary tradition, operate only in a casual, not a causal, way will help us to comprehend, and that in a set of minimal comments rather than grand narratives, how the unusual features of this whole tradition can be seen as authentic to its meaning, mission and multiple validity.

Random connections are familiar between distant growths on the plateau. Douglas Fairbanks, not yet known as Senior, fresh from sword-wielding in *The Mark of Zorro* and *The Three Musketeers*, was doubtful about the idea of playing Robin Hood, reportedly saying, 'The spectacle of a lot of flat-footed outlaws in Lincoln green did not strike me as anything to make a picture about.'[12] But he was persuaded when he studied a synopsis of Alfred Noyes's idealistic, even somewhat grandiose, verse play *Sherwood* (1908), and the film appeared in 1922. Temporal rhizomatics lie in the fact that the play itself was not performed until 1926: a commentator might well feel other forms of imaginative misconnection lay behind the name of Fairbanks's script adviser and synopsiser, Lotta Woods, but this apparent outlaw pseudonym was in fact used well before this Robin Hood encounter by Charlotte Nelson, script-writer and member of Fairbanks's coterie.

In a sort of parallel of random connections, the 1991 Kevin Costner vehicle *Robin Hood: Prince of Thieves* took its differentiating subtitle from a novel by Alexandre Dumas published in 1872 in French and not translated until 1903. In rhizomatic asides, it is possible that the very early Robin Hood films were themselves the stimulus for the translation, or at least the triumphs in the USA, of the de Koven–Bache Smith and Tennyson–Sullivan musicals in the 1890s; and as it had appeared two years after his death, it is highly likely that Dumas was not in fact the author at all. But the subtitle was itself required because the late 1980s

American interest in a new Robin Hood movie had been stimulated by the great success there of the Harlech television series *Robin of Sherwood* with the dashingly handsome and innovatively student-radical-style Robin Hood played by Michael Praed. In the USA it was simply titled *Robin Hood*, presumably because the implications that English audiences would find in 'Sherwood' were not expected to be transatlantically shared. The other film of 1991, starring Patrick Bergin, less effectively differentiated itself through spelling his name as Robert Hode. Yet a third, planned to star Mel Gibson, did not get to production, though some feel that he kept on with the concept and it led, with lateral plateau movement, to his starring in *Braveheart*, based on William Wallace, who, it has been argued above (see pp. 48–50), is an influential avatar of Robin Hood.

Another notable rhizomatic Robin Hood feature is the frequent appearance of new characters with either no connection at all with the tradition or, as commonly, with no basis beyond the current author's imagination. Deep in the quiet backwaters of the Robin Hood tradition are characters like the Earl of Pembroke, who is Robin's amatory rival in the 1730 opera. No doubt invoked by the theatrical need – whether on stage or in fiction – for a villain, and a male rival to the hero, he never reappears. In something of the same elusive spirit, when in 1958 Twentieth Century Fox made *Son of Robin Hood*, one of the many films which both deferred to and tried to share the riches of the all-conquering Errol Flynn vehicle of 1938, they double-plated difference by making the central figure in fact a daughter of Robin Hood, acting as a boy – played by the under-emphatic English actress June Laverick. This film also effloresced in villainy with a dastard named 'Simon, the Black Duke des Roches'. A parallel of this weirdness emerged in the almost equally negligible Disney-produced early Keira Knightley vehicle *Princess of Thieves* (2001), in which she plays Robin's daughter, named Gwyn. Nothing is made of the fact that this is in fact a male name, the Welsh masculine version of the female Gwen – and ultimately, for the real rhizomophile, is the basis of Gwenivere, whom Knightley will play in the 2004 *King Arthur*. But she loves a noble called Philip, a previously unknown son to Richard the Lionheart, who will, in a conclusion that must have surprised the Brits but apparently not made them stampede the box office, become King Philip: in a moment at once ancient and modern, this deutero-Marian will apparently be his faithful mistress, good enough to rob the rich but not rule among them.

The roots of outlawry

These slender rhizomatic irruptions into the light of the outlaw tradition make an appropriately frail but suggestive prologue to a grasp of the whole tradition as having major rhizomatic tendencies. One striking feature of some strength is the existence at any particular period of quite parallel strands of the tradition, which do not cohere or rank themselves in a single shape – the absence of arboreality. It is possible to view this feature of the outlaw tradition through a series of equidistant time slots, without any sign of ascent or descent between them, merely the flat, plateau-like variation as described by Deleuze and Guattari.

Around the year 1400 there were in existence and in different ways flourishing a range of Robin Hood responses. One is a set of general references to the yeoman outlaw as a force connected with the forest and some sort of resistance to authority, like Andrew of Wyntoun's c.1420 reference to Robin and John as 'waythemen' who were 'commendit gud'. More general, in reference and implication, are a set of proverbs indicating both the popularity and the elusive strength of the hero; a sermon from 1405–10 provides the first instance of the very popular proverb 'Many men speak of Robin Hood, who never drew his bow' – here reading 'that schotte never in his bowe'. Then there are the *Piers Plowman* references to existing 'rhymes of Robin Hood' and even a few lines from one, in a Lincoln Cathedral manuscript, of 1400–25:

> Robyn Hode in Sherewod stod
> Hodud and hathut
> Hosud and schod
> Foure and twunti arowus
> He bar in hus hondus.[13]

Against these three popular and not unrelated forms of noting and celebrating the active outlaw figure there stands church disapproval – the figure who knows the 'rymes of Robin Hood' in *Piers Plowman* is a priest who now represents Sloth; there is a negative reference in the devout poem of 1405–10 *Dives and Pauper* to those who would 'levir to heryn a tale or a song of Robin Hood or of sum rubaudry than to heryn messe or matynes'. Helen Phillips has shown how this church dissent to the outlaw myth only strengthens in the context of reformation, and the anti-Robin Hood rhizome is a real force into the seventeenth century when it comes to serve the interests of anti-radical conservative social politics.[14]

Where that might be seen as negatively linked to the three strands of outlaw celebration, the other strong Robin Hood realisation of the late medieval period is quite separate in both location and content. The Robin Hood play-games are located mostly in the English south-west, with a few traces in the south-east, and a whole separate settlement, with no clear sign of a direct link with England, in lowland Scotland. In the play-games Robin is clearly not opposed to authority but is rather the emblem of a positive communal spirit: the earliest of the references is from 1426–27 in Exeter, but it appears that this had been going on for some time. But the outlaw story seems at least a century earlier, as suggested by the striking fact that in 1346 a poacher arrested in Rockingham Forest gave his name to the authorities, in the true trickster spirit of minor criminals, as Robin Hood. A sequence in *The Anonimalle Chronicle* relates an apparently staged encounter at Whitsun between the captured French king and dauphin with bow-wielding forest outlaws as early as 1357.[15] A Patent Roll of 1344 gives a list of men accused of tin-raiding in Cornwall including, in order, William Pipere, William Taborer and Robert Hodyn.[16] As Robert Hodyn is preceded by a piper and a taborer this seems the earliest reference to a play-game, but the figure is now involved in crime. It also seems probable that the name of Gilbert Robynhood, recorded in 1296 in Sussex, with some other instances of the surname to follow in the area, may refer to a man who traditionally played the outlaw in some form of public performance.[17]

So there are five early Robin Hood formations in around 1400 – three are generically varied and in terms of appearance unrelated outlaw elements (references, proverbs, literary citations), one is a hostile response to that (church negativity), and one is a quite unrelated formation without outlawry (the play-games). These may well all have an ultimate origin in the Robin who is a leader in the French *bergerie* poems, as has been noted above (see p. 189), but if that is the case it is not an origin of any formative strength, and it is notable that the English transmutation varies the name, adding Hood, and, outside the play-games, foregrounds the outlaw's distance from social authority, as well as in the outlaw story finding a new location in forests adjacent to towns in the English midlands and north.

Around the year 1600, some of these elements are still identifiable, but under considerable variation, and other growths have appeared. The yeoman outlaw is still quite well known in casual references, and by now place-name connections have emerged, usually of landscape features like Robin Hood's Butts for an isolated set of rocks, and the proverbial Robin Hood is also still about – the simplest forms or references seem the most unchanging. The yeoman outlaw in action has been recorded in two manuscript ballads and some plays, and this figure is beginning to move into very popular broadside ballads, which are, as has been argued in Chapter 4, a new development, rhizomatically distant from the previous yeoman outlaw activities. Church dissent has not disappeared: Phillips cites and discusses from this period, as well as previously, various anti-Robin positions held by both reformers and their opponents.[18] The new formation, gentrification, is an aristocracy-focused dissent to and appropriation of the anti-state outlaw, making the hero resist a bad authority, not authority itself. This includes bad Prince/King John, though the Reformation makes the church itself now the major enemy of Lord Robin. Drama as a form of gentrification fills a generic gap, as the play-games have come under constraint across the country, not it seems because Robin Hood in them is a figure of social dissent, but as the occasions themselves are seen as either potentially carnival turned to riot – as happened in 1561 in Edinburgh – or too communally cheerful for a Puritanical cast of official mind. The play-games will survive sparsely, usually in out-of-the-way places. Although gentrification, in the potentially canonical modes of drama and poetry, is planned to be a reversion to arborescence for the outlaw, in making him a displaced lord and faithful to true aristocratic and royal authority, in fact the gentrified element itself operates as a less than potent rhizome, with Lord Robin appearing in very varied and multidirectional forms through theatre and novel and even into film.

In another segment of rhizomatic time, around 1800, the broadside ballad has been recuperated in the collections by Evans and Ritson, but is also still alive in its original print collections known as garlands. The proverbs seem by now to have faded away, but there are still Robin Hood location references, notably in the Sherwood school of poets celebrating both nature and liberal politics (see pp. 110–13), and the older place-name memorialisation is now often transmuted into Romantic locationism, including in the poetry of Keats and Reynolds (see pp. 113–20). The resistant element of the original references and ballads is still available, and the year of social challenge, 1818, is rhizomatically rich for the outlaw, principally found in ungentrified form, but adding to his local identity the potent force of national meaning as Robin is by

Scott reconstructed as a Saxon hero, a new rhizome which does have some quasi-arboreal force as it runs through so many of the novels and films to come, gaining strength from the encounter with other hostile nationalisms – the Norman thuggery of the 1938 Errol Flynn appears to be based on German Brownshirt violence of the time, and not casually: Warner Brothers' Berlin agent had been killed on the street for being Jewish.

Around 1800 the theatre tradition was, in its own highly rhizomatic way, alive and would strengthen, but the rich, if erratic, growth of the novel was in waiting. Dissent to Robin Hood, whether from bishops or princes, seems largely silent, but it is notable that the conservative Scott diverts the gentrification motif into Ivanhoe himself, leaving Robin operating as a very tough, so also very useful, lower-class soldier. This is a form of control of the power of the yeoman figure, but Peacock saves Lord Robin for the tradition largely by, for the first time, condensing his nobility with the energetic action of the yeoman outlaw, and indeed with the spirited romance of Marian herself. His novella operated fairly slowly as an influence on the tradition – there were other rhizomes at work, as Chapter 6 recurrently discusses, but Peacock's influence would be considerable on the stage, where from now on Robin and Marian were secure as the leads (with the incursive Clorinda forgotten); there would usually be a male rival, and also some moderately exciting action, but while Robin in theatre and cinema would not be quite as wildly rhizomatic as he had been on the eighteenth-century stage, the tradition would have none of the rigid arboreality of, say, the Tristan and Isolde tradition.

If soon after 1800 Robin was remade as both a national and a masculine hero, then around 2000 that is still a dominant element in fiction and film, the two dominating modes of English outlaw realisation, but the viewpoints of both have changed by the present – national to international and masculine to a less romantically assertive mode. Proverb and casual reference have now disappeared, though it could be held that the historicist obsession with the real Robin Hood, so concerned with date and place, is a modern form of sentimental localism, and it seems clear that a new mode of referentiality is the recurrent use in headlines and cartoons of the outlaw figure as a trope for financial redistribution – sometimes, as in recent Republican images of Obama, with some hostility. Historicism has also entered the novel with a writer like Parke Godwin, to make Robin a credible Saxon, in *Sherwood* (1991) taking the date back into the late eleventh century,[19] and a different new fictional and political rhizome has been the feminism which, as discussed in Chapter 7, has worked with some vigour through novelists like Roberson and Tomlinson, while in film it has been at most a passing element or substantially diluted into farce.

The strongest growth of the modern period has been in film and then television. It has always seemed that the outlaw tradition is in some way a theatrical form: the ballads themselves are highly active, not internally revealing, and what Gummere famously called their 'leaping and lingering' style is a good way of describing the changes of pace and place that theatre stagily represents, but which film in long-shot and close-up can convey so effectively. It can be argued that while the whole Robin Hood tradition in print has had no masterpieces, at least two of the films, 1922 with Fairbanks and 1938 with Flynn, have reached that level, and the Flynn vehicle had a central influence that is at least quasi-arborescent. Its Little John, Alan Hale, had appeared in the same character in the 1922 film and would do so again in the 1950 *Rogues of Sherwood Forest*: and as that shows, the 1940s and 1950s producers avoided the title *Robin Hood* as an apparent sign of deference – or caution in marketing – which recognises the arboreal potential of the 1938 film, but eludes it for other kinds of growth.

What can also be seen in terms of the present is the range of Robin Hood formations that in previous periods may well have been lost or never recorded – children's literature, school plays and pageants, references in advertisements, dressing up and the constant activity in journalistic references, verbal and visual. This is also by now international. There are, as Hobsbawm and Seal have noted, bandits and outlaws everywhere.[20] Everywhere I go I am always made aware of the existence of the local outlaw – sometimes vividly alive in time as well as place. After lecturing on Robin Hood to students at the University of Santiago de Compostela I asked about the local hero, of whom I had heard, Foufillaz. A young woman pointed across the room and said, 'That boy, his grandfather was executed with Foufillaz.' They were Galician Marxist anti-Francoists: their story still had vivid presence; yet it seemed to mesh with the dynamism of the Robin Hood tradition, not obscure it. It appears that Robin Hood is today the über-outlaw, the archetype of resistance to the authorities, arborescent only in an essentially rhizomatic way.

If as has been argued, in those ways four periods from 1400 to 2000 are themselves replete with outlaw generic variety and separation, there are two other modes in which the multiplicity of the tradition can be appreciated. One is to look at a thematic structure across periods and cultural formations and see how it has been introduced and has varied, and been falsely back-dated, as an example of a non-arboreal emblem of structure across time and genre. Then, to complete this ranging across the field, or plateau, of outlaw growth, it will be appropriate to discuss how, and from where, new rhizomes have developed in the tradition.

The forest laws rhizome

The default opening of a modern Robin Hood story is: a peasant has killed a deer; an agent of authority is about to arrest him, for execution or at least maiming, as having broken the forest laws; Robin Hood rescues him – and so becomes himself an outlaw, a denizen of the forest. This opening is in most of the films and television series, appearing very influentially in Henry Gilbert's novel of 1912. The forest laws are indeed medieval, but their centrality in the Robin Hood tradition is a post-medieval emphasis. However, this is not one of those cases where a feature suddenly enters the tradition, like gentrification, or Saxonism. Killing the king's deer is in fact quite an old element in the tradition, but early on it is one with little emphasis or indeed continuity. There appear to be certain conditions under which it becomes of compelling interest and is then narrativised as the reason for Robin's outlaw status.

F. J. Child remarks in his wide-ranging account of Robin in his headnote to the *Gest* that 'he lives by the king's deer' and that 'Bishops, sheriffs and game-keepers [were] the only enemies he ever had.'[21] But his own editing tended to force the forest laws card on us. Before the *Gest*, which his order implies (incorrectly) is the first of the Robin Hood texts, he prints 'Robin and Gandelyn', where Robyn is a deer-killer: he and Gandelyn 'wentyn to wode to getyn hem fleych',[22] though their enemy is not a forester, or not said to be one at least. Before that Child, presumably through his forest laws emphasis, printed 'Johnie Cock', where the hero is a poaching outlaw from the Scottish borders who is killed by foresters. Last before the *Gest* he prints *Adam Bell*, the only early printed text which does emphasise the forest laws issue. Child's order, his own manipulation, has entered the consciousness of Robin Hood readers and rewriters.

Poaching the king's deer is not absent from the late medieval materials and the earliest use of the name is as a poacher's alias in 1346, but this is not an emphasised early Robin Hood activity. The

Gest recognises, if in passing, the forest laws: '"We lyue by oure kynges deere,"' says Robin (line 1507), but in the other early texts they are almost completely absent. In 'Robin Hood and the Monk' they eat venison pasties[23] but there is no other early reference of even this indirect sort to the forest laws. On the forest laws the *Gest* is, as in many other instances, ambivalent. The feast that the outlaws give the knight includes venison: it has presumably been poached before it was roasted, but this is not an important enough matter to be specified. When the king goes looking for Robin Hood he does come to Plompton Park, and finds the antlered deer gone – but this is not the reason why he is looking for Robin: it is his habit of stealing money from important people like monks and the sheriff.

Most of the seventeenth-century broadside ballads are like the early ballads in making occasional and almost casual references to deer: in the conservative semi-epic *A True Tale of Robin Hood* (1632), there is one mention of them eating 'venson fat and good' in the forest,[24] but nothing more on the topic: the poem is nervous only about Robin Hood's danger to the state, not to gentry land-owning. The apparent lack of interest in the forest laws theme in the early ballads might simply be taken as reality. Barbara A. Hanawalt sees a strong fit between the early Robin Hood poems and criminal reality: her analysis of what outlaws actually did against the law indicates that robbery and assault were normal and that breach of the forest laws was never an issue.[25]

The forest laws do enter the tradition in the ballad 'Robin Hood and Three Young Men',[26] where the men are condemned to death for killing the king's deer. Robin rescues them, and this can be referenced back through the use of the story in Munday and some knowledge of it, or at least its opening, in the late sixteenth-century Sloane 'Life of Robin Hood'. However, this specificity seems unusual. The vividly anti-authoritarian 'Robin Hood's Progress to Nottingham' is only implicitly about forest laws: before Robin's fight with the foresters, it is his youth and assertion of his skill that makes them aggressive.

The broadside ballads include some engagement with forest law discourse. In 'Robin Hood and the Tanner', the tanner pretends to be 'a keeper of the forest', but there is no sign that Robin believes this, or takes it seriously: it is just a fight, as if the broadside creator was aware of the forest laws motif and fitted it in, but with no real structural or thematic impact. In 'Robin Hood and the Tinker', the tinker is bounty-hunting after Robin Hood, and the host of the inn tells him that Robin is off 'killing of the kings deer' (Child no.127, vol. 3, p. 142, st. 27, line 4). But neither tanner nor tinker is a real forester: they are just pretend ones that Robin defeats and incorporates. In 'Robin Hood and the Ranger', the opponent is a genuine forester, and Robin is off 'to kill a fat buck', but then after the equal fight the ranger joins the outlaw band: this complete reversal of 'Robin Hood's Progress to Nottingham' indicates that the forest laws were of relatively trivial weight at this early stage.

The evidence of the lives of Robin Hood confirms the pattern found in the ballads of an intermittent but slowly growing interest in the forest laws motif, though it seems if anything a little later than in the ballads. The Sloane 'Life' speaks of rangers insulting the young Robin, but does not mention forest laws or indeed deer-killing. But in the 1662 *Noble Birth and Gallant Atchievements of the Remarkable Outlaw Robin Hood*, Robin fights against 'keepers of the Kings game' and the author retells the stories of 'Robin Hood and the Tanner' and 'Robin Hood Rescuing Three Young Men'. Of the eighteenth-century prose lives of Robin Hood, the *Whole Life* of 1712 does not advance on this, but the Captain Smith *Life* of 1714 tells the story of 'Robin Hood's Progress to Nottingham' with a difference: the foresters pursue Robin for attempting to kill the king's deer, so moving the story forward into Robin's adult life when he breaks forest laws with his men. But this sense of resistance can also rhizomatically reverse. In 'Robin Hood's Birth, Breeding, Valour and Marriage', Robin's father was a forester, but still, like his mother, of gentry stock, and he, now as gentry at Gamwell Hall, can go hunting with John, his servant. Robin orders his yeoman to kill six brace of bucks: then they have to fight off some outlaw yeomen who want to take the bucks from him: it is forest laws, but Robin operates from the side of authority.

Gentrification itself seems to have had no early interest in the forest laws. Grafton's account of the outlaw earl made overspending the cause of his outlawry; and in the full gentrification of *The Downfall of Robert, Earle of Huntington* (1598–99) the forest law issues are not noticed at all and Munday seems positively to distance Robin from improper hunting: there is 'venson' in the forest (line 1518), and as Little John notes to the friar (or rather, in the para-play, Sir John Eltham notes to Skelton) there has been 'no hunting song, no coursing of the buck' (line 2213). Though Scathlock and Scarlock, the widow's sons, are rescued from the sheriff, there is no forest law reason for their intended fate – unlike in the ballad version. When the king arrives at the end of *The Downfall* there is no mention of breaking the forest laws, and then in the sequel *The Death*, the king and Robin go hunting together: in his later masque *Metropolis Coronata* (1615) Munday links Robin with hunting more positively as he sings 'Now wend we together, my merry men all, Unto the forest side a' and sums up: 'Our lives are wholly given to hunt, And hunt the merry greenwood.'[27]

In the light of this evidence there is at most slow early growth in the force of the forest laws motif, building up to a moderate level by the early eighteenth century in the late broadside tradition, but nothing like the very strong interest of the nineteenth century (including among scholars like Child), which has carried on to the present. The question is – what was going on in the context to cause this? What made these forest law issues of increasing interest so that they started to grow, unevenly, but clearly enough?

The history of enclosure is complex and still not fully grasped – the timings, locations and public responses are quite controversial, with a clear politics behind the way the scholars fall into, effectively, lords and commoners. But it is agreed that there were two major periods. From the sixteenth century until the early to mid eighteenth century, enclosures were by local agreement – that is, the lords persuaded or forced people to give up their traditional rights and very often to move. Some historians call it enclosure by consent. There are records of dissent through the period, and by the eighteenth century there is strong evidence of it as recorded in E. P. Thompson's book *Whigs and Hunters*. The 'Black Acts' of the 1720s were brought in against those who broke into forests with blackened faces, which were used from the medieval period, apparently as disguise. The ballad evidence I have discussed above makes it clear that this resistance feeling did not significantly enter the early Robin Hood broadside tradition, but was making itself visible by the later seventeenth century, and there is some sign of it gaining strength in the eighteenth century.

It seems that it was the parliamentary enclosures, rather than the consent enclosures, which stimulated the new intensity of interest in the forest law material in the Robin Hood tradition, but why so late? Partly because they became common only in the second half of the eighteenth century and perhaps partly because of their uneven distribution across Britain: the acts mostly applied to areas in the north and west, the best lands having already been enclosed by the lords via consent, and there is as we know little sign that Robin Hood is strongly associated with the south, the south midlands and East Anglia, the primary consent enclosure areas. Also the parliamentary acts were mostly to do with forest and wild enclosures, those used for hunting, while the earlier allegedly consensual reclamation dealt mostly with the previously common village fields, where Robin Hood had no specific meaning.

In the 1730s, when the blacks were invading newly enclosed forest land, they had a mythical leader, but as Thompson notes, although he was like Robin Hood in many ways the only mythic name he was given, in Hampshire's Farnham Park, was 'King John' – perhaps a reference to the mythic reformist powers of Magna Carta.[28] And then in 1765, when royalty enclosed Richmond Park, it was not Robin Hood who was associated with the resistance, but Merlin. No doubt this was because the Merlin's Cave that Queen Caroline had built there in 1735 had just been destroyed as part of Capability Brown's manoeuvres, which included the enclosure. Merlin was held to have predicted both this destruction and the civil resistance, which included breaking into the park in daylight to walk about and use it.

As has been noted in Chapter 6 (see pp. 154–5), the idea of the forest laws is strong in the nineteenth-century novels, especially in the early ones where a general liberal politics is espoused, engaging as a basis of democratic politics the anti-royal hostility that stretches from Pope's critique of the Norman forest laws in *Windsor Forest* (1713) through to Peacock's more personal critique of the enclosing of Windsor Forest, as Gossedge explains the thrust of *Maid Marian* (see pp. 131–2). The idea was widely and strongly felt in the ways Thompson has explored (as also by Thomas Miller: see pp. 155–7), and while this certainly explains why the incident where a peasant, often Much the Miller's son, is about to be taken and probably executed for forest poaching is made the default opening to the story and the basis of Robin's commitment to resisting authority, this is still not common until the twentieth century. As a general idea of freedom curtailed, the forest laws respond very favourably with the general idea of a natural forest freedom, and they have remained emotionally close to the core of the developed tradition, but they do not relate directly with their original contexts: they are medievalist, not medieval.

Routes to rhizomes

Such developments of a theme into central importance from being of underemphasised recurrence, through specific contextual politics to a general idealistic acceptance, are common across the tradition – parallels in this mode to the forest laws are Robin's nobility, his Englishness, the horse and cavalry, his link to the crusades, Marian's possession of agency. This process of rhizomatic recurrence on the Robin Hood plateaus largely replaces the general acceptance and careful variation of plot patterns which is normal in the canonical and arboreal mythic traditions. Origins are very often mysterious in constructing a history of the Robin Hood tradition, from the very beginning and right into the well-recorded present.

To explain the shift from the benign socialised Robin Hood of the play-games to the chronologically overlapping forest-based enemy of the state who appears in the early ballads, the historicists resort to imitation, looking for a suitable law-breaker of the preceding period. But as none exists with any fame at all, just a few Robert Hoods who got into minor bother, the idea of a Jack Sheppard or Dick Turpin of the medieval north midlands seems to be self-cancelled. If the *bergerie* Robin is the source of both play-game benignity and social aggression – and he does have elements of both, if mostly the former – then a major change occurred in England, by the early fourteenth century at the latest.

It may well be credible to relate this negative refocusing of the hero to the dire circumstances of the fourteenth century, yet that is still an act of faith to some extent. But it is worth noting that in popular poetry there are parallels, at least a comparable rhizome in the same part of the plateau. *Gamelyn*, as has been discussed in Chapter 3 (see pp. 66–7), has some patterns that converge with the Robin Hood story, if at a higher social level, but this may indicate not just a path to gentrification for Robin (though it is that, as is there argued), but also a common sense of dissent and disinheritance shared across the less elevated orders of free men – Holt's linking of the Robin Hood ballads to the concerns of the lower gentry remains persuasive. There are some other whispers of this formation in popular romance, like the humiliated hero of *Sir Launfal*, who is happily relocated through a fairy mistress, and there are varied, and always redeemed, elements of this gentry outcast figure in the other popular romances *Sir Cleges*, *Sir Degrevant* and *Sir Amadace* and also in the 'Fair Unknown' stories like *Libeaus Desconus* and Malory's 'Tale of Sir Gareth'. A closer generic parallel may be the remarkably under-discussed series of 'King and Subject' romances (see pp. 68–9), where the king, travelling incognito, meets some skilled tradesman or minor landholder, listens to his complaints and notes his breaches of law and order, and the whole ends back at court, where royalty is revealed and the subject is in some way – through either generosity or constraint – brought back into non-dissenting line. The *Gest* evidently shares this path towards the end, but the striking feature is that these texts are beginning to find a way of providing a voice, and an outcome, for the interests of a class well below the chivalric self-identifiers who have dominated the expanses of romance.

If this originary outlaw moment is largely a puzzle, and one overlaid by the gentrification that has been argued for above in the *Gest* in Chapter 3, then the next major generic move in the relating of Robin Hood's adventures is just as formally enigmatic – or rhizomatic. As Chapter 4 has argued, there is no simple development from peasant song to urban print, and nor is there a general transition from the early long ballad form into the single-page sung broadsides. What appears to have happened is that the popularity of the Robin Hood theme led a new productive format – the printed broadside – to adopt it. Perhaps there are hangovers from before, as seems likely with 'Robin Hood and the Pinder of Wakefield', but basically a busy new productivity both moves into the verbal slickness of seventeenth-century commercial verse and also responds in some ballads to the parallel rhizome of gentrified Robin.

It is possible to see some seventeenth-century concerns in the broadsides. At times the gentry are favoured, the enemy is much more likely to be a Catholic religious than a state official, and the shape of something approaching a biographic life consistent with early modern individualism is to be discerned in the garlands and the emergent prose lives. But at the same time a newly formed antiauthoritarian rhizome is lustily announced in the popularity of the distinctly direct 'Robin Hood's Progress to Nottingham' and the popularity of the gallows-rescue ballads, both probably having a pre-1600 origin.

That mix of formal innovation, sub-generic incoherence, porosity to other influences and sometimes apparently random inclusion of material seems the model – the anti-arboreal model – for each new set of Robin Hood texts. As from 1730 the musical plays slowly gather, they do not in any way look back to the models of the earlier plays, which were staged ballad-type adventures, with their structural, indeed royalist, reversal in the 1661 *Robin Hood and his Crew of Souldiers*. The occurrence of rhizomatic reversal seems a regular, if occasional, feature, and such a sense of opposition is almost the only sign of an assumed coherence in the other materials. The *Gest* opposes by semi-gentrification the earlier ballads; Munday definitely relocates the yeoman tradition socially; the few gentrified ballads in their turn implicitly resist the thrust of the main broadside direction.

Without any such sense of any coherence worth resisting, the eighteenth-century plays respond to theatre requirements in the gender of the characters and the nature of the plots, then draw in elements from all over the theatrical place. Only for Christmas 1795 do they recognise something beyond a generic rhizomatic connection in using ballad material from Ritson's new collection – but with plenty of other non-arboreal growth as well.

As the discussion of the novels has shown, the same centreless conditions occur when the first five just start off in radically different directions, which might be identified as Gothic (Anon), Nationalist (Scott), Romantic (Peacock), Radical (Miller) and Liberal (James). Only with Egan's determinedly popular hand, and his realisation of the archetypally Victorian core of a para-bourgeois family in a patriotic context, does the novel settle to anything like a consistent shape, though the first response to its pattern is Stocqueler's spirited, if also casual and partly incoherent, rhizomatic reversal of almost all its details – except the bourgeois familial patriotism at the core.

Film too establishes itself on a random range of variant sources: as far as we can tell the five made before 1914 are hybrids of some ballad story (basically known through Pyle) and petty-bourgeois modern ideologies, with Robin as active bread-winner, Marian as lovely but timid partner, the pair facing ugly authoritarian enemies, with faithful grotesques in support. Via Noyes, as noted above, the Fairbanks film is both entirely gentrified and entirely romantic, doing with some vitality the work Munday might well have aspired to – and then Warner Brothers went off in a direction varied not only through having sound and colour, but also enjoying in its script-writing process a positive carnival of difference, as Rudy Behlmer's detailed account records.[29]

There were multiple rhizomatic moves at first. An MGM musical was planned, following the de Koven–Bache Smith stage version, with Jeanette MacDonald and Nelson Eddy – what a loss that was – then there was a Warner Brothers' plan for a vehicle starring James Cagney. However unlikely that may seem in the light of his later work, he had done well in *A Midsummer Night's Dream*, and as what would become the Hays Office was closing in on what it felt was modern indecent realism, the historical romance was an attractive option for studios – the audiences seemed entirely adaptable. There were apparently two other studios with Robin

Hood film plans which did get to scripting stage, but little is known of them, even to Behlmer.

The first writer whom Warner Brothers employed did not want to use Marian because he felt she was basically outside the tradition (he was English and something of a scholar). Other random moves were raised and abandoned: initially Robin was to be a yeoman, and, also remembering Scott, there was to be a major siege of Nottingham Castle by the returning King Richard. In a new writer's version this climax was dropped as too costly, Robin became a Saxon knight, and Marian, now in the script, was herself a Saxon, but also a true lady. At this stage she was loved by Sir Guy, who was left out of the next writer's version, where Robin went on crusade, eventually returning to the greenwood, but was finally given as hostage to make John sign Magna Carta – and then John had him bled to death. After this forcefully new script, more changes followed with a new writer – Robin went back to being a Saxon yeoman and there was to be a great night battle, but this was rapidly judged far too expensive. Finally, close to production Robin was promoted to noble and, changing everything, the appointed director William Keighley wanted to start with a great tournament, as in the Fairbanks picture. Presumably cost defeated this whisper of canonicity, and neither the idea nor Keighley survived. Somehow, out of that apparently out-of-hand rhizomaticity, Michael Curtiz's well-organised and highly effective film was generated, and it dominated its successors – not by being copied and altered, like Malory or Tennyson, but by inspiring completely different formations. It did have impact, but that was expressed negatively, in recurrent quests for difference in succeeding Robin Hood films. Kevin Costner's ungainly trousers are apparently to be blamed on his wish not to appear in Flynn-type well-filled green tights.

Growth across a critical field

The creative forces of the Robin Hood tradition are, as has been argued here, quite unlike the canonical and hierarchical traditions of the stories of those like Arthur or Tristan and Isolde that are rich in both literary and social authority. Teaching and writing about the tradition have to recognise that its structure responds to the rhizomatic, not the arboreal models, as outlined by Deleuze and Guattari. Whether seen at randomly selected periods, like 1400, 1600, 1800 or 2000, or assessed in terms of one of its major domains of meaning, both intermittent and recurrent, like the forest laws, or understood in terms of its processes of re-formation, the tradition is constantly untraditional. It renews itself in terms of current political forces and media of dissemination, and consistently has as scant a respect for literary and formalistic authority as it has for social and legal forces of order: even disseminated rhizomes have an underlying interconnecting root.

It is worth considering whether this is also true of the scholarship and criticism about Robin Hood. When I gathered a bulky set of essays for reprinting in 1998, responding to the four areas of Literary, Historical/Political, Mythic and Film, my express intention was to make standardly available facilities for scholarship and analysis of the outlaw myth. In the past fifteen years there has been a growing, though not huge, amount of this kind of material, but it does not appear that wide or purposive reference has been made to that notionally arboreal resource. It would be possible to suggest that Robin Hood scholarship itself has rhizomatic characteristics and is more notable for fine *aperçus* and interventions than for essays dealing quasi-canonically in terms of the overall coherence and constructive comprehension of the tradition.

While I would in intellectually traditional terms probably prefer to see the present book as a tree of knowledge, it might itself well be read as a set of unusually detailed, or perhaps obsessive, rhizomatic sequences, and could even be welcomed as such. It might in fact be better advised to think of ourselves, as Robin Hood scholars, as light of foot and multiple of focus. The present certainly offers challenges of a parallel volatility. Only fifteen years ago Osama bin Laden was being spoken of as 'the Saudi Robin Hood' – the internet is rich in material on this strange by-way of misguided discourse. And, not unrelated, the crusades have returned to the core of the Robin Hood material, having been largely ignored at the time – the knight of the *Gest* thought that would really be the last resort for a fighting gentleman, but for the noble outlaw as recently portrayed by Jonas Armstrong and Russell Crowe, that was where their fidelity to truth was annealed.

Soldier Robin assisting his king, however briefly, might suggestion a relation to another mythic structure, that of King Arthur with its rich tone of hierarchy and canonicity. Membership of university research committees had led me to admire, if from a distance, the scientists' pleasure in negative results, which they saw as tidy, economical of effort and providing guidance for a different direction, a process not unrhizomatic in its way, and so in this spirit I embarked on a study of the relations or, as I thought, lack of them between Robin and Arthur.[30] At first I found a gratifying absence of contact between the two – and then to my surprise I found evidence in very recent films for an apparent cohering of the heroic myths, notably in the 2004 film *King Arthur*, usually regarded as fairly dire, but in a way fascinating as Keira Knightley continued as underdressed archeress, Merlin was a forest lord, and best of all Ray Winstone as Sir Bors offered again his soccer-hooligan rendering of Will Scarlett from *Robin of Sherwood*. I also noted that this was the first film to dare to use *King Arthur* as its title, whereas the title *Robin Hood* was usual, except when Flynn ruled for a while: so Arthur here drew on Robin's strength. The essay ended by speculating whether the two might converge further now that kings had to pretend to be common men, and free forest spirits could lord it in modern celebrity. Robin might become arboreal in more than the terms of his environment.

However, in both film and fiction it seems that twenty-first-century anxieties about order and authority have put that post-1980s egalitarian romanticism to flight, but maybe a future Robin, when reading has been lost to the machines, and canons are only technological, may face the ultimate threat of being as constrained and ultimately as tragic as a king. Or perhaps not: the future of the tradition may lie in no more than the sub-rhizomatic incoherence of electronic games and Twitter tags; or maybe it will avoid royal tragedy and operate in ultra-modernity less ignobly as an avatar of the world-challenging individualism of figures in the mould of Julian Assange, Bradley Manning, Edward Snowden and, already in fiction, Lisbeth Salander.

In whatever mode Robin returns, it will definitely not be as a merely revamped version of himself: his multiform vigour is rooted in the contextual ground itself, and however full our knowledge of the tradition and however well advised our critical arsenal of explanation, commentators will need an equally volatile capacity to comprehend – meaning both understand and hold onto – the continuing rhizomaticity of Robin Hood.

Notes

1 W. W. Greg, *The Calculus of Variants: An Essay on Textual Criticism* (Oxford: Clarendon, 1927).
2 For a discussion of editorial ideology see Stephen Knight, 'Textual Variants, Textual Variance', *Southern Review* (Adelaide), 16 (1983): 44–54.

3 Stephanie Barczewksi, *Myth and National Identity in Nineteenth-Century Britain: The Legends of King Arthur and Robin Hood* (Oxford: Oxford University Press, 2000). For details of the non-English British Arthurians see Rob Gossedge and Stephen Knight, 'Arthur in the Sixteenth to the Nineteenth Centuries', in Elizabeth Archibald and Ad Putter (eds), *The Cambridge Companion to the Arthurian Legend* (Cambridge: Cambridge University Press, 2009), pp. 103–19, at pp. 109–11.
4 For a discussion of this little-known figure see Stephen Knight, 'The Arctic Arthur', *Arthuriana*, 12 (2011): 59–89.
5 The material by R. B. Dobson and John Taylor is the 'Introduction' to their edition *Rymes of Robin Hood: An Introduction to the English Outlaw* (London: Heinemann, 1976), rev. edn (Stroud: Sutton, 1999). Douglas Gray's essay is 'The Robin Hood Poems', *Poetica* (Tokyo), 18 (1984): 1–18. The latter and the segment of Dobson and Taylor entitled 'The Legend since the Middle Ages' are reprinted in Stephen Knight (ed.), *Robin Hood: An Anthology of Scholarship and Criticism* (Brewer: Cambridge, 1999).
6 Thomas Hahn, 'Robin Hood and the Rise of Cultural Studies', in Ruth Evans, Helen Fulton and David Matthews (eds), *Medieval Cultural Studies* (Cardiff: University of Wales Press, 2006), pp. 39–54.
7 Stephen Knight, *Robin Hood: A Complete Study of the English Outlaw* (Oxford: Blackwell, 1994).
8 See in Knight (ed.), *Robin Hood: An Anthology*, Jess Bessinger, 'The Gest of Robin Hood Revisited', pp. 39–50; Douglas Gray, 'The Robin Hood Poems', pp. 3–37; R. H. Hilton, 'The Origins of Robin Hood', pp. 197–210; J. C. Holt, 'The Origins and Audience of the Ballads of Robin Hood', pp. 211–32; J. R. Maddicott, 'The Birth and Setting of the Ballads of Robin Hood', pp. 233–55; Christopher Hill, 'On Robin Hood', pp. 285–96; Richard Tardif, 'The "Mistery" of Robin Hood: A New Social Context for the Texts', pp. 345–62; Colin Richmond, 'An Outlaw and Some Peasants: The Possible Significance of Robin Hood', pp. 363–76; Joseph Falaky Nagy, 'The Paradoxes of Robin Hood', pp. 411–25; John Matthews, 'The Games of Robin Hood', pp. 393–410; Jeffrey Richards, 'Robin Hood on the Screen', pp. 429–40; Rudy Behlmer, 'Robin Hood on the Screen: From Legend to Film', pp. 441–60; Stephen Knight, 'Robin Hood: Men in Tights: Fitting the Tradition Snugly', pp. 461–7.
9 Rob Gossedge, 'Thomas Love Peacock, Robin Hood and the Enclosure of Windsor Forest', in Stephen Knight (ed.), *Robin Hood in Greenwood Stood: Alterity and Context in the English Outlaw Tradition* (Turnhout: Brepols, 2011), pp. 135–64; Lois J. Potter, 'Robin Hood and the Fairies: Alfred Noyes's *Sherwood*', in Helen Phillips, ed., *Robin Hood Medieval and Post-Medieval* (Dublin: Four Courts Press, 2005), pp. 167–80.

10 Jean-François Lyotard, *The Post-Modern Condition*, trans. Geoffrey Bennington and Brian Massumi (Manchester: Manchester University Press, 1984; French original 1979).
11 Gilles Deleuze and Félix Guattari, *A Thousand Plateaus: Capitalism and Schizophrenia*, trans. Brian Massumi (London: Athlone Press, 2004; French original 1980), p. xii.
12 See Rudy Behlmer, 'Robin Hood on the Screen', *Films in Review*, 16 (1965): 91–102, at p. 95.
13 The text reads 'thunti'. It seems more likely that a scribe has misread the elaborate 'w' in a late medieval hand for the almost equally elaborate 'h' than that the quite different letters 'n' and 'r' have been confused. In any case 'four and thirty' would be an oddly random number of arrows to have.
14 See Helen Phillips, 'Reformist Polemics, Reading Publics, and Unpopular Robin Hood', in Knight (ed.), *Robin Hood in Greenwood Stood*, pp. 87–117.
15 V. H. Galbraith (ed.), *The Anonimalle Chronicle, 1333 to 1381* (Manchester: Manchester University Press, 1927), pp. 40–1.
16 *The Calendar of the Patent Rolls of Edward III*, vol. 6 (London: Stationery Office, 1902), p. 401, under 20 July 1344, Westminster.
17 See Dobson and Taylor (eds), *Rymes of Robin Hood*, pp. 12–13.
18 Phillips, 'Reformist Polemics', pp. 111–14.
19 Parke Godwin, *Sherwood* (New York: HarperCollins, 1991).
20 See Eric Hobsbawm, *Bandits*, 2nd edn (London: Penguin, 1985); Graham Seal, *The Outlaw Legend: A Cultural Tradition in Britain, America and Australia* (Cambridge: Cambridge University Press, 1996).
21 F. J. Child (ed.), *The English and Scottish Popular Ballads*, 5 vols, reprint edn (New York: Dover, 1965), vol. 3. p. 42.
22 Stephen Knight and Thomas Ohlgren (eds), *Robin Hood and Other Outlaw Tales*, 2nd edn, TEAMS Middle English Texts (Kalamazoo: Western Michigan University Press, 2000), p. 230, line 11.
23 Knight and Ohlgren (eds), *Robin Hood and Other Outlaw Tales*, p. 130, line 1507.
24 Knight and Ohlgren (eds), *Robin Hood and Other Outlaw Tales*, p. 609, line 152.
25 Barbara A. Hanawalt, 'Ballads and Bandits: Fourteenth-Century Outlaws and the Robin Hood Poems', in Barbara A. Hanawalt (ed.), *Chaucer's England: Literature in Historical Context*, Medieval Studies at Minnesota, 4 (Minneapolis: University of Minnesota Press, 1992), pp. 154–75.
26 This ballad has many titles: Child uses 'Robin Hood Rescuing Three Squires' but this seems wrong as they are not always at the social level of squires – they can also be the three sons of a poor widow. The title used here is from Knight and Ohlgren (eds), *Robin Hood and Other Outlaw Tales*.

27 Anthony Munday, *Metropolis Coronata: The Triumph of Ancient Drapery* (London: Purslowe, 1615), pp. 1–2, 21–2.
28 E. P. Thompson, *Whigs and Hunters: The Origin of the Black Act* (London: Allen Lane, 1975); see chapter 5, 'King John', pp. 142–6.
29 See Rudy Behlmer, 'Introduction: From Legend to Film', in Rudy Behlmer (ed.), *The Adventures of Robin Hood* (Madison: University of Wisconsin Press, 1979), pp. 17–24.
30 Stephen Knight, 'Robin Hood versus King Arthur', in David Matthews (ed.), *In Strange Countries: Middle English Literature and its Afterlife* (Manchester: Manchester University Press, 2011), pp. 9–24.

Appendix A

Robin Hood broadside ballads in collections

The Noble Birth and Gallant Atchievements of the Remarkable Outlaw Robin Hood, 1662 (prose)

Robin Hood's Noble Parentage
Robin Hood's Delight
Robin Hood's Progress to Nottingham
Robin Hood and the Tanner
Robin Hood and the Butcher
Robin Hood and the Beggar
Robin Hood and the Stranger (Robin Hood Newly Revived)
Robin Hood and the Bishop
Robin Hood and Queen Katherine
Robin Hood and the Curtal Friar
The Noble Fisherman
Robin Hood's Chase

Garlands of 1663, 1670, 1684–86 and 1689

Robin Hood's Progress to Nottingham
Robin Hood Newly Revived
Robin Hood and the Pinder of Wakefield
Robin Hood and the Bishop
Robin Hood and the Butcher
Robin Hood and Will Stutely
Robin Hood and the Beggar (= Robin Hood Rescuing Three Young Men)
Robin Hood and Queen Katherine
Robin Hood and the Tanner
Robin Hood and the Curtal Friar
Robin Hood and the Shepherd
Robin Hood's Golden Prize

Appendix A

Robin Hood's Chase
Little John Begging
Robin Hood's Delight

The 1663 garland starts with 'Robin Hood and Queen Katherine' and then repeats it in place. There are some name variations in the 1663 garland: 'The Noble Fisherman' is 'Robin Hood's Golden Prize at Sea', and 'Robin Hood's Golden Prize' is 'Robin Hood Robbing Two Priests'.

Dicey garland of c.1740

The Preface dates Robin Hood to the King Richard I period and says he is poor 'having riotously spent his estates' (as in Richard Grafton, *Chronicle at Large and Meere History of the Affayres of England: and Kings of the Same* (London: Tottle and Toye, 1569), but no title is mentioned.

Robin Hood's Birth, Breeding, Valour and Marriage
Robin Hood's Progress to Nottingham
The Jolly Pinder of Wakefield
Robin Hood and the Bishop
Robin Hood and the Butcher
Robin Hood and the Tanner
Robin Hood and the Tinker
Robin Hood and Allen a Dale
Robin Hood and the Shepherd
Robin Hood and the Curtal Friar
Robin Hood Newly Reviv'd
Robin Hood and Queen Katherine
Robin Hood's Chase
Robin Hood's Golden Prize
Robin Hood and Will Stutely
The Noble Fisherman
Robin Hood's Delight
Robin Hood and the Beggar (with rescue)
Robin Hood and the Prince of Aragon
Little John and the Beggars
Robin Hood and the Ranger
Robin Hood and Little John
Robin Hood and the Bishop of Hereford

Robin Hood Rescuing Three Squires
The King's Disguise and Friendship with Robin Hood
Robin Hood and the Golden Arrow
Robin Hood and the Valiant Knight
Epitaph

Thomas Evans (ed.), *Old Ballads, Historical and Narrative, With Some of Modern Date, Now First Collected and Reprinted from Rare Copies*, 2 vols (London: Evans, 1777)

Robin Hood's Progress to Nottingham
Robin Hood and the Pinder of Wakefield
Robin Hood and the Bishop
Robin Hood and the Butcher
Robin Hood and the Tanner
Robin Hood and the Tinker
Robin Hood and Allen a Dale
Robin Hood and the Shepherd
Robin Hood and the Curtal Friar
Robin Hood Newly Reviv'd
Renowned Robin Hood (= Robin Hood and Queen Katherine)
Robin Hood's Chase
Robin Hood's Golden Prize
Robin Hood and Will Stutely
The Noble Fisherman
Robin Hood's Delight
Robin Hood and the Beggar (with rescue)
Little John and the Beggars
Robin Hood and the Ranger
Robin Hood and Little John
Robin Hood and the Bishop of Hereford
Robin Hood Rescuing Three Squires
The King's Disguise and Friendship with Robin Hood
Robin Hood and the Golden Arrow
Robin Hood and the Valiant Knight

This is the c.1740 Dicey garland order, without 'Robin Hood's Birth, Breeding, Valour and Marriage' at the start or 'Robin Hood and the Prince of Aragon' after 'Robin Hood and the Beggar'.

Appendix A

Joseph Ritson (ed.), *Robin Hood: A Collection of All the Ancient Poems, Songs and Ballads Now Extant Relative to the Celebrated English Outlaw (to which are Prefixed Anecdotes of his Life)*, 2 vols (London: Egerton and Johnson, 1795)

In vol. 2, where the broadside ballads are reprinted, Ritson follows Evans exactly (including the omission of 'Robin Hood and the Prince of Aragon') but inserts 'Robin Hood's Birth, Breeding, Valour and Marriage' back at the start as in the c.1740 garland, and adds 'Robin Hood's Death' at the end. In the previous volume Ritson prints the manuscript ballads except for 'Robin Hood and the Monk' (inserted in the second edition, 1823) and also prints *The Gest of Robin Hood* and Parker's 1632 *A True Tale of Robin Hood*.

F. J. Child (ed.), *The English and Scottish Popular Ballads*, 5 vols, reprint edn (New York: Dover, 1965)

* = Broadside or garland ballad from the 17th century
The Gest of Robin Hood
Robin Hood and Guy of Gisborne
Robin Hood and the Monk
Robin Hood's Death
Robin Hood and the Potter
*Robin Hood and the Butcher
*Robin Hood and the Friar
*Robin Hood and the Pinder
*Robin Hood and Little John
*Robin Hood and the Tanner
*Robin Hood and the Tinker
*Robin Hood Newly Reviv'd
*Robin Hood and the Prince of Aragon
*Robin Hood and Scotchman
Robin Hood and the Ranger
The Bold Pedlar and Robin Hood
*Robin Hood and the Beggar I (with rescue)
Robin Hood and the Beggar II
*Robin Hood and the Shepherd
*Robin Hood's Delight
Robin Hood and the Pedlars
*Robin Hood and Allen a Dale

*Robin Hood's Progress to Nottingham
*Robin Hood Rescuing Three Squires
*Robin Hood and Will Stutely
*Little John Begging
*Robin Hood and the Bishop
*Robin Hood and the Bishop of Hereford
*Robin Hood and Queen Katherine
*Robin Hood's Chase
*Robin Hood's Golden Prize
*Robin Hood's Birth, Breeding, Valour and Marriage
*Robin Hood and Maid Marian
The King's Disguise and Friendship with Robin Hood
Robin Hood and the Golden Arrow
Robin Hood and the Valiant Knight
A True Tale of Robin Hood

Child places some emphasis on the presumptive date of a ballad's origin. Without evidence he feels that 'Robin Hood and Little John' and 'Robin Hood's Death' should be early, but does not see a likely early date for 'Robin Hood's Progress to Nottingham'. He also tries to group ballads with avatars, and this can cut across dating, as with 'Robin Hood and the Butcher' after 'Robin Hood and the Potter', two 'bishop' ballads together and 'Robin Hood Newly Revived', 'Robin Hood and Scotchman' and 'Robin Hood and the Prince of Aragon' together (it is puzzling that they are placed apparently so early). He was aware of the lateness of 'The Bold Pedlar and Robin Hood' but placed it strangely early after 'Robin Hood and the Ranger', a broadly similar ballad, but not itself very early. He was doubtful about, but printed, the 19th-century forgery 'Robin Hood and the Pedlars'. His generic linking process also brings 'Robin Hood and Guy of Gisborne' up early, and yet *A True Tale of Robin Hood*, which actually survives before it and most of the broadsides, is placed at the end, presumably as generically different. More recent editors, Dobson–Taylor and Knight–Ohlgren, have also put the early material first and have followed it with generic groupings.

Appendix B

Robin Hood broadside ballads by date

1. Presumably or probably before 1600

Because story known in period

Robin Hood and the Pinder of Wakefield
Sources: Broadside, 1632; Percy Folio, c.1645; garland, 1663.
Note: Story known to the author of the play *George a Greene*, c.1592, so presumably 16th century; may well be mentioned in Stationers' Register reference of 1557/58.
Type: Anti-authority.

Robin Hood Rescuing Three Young Men
Sources: Percy Folio, c.1645; broadsides, 18th century – 10 versions, plus as 'Robin Hood and Will Stukely', broadside, 1623–61; garland, 1663; and as 'Robin Hood and Robin Hood and the Beggar I', broadside, 1623–61, garland, 1663.
Note: Known to Anthony Munday in his 1598–99 plays and Sloane 'Life of Robin Hood' (just disguised as a beggar in Sloane, no rescue). Likely to be 16th century.
Type: Anti-authority/some gentrification in version where rescued men are squires.

Robin Hood's Progress to Nottingham
Sources: Broadside, 1623–61; garland, 1663 (9 versions, including 1662 prose *The Noble Birth and Gallant Atchievements*).
Note Known to Sloane 'Life of Robin Hood', and no other known source so probably 16th century.
Type: Anti-authority.

Robin Hood and Allen a Dale
Source: Broadside, 1674–79; garland, c.1740.

Note: Forresters manuscript variant version a little earlier? Known to Sloane 'Life of Robin Hood' in version where the bridegroom is Will, not Allen, so probably 16th century.
Type: Anti-church, some anti-authority/celebration.

Robin Hood and Little John
Source: Broadside, 1694–1700; garland, c.1740.
Note: Registered in Stationers' Register 1624. Child (ed.), *The English and Scottish Popular Ballads*, vol. 5, p. 297, said 1680–85. Perhaps ballad known to author of the lost 1594 play *Robin Hood and Little John*, or in popular drama tradition. Possibly 16th century.
Type: Celebration.

Because of links to early texts
Robin Hood and the Butcher
Sources: Percy Folio, c.1645; broadside, 1623–61; garland, c.1740.
Type: Anti-authority.

Robin Hood and Friar Tuck
Sources: Broadside, 1625;'Robin Hood and the Curtal Friar', Percy Folio, c.1645; garland, 1663.
Note: Apparently known to Sloane 'Life of Robin Hood' (or just from popular drama?) so probably 16th century.
Type: Anti-church?/celebration.

Robin Hood's Death
Sources: Percy Folio, c.1645; garland, 1786.
Note: Added to texts in Forresters manuscript, and 'Robin Hood and the Valiant Knight' in garlands – presumably known from *The Gest of Robin Hood* though Percy's use may suggest an early 17th-century or even 16th-century ballad.
Type: Anti-church (minor)/celebration.

2. Early to mid-17th-century texts dealing with anti-authority themes (most first recorded in the 17th century)

Robin Hood and the Bishop
Sources: Broadside, 1623–61.
Note: See also 'Robin Hood and the Bishop of Hereford', broadside, 1740 see also Forresters manuscript but it is named there 'Robin Hood and the 'Bishop', not 'Robin Hood and the Bishop of

Hereford', as the usual 'Robin Hood and Bishop' ballad there features sheriff not bishop as enemy and so is renamed 'Robin Hood and the Old Wife'.
Type: Anti-church (and also church as authority).

Little John a-Begging
Sources: Percy Folio, c.1645; broadside, 1640–65; garland, 1663.
Type: Anti-church.

Robin Hood's Golden Prize
Sources: Broadside, 1623–61 (by L.P. = Laurence Price); garland, 1663.
Type: Anti-church.

3. Early to mid-17th-century texts celebrating Robin Hood

Robin Hood and the Tanner
Source: Broadside, 1640–65; garland, 1663.
Note: Dated 1657 in English Short Title Catalogue.
Type: Celebration.

Robin Hood and the (Jovial/Jolly) Tinker
Source: Broadside, 1623–61; garland, c.1740.
Type: Celebration.

Robin Hood and the Shepherd
Sources: Broadside, 1654–62; garland, 1663.
Type: Celebration.

Robin Hood's Fishing
Sources: Broadside, 1631; as 'The Noble Fisherman', broadside, 1663–74; garland, c.1740.
Note: Early English Books Online, www.eebo.chadwyck.com/home (accessed 6 March 2014), suggests a date from 1658.
Type: Celebration (?nationalistic).

Robin Hood and the Scotchman
Sources: Broadside, c.1650; garland, 1663 (only as final stanzas added to 'Robin Hood Newly Revived', before 'Robin Hood and the Prince of Aragon' addition). As a separate ballad in John Mathew Gutch (ed.), *A Lytell Geste of Robin Hode, with Other Ancient & Modern Ballads and Songs Relating to this Celebrated*

Yeoman, 2 vols (London: Longman, 1847) from a 1796 Irish version.
Type: Celebration (?nationalistic).

Robin Hood's Delight
Sources: Broadside, 1655; garland, 1663.
Type: Celebration.

Robin Hood Newly Revived
Sources: Broadside, c.1660; garland, 1663.
Note: Known in garlands, Forresters manuscript and Ritson (ed.), *Robin Hood* as 'Robin Hood and the Stranger': tune used widely so probably early 17th century.
Type: Celebration/some gentrification.

4. Later texts related to earlier themes

Robin Hood and Little John
Source: Broadside, 1694–1700; garland, c.1740.
Note: Registered in Stationers' Register, 1624. Child (ed.), *The English and Scottish Popular Ballads*, vol. 5, p. 297, said 1680–85.
Type: Celebration.

The King's Disguise and Friendship with Robin Hood
Source: Garland, c.1740; broadside, 1750?
Note: Forresters manuscript, c.1670, uses this as the basis for the edited version that it contains.
Type: Anti-authority?/celebration.

Robin Hood and the Golden Arrow
Source: Garland, c.1740.
Note: Forresters manuscript, c.1670, uses this as the basis for the edited version that it contains.
Type: Anti-authority?/celebration.

Robin Hood and the Beggar II
Source: Broadside, late 18th century.
Type: Celebration.

Robin Hood and the Ranger
Source: Garland, c.1740.
Type: Celebration.

The Bold Pedlar and Robin Hood
Source: J. H. Dixon (ed.), *Ancient Poems, Ballads and Songs of the Peasantry of England*, Percy Society, 17 (London: Percy Society, 1842).
Note: Child (ed.), *The English and Scottish Popular Ballads*, vol. 5, p. 240, cites a 'Proud Pedlar' version, c.1775.
Type: Celebration.

5. Texts appearing thematically variant

Robin Hood's Birth, Breeding, Valour and Marriage
Source: Broadside, 1681–84; garland, c.1740).
Type: Gentrification/celebration.

Robin Hood and Queen Katherine
Sources: Broadside, 1630; Percy Folio, c.1645; garland, 1663.
Note: Also known as 'Renowned Robin Hood' and 'Robin Hood, Scarlet and John'.
Type: Pro-authority/celebration.

Robin Hood and Maid Marian
Source: Broadside, 1623–61.
Type: Gentrification/celebration.

Robin Hood's Chase
Source: Broadside, 1663–65; garland, c.1740.
Type: Pro-authority/celebration.

Robin Hood and the Valiant Knight
Source: Garland, c.1740.
Type: Pro-authority?/celebration.

Robin Hood and the Prince of Aragon
Sources: Broadside, 1675–1725; broadside, 1695; garland, c.1740.
Note: Also known as 'Robin Hood, Will Scarlett and Little John', plus variants of that title: found as second part of 'Robin Hood Newly Revived', as broadside, 1660–73, and in garland, 1663.
Type: Pro-authority/celebration.

Bibliography

Primary texts
Anon., *Robin Hood: An Opera* (London: Watts, 1730)
Anon., *Robin Hood: A Tale of the Olden Time*, 2 vols (Edinburgh: Oliver and Boyd, 1819)
Bartsch, K. (ed.), *Altfranzösische Romanzen und Pastourellen* (Leipzig: Vogel, 1870)
Bodleian Library Broadside Ballads, www.bodley.ox.ac.uk/ballads/ (accessed 9 October 2014)
Bower, Walter, Continuation of John of Fordun, *Scotichronicon*, extract in Knight and Ohlgren (eds), *Robin Hood and Other Outlaw Tales*, pp. 25–6
Brontë, Charlotte, *Shirley*, World's Classics Series (Oxford: Oxford University Press, 1979)
Burgess, Glyn S. (trans.), *Two Medieval Outlaws: Eustace the Monk and Fouke Fitz Waryn* (Cambridge: Brewer, 1997)
Byron, Lord, *Poetical Works* (London: Oxford University Press, 1933)
The Calendar of the Patent Rolls of Edward III, vol. 6 (London: Stationery Office, 1902)
Chaucer, Geoffrey, *Troilus and Criseyde*, in *The Riverside Chaucer*, ed. Larry Benson (New York: Oxford University Press, 1988), vol. 5, pp. 473–585
Chestre, Thomas, *Sir Launfal*, ed. A. J. Bliss (Nelson: London, 1960)
Child, F. J. (ed.), *The English and Scottish Popular Ballads*, 5 vols, reprint edn (New York: Dover, 1965)
Dixon, J. H. (ed.), *Ancient Poems, Ballads and Songs of the Peasantry of England*, Percy Society, 17 (London: Percy Society, 1842)
Dobson, R. B., and John Taylor (eds), *Rymes of Robin Hood: An Introduction to the English Outlaw* (London: Heinemann, 1976); rev. edn (Stroud: Sutton, 1999)
Drayton, Michael, *Poly-Olbion*, in *The Works of Michael Drayton*, ed. J. William Hebel, vol. 4 (Oxford: Blackwell, 1961)
Dunbar, William, *Selected Poems*, ed. Priscilla Bawcutt, 2 vols (Glasgow: Association for Scottish Literary Studies, 1988)

Bibliography

Egan, Pierce, the Younger, *Robin Hood and Little John: or, The Merry Men of Sherwood Forest* (London: Forster and Hextall, 1840)

Emmett, George, *Robin Hood and the Outlaws of Sherwood Forest* (London: Temple, 1869)

Evans, Thomas (ed.), *Old Ballads, Historical and Narrative, with Some of Modern Date, Now First Collected and Reprinted from Rare Copies*, 2 vols (London: Evans, 1777)

Feyrer, Gayle, *The Thief's Mistress* (New York: Dell, 1996)

Galbraith, V. H. (ed.), *The Anonimalle Chronicle, 1333 to 1381* (Manchester: Manchester University Press, 1927)

Gilbert, Henry, *Robin Hood and the Men of the Greenwood* (Edinburgh: Jack, 1912)

Gilliat, Edward, *In Lincoln Green: A Merrie Tale of Robin Hood* (London: Seeley, 1897)

Godwin, Parke, *Sherwood* (New York: HarperCollins, 1991)

Grafton, Richard, *Chronicle at Large and Meere History of the Affayres of England: And Kings of the Same* (London: Tottle and Toye, 1569)

Green, Simon, *Kevin Costner is Robin Hood Prince of Thieves* (New York: Berkley, 1991)

Gutch, John Mathew (ed.), *A Lytell Geste of Robin Hode, with Other Ancient & Modern Ballads and Songs Relating to this Celebrated Yeoman*, 2 vols (London: Longman, 1847)

Hall, Spencer T., *The Forester's Offering* (London: Whitaker, 1841)

Howitt, William and Mary, *The Forest Minstrel* (London: Baldwin, Cradock and Day, 1823)

Hunt, Leigh, *Foliage, or Poems Original and Translated* (London: Ollier, 1818)

Hunt, Leigh, *Selected Writings*, vol. 5: *Poetical Works, 1801–21*, ed. John Strachan (London: Pickering and Chatto, 2003)

James, G. P. R., *Forest Days: A Romance of Old Times*, 3 vols (London: Saunders and Otley, 1843)

Jonson, Ben, *The Sad Shepherd*, in *The Cambridge Edition of the Works of Ben Jonson*, ed. David Bevington, Martin Butler and Ian Donaldson, 7 vols (Cambridge: Cambridge University Press, 2012), vol. 7, pp. 417–80

Keats, John, 'Robin Hood: To a Friend', in *Collected Poems*, ed. Jack Stillinger (Cambridge, MA: Harvard University Press, 1982), pp. 169–70

Knight, Stephen (ed.), *Robin Hood: The Forresters Manuscript* (Cambridge: Brewer, 1998)

Knight, Stephen, and Thomas Ohlgren (eds), *Robin Hood and Other Outlaw Tales*, 2nd edn, TEAMS Middle English Texts (Kalamazoo: Western Michigan University Press, 2000)

Laing, D. (ed.), *The Orygynale Chronicle* (Edinburgh: Edmonston and Douglas, 1903–14)

Major, John, *Historia Majoris Britanniae* (Edinburgh: Fribarn, 1740)

Miller, Thomas, *Royston Gower, or The Days of King John: An Historical Romance*, 3 vols (London: Colburn, 1838)
Millhouse, Robert, *Sherwood Forest, and Other Poems* (London: the author, 1827)
Muddock, Joyce E., *Maid Marian and Robin Hood: A Romance of Old Sherwood Forest* (London: Chatto and Windus, 1892)
Munday, Anthony, *The Death of Robert, Earle of Huntington,* in Knight and Ohlgren (eds), *Robin Hood and Other Outlaw Tales*, pp. 402–28
Munday, Anthony, *The Downfall of Robert, Earle of Huntington,* in Knight and Ohlgren (eds), *Robin Hood and Other Outlaw Tales*, pp. 303–84
Munday, Anthony, *Metropolis Coronata: The Triumph of Ancient Drapery* (London: Purslowe, 1615)
Newbolt, Sir Henry, *The Greenwood*, Teaching of English Series, 40 (London: Nelson, 1925)
Noyes, Alfred, *Sherwood*, in *Collected Poems*, 4 vols (London: Blackwood, 1928), vol. 1, pp. 45–7
Ohlgren, Thomas H., and Lister E. Matheson (eds), *Early Rymes of Robyn Hood: An Edition of the Texts ca. 1425 to ca. 1600* (Tempe: Arizona Center for Medieval and Renaissance Studies, 2013)
O'Keeffe, John, *Airs, Duetts and Choruses in the Operatical Pantomime of Merry Sherwood or Harlequin Forrester* (London: Longman, 1795)
Paden, William (ed. and trans.), *The Medieval Pastourelle* (New York: Garland, 1987)
Peacock, Thomas Love (originally 'By the author of Headlong Hall'), *Maid Marian* (London: Hookham and Longman, Hurst, Rees, Orme, and Brown, 1822)
Percy, Stephen, *Robin Hood and his Merry Foresters* (London: Tilt and Bogue, 1841)
Percy, Thomas (ed.), *Reliques of Early English Poetry*, ed. Henry B. Wheatley, 3 vols (London: Sonnenschein, Swan, Lebus and Lowrey, 1886)
The Percy Folio Manuscript, ed. F. J. Furnivall and J. W. Hales, 3 vols (London: Trübner, 1867)
Pyle, Howard, *The Merry Adventures of Robin Hood, of Great Renown in Nottinghamshire* (New York: Scribners, 1883)
Reynolds, J. H., *Poetry and Prose*, ed. George L. Marsh (London: Oxford University Press, 1928)
Ritson, Joseph (ed.), *Robin Hood: A Collection of All the Ancient Poems, Songs and Ballads Now Extant Relative to the Celebrated English Outlaw (to which are Prefixed Anecdotes of his Life)*, 2 vols (London: Egerton and Johnson, 1795)
Rivière, Jean-Claude (ed.), *Pastourelles*, 3 vols (Geneva: Droz, 1974–76)
Roberson, Jennifer, *Lady of the Forest* (New York: Kensington, 1992)
Robin Hood: A High Spirited Tale of Adventure (Los Angeles: Boom Studios, 1980)

Scott, Walter (originally 'The Author of Waverley'), *Ivanhoe: A Romance*, 3 vols (Edinburgh: Constable, 1820)
Shield, William, and Leonard McNally, *Robin Hood, or Sherwood Forest* (London: Almon, 1784)
Sidney, Sir Philip, *A Defence of Poetry*, ed. J. A. van Dorsten (Oxford: Oxford University Press, 1966)
Southey, Robert, *Later Poetical Works, 1811–1838*, vol. 4: *Fragments and Romances*, ed. Tim Fulford and Rachel Crawford (London: Pickering and Chatto, 2012)
Squire, J. C., *Robin Hood: A Farcical Romantic Pastoral* (London: Heinemann, 1928)
Stocqueler, J. H., *Maid Marian, the Forest Queen, being a Companion to 'Robin Hood'* (London: Peirce, 1849)
The Tale of Gamelyn, in *Chaucerian and Other Pieces*, vol. 3 of *The Works of Geoffrey Chaucer*, ed. W. W. Skeat, 7 vols (Oxford: Clarendon, 1884)
Tennyson, Alfred, *The Foresters*, in *Poems and Plays*, 2 vols, Oxford Standard Authors (Oxford: Oxford University Press, 1965)
Tiddy, R. E., *The Mummers' Play* (Oxford: Clarendon, 1923)

Secondary literature
Andrew, Donna T., *London Debating Societies, 1776–99*, www.britishhistory.ac.uk/report.aspx?pubid=238 (accessed 10 April 2013)
Barczewksi, Stephanie, *Myth and National Identity in Nineteenth-Century Britain: The Legends of King Arthur and Robin Hood* (Oxford: Oxford University Press, 2000)
Barnard, John, 'Keats's "Robin Hood", John Hamilton Reynolds, and the "Old Poets"', *Proceedings of the British Academy*, 75 (1989): 181–200
Behlmer, Rudy, 'Introduction: From Legend to Film', in Rudy Behlmer (ed.), *The Adventures of Robin Hood* (Madison: University of Wisconsin Press, 1979), pp. 11–41
Behlmer, Rudy, 'Robin Hood on the Screen: From Legend to Film', *Films in Review*, 16 (1965): 91–102; reprinted in Knight (ed.), *Robin Hood: An Anthology* pp. 441–60
Bessinger, Jess, '*The Gest of Robin Hood* Revisited', in Knight (ed.), *Robin Hood: An Anthology*, pp. 39–50
Bevington, David, *Tudor Drama and Politics: A Critical Approach to Topical Meaning* (Cambridge, MA: Harvard University Press, 1968)
Blamires, David, 'Maid Marian in Twentieth-Century Children's Books', in Phillips (ed.), *Bandit Territories*, pp. 44–57
Blunk, Laura, 'Red Robin: The Radical Politics of Richard Carpenter's *Robin of Sherwood*', in Hahn (ed.), *Robin Hood in Popular Culture*, pp. 29–39
Blunk, Laura, 'And for Best Supporting Hero ... Little John', in Phillips (ed.), *Bandit Territories*, pp. 196–216

Boerch, Marianne, 'Preface'. in *Text and Voice: The Rhetoric of Authority in the Middle Ages* (Odense: University Press of Southern Denmark, 1999)

Bradbury, Nancy Mason, *Writing Aloud: Storytelling in Late Medieval England* (Urbana and Chicago: University of Illinois Press, 1998)

Brandin, Louis, 'Nouvelles récherches sur *Fouke Fitz Waryn*', *Romania* 55 (1929): 17–44

Bromwich, Rachel, 'Concepts of Arthur', *Studia Celtica*, 10–11 (1975–76): 163–81

Bronson, Bertrand, *The Traditional Tunes of the Child Ballads*, 4 vols (Princeton: Princeton University Press, 1959–72)

Brown, P. Hume (ed.), *Scotland before 1700 from Documents* (Edinburgh: Douglas, 1893)

Butler, Marilyn, 'The Good Old Times', chapter 5 of *Peacock Displayed* (London: Routledge, 1979)

Butler, Marilyn, *Romantics, Rebels and Reactionaries* (Oxford: Oxford University Press, 1981)

Carpenter, Kevin (ed.), *Robin Hood: The Many Faces of that Celebrated Outlaw* (Oldenburg: Bibliotheks- und Informationssystem der Universität Oldenburgs, 1995)

Chambers, E. K., *English Literature at the Close of the Middle Ages*, Oxford History of English Literature, 2/2 (Oxford: Clarendon, 1945)

Chandler, James, *England in 1819* (Chicago: University of Chicago Press, 1998)

Chandler, John, 'Batman and Robin Hood: Hobsbawm's Outlaw Heroes Past and Present', in Knight (ed.), *Robin Hood in Greenwood Stood*, pp. 187–206

Chaytor, H. J., *From Script to Print* (Cambridge: Cambridge University Press, 1945)

Clanchy, M.T., *From Oral Memory to Written Record: England 1066–1377* (Cambridge, MA: Harvard University Press, 1979)

Clawson, William H., *The Gest of Robin Hood* (Toronto: University of Toronto Library, 1909)

Coleman, Joyce, *Public Reading and the Reading Public in Late Medieval England and France* (Cambridge: Cambridge University Press, 1996)

Cox, Jeffrey N., *Poetry and Politics in the Cockney School*, Cambridge Studies in Romanticism (Cambridge: Cambridge University Press, 1998)

Crawford, Robert, *Devolving English Literature* (Oxford: Clarendon, 1992)

Deleuze, Gilles, and Félix Guattari, *A Thousand Plateaus: Capitalism and Schizophrenia*, trans. Brian Massumi (London: Athlone Press, 2004; French original 1980)

Dickstein, Morris, *Keats and his Poetry: A Study in Development* (Chicago: University of Chicago Press, 1971)
Ebsworth, J. W., rev. Megan A. Stephan, 'Egan, Pierce Junior (1814–80)', *Oxford Dictionary of National Biography* (Oxford: Oxford University Press, 2004), www.oxforddnb.com/view/article/8578 (accessed 10 April 2013)
Ferguson, A. B., *The Indian Summer of English Chivalry* (Durham, NC: Duke University Press, 1960)
Finny, W. E. St Lawrence, 'Mediaeval Games and Gaderyngs at Kingston-upon-Thames', *Surrey Archaeological Collections*, 44 (1936): 102–36
Forrest, John, *The History of Morris Dancing, 1458–1750* (Toronto: University of Toronto Press, 1999)
Fowler, David C., *A Literary History of the Popular Ballad* (Durham, NC: Duke University Press, 1968)
Freeman, Arthur, and Janet Ing Freeman, *John Payne Collier: Scholarship and Forgery in the Nineteenth Century* (New Haven: Yale University Press, 2004)
Gable, J. Harris, *Bibliography of Robin Hood*, University of Nebraska Studies in Language, Literature and Criticism, 17 (Lincoln: University of Nebraska Press, 1939)
Gellrich, Jesse M., *Discourse and Dominion in the Fourteenth Century: Oral Contexts of Writing in Philosophy, Politics, and Poetry* (Princeton: Princeton University Press, 1995)
Gossedge, Rob, 'Thomas Love Peacock, Robin Hood and the Enclosure of Windsor Forest', in Knight (ed.), *Robin Hood in Greenwood Stood*, pp. 135–64
Gossedge, Rob, and Stephen Knight, 'Arthur in the Sixteenth to the Nineteenth Centuries', in Elizabeth Archibald and Ad Putter (eds), *The Cambridge Companion to the Arthurian Legend* (Cambridge: Cambridge University Press, 2009), pp. 103–19
Gray, Douglas, 'The Robin Hood Poems', *Poetica* (Tokyo), 18 (1984): 1–19; reprinted in Knight (ed.), *Robin Hood: An Anthology of Scholarship and Criticism*, pp. 3–37
Green, Richard Firth, 'The Ballad in the Middle Ages', in Helen Cooper and Sally Mapstone (eds), *The Long Fifteenth Century: Essays for Douglas Gray* (Oxford: Clarendon, 1997), pp. 163–84
Greg, W. W., *The Calculus of Variants: An Essay on Textual Criticism* (Oxford: Clarendon, 1927)
Gummere, Francis B., *The Popular Ballad* (New York: Houghton Mifflin, 1997)
Hahn, Thomas G., 'Robin Hood and the Rise of Cultural Studies', in Ruth Evans, Helen Fulton and David Matthews (eds), *Medieval Cultural Studies* (Cardiff: University of Wales Press, 2006), pp. 39–54
Hahn, Thomas G. (ed.), *Robin Hood in Popular Culture: Violence, Transgression and Justice* (Cambridge: Brewer, 2000)

Hanawalt, Barbara A., 'Ballads and Bandits: Fourteenth-Century Outlaws and the Robin Hood Poems', in Barbara A. Hanawalt (ed.), *Chaucer's England: Literature in Historical Context*, Medieval Studies at Minnesota, 4 (Minneapolis: University of Minnesota Press, 1992), pp. 154–75

Harty, Kevin, *The Reel Middle Ages: American Western and Eastern Europe, Middle Eastern and Asian Films about Medieval Europe* (Jefferson: McFarland, 1999)

Harty, Kevin, 'Robin Hood on Film: Moving beyond a Swashbuckling Stereotype', in Hahn (ed.), *Robin Hood in Popular Culture*, pp. 87–100

Hill, Christopher, 'Robin Hood', chapter 5 of *Liberty against the Law: Some Seventeenth-Century Controversies* (London: Lane, 1996), pp. 71–82

Hilton, Rodney, 'The Origins of Robin Hood', *Past and Present*, 14 (1958): 30–44; reprinted in Knight (ed.), *Robin Hood: An Anthology*, pp. 197–210

Hobsbawm, Eric, *Bandits*, 2nd edn (London: Penguin, 1985)

Hodgart, M. J. C., *The Ballad*, 2nd edn (London: Hutchinson, 1962)

Holt, J. C., 'The Origins and Audience of the Ballads of Robin Hood', *Past and Present*, 18 (1960): 89–110; reprinted in Knight (ed.), *Robin Hood: An Anthology*, pp. 211–32

Holt, J. C., *Robin Hood*, 2nd edn (London: Thames and Hudson, 1990)

Hopkins, Lisa, *Drama and the Succession to the Throne* (Aldershot: Ashgate, 2011)

Johnson, Edgar, *Sir Walter Scott: The Great Unknown*, 2 vols (London: Hamish Hamilton, 1970)

Johnson, Valerie B., 'Agamben's *homo sacer*, "the State of Exception" and the Modern Robin Hood', in Knight (ed.), *Robin Hood in Greenwood Stood*, pp. 207–27

Joukovsky, Nicholas, 'Peacock's Sir Oran Haut-ton, Byron's Bear or Shelley's Ape', *Keats–Shelley Journal*, 29 (1980): 173–90

Kaufman, Alexander L., 'Nietzsche's Herd and the Individual Construction of Alterity in *A Lytell Gest of Robyn Hode*', in Knight (ed.), *Robin Hood in Greenwood Stood*, pp. 31–46

Kelly, Thomas E., 'Introduction' to *Fouke Fitz Waryn*, in *Medieval Outlaws: Twelve Tales in Modern English Translation*, ed. Thomas H. Ohlgren, 2nd edn (West Lafayette: Parlor Press, 2005)

Knight, Stephen, 'Textual Variants, Textual Variance', *Southern Review* (Adelaide), 16 (1983): 44–54

Knight, Stephen, 'Robin Hood and the Royal Restoration', *Critical Survey*, 5 (1993): 298–312

Knight, Stephen, *Robin Hood: A Complete Study of the English Outlaw* (Oxford: Blackwell, 1994)

Knight, Stephen, *Robin Hood: A Mythic Biography* (Ithaca: Cornell University Press, 2003), pp. 136–9

Knight, Stephen, '*Robin Hood: Men in Tights*: Fitting the Tradition Snugly', in Knight (ed.), *Robin Hood: An Anthology*, pp. 461–7

Knight, Stephen, '"Meere English flocks": Ben Jonson's *The Sad Shepherd* and the Robin Hood Tradition', in Phillips (ed.), *Robin Hood: Medieval and Post-Medieval*, pp. 129–44

Knight, Stephen, 'Afterword', in Howard Pyle, *The Merry Adventures of Robin Hood* (New York: Signet, 2006), pp. 377–88

Knight, Stephen, 'Rabbie Hood: The Development of the English Outlaw Myth in Scotland', in Phillips (ed.), *Bandit Territories*, pp. 99–118

Knight, Stephen, 'Robin Hood and the Crusades: When and Why Did the Longbowman of the People Mount Up Like a Lord?' *Florilegium*, 23 (2008, for 2006), 201–22

Knight, Stephen, 'Robin Hood: The Earliest Contexts', in Potter and Calhoun (eds), *Images of Robin Hood*, pp. 21–40

Knight, Stephen, *Merlin: Knowledge and Power through the Ages* (Ithaca, NY: Cornell University Press, 2009)

Knight, Stephen, 'Alterity, Parody, Habitus: The Formation of the Early Literary Tradition of Robin Hood', in Knight (ed.), *Robin Hood in Greenwood Stood*, pp. 1–29

Knight, Stephen, 'The Arctic Arthur', *Arthuriana*, 12 (2011): 59–89

Knight, Stephen, 'Robin Hood versus King Arthur', in David Matthews (ed.), *In Strange Countries: Middle English Literature and its Afterlife* (Manchester: Manchester University Press, 2011), pp. 9–24

Knight, Stephen (ed.), *Robin Hood: An Anthology of Scholarship and Criticism* (Cambridge: Brewer, 1999)

Knight, Stephen (ed.), *Robin Hood in Greenwood Stood: Alterity and Context in the English Outlaw Tradition* (Turnhout: Brepols, 2011)

Leland, John, *Joannis Lelandi antiquarii de rebus britannicis collectanea*, ed. Thomas Hearne, 3 vols (Oxford: E Theatro Sheldoniano, 1715)

'List of Publications March to July 1819', *Edinburgh Review*, 32 (1819–20): 257

Livingston, Carole Rose, *British Broadside Ballads of the Sixteenth Century: A Catalogue, the Extant Sheets, and an Essay* (New York: Garland, 1991)

Lord, A. B., *The Singer of Tales* (Cambridge, MA: Harvard University Press, 1960)

Lux, Sherron, 'And the "Reel" Maid Marian', in Hahn (ed.), *Robin Hood in Popular Culture*, pp. 151–60

Lyotard, Jean-François, *The Post-Modern Condition*, trans. Geoffrey Bennington and Brian Massumi (Manchester: Manchester University Press, 1984; French original 1979)

Maddicott, J. R., 'The Birth and Setting of the Ballads of Robin Hood', in Knight (ed.), *Robin Hood: An Anthology*, pp. 233–55

Marshall, John, 'Playing the Game: Reconstructing Robin Hood and the

Sheriff of Nottingham', in Hahn (ed.), *Robin Hood in Popular Culture*, pp. 161–74

Marshall, John, 'Picturing Robin Hood in Early Print and Performance: 1500–1509', in Potter and Calhoun (eds), *Images of Robin Hood*, pp. 60–81

Marx, Karl, *Capital*, 3 vols (London: Penguin, 1976–81)

Matthews, John, 'The Games of Robin Hood', in Knight (ed.), *Robin Hood: An Anthology*, pp. 393–410

Matthews, Tom Dewe, 'The Outlaws', *The Guardian*, 6 October 2006, http//books.guardian.co.uk (accessed 1 March 2014)

Nagy, Joseph Falaky, 'The Paradoxes of Robin Hood', in Knight (ed.), *Robin Hood: An Anthology*, pp. 411–25

Neale, Steve, 'Swashbuckling, Sapphire, and Salt: Un-American Contributions to TV Costume Adventure Series in the 1950s', in Frank Krutnik, Steve Neale, Brian Neve and Peter Stanfield (eds), *'Un-American' Hollywood: Politics and Film in the Blacklist Era* (New Brunswick: Rutgers University Press, 2007), pp. 198–209

Nelson, William, 'From "Listen, Lordings" to "Dear Reader"', *University of Toronto Quarterly*, 46 (1976–77): 110–24

Nollen, Scott Allen, *Robin Hood: A Cinematic History of the English Outlaw and his Scottish Counterparts* (Jefferson: McFarland, 1999)

Ohlgren, Thomas H., 'The "Marchaunt" of Sherwood: Mercantile Ideology in *A Gest of Robyn Hode*', in Hahn (ed.), *Robin Hood in Popular Culture*, pp. 175–90

Ohlgren, Thomas H., *Robin Hood: The Early Poems, 1465–1560: Texts, Contexts, and Ideology* (Newark: University of Delaware Press, 2007)

Ong, Walter J., *Orality and Literacy: The Technologizing of the Word* (London: Methuen, 1982)

Palmer, Roy (ed.), *A Touch on the Times: Songs of Social Change, 1770–1914* (London: Penguin, 1974)

Peacock, Thomas Love, *The Letters of Thomas Love Peacock*, ed. Nicholas A. Joukovsky, 2 vols (Oxford: Clarendon, 2001)

Phillips, Helen, 'Robin Hood, the Prioress of Kirklees, and Charlotte Bronte', in Phillips (ed.), *Robin Hood Medieval and Post-Medieval*, pp. 154–66

Phillips, Helen, 'Reformist Polemics, Reading Publics and Unpopular Robin Hood', in Knight (ed.), *Robin Hood in Greenwood Stood*, pp. 87–117

Phillips, Helen (ed.), *Robin Hood Medieval and Post-Medieval* (Dublin: Four Courts Press, 2005)

Phillips, Helen (ed.), *Bandit Territories: British Outlaws and their Traditions* (Cardiff: University of Wales Press, 2008)

Pollard, A.J., *Imagining Robin Hood: The Late-Medieval Stories in Historical Context* (Routledge: London, 2004)

Potter, Lois J., 'The Apotheosis of Maid Marian: Tennyson's *The*

Foresters and the Nineteenth-Century Theater', in Lois J. Potter (ed.), *Playing Robin Hood: the Legend in Performance in Five Centuries* (Newark: University of Delaware Press, 1998)

Potter, Lois J., 'Sherwood Forest and the Byronic Robin Hood,' in Hahn (ed.), *Robin Hood in Popular Culture*, pp. 215–24

Potter, Lois J., 'Robin Hood and the Fairies: Alfred Noyes's *Sherwood*', in Phillips (ed), *Robin Hood Medieval and Post-Medieval*, pp. 167–80

Potter, Lois J., and Joshua Calhoun (eds), *Images of Robin Hood: Medieval to Modern* (Newark: Delaware University Press, 2008)

Prideaux, W. F., 'Who Was Robin Hood?', *Notes and Queries*, 7th series, 2 (1886): 421–4

Priestley, J. B., *Thomas Love Peacock* (London: Macmillan, 1927)

Raglan, Lord, *The Hero* (London: Watts, 1949)

Richards, Jeffrey, 'Robin Hood on the Screen', in Knight (ed.), *Robin Hood: An Anthology*, pp. 429–40

Richmond, Colin, 'An Outlaw and Some Peasants: The Possible Significance of Robin Hood', in Knight (ed.), *Robin Hood: An Anthology*, pp. 363–76

Roe, Nicholas, *John Keats and the Culture of Dissent* (Oxford: Clarendon, 1997)

Saintsbury, George, 'Introduction' to Thomas Love Peacock, *Maid Marian* (London: Macmillan, 1895), pp. vii–xxix

Sands, D. B., *Middle English Verse Romances*, reprint edn (Exeter: University of Exeter Press, 1986)

Seal, Graham, *The Outlaw Legend: A Cultural Tradition in Britain, America and Australia* (Cambridge: Cambridge University Press, 1996)

Sedgwick, Eve Kosofsky, *Between Men: English Literature and Homosocial Desire* (New York: Columbia University Press, 1985)

Singman, Jeffrey L., *Robin Hood: The Shaping of a Legend* (Westport: Greenwood, 1998)

Spence, Lewis, 'Robin Hood in Scotland', *Chambers Journal*, 18 (1928): 94–6

Stock, Brian, *The Implications of Literacy: Written Language and Modes of Interpretation in the Eleventh and Twelfth Centuries* (Princeton: Princeton University Press, 1980)

Stock, Lorraine Kochanske, 'Recovering Reginald de Koven and Henry Bache Smith's "Lost" Operetta *Maid Marian*', in Potter and Calhoun (eds), *Images of Robin Hood*, pp. 256–65

Stokes, James (ed.), *Records of Early English Drama: Somerset*, 2 vols (Toronto: University of Toronto Press, 1996)

Tardif, Richard, 'The "Mistery" of Robin Hood: A New Social Context for the Texts', in Stephen Knight and S. N. Mukherjee (eds), *Words and Worlds: Studies in the Social Role of Verbal Culture* (Sydney: Sydney Association for Studies in Society and Culture, 1983), pp. 130–4; reprinted in Knight (ed.), *Robin Hood: An Anthology*, pp. 345–62

Tennyson, Hallam, *A Memoir of Lord Tennyson* (London: Macmillan, 1897)
Thompson, E. P., *Whigs and Hunters: The Origin of the Black Act* (London: Allen Lane, 1975)
Troost, Linda V., 'Robin Hood Musicals in Eighteenth-Century London', in Hahn (ed.), *Robin Hood in Popular Culture*, pp. 251–64
Troost, Linda V., 'The Noble Peasant', in Phillips (ed.), *Robin Hood Medieval and Post-Medieval*, pp. 145–53
Vitz, Evelyn Burge, Nancy Freeman Regalado and Marilyn Lawrence (eds), *Performing Medieval Narrative* (Cambridge: Brewer, 2005)
Wiles, David, *The Early Plays of Robin Hood* (Cambridge: Brewer, 1981)
Wright, Allan W., '"Begone, knave! Robbery is out of fashion hereabouts": Robin Hood and the Comics Code', in Phillips (ed.), *Bandit Territories*, pp. 217–23

Index

Films, plays and anonymous texts, mostly ballads, are listed under Robin Hood

Adam Bell 3, 23, 40, 57, 69, 86, 244
Andrew of Wyntoun 38, 41–2, 46, 239
Arcejaeger, R. M. 216
Armstrong, J. 219, 253
Austen, J. 229

Barclay, A. 19
Barczewski, S. 227
Barlowe, J. 19
Barnard, J. 115, 116, 119
Barnsdale Forest 44–6
Bateson, G. 236
Behlmer, R. 236, 251
Bessinger, J. 234
Bevington, D. 45
Bin Laden, Osama 253
Blamires, D. 213
'Blind Harry', *see* Henry the Minstrel
Bliss, A. J. 66
Blunk, L. 7
Boece, H. 44
Boerch, M. 15
Bower, W. 18, 19, 24, 42–3, 48, 59, 158
Bradbury, N. M. 17
Bradley, M. Z. 220, 228
Breton, N. 18
Brewer, D. 6, 233

Bromwich, R. 38
Bronson, B. 4, 20–1, 27, 86
Bronte, C. 7, 134–5
Brooke, F. 106
Burgess, G. 71
Burney, C. 105
Butler, M. 116, 127, 130
Byron, Lord 110–11, 113, 116–17, 132, 152

Cagney, J. 251
Carpenter, K. 5
Chadwick, N. K. 38
Chambers, E. K. 4, 189
Chandler, James 151
Chandler, John 7
Chandler, R. 50
'Chase, N.', *see* Hyde, A. and C.
Chaucer, G. 17, 119, 225
Chaytor, H. F. 14
Chevy Chase 22, 57, 86
Child, F. J. 3, 4, 8, 17, 23–4, 25, 26, 28, 64, 83, 84, 85, 86, 88, 89, 91, 92, 93, 97, 98–9, 101, 184, 244, 247
Churchyard, T. 26
Clanchy, M. T. 14
Clawson, W. 4, 63, 71, 72, 73
Coleman, J. 15–16
Coleridge, S. T. 131
Collier, J. P. 84

Copland, W. 24, 57, 87, 190
Costner, K. 139, 252
Cox, J. N. 120
Crawford, R. 50–1
Crowe, R. 139, 253
Cundall, J. (= 'S. Percy') 30, 162–4, 180–1, 182, 204
Curtiz, M. 138–9, 252

Daly, A. 135
Davenant, W. 226
de la Halle, A. 188
de Koven, R. 30, 237
Deleuze, G., and Guattari, F. 235–7, 239, 252
de Montfort, S. 43, 145, 158, 159, 160, 174, 207
Dickens, C. 14, 16, 178
Dickstein, M. 115
Dives et Pauper 18, 19, 239
Dixon, J. H. 28
Dobson, R. B., and Taylor, J. 5, 44–5, 83, 231, 232
Dodsworth, R. 109
Douglas, G. 49
Doyle, A. C. 173
Drayton, M. 52, 53, 75, 77, 192, 194, 195
Drinkwater, J. 137, 210
Dryden, J. 226, 227
Dumas, A. 165, 237
Dunbar, W. 23, 49

Eaton, M. 51
Eddy, N. 30, 251
Egan, P. 9, 154, 164–9, 170, 171, 173, 174, 177, 182, 204–6, 207
Ellis, G. 107
Emmett, G. 174–8, 181, 207
Evans, T. 2, 8, 97, 101, 105, 107, 145, 198

Fairbanks, D. 138, 210, 237
Ferguson, A. B. 65

Feyrer, G. 214
Fielding, H. 143, 227
Flynn, E. 138, 201, 211
Forresters manuscript 6, 24, 27, 73, 83, 87, 92, 94, 96, 101
Foufillaz 243
Fowler, D. C. 8, 16, 17
Forrest, J. 190
Frank, B. 22
Fraser, A. 183, 214
Fulk Fitz Warren 43, 56, 70–4, 76, 77, 78
Furnivall, F. J. 107

Gable, J. H. 103
Gale, T. 109
Gamelyn 8, 17, 55, 66, 67, 71, 74, 77, 117, 122, 249
Gellrich, J. H. 15
Gibson, M. 238
Gilbert, H. 123, 183, 208–9, 244
Gilliat, E. 183, 208
Glyndŵr, O. 50
Godwin, P. 183, 242
Gollancz, I. 107
Gossedge, R. 7, 127, 131–2, 235, 248
Grafton, R. 43, 44, 70
Gray, D. 5, 6, 231, 233, 234
Green, R. F. 17, 234
Green, R. L. 183
Greene, R. 51
Greg, W. W. 225
Griffiths, L. 219
Guattari, F., *see* Deleuze, G.
Gummere, F. B. 22, 23, 243
Gutch, J. M. 2, 84, 98, 112, 145, 162, 165, 173, 174

Hahn, T. 5, 6, 232, 234
Hale, A. 243
Hall, S. T. 112, 113
Hanawalt, B. 245
Harty, K. 6
Harvey, G. 20

Index

Hawkins, J. 108
Hazlitt, W. 120, 128
Henry the Minstrel (= 'Blind Harry') 47, 48
Hepburn, A. 212
Hill, C. 234
Hilton, R. 4, 234
Hobsbawm, E. 243
Hodgart, M. 23
Holt, J. 4–5, 64, 234
Hone, W. 116
Hopkins, L. 45, 46
How the Plowman Lerned his Paternoster 18, 19
Howitt, M. and W. 110–12, 113
Hunt, J. 120
Hunt, L. 110, 117, 120–6, 127, 128, 133, 155, 200, 202
Hunter, I. M. 51
Huntingdon, Earl of 45
Hwde of Ednam 46
Hyde, A. and C. (= 'N. Chase') 183

Irving, H. 135
Isolde 1, 10, 187, 207, 224, 242

James, G. P. R. 119, 158–62, 164, 174, 177, 178, 204
Jerrold, D. 174
'Johnie Cock' 3, 244
Johnson, S. 108
Johnson, V. B. 7
Johnston, N. 109
Jonson, B. 77, 106, 120, 134, 194–5, 197, 199, 211

Kaufman, A. 7
Keats, J. 110, 111, 113–20, 125, 126, 127, 128, 131, 137, 155, 158, 169, 199–200, 204, 209, 241
Keighley, W. 252
Kelly, I. 148
Kelly, N. 31

Kelly, T. E. 71
'King and Subject' ballads 8, 68–9, 72, 77, 86, 249–50
King Arthur 1, 10, 36, 38–9, 50, 69, 110, 224, 227–8, 253–4
King Arthur (film) 254
King Charles II 103
King Edward I (also as Prince) 43, 51, 159, 160, 177, 204
King Edward III 46
King Henry III 42, 174, 177, 204
King John (also as Prince) 2, 43, 55, 71, 73, 74, 76, 77, 126, 129, 130, 133, 136, 144, 145, 152–3, 156, 168, 169, 170, 172, 173, 182, 192, 205–6, 241
King Richard I 77, 129–30, 141, 161, 194, 208, 238
Knightley, K. 219, 238, 254
Korngold, W. 31, 138

Langland, W. 17–18, 19, 48, 73, 225, 239
Lardner, R. 51
Lawhead, S. 183
Leavis, F. R. 4, 226
Legat, H. 19
Leland, J. 7
Lewis R. (= 'P. Porrence') 183
Livingston, C. R. 86
Lynne, W. 19–20
Lyotard, J.-F. 235
Lytton, E. B. 148

MacDonald, J. 30, 251
McKinley, R. 183, 214
Maclise, H. 179
McNally, L. 105, 106
McSpadden, J. W. 187
Maddicott, J. R. 234
Magna Carta 3, 136, 145, 248
Major, J. 18, 19, 43, 44, 56, 70, 74, 109

Malory, T. 70, 77, 187, 227, 228, 237, 249
Marian 9, 75, 95–6, 104–5, 111, 114, 116, 117, 120, 125, 126–32, 137, 174–5, 181–2, 187–221
'False Marian' 188, 193, 195, 210, 212, 214, 219
Marshall, J. 7, 67
Mendez, M. 105
Merlin/Myrddin 38–9, 248
Miles, B. 214
Miller, T. 123, 145, 155–8, 162, 164, 165, 178, 203–4, 220, 248
Millhouse, R. 111–2, 113
More, T. 7, 18
Morris, W. 179
Muddock, J. E. 183, 208
Munday, A. 43, 45, 50, 55, 70, 71, 74–7, 90, 103, 109, 127, 146, 173, 192, 193, 195, 197, 198, 199, 200, 203, 210, 246–7, 250–1

Nelson, C. (= 'L. Woods') 237
Newbolt, H. 138
Newgate Calendar 106
Nollen, S. 6
Noyes, A. 6, 137–8, 210, 235, 237

Obama, B. 242
Ohlgren, T. 6, 7, 48, 56, 67, 69, 73, 83, 232
O'Keeffe, J. 106, 130
Oman, C. 183, 214
Ong, W. J. 15, 16

Parker, M. 93, 101, 109, 163, 245
Peacock, T. L. 7, 9, 30, 110, 126–32, 143, 144, 145, 154, 155, 164, 169, 173, 182, 200, 201–3, 204, 207, 208, 214, 221, 242
Pearce, W. 106
Pepys, S. 27, 94

'Percy, S.', *see* Cundall, J.
Percy, T. 23, 24, 26, 30, 49, 57, 60, 87, 90, 91, 92, 94, 96, 101, 107, 127, 168, 181
Phillips, G. S. (= 'Searle, J.') 112
Phillips, H. 7, 134–5, 239, 241
Planché, J. R. 201
play-games 20, 38, 40, 50, 56, 189–90, 240
Poe, E. A. 61
Pope, A. 127, 248
'Porrence, P.', *see* Lewis, R.
Potter, L. 6, 110, 111–13, 135, 235
Praed, M. 139, 238
Prideaux, W. F. 71
Priestley, J. B. 126
Pyle, H. 30, 164, 179–84, 207–8

Queen Caroline 248
Quiller-Couch, A. 137, 184

Raglan, Lord 64, 233
Randolph, Earl of Chester 73
Rastell, J. 18
Rathbone, B. 201
Reynolds, G. W. M. 14, 16, 32, 156, 158, 178
Reynolds, J. H. 110, 111, 113–20, 125, 128, 131, 137, 139, 199–200, 241
Rhead, L. 179, 184
Richards, J. 234
Richmond, C. 234
Ritson, J. 2, 3, 8, 42, 84, 97–8, 101, 106, 107, 108–10, 126, 127, 128, 132–3, 144, 145, 148, 155, 162, 165, 173, 174, 193, 198, 251
Roberson, J. 9, 127, 214, 243
Robin and Gandelyn 3, 73–4, 86, 244
Robin des Bois 41, 50, 188, 189
Robin et Marion (*pastourelle* and *bergerie*) 17, 58, 74, 188, 240

Index   283

Robin Hood Society, early 18th
    century 155
  c.1800 107
Robin Hood anonymous fiction
  *Robin Hood: A High-Spirited
    Tale of Adventure* (Muppets
    comic) 216–17
  *Robin Hood: A Tale of the Olden
    Time* (1819 novel) 52, 143,
    144, 145, 146–51, 155, 164,
    165, 200–1, 202, 205, 206
Robin Hood ballads
  'The Birth of Robin Hood' 84
  'The Bold Pedlar and Robin
    Hood' 84
  The Gest of Robin Hood 8, 22,
    23, 24, 29, 45, 47, 48, 49,
    55–8, 59, 62, 63–7, 69, 71, 72,
    73, 74, 75, 87, 90, 92, 93, 99,
    129, 130, 136, 145, 159, 163,
    167, 168, 169, 176, 177, 178,
    182, 191, 205, 206, 208, 209,
    212, 230, 234, 244–5, 250,
    253
  'The King's Disguise and
    Friendship with Robin Hood'
    99–100
  'Little John Begging' 94
  'The Noble Fisherman' (=
    'Robin Hood's Preferment',
    'Robin Hood Fishing') 95,
    169, 177, 207
  'Robin Hood and Allen a Dale'
    27, 87, 90, 93, 162
  'Robin Hood and the Beggar' I
    and II 26, 84, 90, 93; II 163
  'Robin Hood and the Bishop'
    47, 75, 94, 191
  'Robin Hood and the Bishop of
    Hereford' 94, 175
  'Robin Hood and the Butcher'
    26, 90–1, 92, 93, 98, 162, 168
  'Robin Hood and the Curtal
    Friar' (= 'Robin Hood and
    Friar Tuck') 23, 26, 87–8, 93

'Robin Hood and the Golden
    Arrow' 63, 84
'Robin Hood and Guy of
    Gisborne' 22, 24, 49, 57, 58,
    60, 61, 64, 71, 76, 88–9, 93,
    162–3, 168
'Robin Hood and Little John'
    28, 85, 93, 98–9
'Robin Hood and Maid Marian'
    95–6, 192, 195–6
'Robin Hood and the Monk' 17,
    22, 24, 47, 48, 49, 56, 58, 59,
    60, 61, 68, 71, 77, 86, 88–9,
    93, 98, 245
'Robin Hood and the Pedlars' 84
'Robin Hood and the Pinder
    of Wakefield' (= 'The Jolly
    Pinder of Wakefield') 23, 24,
    29, 58, 76, 86, 89, 90, 93, 163,
    250
'Robin Hood and the Potter'
    17, 22, 24, 26, 47, 48, 49, 56,
    58, 59, 60, 61, 71, 77, 86, 89,
    91–2, 93, 96, 98
'Robin Hood and the Prince of
    Aragon' 28, 98, 99
'Robin Hood and Queen
    Katherine' 96, 98, 101, 150,
    163, 181, 191
'Robin Hood and the Ranger'
    83, 162, 246
'Robin Hood Rescuing Three
    Young Men' (= 'Robin Hood
    Rescuing Three Squires') 60,
    76, 89, 90, 191, 245, 246
'Robin Hood and the
    Scotchman' 28, 98, 99
'Robin Hood and the Shepherd'
    95
'Robin Hood and the Tanner'
    94, 245, 246
'Robin Hood and the Tinker'
    25, 95, 245
'Robin Hood and the Valiant
    Knight' 84, 92

Robin Hood ballads (*cont.*)
  'Robin Hood and Will Scarlet' (= 'Robin Hood Newly Revived') 27–8, 87, 90, 98, 121, 195; as 'Robin Hood and the Stranger' 26, 28, 98
  'Robin Hood's Birth, Breeding, Valour and Marriage' 25, 97, 99, 105, 191, 246
  'Robin Hood's Chase' 96, 98
  'Robin Hood's Death' 24, 92, 93, 163
  'Robin Hood's Golden Prize' 47, 63, 94
  'Robin Hood's Progress to Nottingham' 47, 73, 87, 90, 93, 96–7, 101, 245, 246, 250
  A True Tale of Robin Hood, see under Parker, M.
Robin Hood films and television
  The Adventures of Robin Hood (1938) 31, 123, 201, 224, 227–8, 230, 242, 243, 251–2
  The Adventures of Robin Hood (television, 1955) 31, 51, 211
  Maid Marian and Her Merry Men (television, 1988) 127, 218
  The New Adventures of Robin Hood (television, 1997) 219
  Princess of Thieves 219, 238
  Robin and Marian 25, 212, 219, 237
  Robin Hood (1922) 210, 212, 230, 243
  Robin Hood (1991) 193, 212, 213, 237
  Robin Hood (television, 2006) 219, 253
  Robin Hood (2010) 145, 220
  Robin Hood: Men in Tights 30–1, 216
  Robin Hood: Prince of Thieves 31, 192, 212–3, 238, 252

Robin of Sherwood 31, 139, 192, 210, 238, 254
Rogues of Sherwood Forest 247
Son of Robin Hood 238
The Story of Robin Hood and the Merry Men of Sherwood Forest 31
The Zany Adventures of Robin Hood 216
Robin Hood garlands 84, 95, 96, 98, 101,103
  The Noble Atchievements of Robin Hood (prose garland, 1662) 96, 97, 99
  Robin Hood's Garland (1663) 95, 96, 98, 100, 101
  Robin Hood's Garland (c.1740) 92, 94, 97, 107
Robin Hood plays
  The Adventures of Robin Hood: A Play (1774) 104
  George a Green 24
  Looke About You 193–4
  Merry Sherwood: or Harlequin Forester 106, 198
  'Robin Hood' (Paston manuscript play) 57, 60
  Robin Hood: A New Musical Entertainment 105, 197–8
  Robin Hood: An Opera 104, 197
  Robin Hood and his Crew of Souldiers 92, 103–4, 250
  'Robin Hood and the Friar' 56, 59, 190
  Robin Hood and Little John 28, 84–5, 94, 104
  'Robin Hood and the Potter' 56
  Robin Hood, or Sherwood Forest 105–6, 198
Robin Hood themes
  anti-authority 84
  anti-clerical 214
  aristocratic 109
  celebration 84
  'meets his match' 58–9, 76, 87–8

Index

money 61–2
nationalism 151–2, 227–8
place-names 240–1
'real Robin Hood' 1, 42, 109, 232, 242
Rockingham Forest 46
Roe, N. 116, 117, 119, 120
Roye, W. 19

Saintsbury, G. 201
Sands, D. B. 66–7
Schiller, F. 108, 132
Scott, R. 220
Scott, W. 3, 36, 37, 51–2, 126, 138, 133, 143, 144, 145, 146, 147, 148, 151–5, 158, 160, 161, 164, 170, 171, 173, 179, 182, 200, 201, 242, 252
Seal, G. 243
'Searle, J.', see Phillips, G. S.
Sedgwick, E. K. 128, 201–2, 220
Shakespeare, W. 18, 46, 119, 225, 226–7
Shelley, M. 127, 202
Shelley, P. B. 126, 127
Shield, W. 105
Sidney, P. 22
Singman, J. 5
Sir Launfal 55, 65, 66, 71, 97, 249
Skeat, W. W. 66, 71
Sloane 'Life of Robin Hood' 24, 27, 57, 76, 87, 88, 89, 90, 93, 101, 245, 246
Southey, C. 133–4, 135
Southey, R. 129, 132–4, 135
Spence, L. 37, 45, 48
Spenser, E. 227
Squire, J. C. 137–8, 210
Stock, B. 14–15
Stock, L. 6, 234
Stocqueler, J. H. 9, 30, 165, 169–74, 200, 206–7, 251

Stow, J. 44, 45
Stukeley, W. 109
Sullivan, A. 135, 237
Sussex, L. 38, 232

Tardif, R. 234
Taylor, J., see Dobson, R. B.
Tennyson, Alfred, Lord 30, 65, 135–7, 139, 178, 182, 209–10, 237, 238
Thackeray, W. M. 158, 173
Thompson, E. P. 112, 247, 248
Thorpe, A. 183
Thurman, U. 193
Tomlinson, T. 127, 183, 215–16, 220, 243
Trease, G. 183
Tristan 1, 10, 187, 242
Troost, L. 6, 104, 105, 107
Tyndale, W. 19
Twm Siôn Cati 31

Udall, N. 18

Wager, L. 18
Wallace, W. 42, 43, 44, 47, 48–50, 238
Walpole, R. 107
Wasserman, J. 8
Watson, E. 216
Weinstein, H. 51
Wellington, Duke of 158, 162
White, T. H. 228
Wiles, D. 5
Williams, R. 7
Wilson, R. 19
Winstone, R. 139, 254
Wollstonecraft, M. 202
Wood, A. 94
'Woods, L.', see C. Nelson
Wright, A. W. 7
Wyeth, N. C. 179, 184–5

EU authorised representative for GPSR:
Easy Access System Europe, Mustamäe tee 50,
10621 Tallinn, Estonia
gpsr.requests@easproject.com

www.ingramcontent.com/pod-product-compliance
Lightning Source LLC
Chambersburg PA
CBHW070235240426
43673CB00044B/1801